Congress in the Politics of West Bengal

From Dominance to Marginality (1947-1977)

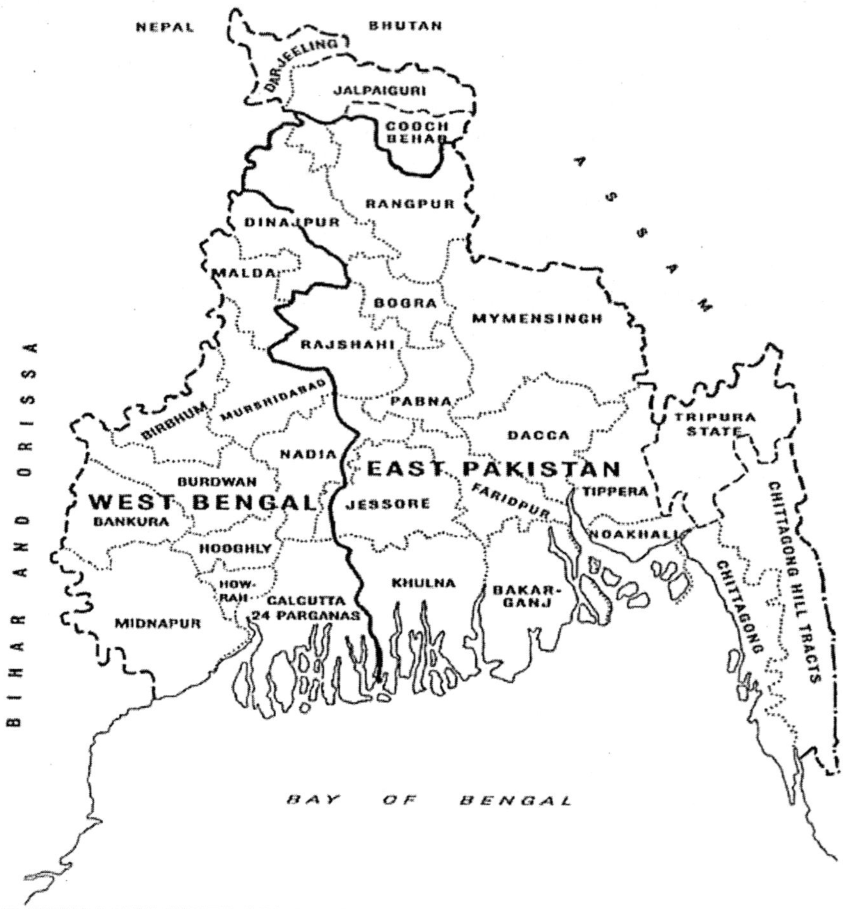
NEPAL
BHUTAN
DARJEELING
JALPAIGURI
COOCH BEHAR
ASSAM
RANGPUR
DINAJPUR
MALDA
BOGRA
MYMENSINGH
RAJSHAHI
BIHAR AND ORISSA
BIRBHUM
MURSHIDABAD
PABNA
TRIPURA STATE
DACCA
NADIA
EAST PAKISTAN
BURDWAN
WEST BENGAL
JESSORE
FARIDPUR
TIPPERA
BANKURA
HOOGHLY
NOAKHALI
CHITTAGONG HILL TRACTS
HOW-RAH
CALCUTTA
24 PARGANAS
KHULNA
BAKAR-GANJ
CHITTAGONG
MIDNAPUR
BAY OF BENGAL

Congress in the Politics of West Bengal

From Dominance to Marginality (1947-1977)

Babulal Bala

Foreword by:

I. Sarkar

KUNAL BOOKS

New Delhi - 110002. (India)

KUNAL BOOKS
4648/21, 1st Floor, Ansari Road,
Daryaganj, New Delhi-110002.
Phones: 011-23275069, 9811043697
E-mail: *kunalbooks@gmail.com*
Website: *www.kunalbooks.com*

Congress in the Politics of West Bengal: From Dominance to Marginality (1947-1977)

First Published 2022
ISBN: 978-93-91908-38-6

Published in India by **Prem Singh Bisht for Kunal Books** and printed at Trident Enterprises, Noida, U.P.

Dedicated to

My Father

Shanti Charan Bala

Eldest and Youngest brothers

Bhaduri Bala and **Nikhil Bala**

who ever dreamt to see my success in life, but are no more in this world to share with me.

FOREWORD

The definition of marginality in the historical arena has been a matter of debate and analysis through generations. What stands for marginality and how we discern it when looked at in comparison to dominance or oppression is dependent on the historical narrative prevalent at a certain time period. During rebellions or wars, we may find such differentiation but if we are to look against the grain, many a times what we know as dominance is merely a defense as opposed to submission. The political fervour or governance, to a large extent, decides the severity of these terms in a narrative. The time period of 1947- 1977 is crucial in terms of understanding how political machinery became a tool in shaping the general history of a region, province or country. In addition to this, there are also roles performed by various individuals or political figures that happen to influence the map of diplomacy. Dr. Bidhan Chandra Roy in the history of post independence Bengal has been an instrumental figure in this regard. Apart from the political scenario that has been described in this text, the idea that a political party could be the element behind changing the shape of history at a certain point is a matter worth analysis. The time period is ripe for such studies and hence enables other branches of political history like nationalism and diplomacy to become themes for discussion in conference rooms and make for study materials in higher education. Like it this has been established by various scholars of political history that facts play a major role in developing perspectives about bodies of governance and administration, this text highlights events with ample substantiation of documents from repositories of information.

The significance of the research under consideration lies on the fact that the scholar (Dr Babulal Bala) has taken up a very significant phase of Indian history with reference to the politics of West Bengal from 1947 to 1977. In the study one may come across various waves of political events of West Bengal during this period and particularly right from 1947, gradually the follow-up of the incidents witnessed many ups and downs in the politics of West Bengal. The tasks and goals of the Indian National Congress in West Bengal and the activities of the Congress Party during the era of Dr. Bidhan Chandra Roy have been analyzed by the scholar with the support of available archival and primary sources. Fact remains that at a certain moment especially from 1967 onward, there were certain strains and challenges of the congress party and the author has minutely detailed the period of marginalization (1967-1971). In addition to that at certain circumstances, non-congress coalition government was formed and thereafter presidential rule within this period in this province had a direct impact on the Congress Party of West Bengal. The formation of PDA Government (Progressive Democratic Alliance) from 1972-1977 is another important chapter of the politics of West Bengal and the Congress Party emerged as a powerful force in West Bengal politics. In this way this chapter is an important part of the thesis and the scholar has tried to put up sufficient arguments to establish all the facts. In fine this study tends to indicate the results of the gradual impotence and irrelevance of the congress party and its leadership in the political arena of the province and that it led to the development of various divisive forces in the politics of West Bengal. In this way the scholar has studied the entire premise thoroughly and with lucid language he established his arguments up to mark. He has collected and analyzed enough materials both from primary and secondary sources and graphically narrated the various aspects of the dissertation by adopting thematic, narrative and analytical methods.

Some historians may attempt to speak of divisive politics in the manner of playing one group against the other and in the process leave no scope for reading against the grain. Studies related to political parties and individuals responsible for decisions taken for national interest are many but an accurate study would be rare. This work is an attempt to touch on a subject as such hence it has covered aspects that could be regarded as vital for the understanding of West Bengal political scenario during the Partition and even after, repercussions of which may be seen in formation of smaller political bodies with equal enthusiasm and sense of purpose.

In an aggregate, this work is an assimilation of political narrative coupled with deeper understanding of how political events shaped the history of a particular region (i.e. West Bengal) during other major political developments. It is really notable that Dr. Bala has brought to our notice many issues and facts which have hardly been focused by the scholars of our time and in this sense his work may claim an extraordinary research to open new dimensions in the field of further research on post- independent

Bengal. Incidentally, Joya Chatterjee has produced a book in recent years titled *Spoils of Partition*: *Bengal and India, 1947-67* (Cambridge University Press, 2007). This work is no doubt commendable being able to highlight a few issues of post-partition Bengal along with India but her research has abruptly stopped in 1967. In this light Dr. Babulal Bala's research makes a meaning as it fairly covers some crucial decades of West Bengal politics which dictated the course of history of India as well as that of the region under consideration in the subsequent period.

I am glad to know that Babulal's dissertation is coming out in book form shortly and there cannot be any good news for a supervisor as I am, and I wish him success in every step of his life.

4th March, 2022

I. Sarkar
Former Professor of History
University of North Bengal
Raja Rammohonpur
Darjeeling, West Bengal

PREFACE

It would be proper on my part to deal with the genesis of the present work titled 'Congress in the Politics of West Bengal: From Dominance to Marginality (1947-1977)'. It is in fact the days of my Post–Graduate studies in the Department of History, University of North Bengal, during the initial years of the 21st century; I was deeply impressed by some discussions in the classes by our revered teachers of the Department. Some of these deliverances used to pick up some issues of the politics of Bengal in the first half of the 20th century and other times some historical events related to the politics of West Bengal in the post independent period. It is a fact that national movement in India had found its organized expression in the Indian National Congress. As a student as well as a teacher of the Modern Indian History it was a query in my mind that as the main protagonist of the Indian national movement congress came in power in West Bengal like other states in India and maintained its control and dominance over the politics of West Bengal for long two decades after independence; but how was it subsequently marginalized in the later period. When I got a rare opportunity to carry on my Ph. D work in the said Department, I got a privilege to think over such a theme after my choice and in the long run it was finalized in consultation with my supervisor Professor Ichhimuddin Sarkar, Former Professor, Department of History, University of North Bengal.

In course of my study I was lucky enough to come in touch and to meet and consult a good number of stalwarts, both veteran politicians and renowned journalists who like living historians explained and analyzed many points which are not only rare but can hardly be found in any written documents. Incidentally, either they were participants in many political events of the period or could observe and record in the form of memoires or written books. I have tried my best to examine such sources in the light of connected documents or to test such materials from historical point of view. By the way I had also opportunities to consult many documents and research materials in some academic centers but I could not insert all of them in the present work for some reasons or other. But I hope to utilize them, if possible, in my research in the days to come.

It is expected that the present work would encourage the next generation to take up and explore some other areas of research which have not been highlighted in course of my study.

Raiganj **Babulal Bala**

11th March, 2022

ACKNOWLEDGEMENT

The present book titled *Congress in the Politics of West Bengal: From Dominance to Marginality (1947-1977)'* is an outcome of a revised and updated version of the research work of my Ph. D degree at the University of North Bengal, Raja Rammohanpur, Darjeeling, West Bengal. The work is a study which neither may claim full credit for new discoveries nor is a major breakthrough in the study of the Congress in the Politics of West Bengal. It thus stands as an attempt to explore the research theme, which, in some respect, may appear to be an introductory in modern historiography but the depth and approach of the study may claim its originality as per the material consulted and the structure that has been built up might open a new area of research for the coming generation.

Acknowledgement of cooperation is not a mere routine affair, but is a very sincere and genuine recognition of gratitude to those who have always helped and supported in the entire process at the different levels in course of the study. At the outset, I have no word to express my deep sense of gratitude and indebtedness to my revered Guide and Supervisor Dr. Ichhimuddin Sarkar, former Professor, Department of History, University of North Bengal, without whose ungrudging cooperation and timely grooming in a systematic manner in the form of creation of 'research mind', I might not be able to complete the work in the present form of a book. As a cordial supervisor, he has not only inflamed me the desire of extensive study and guided the way of collection of research material but also helped to resolve many tangled issues as and when necessary by offering valuable suggestions. Whatever I might say to thank him will never be enough as he deserves. Further, Professor Sarkar deserves special thanks and heartfelt gratitude for writing a brief 'Forward' to this work.

In this opportunity, I would like to record my heartiest gratitude to all the faculty members of the Department of History, University of North Bengal for providing me all kinds of necessary assistance in time.

In that connection I would like to convey my gratitude to the various academic institutions and their employees from where I have received sincere cooperation according to my needs for the work. In that queue the most notable names of academic institutions are National Archives of India, New Delhi, Nehru Museum and Memorial Library, New Delhi, National Library, Kolkata, West Bengal State Archives, Kolkata, Secretariat Library, Kolkata, Asiatic Society, Kolkata, Ramkrishna Mission Library, Goalpark, Kolkata, Bidhan Sishu Uddyan, Ultodanga, Kolkata, Bidhan Bhavan, head quarter of the West Bengal Pradesh Congress Committee, Kolkata, Hemanta Basu Bhavan, State Committee office of the Forward Bloc, Kolkata, Old Congress Bhavan, Kolkata, Nimtairi Smriti Saudha, Midnapore, Central Library, University of North Bengal, Central Library, Raiganj University, District Library, Konnogarh, Hooghly, West Bengal etc.

I have taken so many personal interviews viz. Mr. Kumud Bhattacharyay, former state president of Chhatra Parishad from 1973-1977; Mr. Sukharanjan Sengupta, veteran journalist of the time, Mr. Deba Prasad Roy, veteran Congress leader, Mr. Somen Mitra, veteran Congress leader, Mr. Ashim Chatterjee, former Naxalite leader, Mr. Mihir Ganguly, veteran journalist and Mr. Sarder Amjad Ali, former Bangla Congress MP, who gave me a rare opportunity to record their statements regarding the various unexplored areas of present work. Without their help and cooperation there would have been many gaps to reconstruct my idea so as to complete the work. I must express my indebtedness to them.

It is high time to express my greetings to Madam Mrs. Ayesha Sarkar who at the time of fatigue or indifference during the entire course of my work as if she appeared to me as like Florence Nightingale with the lamp beside a wounded minded soldier.

I am also thankful to my colleagues particularly to Dr. Debasish Biswas, Department of Economics, Mr. Barendra Nath Giri, Department of History, Dr. Iti Chottopadhyay, Department of Philosophy, Professor Prasanta Kumar Mahala, Department of Sanskrit, Dr. Md. Rabiul Islam, Department of Physics and my friend Hemanta Kumar Sinha, my father-in-law Mr. Arup Narayan Basak and mother-in-law Manjushree Basak for their encouragement to complete the work.

I should not miss to extend my sense of gratefulness to my family members who have maintained a congenial atmosphere throughout the course of the research study. My wife Ananya Basak (Bala), Assistant

Teacher in English of a High School, has been a profound source of inspiration. Her contribution is much more impressive than she would ever realize. My son Sasanka (Ananyo) and my nephew Jayanta (Rajib), too have helped and inspired me in their own way. Moreover, without whose wish even I could not be able to go forward in every aspect of my life I convey my complete surrender and homage to my mother Smt. Dhakeswari Bala who ever prayed for me and desired every success in my life.

I am indebted to several authors and academicians whose works I have utilized in writing and ultimately it is now in the form of a book. They have been humbly acknowledged.

All the more, it is a time to express my heartfelt gratitude to Mr. Prem Singh Bisht of Kunal Books, New Delhi for undertaking the task of publication of this book.

Finally, in spite of my best efforts to make this work up to date and above question, there may be some obscure mistakes and errors, in that case the responsibility, of course, goes to me alone and latter on in the light of available authentic source materials the errors (if there is/are any) will be rectified in the next edition.

Raiganj **Babulal Bala**

11th March, 2022

Abbreviations

ABTA	:	All Bengal Teachers' Association
AICC	:	All India Congress Committee
AIMC	:	All India Medical Council
AIML	:	All India Muslim League
AIVDO	:	All India Village Development Organization
BKD	:	Bharatiya Kranti Dal
BPCC	:	Bengal Provincial Congress Committee
BPML	:	Bengal Provincial Muslim League
CAP	:	Congress Assembly Party
CLP	:	Congress Legislative Party
CP	:	Chhatra Parishad
CPI	:	Communist Party of India
CSS	:	Chittaranjan Seva Sadan
CVC	:	Congress Volunteer Corps
DDA	:	Dandakaranya Development Authority
DIR	:	Defense of India Rules
FB	:	Forward Bloc
HM	:	Hindu Mahasabha
ICL	:	Indian Chemical Industries
INC	:	Indian National Congress
INDF	:	Indian National Democratic Front
INTUC	:	Indian National Trade Union Congress
JS	:	Jana Sangha
KMPP	:	Krishak Mozdoor Praja Party.

KPP : Krishak Praja Party
MDCC : Midnapore District Congress Committee
MISA : Maintenance of Internal Security Act
MLA : Member of Legislative Assembly
MLC : Member of Legislative Council
MP : Member of Parliament
MPHS : Medical and Public Health Service
NBBKP : Nikhal Banga Bastuhara Karma Parishad
NDC : National Defense Certificate
NDC : National Development Council
NHH : Nirmal Hriday Home
NMCU : National Malaria Control Unit
NNS : Nava Nirman Samity
PDA : Protective Detention Act
PIFRC : Price Increase and Famine Resistance Committee
PSP : Praja Socialist Party
PULF : Peoples United Left Front
RPI : Republican Party of India
SDC : State Defense Committee
SRC : State Reorganization Commission
SSP : Samyukta Socialist Party
ULF : United Left Front
UMP : United Muslim Party
USO : United Socialist Organization
WBCUTA : West Bengal College and University Teachers' Association
YC : Yuba Congress

Contents

Introduction

The history of the congress politics of colonial Bengal is no less fascinating than that of India. In fact, many phases of the national movements of India had its exposition in different forms. It is clear that prior to independence this party was essentially involved in a political-oriented process of activities. All the more, it was neither in a position to suggest any complete autonomy of politics nor with any concern of material development of the people. As a result, until the time of the First World War the congress in Bengal as well as in India had a relatively narrow set of aims either in the form of political representation for western educated Indians or movement for Home Rule as well as some insignificant programmes. During the inter war period Mahatma Gandhi was successful in turning the Indian national congress into a political organization of the masses. But in the context of Bengal the factional politics could not be minimized and it resulted in the form of the emergence of numerous political platforms dominated by a few political parties like Swarajya Party, Krishak Praja Party and so on. The decade before Indian partition (1947) was again critical as Bengal was turned gradually as an epicenter or nerve-centre of Indian politics. All these issues may be taken as significant features of Bengal politics and its relevance has been thoroughly investigated as the prefatory part of the present work.

One of the important features of Bengal politics during the first half of 20th century was that the scheme of partition (1905) proved to be a significant point as because with the annulment of the Bengal partition in 1911, there was a clear picture of the doldrums of the politics that prevailed in Bengal and its consequences were followed in the decades to come. In fact from 1911 all most all the politicians of Bengal lost power in Indian politics and eventually their political platform 'shrank from the national to the regional level.' In another way the divisions of Bengalese on regional terms by and large strengthen the identity of the 'Bengalines' in many respects. At the same time the trend of the regional politics with special reference to Bengal from 1905 to 1911 took inevitably a new turn in the form of religious identity which had virtually surpassed all regional or class identities. Thus the history of colonial Bengal as we have stated in our research had experienced one of the most critical times where the Muslims and the Hindus irrespective of their class identity appeared in the frontiers of 'separate and antagonistic identity politics.'

It is thus quite clear that the 1940s, immediately after the Second World War, the nature of the Bengal politics represented a critical moments of its own and most of the political parties were deeply concerned in politics of separatism rather than to look after the conditions of the people at large. In the meanwhile, the repeated disillusions and formations of Bengal Governments in one side and the natural calamities and communal riots (the Great Calcutta Killings, August, 1946 and Noakhali riots, October, 1946) on the other turned Bengal to be a burning centre of Indian politics. This trend of politics got intensified in course of time and the destiny of India particularly of Bengal was thus decided by the disaster in the name of partition.

A new phase of politics after partition started in West Bengal. The first Chief Minister was Dr. Prafulla Chandra Ghosh and after a short term he was replaced by Dr. Bidhan Chandra Roy. Fact remains that the province of West Bengal had to bear the full brunt and first of all the undivided Bengal was divided into two new states. Naturally, the immediate task of the West Bengal Government was to reconstruct the province keeping pace with the process of building a new India. It may be noted that partition of India and obviously that of Bengal was a geographical solution and naturally West Bengal was over burdened with various problems including the migration of the refugees from East Pakistan and of course the factional politics that dictated the era of Dr. B.C. Roy and afterwards. In the meantime, West Bengal had to experience the consequences of the sudden death of Dr. B.C. Roy (1st July, 1962) and no less was the impact that shaped Indian politics after the death of Jawaharlal Nehru (27th May, 1964), the then prime minister of India. In our study we have tried to pick up all these issues and to present a systematic analysis in the light of available materials related with the theme.

This may also be seen that the situation as it appears in the subsequent period was such that there was internal conflict within the congress party in West Bengal as well as in the centre and the entire political picture was a crisis moment in the politics of West Bengal. It has been stated that the central government headed by Smt. Indira Gandhi had to take up steps to tackle the situations but the inner crisis of the congress party was such that a few disgruntled congress leaders could not find any alternative but to form new political party. Thus the emergence and creation of 'Bangla Congress' came to a reality and the following years witnessed the emergence of new government namely United Front Government headed by Sri Ajay Kumar Mukherjee. But a grand reality of the politics of the then Bengal was that the congress as a political party became gradually unpopular being de-touched from the people of Bengal. It lost the support base and in course of time the leaders were much more concerned about clash of interest rather than political solidarity or well being of the people.

Although in the meantime there were presidential rules in West Bengal for three consecutive times. At long last so far as our research period is concerned the West Bengal Government under the congress headed by Siddhartha Shankar Ray came into existence in 1972. But this government had not only to face the consequences of the emergence of Bangladesh, its huge number of refugees and also the peasant movement of the Naxalites. Incidentally, there was also crisis in the central government and through various ups and downs the government under Siddhartha Shankar Ray had to suffer in some way or other. Side by side, taking advantage of the crisis and political instability of West Bengal the communist parties and a few other non-congress political parties came forward to utilize the political crisis and the time was not far to bring about the end of the congress rule in West Bengal and in the long run there was the formation of the left front government under Jyoti Basu in 1977.

Keeping in view the above background and facts the present study titled *'CONGRESS IN THE POLITICS OF WEST BENGAL: FROM DOMINANCE TO MARGINALITY (1947-1977)'* is a humble attempt to represent the congress politics from dominance to marginality with an outcome of its collapse. All the more the arguments and explanations have been scanned carefully through some chapters and a short sketch is presented as follows:

The 'Introduction' of the work is intended to highlight the basic concept and the theme of the study. It also focuses the main approach of the work and in short the issues of politics of Bengal that dictated the subsequent political atmosphere of the region as a whole.

This has been followed by the first chapter 'The Partition Colossus and the Politics of Bengal' which deals with exploring the very roots of the spread of hated communal politics in the country particularly in Bengal. In that context, Role of Deshbandhu Chitta Ranjan Das and his famous 'Bengal

Pact' for the sake of Hindu-Muslim unity in Bengal and the troubled politics with the rejection of the pact have been detailed in this chapter. There was also dissolution of a large number of congress leaders due to various factors that dominated the politics of the time. Incidentally the emergence of the Krishak Praja Party under Abul Kashem Fazlul Huq came to the surface of Bengal politics and how did it get involved in communal politics have been included in detail.

The astonishing silence of the top congress leaderships to the call of Fazlul Huq forced him to catch the hand of the Muslim League – which one may considered as the most eventful inclination in the history of the nation as well as Bengal in terms of importing communal politics and consolidating it for their future course of action which ultimately led to the partition of the country and of course Bengal.

The communist party's support behind the 'Pakistan Demand' of the Muslim nationalists on the plea of self-determination but when the flame of communal violence engulfed the country instead of taking up any effective measures it preferred to remain as silent spectators.

After the acceptance of the Cabinet Mission Plan which 'guaranteed the unity of India' by both the main political parties i.e. the All India Muslim League and the Indian National Congress, the sudden controversial faux pass (10th July, 1946) of Pundit Jawaharlal Nehru regarding the accepting the terms and conditions of Cabinet Mission proposals in to-to, that grounded the outbreak of the Great Calcutta Killings and others holocausts undoubtedly sabotaged the unity of India and ultimately India along with of course Bengal was partitioned

In this chapter it has also been scanned on the basis of available documents regarding the much talked political controversy of Jogendra Nath Mondal in terms of his inclusion in the Cabinet headed by the Muslim Leaguers. It is generally used to say that J.N. Mondal cooperated with the communal politics of Muslim League Coalition Government headed by Khwaja Najimuddin and H.S. Suharawardy, but it is found that besides Mondal, many caste Hindus specially 3 Caste Hindu leaders namely Tulsi Charan Goswami, Baroda Prasanna Pyne and Tarak Nath Mukhopadhyay and 3 Scheduled Caste leaders i.e. Premhari Burman, Pulin Behari Mullick and Jogendra Nath Mondal became the member of Nazimuddin's Muslim League Coalition Government (24th April, 1943 —28th March, 1946).

After the induction of J.N. Mandal in the central cabinet then H. S. Suharawardy reconstituted his cabinet (24th April, 1946 -14th August, 1947) where three Hindu Ministers namely Tarak Nath Mukherjee, Nagendra Narayan Roy and Dwarakanath Barori were included respectively.

In the second chapter under the caption 'Task and Goals of the Indian National Congress in Bengal after Independence (1947-1948)' – is to focus the position of the Congress Party and the Muslim League in West Bengal after Partition, acute factionalism within the congress party in the politics of West Bengal in the name of Gandhian Group, Jugantor Group and Hooghly Group, background of the formation of the 'Shadow Ministry', Mahatma Gandhi along with H.S. Suharawardhy's attempts to restore communal amity between the Hindus and the Muslims, background of the resignation of Dr. Prafulla Chandra Ghosh from the seat of the first Premier of West Bengal and how Dr. B. C. Roy took up the responsibility of West Bengal as its Chief Minister etc. have been discussed systematically.

The third chapter 'State Entrepreneurship and the Congress Party in the Era of Dr. Bidhan Chandra Roy:Ideology verses Necessity and Reconstruction' is on a thorough analysis as to how Dr. Bidhan Chandra Roy perpetrated various numerous welfare schemes for the all round development of the 'problematic state in India' i.e. West Bengal.

Side by side, attempts have been made to show Dr. Bidhan Chandra Roy and his mechanisms to overcome the crises that had befallen on him and his Government at that point of time. Dr. Bidhan Chandra Roy had however, explore mechanism to overcome all the problems and to some extend he was successful.

The forth chapter is a study to bring out all the issues related to a peculiar politics of West Bengal which denoted to highlight the nature of politics dealing with 'Dominance with Difference: Strains and Challenges (1962-1967)'. Many issues such as factionalism within the congress party, emergence of Bangla Congress and the leadership crisis due to the sudden death of Dr. B.C. Roy, Jawaharlal Nehru and also that of Lal Bahadur Shastri have been discussed in detail. In the long last a part of the chapter is devoted to scan the issues which led to the fall of the Congress Government in 1967 for the first time after independence.

The period of marginalization of the Congress party is the main theme of the fifth chapter of the dissertation. The entire chapter under the caption of 'Period of Marginalization (1967-1971)'has however been examined from two angles – (i). Non-Congress Coalition Government and (ii). Impositions of Presidential Rule. In this chapter, attempt has been made to explore the various ups and downs of the political parties in West Bengal. It has categorically discussed about dissolution and formation of the Non-Congress Coalition 'United Front' Government. A significant issue has also been taken up here to show how acute anti-congress feelings helped to unite the various political parties keeping aside their ideological differences. This chapter has also incorporated the historical development about the formation of the various governments consecutively i.e. first (2nd March, 1967 to 21st November, 1967); second (25th February, 1969 to 16th March, 1970) United Front and Democratic Coalition Front (2nd April, 1971 to 28th June, 1971)) Government headed by Ajay Kumar Mukherjee and of course the declaration of the presidential rule as many as three times in the stop gaps ((20th February, 1968 to 25th February 1969; 19th March, 1970 to 2nd April, 1971; and 29th June, 1971 to 20th March, 1972). Most interestingly, another Government namely 'Progressive Democratic Front' (21st November, 1967 to 20th February, 1968) headed by Dr. Prafulla Chandra Ghosh, and its activities have also been discussed in this chapter.

The sixth chapter captioned 'Progressive Democratic Alliances (PDA) Government – Promises and Performances' concentrates to discuss the causes behind the landslide victory of the congress party in the election of 1972. In this regard, the role of the Chhatra Parishad under the mighty leadership of Shri Priya Ranjan Dasmunshi during the bloody activities of the Naxalites and the left communists at the time of first and second United Front government has been discussed meticulously. In that context, the role of Siddhartha Shankar Ray as the leader of the opposition during the very odd moment of the congress party in West Bengal and his fearlessness as well as dynamic leadership have also been included.

In spite of the victory of the congress party in West Bengal in 1772, what circumstances led to the landslide defeat of the congress party in the election of 1977, has also been taken into account as a part of this chapter.

The last part of the dissertation happens to be the 'Conclusion' that tends to make a survey of the entire dissertation which has been depicted in the relevant chapters. By the way some of the issues have been incorporated here in order to identify some gaps which could not be successfully dealt with in spite of our efforts. There are controversies, counter arguments and debates as to our analysis and these may be handled and clarified afterwards in the light of fresh look at the available documents.

CHAPTER

1

The Partition Colossus and the Politics of Bengal

In spite of a common language of which every Bengalese is proud, a shared culture and lifestyle and a common history since at least a thousand years, no Bengalese wanted the partition of Bengal from the core of their heart, yet the partition happened due to the gradual deterioration of communal harmony and thereupon undivided Bengal disappeared from the atlas on 15th August, 1947. In fact, the deterioration of communal harmony began with the unexpected and untimely demise of Desh Bandhu Chittaranjan Das (henceforth C.R. Das) on16th June, 1925, who was no doubt a pioneer of the emergence of joint Hindu-Muslim front in Bengal politics on the basis of the historic Bengal Pact[1] of 1923, a shining example of an ambitious instrument that could bring the Muslims and Hindus of Bengal together. Chittaranjan Das was the only national leader whom both the Hindus and Muslims relied, that is why with his death the very emotional comments was made by a Muslim daily paper, titled *'MUHAMADI'* (in Bengali) as – 'God's extreme punishment to our countrymen'.[2] Not only that the Daily News of London commented with the death of Chittaranjan Das as "For there is apparently no one to replace Das, who stood in an absolutely unique position."[3] In that context, Aparna Devi, daughter of Chittaranjan Das wrote in his (C. R. Das's) biography titled *Manush Chittaranjan* (in Bengali) "If the country would advance along with the path indicated by my father at Faridpur (1st May, 1925) with the leaders giving up the illusion of their leadership and egoism, we would have obtained complete independence long ago and India would not be partitioned for gaining independence".[4]

During the lifetime of Chittaranjan Das, though the Bengal Pact (1923) was rejected by the Congress Session at Kakinada (1923) which was presided over by Mohammad Ali, but it was endorsed by Bengal Provincial Congress Committee (henceforth BPCC) of Sirajganj (1924), presided over by M. M. Akram Khan and thereafter majority of the congress leaders defied their own central leadership and decided to go along with C. R. Das in which they gave utmost priority to the Bengal's larger and long term interests. But, after C. R. Das's untimely and unexpected sudden demise the Krishnagar Session of Bengal Provincial Congress Committee (BPCC) rejected the Bengal Pact in 1926, under the Presidentship of Birendra Nath Sasmal,[5] and thereupon most of the Muslim leaders bonhomie with the congress party ended and in the election of the Calcutta Corporation of 1927 Muslims fought separately which was a clear signal in terms of returning separatism and the end of the nascent Bengali nationalism.[6]

In that situation, the Arya Samajists during their procession would play music near Mosques that was objected by the Muslims for their disturbances at the time of prayers, and during the time of *Bakr-Id,* some of the people of Muslims community would slaughter cows in the open places that would hurt the religious sentiments of the Hindus. This made the situation worse and aggravated the process of communal polarization in Bengal. Kaji Nazrul Islam, the famous rebel poet who at that time of budding communalism wrote his most inspiring song named *Kandari Hushiar* (1926),[7] in which Hindus and Muslims were asked to unite, but by and large his dictum as well as appeal was unheeded. The widely circulated and much talked composite culture of Bengal and societal tradition gave way to the political stance of 'Islam in Danger' which was primarily the slogan of non-Bengali Muslims and later on accepted by the large section of Bengali Muslims to consolidate the Muslim community. In that context, the non-existence of C. R. Das created a void in Bengal politics which was not filled up by anybody. Incidentally, after C. R. Das there was only one politician i.e. Subhas Chandra Bose who had the enormous abilities to keep the Hindus and Muslims together, but unfortunately, he was kept far away from the ongoing political scenario of the country particularly Bengal due to his long period of detention at home or at Mandalay or in exile in Europe.[8]

The promise for united movement against the British rule was seen during the period from 1914 to 1925. But the move for joint action was belied during the time from 1926 to 1935 and it was more deteriorated thereafter, especially on the eve of the independence as well as partition of India along with Bengal. Actually, after C. R. Das there was none in Bengal politics who could retain the general loyalty of both the communities. From a Special Correspondent, under the caption of 'MASTER ORATOR: "LLOYD GEORGE" OF INDIAN POLITICS' wrote as "Das revealed all through his life an intensely anti- British trait, and although suspect by the Mohammedans, who always referred to Das as being "far too good a

'Hindoo' for them," he was a remarkable personality; a man of great culture and deep learning."[9] Naturally, after the death of C.R. Das and rejection of the Bengal Pact (1923) in the Krishnagar Session of Bengal Provincial Congress Committee (BPCC) held in the year of 1926 under the Presidentship of Birendra Nath Sasmal, the Muslim separatists started asserting themselves at the aim of claiming to political power of the Bengal province. They adopted various policies and programmes to counteract Hindu bhadraloks' control over different institutions in the soil of demographic preponderance of the Muslims community in Bengal. In that juncture, the process of communal polarization was accentuated by the attitude of the Hindus particularly the leaders of the congress party along with the Swarajyists regarding the opposition to the passing of the Bengal Tenancy (Amendment) Bill in 1928 in the Bengal Legislative Council. It may be mentioned that during the time of the passing of the proposed Bill, the Hindu members of the Legislative Council those who mainly belonged to the congress party showed their support in favour of the interest of the Zaminders and neglected the interests of the Prajas, because most of the leaders of the congress party were Zaminder in class. In that context Abul Mansur Ahmed remarked, "Neither in terms of the Muslim interest, nor on the Praja interest, was it possible for any longer to rely on the Congress."[10] Centering the passing of the Bengal Tenancy (Amendment) Bill in 1928 in the Bengal Legislative Council, many congress minded leaders among the Muslim communities were disillusioned about the aim and objectives of the congress party and subsequently they automatically joined anti congress parties.[11]

The Bengali Muslims who were initially loyal to the congress party started getting disillusion due to opposing the Bengal Tenancy Act of 1928. This processes of disillusionment continued with the dominance of Hindu bhadraloks and wealthy non-Bengali Muslims. At the same time a powerful Praja movement spawned among the Bengali Muslims for attaining freedom from economic bondage. In the question of forming organization among the Muslims of Bengal- Huseyn Shaheed Suhrawardy (henceforth H.S. Suhrawardy) and Khaja Nazimuddin i.e. non Bengali Muslims completely favoured a purely Muslim organization, but Abul Kashem Fazlul Huq popularly known as A. K. Fazlul Huq (henceforth Huq), Tamijuddin Khan and some others Bengali Muslims favoured a concrete non-communal organization. Being influenced by the sentiment and fire brand oratory of Huq, the supporters of the non communal organization among the Muslims formed the Council Praja Party (later known as Bengal Praja Party) to work for 'safeguarding the interests of tenants and labouring classes of the province' against the economic oppression. A.K. Fazlul Huq was elected leader of the newly formed Council Praja Party. Soon the Council Praja Party was expanded and it was renamed as the Nikhil Banga Praja Samity towards the end of 1929. Thereafter with the broadening of the support base of the Nikhil Banga Praja Samity, subsequently it turned into as the historic Krishak Praja Party (henceforth KPP) in the year of 1936. A.K. Fazlul Huq's prime motive was to protect the interests of the prajas from the oppression of the Zamindars and money-lenders that is why, he opened the door of the praja movement to all.[12] In the question of the interest of the prajas, Huq remarked "Hindus are not the enemy of the Muslims. Due to lack of proper education fanaticism has grown up into the minds of both communities and as a result of that they sometimes engaged themselves in communal violence. In case of the exploitation of the Hindu Zamindars, money lenders and lawyers, Huq categorically told that practice was not confined only within a particular community, at the same way the Muslim Zamindars, money lenders and lawyers also exploited the poor peasants as well as prajas irrespective of caste and communities"[13] It is mention worthy that parallel to the praja movement, there was all along another movement among Muslims in Bengal, primarily of non-Bengali Muslims who were harping the slogan of 'Islam in Danger' and who aimed consolidating only the Muslims, but at the beginning that slogan was not greeted by the Bengali Muslims.[14]

In that context of Bengal politics there were five separate groups which were- i. A upper class Muslim group that was mainly influenced by the non-Bengali Muslims like Khwaza Najumuddin and H.S. Suhrawardy, ii. Muslim peasantry and professional classes consisted by rural and middle class Muslims of Bengal, dominated by A. K. Fazlul Huq, iii. Hindu bhadralok class of Bengal under the fold of the congress party dominated by the so-called 'big-five' of Bengal namely Sarat Chandra Bose, Dr. Bidhan Chandra Roy, Nalini Ranjan Sarkar, Tulsi Charan Goswami and Nirmal Chandra Chunder, iv. A non-congress powerful and vocal Zamindar class and v. Scheduled Castes people particularly the Namasudras of Bengal led by Jogendra Nath Mandal. These five distinct groups were pulling the strings of political scenario of Bengal for two decades before 1947. However, the formal Hindu domination in Bengal politics was ended from the year of 1927, because since then, each and every successive Ministry was headed by a Muslim politician who could receive the joint support of the elected Muslim MLAs, the Scheduled Castes Federation MLAs and the European MLAs along with the nominated official members. In that time the policy of the congress party was successively sending congressmen into the legislative council only for the aim of wrecking the diarchyal constitution.

Muslim leaders in Muslim majority provinces would receive every possible support from the British Government and developed a vested interest in separatism which ultimately accentuated the bitterness between the Hindus and the Muslims and paved the way towards partition of the country.[15]

In the meantime, Ramsay Mac Donald, the then Prime Minister of England had declared his much-talked 'Communal Award' on 10th August 1932. Keeping in mind the 'Communal Award' under the Government of India Act of 1935, out of 250 seats of the Bengal Legislative Assembly, Muslims of Bengal were provided 119 seats i.e. 47.6 % of the total seats, against their 54.8 % of total population. The Hindus were given altogether 80 seats i.e. 32% of the total seats while they constituted 44% of the total population in Bengal. On the other hand as many as 25 seats i.e.10% of the total seats were fixed for the Europeans living in Bengal who were a little more than 14 thousand in number and constituting merely 0.25% of the total population. The Anglo-Indians were also given more seats compared to their position in the population ratio of Bengal. The main objective of the British Rulers behind the arrangement of the disproportionate representations in the Bengal Legislative Assembly was to regulate the politics of Bengal by broadening the gap between the Hindus and the Muslims.[16] The ratio of the division of seats in between Hindus and Muslims was opposed by the newly formed Hindu Mahasabha by all means. They accused the congress party for betraying with the interests of the Hindus of Bengal.[17]

Under the circumstances, the Muslim League was almost insignificant in the politics of Bengal, but the most influential party among the Muslim communities particularly the East Bengali Muslims was the Krishak Praja Party (KPP) of A. K. Fazlul Huq. It was fact that the KPP was nominally a secular political party but it had strong Muslim orientation and dedicated mainly for protecting the interests of farmers and ryots from any kind of exploitation and ameliorating their conditions.[18] After establishing the Krishak Praja Party, A. K. Fazlul Huq categorically stated that his fight was with landlords, capitalists and holders of vested interests. Huq also said, "I am fighting for a satisfactory solution of the bread problem or in our words, of the 'Dal-Bhat' problem of Bengal and also for the through overhauling of the Tenancy Laws in Bengal so as to give some relief to agriculturists. This cannot be effected by the Muslim League Parliamentary Board because in that Board out of 28 members, as many as 11 are non-Bengalees who hail from Ispahan, Teharan, Badakshan and Samarkand and other places of outside Bengal and 89 percent are landlords and capitalists. These landlords and capitalists cannot certainly join us in this fight, because they are the very people with whom we will have to carry on a life and death struggle."[19]

It is important to note that with the creation of strong support base among the peasants as well as prajas of the Bengal, the KPP became cynosure of unscrupulous elements of Bengal politics. As per the version of Fazlul Huq, "Attempts were made to misrepresent our real aims and aspirations and to delude the public about our programme and ultimate goal. Among the Mussalman masses, interested parties carried on propaganda against us, and accused us of dividing the Mussalmans among themselves, and thus impairing Muslim solidarity. Among the Hindu masses, propaganda was carried on against us that we were in fact a communal party, masquerading under the cloak of the economic interest of the masses. These two criticisms quite obviously cancel one another, and hardly demand any reply from me. But I should like to take this opportunity of stating once again in unambiguous terms what are the aims of our party and what we ultimately seek to achieve. All talks of Muslim unity and solidarity for merely political ends are worse than useless when it is remembered that the Mussalmam cultivating classes constitute more than 90 per cent of the total Muslim population of Bengal, and it is therefore their interest which must be fundamental an any scheme we may lay down for ourselves, or for the sake of any ideal which we may seek to achieve. On the fundamental question of the interest of the *Prajas* and *Krishaks*, the tillers of the soil who sweat so that others might enjoy the fruits of their labour, there is no difference whatever between the Hindus and the Mussalmans, for their interests are welded into one another, together they stand and we are confident, they shall triumph."[20]

Meanwhile, to meet the challenge of the KPP, some of the Muslim leaders, notably Nawab Khwaja Habibullah, H. S. Suharawardy and M. A. H. Ispahani founded the United Muslim Party (henceforth UMP) on 25th May, 1936.[21] In that context, criticizing the UMP, Fazlul Huq described it as a 'Ministerial party, a Zaminder party, formed to mislead the Bengal Muslim community'. Nawab Khwaja Nazimuddin, leader of the UMP accusing the KPP retorted that the Praja Party was not a purely Muslim organization. By this time , the All India Muslim League (henceforth AIML) led by Mahammad Ali Jinnah (henceforth M A Jinnah) made their sincere attempts to win over the support of the Bengal Muslims by ignoring the Bengal Provincial Muslim League (henceforth BPML) and invited directly some non-Benglee Muslim leaders like A. R. Siddiqui, M. A. H. Ispahani and K. Nooruddin. Thereafter Jinnah came to Calcutta to discuss with KPP leaders for further coordination. In course of discussion with M A Jinnah, the KPP leaders categorically demanded- i) abolition of Zamindari system without compensation, ii) The right to maintain KPP's separate identity and iii) that there will be no nomination from Jinnah. Though, BPML expressed its full accord with the demands of the KPP leaders but the UMP led by non-Bengali Muslims vehemently opposed the abolition of Zamindari system. Naturally it was impossible to reach any fruitful solution regarding the unity between the AIML and KPP. During this time the leaders of the KPP and the AIML would represent two contrasting ideologies for obtaining the support of the Bengali Muslim. The KPP particularly fought for the interest of the tenants and peasant class people while the AIML represented the interests of the Zaminders and Business communities. So, Fazlul Huq emphatically declared, 'From this day onwards begins a grim fight between Zaminders and Capitalists on the one hand, and the poor people on the other. It is not at all a civil war in the Muslim Community but it is a fight in which the people of Bengal are divided on a purely economic issue."[22]

It is noteworthy that from the days of the formation of Muslim League in 1906 to the publication of the activities of the League Parliamentary Board in 1936, Muslim League never took any resolution regarding the abolition of the permanent settlement.[23] Though, there was a long history of peasants movement in Bengal and from 1920 to 1934 the peasants also participated in the movements of some regions under the congress party, but the congress leadership also did not take any initiative to form any separate organization for the peasants.[24] But peasant conference was convened in Kolkata in the month of August in 1936, by the then illegal communist party. After that in March, 1937, the first 'Bengal Provincial Peasants Conference' was held at *Patrasayar* in Bankura District.[25] Though, at that time the influence of *prishak sabha* under the communists was very limited, so in the election of 1937 the *krishak sabha* extended its major support to the krishak praja party of Fazlul Huq and some to the congress party.[26] At that time the K.P.P. of Fazlul Huq was the most influential party in the rural Bengal. That time Fazlul Huq organized the *krishak-prajas* at the aim of the abolition of the permanent settlement as well as to protect them from the atrocities of the zamindars and money-lenders. Actually, no political leader in contemporary Bengal like Fazlul Huq demanded the abolition of the permanent settlement in a loud voice.[27]

It has already mentioned that through the Government of India Act of 1935, the Muslims, Hindus, Scheduled Castes and Europeans were allotted 119, 50, 30 (30 out of 80 in the Hindu constituency being reserved for Scheduled Castes under the Poona Pact) and 25 Assembly seats respectively which once again foreshowed that Bengal politics would be dominated in future by Muslims and it would be inevitable that the caste Hindus would lose their long standing privileged position which they had enjoyed since the beginning of the British rule. Incidentally, the allocation of seats in the Bengal Legislative Assembly was not willingly acceptable to a section of the caste Hindus and as a result of that they refused to cooperate with the Muslim leaders which further intensified the communal divide. It is important to note that the failure of the caste Hindus as well as the congress leadership in Bengal to win over the political support of the Schedule Castes Federation whose steady support to the Muslim League must be considered as a decisive failure of the Congress politics in Bengal.[28]

Under the Government of India Act of 1935, the first general elections to the Provincial Legislatures were held in between 16-25 January, 1937. Out of 250 seats of the Bengal Legislative Assembly, the party wise position of the election were as follows: Congress - 54, Muslim League - 40, KPP - 36, Independent Muslim - 42, Independent Hindu - 37, European - 25, TKP (Tippera Krishak Party) - 5, Anglo Indian - 4, Nationalist - 3, Hindu Mahasabha - 2, and Indian Christian - 2. [29] As a result of Huq's acceptance among the Krishak-Prajas, in the election of 1937, Fazlul Huq was able to defeat Muslim League. The personal prestige and influence of Fazlul Huq increased greatly when he emerged victorious by defeating Sir Khwaja Nazimuddin in the election in his Zamindary at Patuakhali. It is important to note that during that time of election Khwaza Nazimuddin was a member of the Governor's Executive Council and was an important member of the Muslim League. Fazlul Huq's KPP returned with considerable number of Muslim members to the Bengal Provincial Legislative Assembly and as a result of that he occupied a dominant position in the legislature.[30] The Congress Party also became successful in that election. Actually in that election the reactionary forces were defeated and progressive forces were came into victorious.[31]

After the election of 1937 when it was found that no party was in a position to form Government due to lack of absolute majority, then Governor Sir John Herbert invited Sarat Chandra Bose, leader of the single largest party i.e. the congress to form the Ministry, but he declined the offer because of the decision of congress high command. This time congress high command committed a Himalayan blunder for that Bengal had to pay heavy cost. It was decided by the congress high command that the congress would form ministries only in those provinces where it got an absolute majority in the assembly election and would not join hands with any other parties for ministry making. Though, Fazlul Huq, leader of the krishak praja party requested Kiran Sankr Roy of the congress party to join him in a coalition government under his leadership. Sarat Chandra Bose was intending to agree and requested Abul Kalam Azad, one of the members of the Congress High Command for permission to join hands with Huq, taking into account the special situation in Bengal, but the congress high command turned it down despite repeated requests. History would have been different if the congress party agreed to Huq's offer at this juncture. Lastly, Huq was compelled to take the support of the Muslim League, which promptly seized the initiative and agreed to join the coalition under Huq's leadership. As a result of the formation of Huq - League Ministry, the support base of the Muslim League among the Bengali Muslims increased many times which gradually paved the way for the partition of Bengal as well as India. In that context, Amalesh Tripathy, a noted historian wrote "if the congress would have supported the Ministry headed by A.K. Fazlul Huq from outside, then possibly he would not have to go to the Muslim League and Bengal also would not have divided."[32]

Another costly blunder that had long term impact in all India politics was made by the congress party in the United Province, where the Congress and the Muslim League jointly fought for the electoral battle, but as soon as the Congress party itself got an absolute majority and hereafter it forgot the understanding with the Muslim League about forming a government together and dumped the latter. The League leadership never forgave the Congress party for this reason and considered it as a breach of faith and went on life and death struggle against the Congress which embittered Hindu Muslim relations and paved the way for adopting the 'Pakistan Slogan' and materialization of it. However, cutting across the party line Fazlul Huq selected the ministers from both the Hindu and Muslim communities those who were 'the very best man, the very ablest man, man of sterling character and integrity.'[33] From that point of view, the first problem before A.K. Fazlul Huq was to satisfy the members of Muslim League and Krishak Praja Party and side by side accommodate minister from Hindu community also. At last, Fazlul Huq formed his ministry with 5 Muslim and 5 Hindu ministers. The Muslim ministers were 1. Sir, Khaja Nazimuddin 2. Nawab Habibullah of Dhaka 3. H. S. Suharawardy 4. Sayyid Nauser Ali, and 5.Nawab Mosharraf Hussain. The Hindu ministers were 1. Nalini Ranjan Sarkar 2. Maharaja Srishchandra Nandi of Kashimbazar 3. Bijay Prasad Singha Roy 4. Mukunda Bihari Mallick and 5. Prasannya Dev Roykat. Huq himself took the chair of Prime Minister of Bengal.[34]

From the beginning, there was a discontent within the Krishak Praja Party regarding the selection of ministers as because there were only two ministers from the praja party including Huq. It was commented from a section of Muslim community that "too much favoured had been shown to the Hindus" and the AZAD Patrika i, e, the mouthpiece of the Muslim

League reported on 18th March in such a way that 'so far as we know the Bengal Moslems will never acquiesce in the fifty -fifty proposal out of their own accord'.[35] Though, on behalf of the Hindu community, the editorial of the Amrita Bazar Patrika congratulated Fazlul Huq for the formation of such type balanced Ministry.

The newly formed ministry faced uneasy times from the beginning. Huq pressed his most important election agenda i.e. abolition of the Zamindari system. But it was met with sharp opposition from one of the League ministers named Nawab Mosharraf Hussain who declared that "he is willing to spend all his money to get Huq removed from the Cabinet".[36] Many members of the KPP were very much dissatisfied regarding the selection of ministry by Fazlul Huq and his failure to abolish the Zamindari system, the main election pledges of the KPP, due to the strong opposition from the League members and thereupon 20 MLAs of KPP under the leadership of Shamsuddin Ahmed accused Fazlul Huq for this failure.[37] In that circumstances, A. K. Fazlul Huq, the supreme leader of the KPP took a stern action against the agitators of the party and lastly at the aim of controlling the internal fray of the party Fazlul Huq expelled 17 MLAs from the KPP. But that action of Fazlul Huq was reversed to him because the expulsion of 17 MLAs prompted more members to leave the party and as a result of that Fazlul Huq instantly became a minority within the ministry. In that situation, with severe opposition from his coalition partner i, e, Muslim League and the Congress Legislatures in the Assembly, Fazlul Huq realized that without understanding with the communal policy of Muslim League it was almost impossible for him to save his ministry and to counter the opposition in Bengal.[38] Though, there was no pre- election alliance with Muslim League as well as Jinnah, in spite of that in order to overcome his 'crisis of existence' and 'save ministry', Huq prepared to join hand with Jinnah as because he (Huq) clearly realized that he could save his ministry only with Jinnah's support. Considering the gravity of the situation Huq joined the Muslim League in its annual session at Lucknow in October 1939 along with Siquander Hayat Khan of Punjab.[39] After joining Muslim League, A.K. Fazlul Huq, declared "I submit to my leader Mr. Jinnah for all my future work and assured him that I shall abide by his decision… I have entirely thrown myself at the disposal of Mr. Jinnah… I am prepared for any sacrifice when Islam demands it"[40]

It may be considered as a turning point in the political history of Bengal, because it became clear to Jinnah that Fazul Huq was very popular among the Bengali population and it would be impossible to create a strong support base of Muslim League in Bengal defying Huq. At that point of time considering the stature of Fazlul Huq, from that time and onwards Jinnah started using Huq for the purpose of the development of the organization of the Muslim League and inducted him in various important portfolios in the All India Muslim League. The inevitable consequence was that the Muslim League gradually emerged as a strong organization with mass support base in Bengal which completely changed the balance of political scenarios of Bengal.[41]

Keeping in mind the enormous contributions of Fazlul Huq behind the organization of the Muslims of Bengal under the banner of the Muslim League, Humayun Kabir, one of the important personalities of the KPP, remarked "...forced into the arms of Muslim League, Fazlul Huq did perhaps more than anybody else in India to restore the prestige of the League and win for its support among the masses of the land. Thus an awakened mass consciousness contributed to the growth of popularity for the League."[42] In the meanwhile, by a series of administrative and legislative measures such as – the Bengal Tenancy (Amendment) Act of 1938, the Debt Settlement Boards and the Money-lenders Act of 1940; Fazlul Huq enhanced his popularity among the Muslim peasants. Though, he was not able to become completely successful due to strong opposition of the Zamindar Class of both the Congress and the Muslim League, but people specially the rural Muslims realized that this government always tried to save their interests from the exploitation of Zamindars and Money-lenders etc.[43]

Two other contemplated legislations of the Huq ministry ran into serious controversies, namely the Secondary Education Bill and the Communal Ratio Bill. The first aimed at shifting secondary education from the Hindu controlled Calcutta University to a proposed Board of Secondary Education with fifty members, of whom each twenty members were to be nominated from among the Hindus and Muslims, five from the Europeans and five from other categories. Among the total members nineteen were to be directly nominated by the government. There was to be an executive council of fourteen of whom six were to be ex-officio government officials and others members were nominated by the boards.[44] Communal bitterness between the Hindus and the Muslims increased many fold by centering the proposed Secondary Education Bill. Shyamaprasad Barman, one of the members of the Legislative Assembly criticizing the proposed Bill remarked, "The main object of the Bill was to make all secondary schools, the training ground in ideas and theories of the League".[45] This move was interpreted by the Hindu intellectuals like Kiran Sankar Roy, Shyama Prasad Mookherjee etc. as a politically motivated move to communalize school education. Rabindra Nath Tagore, the Nobel laureate poet with international reputation and Acharya Prafullya Chandra Roy, the great nationalist scientist were very much astonished and pained after seeing the communal character of the proposed bill. Even Moulavi Abul Hossain Sarkar, an MLA from Gaibandha (North), criticized the proposed Bill and accusing the influence of non – Bengalese in Bengal politics, said , " They have also discovered that a strong religious feeling pervades the mass mind of Bengal, so these Iranis, Ispahanis, Dadabhais and Adamjis in collaboration with Ghaznavis, Suharawardys and Khwajas, none of whom are Bengalese, have invented the cry of 'Islam in danger' only for the purpose of exploiting Bengal politically and economically."[46]

The various efforts were formulated by the Huq-League coalition ministry regarding the long standing demands of the Muslim community in Bengal. First of all, by the Communal Ratio Act, the ministry was attempted to ensure higher percentage of Government job for the Muslims. It was decided that at least 50% government jobs would be reserved for Muslim community and in the subsequent period of about six months government would apprise the House about the Ratio of getting government service of different communities and in order to execute this decision a 'Communal Ratio Officer' was appointed.[47] Actually, by the Communal Ratio Act what Fazlul Huq attempted to do was nothing more than what Desh Bandhu Chittaranjan Das had assured Bengal Muslims through his historic 'Bengal Pact' (1923). Naturally, the Communal Ratio Act was welcomed by the Muslim community specially the educated rural and urban Muslims, but, on the other hand the congress openly calling the ministry a communal ministry as well as Muslim government. As return of the congress as well as Hindu criticism against Communal Ratio Act, supporters of Huq raised the cry of 'Islam in Danger' which embittered Hindu – Muslim relation badly.

Hindu Muslim relation in Bengal thus deteriorated on the controversy centering the 'Communal Ratio Act' then, Muslim demand for the removal of the 'Lotus Flower' and the word 'Shree' from the logo of the Calcutta University on the ground that these were Hindu symbols – also more embittered the Hindu-Muslim relations . Not only that, a severe criticism started regarding the process of the formation of Senate and Syndicate of Calcutta University. Moulavi Abdul Bari, an MLA accused that out of 70 Syndicate and 100 Senate members, the number of Muslim members were only 01 and 21 respectively. Incidentally, after the establishment of the Calcutta University - there was only one Muslim Vice- Chancellor namely Sir Hassan Suhrawardy (Sir Hassan Suhrawardy from 08. 08. 1930 to 07. 08. 1934 and Sir Azijul Haque from 8. 8. 1938 to 12. 03. 1942) and Muslim employees were only 02 in number out of 180 clerical posts. Besides these, there were only 02 Professor belonging to Muslim community out of 88 Professors.[48] The communal mentality was spread out so widely that even the theme of the Poem of *'BICHAROK'* and *'PUJARINI'* of Rabindra Nath Tagore became subject of severe criticism from communal view points. In the Poem *'Bicharok'* Tagore wrote:

Kahe Raghunath
Amar Path Rudhile Hathat
Chalechhi Korite Yavan Nipat
Jogate Jomer Khadya .

(Raghunath said, why are you creating obstruction in my path? I am on my way to terminate the Yavans to feed the God of death.) [49]

In the poem *'Pujarini'* the poet again wrote:

Veda Brahman Raja Chhara Aar
Kichhu Nahi Bhabe Puja Koribar
Eai Kati Katha Jeno Mone Saar
Bhulile Bipad Habe"

(You should keep it in mind that no one could be worshipped other than the Vedas, the Brahmins and the King in this world. Forgetting this may be troublesome.)[50]

In spite of showing adequate respect to Rabindra Nath Tagore, Mustagaswal Haque, MLA from Bagerhat commented, "But, we ,who constitute Muslim Bengal will not tolerate any poem which definitely shocks Muslim sentiments and which outrages Muslim feelings.[51]

Use of Fazlul Huq's Stature by Muslim League and 'Pakistan Resolution'

Fazlul Huque was successfully utilized by the Muslim League after his joining to the League (October, 1939) to enhance the support base among the Bengalese Muslims as because Fazlul Huq was very much popular among them. In the mean time, Second World War broke out and India was declared a wary country against Germany by Viceroy Lord Linlithgow. In that context, as a protest against this type of declaration without consulting any Indian as well as the congressmen and the decision of Praja–League government to support it unconditionally, Nalini Ranjan Sarkar, the then Finance Minister resigned from the ministry and there upon Huq entirely compelled to depend on the European and Muslim League MLAs for the survival of his Ministry. This time, Lahore Session of the Muslim League

(1940) was convened and 400 delegates from Bengal joined the Lahore Session under the leadership of A. K. Fazlul Huq. Jinnah would never trust Fazlul Huq, but, he was aware that Huq was very much popular in Bengal and he had immense influence over both the Hindu and Muslim communities. That was why M.A. Jinnah, a very shrewd and farsighted statesman tried to dissociate Huq from the Hindus first. He created in such a situation that Fazlul Huq had to move the historical "Lahore Resolution" on 23rd March,1940 which was termed by the Hindus as well as nationalist news papers as 'Pakistan Resolution' because it was the basis behind the demand for Pakistan. The word 'Pakistan' was not included in the proceedings of the Muslim League in its Lahore Session of 1940, but it was the Hindus who used the term 'Pakistan Resolution' instead of 'Lahore Resolution'. In that pretext, M.A. Jinnah applauded the Hindus for using the term 'Pakistan' which was later on generally known as 'Pakistan Resolution'.[52]

In his address Fazlul Huq emphatically remarked, "We have stated definitely and unequivocally that what we want is not merely a tinkering with the idea of federation but its thorough overhauling so that the federation may ultimately go. This idea of federation must not only be postponed but abandoned altogether. On many occasion on the platform of the Muslim League and the other day on the floor of the House in the Bengal Legislative Assembly, I made an emphatic and definite assertion that the Mussalmans of India will not consent to any such scheme which is framed without our approval. We will make such a constitution absolutely unworkable. I hope those who may have in their power to shape the future constitution of India will take the Muslims feelings into consideration and not take any step which may be regretted. We have made our position absolutely clear. The problem is very simple. At present the Muslims constitute 80 millions scattered all over India. It may sound a big number but, as a matter of fact, the Muslims are in a weak position numerically in almost every province of India. In the Punjab and Bengal we are in an effective majority and are hopelessly in minority elsewhere. The position is such that whatever may be the constitution, Muslim interests are bound to suffer just as they have suffered during the last three years of the working of provincial autonomy".[53] Though, later time Fazlul Huq was able to realize the limitation of 'Pakistan Resolution' and rectifying his mistake on 8th January, 1942 he commented, " ...There is no diversity really in religion. All religions must be, from the basic point of view, One ... The future of India would be decided not by strife but by harmony and concord would be greatest benefactors of the country".[54] On 20th June of 1942, Fazlul Huq further remarked, "The Hindus and Muslims have to realize the fact that they had got to live together, sink or swim together and if need be, lay down their lives together for the good of their common motherland."[55]

Huq-Jinnah Personality Clash

Though, Fazlul Huq joined Muslim League but, always kept contact with the group of the congress party led by Sarat Chandra Bose. Sarat Chandra Bose and his followers were very much enthusiastic to form a 'Praja–Congress' Ministry excluding Muslim League and in this regard Subhas Chandra Bose initiated discussion with Huq. But in other side Subhas Chandra Bose also started dialogues with Gandhiji. Gandhiji initially showed his flexibility but, he changed his mind after the consultation with G. D. Birla, Nalini Ranjan Sarkar and Moulana Abul Kalam Azad.[56] Nirad Chandra Chaudhury, personal assistant of Sarat Chandra Bose who had the opportunity to see the all letters of Bose brothers during this time and came to the conclusion that if the proposed 'Praja-Congress' coalition Ministry would form, the business interest of Marwari community of Calcutta might be hampered so, Birla tried his best not to form the proposed ministry and he materialized his notion through Gandhiji.

However, after Huq's move to 'Lahore Resolution' as well as "Pakistan Resolution" (23rd March, 1940), M. A. Jinnah wished to defame and isolate Huq from the Muslim masses of the country. As Jinnah would not believe Huq and both of them shared a mutual distrust, so as like as very mature and shrewd politician, M.A. Jinnah inspired Fazlul Huq to move the 'Lahore Resolution' which might be considered as the greatest diplomatic achievement of Jinnah. Fazlul Huq was very much popular among the both Hindus and Muslims in Bengal as well as a strong proponent of Hindu – Muslim unity, but as a result of Jinnah's successful diplomacy behind his (Huq) move for 'Pakistan Resolution' and thereafter though Muslim League was expected to get benefit a lot but Huq's popularity among the Hindus started declining. As a leader of the Muslim League, Jinnah was so sophisticated that he wanted from his associates' complete subordination. But, A. K. Fazlul Huq due to his mass support base in Bengal politics as well as strong views he could not put up with it. Naturally, there was a personality clash between the two leaders. However, at that point of time, the All India Muslim League instructed its followers to observe the '23rd March' as the ''Pakistan Day" throughout the country. As the communal situation of Bengal was getting overheated so, Fazlul Huq with the consultation of H. S. Suharawardy issued a directive to all branches of the Muslim League in Bengal in 1941 regarding the postponement of the public celebration of 23rd March as 'Pakistan Day'. But, completely ignoring the joint appeal of the Premier of Bengal and President of the Bengal Provincial Muslim League, the Calcutta District Muslim League committee organized a public meeting at Mohammad Ali Park in order to observe 'Pakistan Day' on 23rd March.[57] Following the incidents, Fazlul Huq gradually came to the realization that the Muslim League under the leadership of M.A. Jinnah having made full use of his stature and was determined to leave him high and dry. Fazlul Huq as well as the real representative of the Muslim society in Bengal also realized that the Urdu-speaking non–Bengalese Muslim leaders had no attention towards the interests of the Bengal Muslims as because showing Bengal as a Muslim majority province they only wanted to gain more advantage in all India politics. On that pretext, Fazlul Huq protested against the attitude of all India League leaders towards Bengal and emphatically proclaimed that:-"I will never allow the interests of 33 millions of the Muslims of Bengal to be put under the domination of any outside authority however eminent it may be. At the present moment I have a feeling that Bengal does not count much in the councils of political leaders outside our province, although we constitute more than one-third of the total Muslim population in India."[58]

Drama on National Defense Council

In the meantime, in view of the out broke of the second world war, viceroy Lord Linlithgow nominated the Premiers of Bengal, Assam and Punjab i.e. A.K. Fazlul Huq, Mohammad Shadulla Khan and Sikandar Hayat Khan respectively as the members in the National Defense Council in the month of July of 1941. But on 30th July 1941, M.A. Jinnah issued a directive from Hyderabad to the said three League Premiers to resign from the 'National Defense Council' of viceroy as because they were appointed as the members of the 'National Defense Council' by Viceroy without his clearance.[59] Though, Sikandar Hayat Khan of Punjab and Mohammad Shadullah Khan of Assam resigned promptly, but Fazlul Huq, was not a man to be frightened by swashbuckling and refused to resign on the ground that he did not do any anti-League activities by accepting the membership of 'National Defense Council'. Jinnah gave him ten days time for resignation and failing which threatened to take disciplinary action.[60] In that situation, Fazlul Huq resigned under a lot of pressure, but at the same time he showed his anger by resigning from the League working committee simultaneously and accused Jinnah for using arbitrary powers and being 'wholly unconstitutional'. This resulted in an open conflict between the supporters of the Muslim League in Bengal and virtually the League politics moved into two camps one led by Fazlul Huq and the other was guided by the pro-

Jinnah Leaguers led by Khwaja Najimuddin and H.S. Suhrawardy. Incidentally, Khwaja Najimuddin took an avenge at this point what he suffered as defeat in the hands of Fuzlul Huq in Patuakhali constituency in 1937.[61]

Formation of Progressive Coalition Party (3rd December, 1941)

Under the circumstances, Fazlul Huq started looking for sympathizers elsewhere and went for secret negotiation with Sarat Chandra Bose, Shyama Prasad Mookerjee and the Scheduled Caste leaders of the Bengal Legislative Assembly. As a result of the herculean task of Sarat Chandra Bose new combination i.e. Progressive Coalition Party consisting of 119 MLAs among whom 28 from Sarat Chandra Bose group, 19 from KPP, 42 from Progressive Coalition, 12 from Independent Scheduled Caste, 14 from Nationalists, 3 from Anglo-Indian and 1 from Labour. As per the proposal of Sarat Chandra Bose, A. K. Fazlul Huq was selected as the leader of the newly formed Progressive Coalition Party secretly. Fazlul Huq thus showed great political sagacity for his survival.[62] In the meanwhile, as a part of conspiracy to remove Huq from the seat of Premiership of Bengal, four League minister i. e. Khwaja Nazimuddin, H. S. Suharawardy, Nawab Khaja Habibullah of Dhaka and Tamijuddin Khan accused Huq for creating rift in Muslim Unity and they resigned at a time from the Cabinet in its meeting held on December 1st, 1941. The League leaders expected that after the fall of Huq Ministry a new Government would be formed headed by Khwaja Nazimuddin. At that critical situation, in order to give a fitting reply to the anti-Huq group leaders, the very experienced and shrewd politician A.K. Fazlul Huq also resigned on the same day. Thereafter, as a result of secret negotiation with Sarat Chandra Bose and others on 3rd December 1941, Progressive Coalition Party emerged officially. After selecting the leader of the Progressive Coalition Party unanimously, Fazlul Huq declared "that is formation was an augury not only for the cessation of communal strife but also for carrying out of a programme for the good of all sections of the people of the country".[63] Naturally, Jinnah, one of the cleavers politicians of India had no other alternatives but to accuse Fazlul Huq for anti party activities and eventually expelled him from the Muslim League one day before his formation of the 2nd Ministry i.e. on 10th December, 1941. At that point, M.A.H. Ispahani was inducted in the Working Committee of the Muslim League in place of Huq on 13th December. However, supposing the move of M.A. Jinnah and his followers, Fazlul Huq at the aim of averting the intention of Jinnah as well as Muslim League formed his Second Ministry on 11th December, 1941 including Shyama Prasad Mookerjee and Nawab Habibullah of Dhaka.[64] In this way, by dint of long political experience Fazlul Huq dismissed the hope and plan of pro-Jinnah Leaguers.[65]

Huq-League Controversy and Second Ministry of Fazlul Huq (11th December, 1941 to 28th March, 1943)

The Progressive Coalition Ministry headed by A.K. Fazlul Huq consisted of Progressive Assembly Party - 42, Congress (Bose Group) -28,[66] Krishak Praja Party - 19, Hindu Mahasabha -14, Independent Scheduled Caste Group -12, Anglo-Indian -3 and Labour-1. Besides, the official Congress Party in Bengal having 25 members under the leadership of Kiran Shankar Roy promised responsive cooperation to the Progressive Coalition Government led by A.K. Fazlul Huq.[67] The Council of Ministers of Progressive Coalition Ministry were as follows:- 1. A.K. Fazlul Huq – Prime Minister, Home and Publicity; 2. Dr. Shyama Prasad Mookherjee – Finance; 3. Nawab Khwaja Habibulla Bahadur of Dhaka – Agriculture and Industry; 4. Santosh Kumar Basu - Public Health along with Local Self Government; 5. Khan Bahadur M. Abdul Karim, MLC - Education, Commerce and Labour; 6. Pramatha Nath Banerjee – Judicial and Legislature; 7. Khan Bahadur Moulavi Hashem Ali Khan - Co-operative Credit & Rural Indebtedness; 8. Shamsuddin Ahmed – Communication & Works; 9. Upendra Nath Burman - Forest & Excise.[68] It was no doubt that the formation of the second ministry headed by Huq became possible due to the personal charm and the wide acceptance of Fazlul Huq to the non-League leaders and the compliance of a number of Bengalese leaders including Sarat Chandra Bose and Shyama Prasad Mookerjee for the larger interest of Bengal. At this juncture, being a partner of the 2nd Huq Ministry, popularly known as 'the Huq- Shyama Coalition Government' Sarat Chandra Bose and Shyama Prasad Mookerjee had to defy the congress high command as like as Fazlul Huq defied the attitude of Muslim League headed by M.A. Jinnah. Both the leaders felt that the central leadership of the Congress and the Muslim League were only imposing policies in Bengal for their political interest, not for the interest of Bengal. Kazi Nazrul Islam, the rebel poet welcomed the formation of that Ministry as a big step towards Hindu – Muslim unity. Hindusthan Standard, one of the leading Newspapers of India commented the situation thus 'No persons are better fitted at the present moment to restore communal peace and harmony than Mr. Fazlul Huq and Sarat Chandra Bose'.[69] It is important to note that during the tenure of 'Huq-Shyama' Ministry there was not a single incident of communal riot. At the time of presenting budget on 16th February, 1942, the Finance Minister, Shyama Prasad Mookerjee provided one lakh rupees for the promotion of communal harmony, a very unique gesture in the politics of Bengal. Thereafter, Fazlul Huq and Shyama Prasad Mookerjee jointly visited several trouble prone districts of Bengal for propagating the message of communal harmony. Shyama Prasad Mookerjee at the time of his delivering speech at Coronation Park in Dhaka on 21st April, 1942, said that "Bengal Ministry was no longer for any particular community, but for all communities. This would not only solve the communal problem in Bengal, but would show the whole of India how to stand shoulder to shoulder in the face of common danger. He appealed to complete Hindu – Muslim unity and asked the Hindus to defend the Mosque and Muslims to defend the Temples against attacks from goondas."[70]

As a result of the outbreak of the second world war (1st September, 1939), Subhas Chandra Bose's daring escapes from house arrest at midnight on 16th January, 1941 in disguise, when political situation in India as well as world was very exciting, in that critical hour Fazul Huq formed his Second Ministry on 11th December in 1941. In the meanwhile, with Japan's dramatic entry into the Second world war on 7th December, 1941 on the side of Axis power; Congress launched the Quit India Movement from 9th August, 1942; Muslim Leaguers unconditional support to the warfare of the British; a strong demand in the Assembly for an Judicial enquiry on the pretext of police excesses at Tamluk in Midnapore district and Huq's ultimate order for judicial enquiry in Midnapore police atrocities ground worked the bitter relation between Fazlul Huq and John Herbert, the then Governor of Bengal.[71] At this stage , Fazlul Huq was losing the ground of the political platform and became gradually isolated from the main stream politics. The actual winner in the situation created by the above facts was M. A. Jinnah due to untimely death of Sikandar Hayat Khan of Punjab, an assiduous advocate of a United Punjab and the assassination of Allah Bux, the Premier of Sind who was not a friend of the Muslim League led by Jinnah. Activists of the League systematic anti – Huq campaign in and outside the Legislative Assembly and calling him a betrayer against Islam, rapidly isolated Huq among Muslims. The result of the League's propaganda and the deterioration of Huq's popularity were proved in a by-election for a Muslim seat in the Assembly election held in 1942, with a result the League candidate overcame the KPP candidate by 10,843 votes to 840.[72]

Huq-Jinnah Correspondence

Under the circumstances, Muslim League leaders also continuously poisoned the ears of the British authorities in such a way that since one of the coalition partners of the second ministry of Fazlul Huq was Forward

Block, the party of Subhas Chandra Bose who already joined with the Axis Powers against the British in the Second World War. Naturally Fazlul Huq and his ministers had spontaneous sympathy for the anti-British activities of Subash Chandra Bose. Thus, after being failed of the League leaders to combat Fazlul Huq politically, a conspiracy was set on foot jointly by the Muslim League, the Governor and the twenty five European MLAs for the purpose to replace the Progressive Coalition Ministry headed by A.K. Fazlul Huq with a Muslim League led coalition Government. In the meantime, due to Shyama Prasad's sudden resignation from the Cabinet and being severely criticized by the Muslim League each and every action of the Ministry, the very perplexed Fazlul Huq came to the realization that he might overcome from that situation only if he could secure support and grace of M.A. Jinnah. Following the realization Fazlul Huq with a comparatively soft voice wrote a secret letter to Jinnah on 13th November 1942, thus,- "After all that has happened during the last 11 months, I was hesitating how write to you, but what I have heard from Kaji Saheb has encouraged me to write these lines to you. You have known me for over 30 years and you easily realize that I have been longing to meet you and to assure you of my attachment to you and the Muslim League. It is an irony of fate that this rift should have placed between you and me after close cooperation for long span over a quarter of a century. However, I now request you to allow the dead past bury its dead and throw a veil over all that has happened during the past few months"[73]

In response to the secret letter of Huq, Jinnah laid down some condition i.e. a. Huq had to be expressed his sorrow for his previous activities, b. He had to cut off his relation with Progressive Coalition Party and resign from the post of Premiership of Bengal and only then after discussing the matter in the working committee of League, Mr. Jinnah would take necessary step for lifting ban on Fazlul Huq. In order to get appropriate answer from Huq, Jinnah sent a Telegram to Huq on 11th February 1943 in the following way- "Reference your telephone call and our conversation. Have already posted reply to your letter of the 5th Feb. Reply immediately on receiving my letter. I propose releasing correspondence to avoid circulation of incorrect and misleading version."[74] But, before coming any answer from Huq, M.A. Jinnah would hit A. K. Fazlul Huq as like as below the belt by publishing the correspondence in newspaper which would be considered as a clear breach of faith. In that context, the very astonished Huq lost his credibility among both the Hindus and also his own party men.[75]

Secrecy behind the Resignation of Huq

In the meanwhile, as a part of conspiracy against 'Huq-Shyama' coalition Government, Governor Sir John Herbert completely ignoring the ministers started dealing with some crucial matters like removal of food grains from several East Bengal districts, boat removal policy etc. in the name of creating obstruction before Japanese advance, directly with the help of the officials. He did not even consider a memorandum submitted by the ministers about the activities of the officialdom in the Writers' Building that creating obstruction before the smooth functioning of the cabinet headed by Fazlul Huq. Not only that Governor Sir John Herbert also encouraged the various nefarious designs of the Muslim League in order to disband the functioning of Fazlul Huq's Cabinet in every possible way. In that situation, when Governor was running the administration bypassing the ministers, Shyama Prasad Mookerjee, the then Finance Minister and one of the strong pillars of the Progressive Coalition Government under the leadership of Fazlul Huq resigned from the cabinet on 16th November, 1942, accusing provincial autonomy a 'colossal mockery' and charging the governor for taking advice from officials ignoring the ministers in various crucial matters which were concerning the rights and liberties of the common people.[76] In course of time due to the arrogance and atrocities of the British officers regarding the molestation of the womenfolk at sanoa region in Noakhali district, appointment of Home Guards, excessiveness of the implementation of the 'Defense of India Act', appointment of 'Rice Control officer' etc. and continuous support of the Muslim League leaders created in such a situation that it was not possible for any dignified person to continue as a minister. In that critical juncture, Fazlul Huq firstly remarked in the Legislative Assembly and later on wrote a letter to Governor Sir John Harbert on 26th March, 1943 that "Cabinet should be constituted so as to include the representatives of all the political parties in the Legislature. If at any time your Excellency feels that I am an obstacle to the formation of such a Cabinet, I shall be prepared to tender resignation of my office in the interest of the country".[77] Taking advantage of this type of statement made by Fazlul Huq, Governnor Sir John Herbert called upon him in the evening on 28th March at 7.30 P. M. to discuss the possibility of the formation of an all party Government. But all of a sudden, the Governor requested Huq to resign from the Premiership of Bengal in order to facilitate the formation of an all party Cabinet and even placed a typed letter of resignation before him for putting his signature. Governor also gave Fazlul Huq an impression that he would be invited again to form an all – party Government. The letter read as follows:

"My dear John,

Understanding that there is a possibility of the formation of a ministry representative of most of the parties in the event of my resignation, I hereby tender my resignation of my office as minister in the sincere hope that this will prove to be in the best interest of the people of Bengal.

Yours Sincerely

A.K. Fazlul Huq".[78]

Though, A.K. Fazlul Huq simply signed the letter, but it was a very deep rooted conspiracy of the Governor and Muslim League leaders to oust him from power and as a result of that he was never invited to form the new government.

Nazimuddin's Muslim League Coalition Government- (24th April, 1943 —28th March, 1946)

After the forced resignation of A. K. Fazlul Huq, Governor's rule was proclaimed in Bengal under Article 93 of the constitution under the Government of India Act, 1935 for the period of about a month in order to facilitate to install a Government headed by Khwaja Najimuddin, a pro-Jinnah Muslim League leader. On 24th April 1943, Khwaja Nazimuddin, the leader of the Muslim League in the Assembly was invited by the Governor to form a Cabinet. The new Ministry headed by Khwaja Nazimuddin comprised of - 140 MLAs among whom the Muslim League - 79; Bengal Swarajya Party - 5; Bengal Legislative SC Party - 20 (20 S.C. members united into a new party under the leadership of Jogendra Nath Mandal); European Group - 25; Labour - 2, Independent - 4, Indian Christian - 1 and Anglo-Indian - 4.[79] This Cabinet included 7 Muslim members i.e. H. S. Suhrawardy, Tamizuddin Khan, K. B. Saiyed Muzzamuddin Hossain, Mosharraff Hossain, Khwaja Sahabuddin, Moulavi Jalaluddin Ahmed and Khwaja Nazimuddin himself took the Premiership; 3 Caste Hindus namely Tulsi Charan Goswami, Baroda Prasanna Pyne and Tarak Nath Mukhopadhyay and 3 Scheduled Caste leaders i.e. Premhari Burman, Pulin Behari Mullick and Jogendra Nath Mandal.[80] But it is said that though, among the 140 MLAs only 79 MLAs belonged to Muslim League, but the very nature of the Government was essentially a Muslim League government, not a national government at all.[81] The purpose behind the removal of Fazlul Huq and bring a government led by loyalist and pliable Nazimuddin by the British authorities was in the context of the great famine of 1943 and the deteriorating war situation with the spectacular Japanese occupation in South East Asia. Moreover, the formation of the Azad Hind Government led by Netaji Subhas Chandra Bose and his declaration of war against the British Government and his advancement towards India as well as Bengal's borders with the help of the Japanese army, was incongruous for an independent minded and self-respecting Premier like A. K. Fazlul Huq in Bengal.[82]

Famine of 1943 and Role of the Muslim League Coalition Government led by Khwaja Nazimuddin

The main challenge before the Muslim League Coalition Government led by Khwaja Nazimuddin was to tackle the great famine of 1943 and the dearth of cotton textiles. The famine of 1943 was so alarming that it was widely known as *'Panchasher Manbantar'* (1350 in Bengali Calendar) and was compared with another devastating famine of 1770 i. e. the *Chhiattarer Manbantar* (1176 - Bengali Calendar). The famine of 1943 severely damaged the indigenous rural economy as well as rural life of Bengal along with social value system. It was almost a wholly manmade famine which put the death toll at fifteen lakh as per the official enquiry commission headed by Sir John Wood head. Though unofficial estimates spoke of the figures of death toll was as high as five million. It is noteworthy that applying the same method for calculation of the official enquiry commission, Amartya Sen, famous economist and Nobel laureate estimated a figure around three million deaths.[83] In the face of the wide scale confiscation as well as destruction of boats and other means of transport such as bullock carts by the government all over the province in the name of Japanese invasion and forcible removal and destruction of paddy from the warehouses of the rich merchants as well as peasants affected the normal trading system and caused acute scarcity. The Bengal government led by Khwaja Nazimuddin completely failed to tackle the destructive man-made disaster. Such devastation and forfeiture of paddy on a wide scale took place mainly in the districts of Midnapore, 24 Paragana, Khulna, Bakharganj, Noakhali and several others districts. In his memoirs, Ashoke Mitra has categorically described how did Munshiganj Sub division i.e. Bikrampur pargana render completely devoid of rice and paddy in 1942-43 and countless number of people had to die as a result of severe scarcity of food grain.[84] Out of magnitude of the devastating famine of Bengal the *New Statesman* of London in one of its issues of 24th September 1943, under the headline 'Black Death in Calcutta', mentioned: 'The description of life in Calcutta reads like extracts from medieval chronicle of black death'.[85]

The famine coincided with another important man made poverty - that of cotton textiles in 1944-45. This very necessary day to day commodity simply disappeared from the market during Muslim League Coalition Government led by Khwaja Nazimuddin. H. R. Norton, leader of European group of MLAs in Legislative Assembly sharply criticized the incompetence of Nazimuddin Ministry and remarked "...As a businessman of 36 years experience in Calcutta, I have never known such a dearth of cloth as there has been during the last 12 months."[86] Not only that, Governor Sir Richard Casey requested Viceroy Field Marshal Lord Wavell to dismiss the Nazimuddin Government by applying Article 93 due to its failure to tackle the famine properly.[87] Even after his personal visit to study about the Bengal famine, Lord Wavell blamed the Bengal Ministry led by Khwaja Nazimuddin for this man-made famine and is said to have recommended the dismissal of this Ministry and an imposition of Governor's rule under Section 93. Though, it was not possible due to the disagreement of the Home Government.[88]

Historic Rulling of Nauser Ali and Impossition of Governor's Rule

However, Nazimuddin Ministry had lost its popularity in the wake of improper handling of the severe famine situation of Bengal and ultimately became minority in the Legislative Assembly. It is important to note that on 28th March 1945, during the budget session, Agriculture Minister, K. B. Saiyed Muzzamuddin Hossain placed his Agricultural Budget which was defeated on the floor by 106 votes to 97 on the grant for agricultural department.[89] On the 29th March, 1945, in a historic ruling, Nousher Ali, the then Speaker of the Assembly *inter alia,* stated that "refusal by the House of 'Demand for Grant' made by the Ministry for a major department was a censure on the Government and that he could not allow the existing Ministry to function any longer as such in the Legislature, and adjourned the House *sine die"*.[90]

It is noteworthy that due to the combined as well as skillful opposition under the leadership of Fazlul Huq, the Muslim League Coalition Government led by Khwaja Nazimuddin was thrown out in the Bengal Legislative Assembly during the time of Agriculture Budget by 106 to 97 votes on the fateful day of 28th March, 1945. Incidentally, it may be recalled that exactly two years back, on the same day i.e. on 28th March 1943, the Ministry headed by Fazlul Huq had also been terminated. However, on 30th March, 1945 both the Houses of the Legislature were adjourned by the Governor and on 31st March, 1945 the then Governor Mr. R.G. Casey assumed direct administration of Bengal as per the Section 93 of the Government of India Act, 1935.[91]

Though the Muslim League Coalition Government led by Khwaja Nazimuddin failed to tackle the great famine of Bengal (1943) properly, but it became successful in gaining the support base of Muslim League among the Bengal Muslims enormously. At the time of the distribution of relief, the League workers extensively visited the districts of Bengal and utilized that opportunity to make mass contact and propaganda for Muslim League. As a result of the constant campaign for Muslim League many KPP and old Congress leaders joined the League. The Muslim League was successful to take the anti Huq propaganda so high that even A. K. Fazlul Huq himself had to face black flag demonstration from students almost in every town of East Bengal after he left the Muslim League in 1941. Thus by 1945, the Muslim League had become the most dominant as well as mass-based political party among the Muslims of Bengal. In that situation, after Speaker's historic ruling, Governor Casey took over the charge of the administration under section 93 of the Government of India Act, 1935 without directing the ministers to resign. Taking advantage of this situation, in a desperate move Nazimuddin tried his best to get Jinnah's permission to form a coalition with the official congress group, and Jinnah gave his conditional nod so long as the provision was in honorable terms.[92] But, in spite of all attempts made by Khwaja Nazimuddin, it was not materialized. If really it would have happened, most probably a new chapter in the history of Bengal might have opened.

After the defeat of Nazimuddin Ministry on the floor by 106 votes to 97 votes, preparation started among the political parties for next election. It is important to note here that the term of the present Assemblies was extended more than 5 years by a special Act, passed on 2nd October, 1941 after the end of the war period.[93] However, during the campaign for Assembly election in Bengal, the Muslim League made 'Pakistan' the single issue and asked Muslims to vote only for Muslim League candidates to prove that the League alone represents the Muslims. The Muslim League enlisted the support of both 'Muslim Students' and the *Mullahs* at the time of their election campaign and also launched a campaign of terror against all non–League Muslim candidates throughout the Bengal particularly in the various parts of East Bengal. There were a number of complaints of bloody attack on non-League Muslim candidates, their kidnapping in some cases and threatening them not to contest in that election against the Muslim League candidates or forcible detention of some of them in their own houses. Even some well known Muslim personalities like Nousher Ali, Speaker of the Assembly and KPP leaders like Syed Jalaluddin Hashemi and Azhar Ali were not spared from heinous attack.[94] Some of the *Mullahs* and *Pirs* also campaigned in that election in favour of Muslim League and they vividly spread the theory of fear as well as divine punishment to general Muslim people, warned them to vote only for the Muslim League candidates.[95] Even Golam Murshed Lahori, the then Imam of Jama Alamgir Mosque of Lohore emphatically declared in his election campaign that, "this election battle is the first battle of achieving Pakistan, our future depends on victory in the election."[96]

In order to win over the election at the aim of achieving Pakistan, M. A. Jinnah, undisputed leader of the Muslim League declared, "this election is a plebiscite of the Muslims of India on Pakistan".[97] Abul Hashem, the then Secretary of the BPML, in his leaflet 'Let Us Go to War' appealed to the Muslims "to vote for League candidates and clearly declared that this general election is the beginning of our struggle, immediately after recording our votes in favor of Pakistan at the polling centre after winning our plebiscite liquidating the false claims of the Congress to represent the Muslims, we shall direct our attention towards British imperialism and demand immediate transfer of power to the people of India on the basis of Pakistan."[98] However, due to tireless efforts of Muslim League activists during election campaign specially as a result of the vigorous campaign of Abul Hashem ultimately made Muslim League very popular among the Muslim masses in Bengal and they got the result in ballot box. It is important to note that the general election of 1946 was the last election of undivided Bengal and it had a great importance to both the Congress party and the Muslim League. The British Government also intended to understand the minds of the Bengalese as well as Indians through the said election. Amidst the Muslim League's spirited campaign to the Muslims vote for Muslim League candidates in order to materialize their dream of a separate state of Pakistan, campaign of the KPP and the Congress party on the basis of political, social and economic issues could not make any indelible mark in the minds of the Muslims. Even Fazlul Huq's personal charisma also did not work in that election. As a result of that it was clear that the Muslims of Bengal had given their mass support behind the concept of Pakistan of Muslim League.[99] In the result of the election of 1946, it was found that out of total 250 seats, Muslim League secured 115 seats of the 121 Muslims seats and got 83.64% of the total votes. On the other hand, in spite of all efforts, it became impossible for the Congress party to secure even a single seat in the Muslim constituencies. However, altogether 87 seats won by the congress party out of 90 non-Muslims as well as general seats washing out the Hindu Mahasabha, except the university seat was won by Shyama Prasad Mookherjee in that election. KPP of Fazlul Huq secured only 4 seats from

Muhammadan constituencies including 2 seats were contested and won by Huq himself. Communist Party got only - 03 and European Group - 25 out of 250 assembly seats respectively.[100] Naturally, the election result clearly established the fact that as Muslim League polled about 45 lakhs or 4.5 million i.e. 75% of Muslim votes and non-League parties polled only 15 lakhs or 1.5 million i.e. 25% of Muslim votes - which could for the time being justify that not only Bengal Muslims but also over all Muslim community of India extended their support of Jinnah's demand of 'Pakistan' in that election.[101]

Role of the Communists

At that point of time it appears relevant to look at the role of the Communist Party of India (CPI) and its activities on the eve of a full-fledged political crisis of the Indian nation. It is a fact that India as a whole and Bengal was not an exception while there was a communal atmosphere and most of the political parties were involved in heated politics and ill-feeling to each other, the CPI was in their dreams for 'revolutionary seizure of state power' and side by side to bring about 'revolution with a proletarian impress and also armed insurrection' wherever it was necessary. The British imperialist power identified the CPI as the main danger of the imperialist war period and "on March 15, 1940 the Central Government passed an order for the detention of the communists under the defense of India Act all over India ..."[102] One may not be so much sure about the activities of the communists on the question of communalism in Indian politics had they not been jailed but it is clear that those who were then outside were much more concerned about 'Peoples' War' rather than to honour the national sentiment of India.[103] It is again a matter of no less surprise that the communists of India were then much more concerned about "organizing a country wide campaign for national unity and it was in the form of justification of the Pakistan demand of the All India Muslim League on the logic of "the right of self-determination" of the Muslim nationalists", including the right of separation.[104]

It may be concluded here that why the communist party of India had the role as explained and that it is still a matter of surprise when there was acute national crisis they turned attention either in international affairs or peoples' war and that they were either indifferent towards the national crisis of India or wanted to avoid everything just like silent spectators.

Muslim League Ministry headed by H. S. Suhrawardy (24th April, 1946- 1947)

After the result of the general election of 1946, H. S. Suharawardy was elected the leader of the Muslim League in the Assembly and was invited on 2nd April 1946 by Governor Frederick Burrows to form the Ministry. In that situation, in order to develop the communal amity the Congress agreed to cooperate with League. Moulana Abul Kalam Azad, the then Congress president requested Suharawardy to induct at least one non – League Muslim into his cabinet; but, M. A. Jinnah would never agree with this proposal, showing this reason Suharawardy rejected Moulana Azad's proposal.[105] Suharawardy then formed his Ministry on 24th April 1946, only by the Muslim Leaguers excepting Jogendra Nath Mandal who was the lone Hindu minister and represented the Scheduled Caste Federation.[106] The formation of the Cabinet only by the Muslims and omission of Caste Hindus from Ministry hardened the Bengalese Caste Hindus which sent a strong message to them that what was likely to happen if the whole Bengal would become a part of Pakistan. Naturally, in the pretext of the above circumstances the Bengali Hindus those who enjoyed the power of Bengal politics since the beginning by and large, campaigned intensively for the partition of Bengal as well as creation of a separate Hindu majority province that would remain as a part of Indian Union and refused to have anything to do with the United Bengal proposed by Suharawardy - Sarat Bose duo.[107]

Cabinet Mission Proposals

In the meantime, before the end of the provincial election in Bengal (March, 1946), another significant development took place in Indian politics with the arrival of 'Cabinet Mission' on 24th March 1946. The Cabinet Mission consisting of three members namely Sir Staford Crips, A.V. Alexander and Pethik Lorance arrived in India at the aim of discussion the question of transfer of power with the different political parties in India. The Cabinet Mission had prolonged and niminy-piminy meetings for seven weeks at Simla with not only the leaders of the Congress party including Gandhiji who officially was not even a member of the Congress but practically still the Supreme commander, Jawaharlal Nehru, Maulana Abul Kalam Azad, Sarder Ballavbhai Patel and leaders of the Muslim League namely M. A. Jinnah, Liakot Ali Khan etc. but also with the leaders of other political parties like Dr. B. R. Ambedkar and J.N. Mondal of the Scheduled Caste Federation, Master Tara Singh and Baldev Singh of the Akali Dal etc. The members of the Cabinet Mission also discussed with

Bengal Provincial leaders like Kiran Shankar Roy, H.S. Suharawardy, A.K. Fazlul Huq, Shyama Prasad Mookerjee etc. After circumstantial discussion with the leaders of the different political parties, the Cabinet Mission rejected Jinnah's demand for 'Pakistan' on various ground and remarked , ''It would not solve the communal minority problem but would raise more such problems.''[108] When the Indian leaders failed to arrive at a consensus or come to an understanding, then the Cabinet Mission announced its own proposal on 16th May, 1946, which were as follows:

1. "India would constitute as a federal Union with both the British Indian provinces and the princely states of India.
2. The Union will be in charge of Foreign Affairs, Defence and Communications (railways, posts and telegraphs, etc.) and all other subjects will be under the provinces and the princely states.
3. British Indian provinces would be grouped into three sections. Section A would be consisted of the provinces of Madras, Bombay, United Provinces, Bihar, Central Provinces, and Orissa in which Hindus had an overwhelming majority and in a dominant position. Section B would be consisted of the provinces of Punjab, North-West Frontier Province, Sind and Baluchistan in which Muslims had a majority of about 62:38. Section C would be consisted of the Provinces of Bengal and Assam in which Hindus and Muslims are almost equal, but Muslims had a majority of about 52 to 48.
4. The power of the sections to form their Constitution by a majority (as was the intention of the Mission) came near to securing parity between Hindus and Muslims in their respective Sections.
5. The new constitutions both provincial and national would continue for ten years after which any province would have an option to consider the matter and leave the Union and form a separate state.
6. Until the new constitution was in place, the country would be run by the executive council to be designated as an interim government consisting of Indian leaders.
7. The paramountcy of the British Crown over the princely state would lapse. The precise status of the states would have to be negotiated during the building up of the new constitutional structure." [109]

Nehru's Controversial Faux Pas (10th July, 1946) and Muslim League's declaration of Direct Action Day (16th August, 1946)

The above proposal of the Cabinet Mission met a mixed reaction. The two main parties i. e. the Indian National Congress and the All India Muslim League were initially remained silent. On 6th June, 1946 the Muslim League first accepted the Cabinet Mission's three tier formula on communal basis. A few days later, after three weeks of long debate the Congress Working Committee accepted the Cabinet Mission plan on 26th June, though it was still unwilling to accept the proposal for an interim Government and however lastly the All India Congress Committee accepted the plan by a massive majority on 7th July, 1946. At the same date i.e. on 7th July 1946, with the end of Moulana Azad's term as Congress president, Jawaharlal Nehru took the responsibility of the Congress party as the new president. The acceptance of the Cabinet Mission Plan which 'guaranteed the unity of India' along with necessary assurances to the minorities- by both the Congress and Muslim League was a 'glorious event' in the history of the freedom movement of India.[110] At that juncture of Indian history one of the unfortunate and provocative comments made by Jawharlal Nehru, the then President of the Congress party, changed the entire course of history in India. On 10th July, 1946, as a Congress president Nehru held a press conference in Bombay where he was asked by some pressmen whether, the Congress had accepted the Cabinet Mission Plan in to to? Pandit Nehru answered that 'His party was completely unfettered by any agreements and free to meet all situation as they arose'. Not only that in a response to some quires of the press representatives, Nehru emphatically declared that "the Congress had agreed only to participate in the Constituent Assembly and regarded itself free to change or modify the Cabinet Mission Plan as it thought best." [111] Nehru's this type of controversial faux pas once again reopened the issues which sabotaged the cause of Indian Unity. He was bitterly criticized by Moulana Azad, in his Memoirs 'India Wins Freedom' in which Maulana Azad categorically mentioned "I have to say with the deepest of regret that a large part of the responsibility for this development rests with Jawaharlal. His unfortunate statement that the Congress would be free to modify the Cabinet Mission Plan reopened the whole question of political and communal settlement. Mr. Jinnah took full advantage of his mistake and withdrew from the League's early acceptance of the Cabinet Mission Plan".[112] After making this comment Nehru played into the hands of Jinnah and gave him the excuse to repudiate the agreement. Under the circumstances, M. A. Jinnah thought that Jawaharlal's statement represented the real mind of the Congress. He also felt that Congress could change the scheme through its majority in the Constituent Assembly, this would mean that the minorities would be placed at the mercy of the majority.[113] In that context, all hopes of a United India were shattered to the ground and the idea of an Independent Pakistan, which Jinnah had compromised by accepting the Cabinet Mission Plan, was revived. In Jinnah's reckoning the Congress had given a foretaste of how exactly the Hindus would behave towards the Muslim minority after the British had departed. So, on 27th July, 1946 the League Council met to withdraw its acceptance of the Cabinet Mission plan, and instructed its followers to prepare for a 'Programme of Direct Action to organize the Muslims for the coming struggle to be launched as and when necessary.' The Muslim League working committee gave a call for the declaration of 'Direct Action Day' on 16th August, 1946 was to be a 'Universal Muslim Hartal'. M. A. Jinnah also delivered a provocative speech in the course of which he announced that he was 'giving a goodbye to constitutional methods' and threatened to wield a pistol.[114]

The Great Calcutta Killings

The above circumstances directly triggered off the communal holocaust in Calcutta, then India's one of the largest cities with a population of twenty five lakhs. The violence that erupted on and from 16th to 19th August, 1946, following the observance of the 'Direct Action Day' by the Muslim League, sparked off a chain of communal violence that led to the partition of the country within a year. It is a fact that the then Government of Bengal headed by H. S. Suharawardy declared 16th August, 1946 the 'Direct Action Day' as a public holiday for both Muslims and Hindus alike. In order to enthusiastic the Muslims, the Direct Action Day was directed as if an anti – Hindu campaign by top Muslim League Leaders like H.S. Suharawardy and some of his close aids with the impression among the Muslims 'no cause is dearer or nobler than Pakistan' or adopt the slogan of 'Lar ke lenge Pakistan! i. e. 'Pakistan by Force!'.[115] With the full backing and support of Muslim League Ministry of Bengal under H. S. Suharawardy, the Muslim goondas committed worst crime in Calcutta for three days at a stretch. The Hindus were butchered like sheep, their women ravished and their houses looted and burnt. The police and the Military were not allowed to take any action. On this issue we may refer here the observation of Maulana Abul Kalam Azad what he wrote in his autobiography titled 'India Wins Freedom' - "In Calcutta, I found a general feeling that on 16 August, the Muslim League would attack Congressmen and loot Congress property. Further panic was created when the Bengal Government decided to declare 16 August a public holiday."[116] Maulana Azad further mentioned "16 August was a black day in the history of India. Mob violence unprecedented in the history of India plunged the great city of Calcutta into an orgy of bloodshed, murder and terror. Hundreds of lives were lost. Thousands were injured and property worth crores of rupees was destroyed. Processions were taken out by the League which began to loot and commit acts of arson. Soon the whole city was in the grip of goondas of both the communities.... I found there a large contingent of the military waiting in trucks. When I asked why they were not helping in restoring order, they replied that their orders were to stand ready but not to take any action. Throughout Calcutta, the military and the police were standing by but remained inactive while innocent men and women were being killed."[117]

However, on the third day of the ongoing bloodshed, the retaliation on behalf of the general Hindu was spearheaded by the Sikhs from Bhawanipur area and started branching out soon across the city. The Hindus in their vehicles filled with guns and swords started attacking on the Muslims wherever they could be found throughout the city. In that critical juncture, only when the whole Metropolis was involved in the worst form of communal violence and the whole city went under the grip of the goondas, then the army was called for maintaining law and order, following a conversation about the gravity of the situation in Calcutta between the Viceroy Lord Wavell and the Governor of Bengal Frederick Burrows. On the pretext of the Direct Action Day – what happened in Calcutta 'The Great Calcutta Killings' as they came to be known, had indeed changed the course of Bengal's history by making partition certain.

Holocaust in Noakhali and in Bihar

The Great Calcutta killings had triggered off in Noakhali district of East Bengal an anti Hindu riots in October 1946 and in Bihar anti Muslim riots shortly thereafter. Violence erupted in Noakhali which was predominantly Muslim (82 percent) influential district with some adjacent areas of Tippera district, on 10th October 1946, on a day of the worshiping of the Devi Lakshmi, the Hindu Goddess of prosperity. Under the leadership of Golam Sarwar, an ex MLA of the Muslim League, the organized miscreants of Muslim League started attacking Hindu villages one after another, killing them, burning their houses, looting their movable possessions, molesting their womenfolk, abducting and forcibly marrying many of them, forcibly converting Hindu peoples to Islam and desecrating Hindu temples in order to spread out terror so that they would force to emigrate from their hearths and homes. The press reported that around 5,000 Hindus had been killed and about 1.5 lakh lost their homes and possessions.[118] Under this circumstances, Gandhiji felt extremely disturbed and took decision to proceed to Noakhali along with Sucheta Kripalini in order to restore normalcy. Taking into account of the urgency of the happening in Noakhali, the government of Bengal deputed Simpson, a high ranking official for an on the spot study of the situation of Noakhali and Tippera and to make a report, but the report somehow was not released. However, Gandhiji visited Ramganj village and personally witnessed the horrors of the mass killings. He stayed there for about four months and devoted himself to restore normalcy there. He toured the most affected areas on foot, lived in Muslim villages and held numerous meetings in order to reestablish communal understanding. Gandhiji also appealed to both the communities to live peacefully and amicably as they were before. After staying four months at last he left Noakhali on 2nd March, 1947. The communal feeling was so deepened into the minds of both the communities that in spite of Gandhiji's repeated appeal Noakhali and Tippera continued to be in the grip of fear for many months to come.[119]

Holocaust in Bihar

If Noakhali hardened the Hindu sentiment, the Bihar riots had the same effect for the people of Muslims community. In Bihar, the Muslims had to face suffer at the hands of armed murderous of gangs of Hindus who had been incited by the reports from Calcutta where many Bihari rickshaw pullers and milk vendors were killed by Muslim goondas during mass killing in August 1946. With the spread of the news of the atrocities along with Bihari people killing in Calcutta by Muslim miscreants, into the villages in Bihar, invariably they started retaliating action on a large scale that surpassed the great Calcutta killings. Armed mobs of Hindu miscreants went round the countryside and attacked Muslim villages one after another in a planned manner. Village after villages were burnt, the inhabitants were mercilessly killed or injured and the moveable property were looted. So, it was found that after the great Calcutta killing in the wake of 'Direct Action Day' observed by the Muslim League, if Noakhali riots had hardened the Bengalese Hindu opinion in favour of partition then it was obvious that the happenings in Bihar also instigated the attitude of Muslims Bengalese in favour of not staying in 'Hindu India'.[120]

Impact of Communal disturbances and the Idea of Partition of Bengal

The great Calcutta Killings and the holocaust in Noakhali, Tippera and subsequently in Bihar, no doubt antagonized both the Hindus and Muslims attitude against each other and there was no place of trust between the two main communities in India. In that situation of distrust as well as instability a total unforeseen or unexpected development took place, namely the idea of 'Partition of Bengal', which paradoxically Bengal had rejected almost half century ago by the anti-partition movement against the scheme of partition of Bengal by Lord Curzon in 1905. This proposal first mooted in the Tarakeshwar Conference of the Bengal Provincial Hindu Mahasabha, held on 4th to 6th April 1947, and rapidly gained in favour of the proposal i.e. partition of Bengal like a rolling snowball. N. C. Chatterjee, the then President of the Bengal Provincial Hindu Mahasabha, in his Presidential address remarked, “Let us declare today that as the Muslim League persists in its fantastic idea of establishing Pakistan in Bengal, the Hindus of Bengal must constitute a separate province under a strong national government. This is not a question of partition; this is a question of life and death for us, the Bengali Hindus.” One of the principle advocates of the concept of the partition of Bengal was Shyama Prasad Mookerjee, who declared “I conceive of no other solution of the communal problem in Bengal than to divide the province and to lead the two major communities residing here with peace and freedom’.[121] The commissioner of Burdwan Division reported to government that, “the movement was gradually gaining strength in all the districts of the division and local congress organization became active in support of the movement”.[122]

In the meantime on 20th February 1947, Prime Minister of Britain Clement Attlee made the following historic announcement in the British parliament: “His majesty’s government wishes to make it clear that it is their definite intention to take the necessary steps to effect the transfer of power into responsible Indian hands by a date not later than June 1948.”[123] In that situation, the Bengal Congress Committee almost immediately passed the following resolution : “If His Majesty’s Government contemplate handing over its power to the existing Government of Bengal which is determined to the formation of Bengal into a Sovereign state and which by its composition is a Communal Party Government, such portion of Bengal as are desirous of remaining within the Union of India should be allowed to remain so and be formed in a separate province within the Union of India.”[124]

On the basis of the resolution of the Bengal Congress Committee, it is clear that Bengal Congress also agreed with the view of Hindu Mahasabha i. e. the proposal of the partition of Bengal. A group of 11 (eleven) member representatives of Bengal comprising of - Pandit Laxmikanta Maitra , Nagendra Nath Mukhopadhyay, Devendralal Khan, Kshitish Chandra Neogi, Birendra Kanta Lahiri Chaudhury, Ananda Mohan Poddar, Devendra Mohan Bhattacharyaya, Sushil Kumer Roychaudhury, Surpat Singh, Satyendra Kumer Das and J. Ghoshal served a memorandum to the Viceroy in favour of the Partition of Bengal.[125] In this way Bengal Provincial Congress and the Hindu Mahasabha in political and non political forum started debate regarding the feasibility of the partition of Bengal.

H. S. Suhrawardy was totally unprepared for such a move towards the Partition of Bengal. At a press conference in New Delhi on 27th April, 1947, he described it as a suicidal move and pleaded for 'an independent, sovereign, undivided Bengal in a divided India'.[126] Khwaja Nazimuddin also supported the move of undivided Bengal and remarked that 'if independent, sovereign and undivided Bengal would form, the interests of both Hindu and Muslim community would be protected". In another side, Kiran Shankar Roy and Sarat Chandra Bose in accordance with the opinion of H. S. Suharawardy tried to materialize the united, independent, sovereign Bengal. They also sought Gandhiji's support. Gandhi did at one stage extend his half hearted support, but not the full throated support which was very much needed in that hour of crisis in the history of Bengal. Jogendra Nath Mandal, leader of Scheduled Caste Federation was also in favour of United Bengal.[127]

H. S. Suharawardy met M. A. Jinnah in New Delhi on 15th and 16th May 1947, explained the probability regarding the formation of United Bengal. After Jinnah-Suharawardy meeting over the question of United Bengal, Jinnah as well as Muslim League's stand in that matter was published in Amrita Bazar Patrika on 17th May, 1947 in the following way – "The Muslim League can accept Hindustan, Pakistan and United Bengal, but in no case they would agree to the position of Bengal joining into the Indian Union".[128] But the Congress high command did not allow the existence of Independent, United Bengal. Kiran Shankar Roy soon backed out under pressure of the Congress top leaders and was instructed by Sarder Ballavbhai Patel to go forward according to the main guideline of the Congress high command. Thereafter Kiran Sankar Roy never tried to implement the scheme of sovereign Bengal and thereupon all the efforts of H. S. Huharawardy and Sarat Chandra Bose for the materialization of an 'independent sovereign Bengal' was dashed.[129]

At a meeting on 23rd May 1947, when Mountbatten raised Suharawardy's proposal, Nehru made his task simpler by saying that the Congress party would not support the 'balkanization' of India in terms of the scheme of sovereign Bengal.[130] Nehru was however, in favour of United Bengal if it would be an integral part of India.[131]

It may be noted here that J. N. Mandal was also in favour of the same scheme, we noted above, but when it was totally failed then he had to turned to another scheme so as to draw up a separate North Bengal namely 'Rajasthan' after the name of the Rajbanshi community. Incidentally, he was so "pained at this juncture that in the Star of India, a leading news paper of that time, dated, 12th May, 1946 (page.5) he made a statement condemning the leaders of the Indian National Congress as well those of the Hindu Mahasabha of Bengal by saying that 'the caste Hindu leaders from the congress high command down to the petty workers of the Hindu Mahasabha were keeping silent over this vital question', which was life and death problems of the scheduled castes of Bengal".[132] But his plan was again openly rejected and the subsequent history of North Bengal proves that such a scheme was really a practical through which 'could ensure prosperity of the region'... .[133] But, neither of Sarat Chandra Bose, nor H. S. Suharawarthy and even at the last stage of J. N. Mandal's efforts to maintain undivided Bengal were fulfilled and the trend of Bengal politics was rapidly moving towards the final holocaust i.e. partition.

NOTES AND REFERENCE

1. In order to forge unity among the Hindus and the Muslims, C.R. Das drafted the historic Bengal Pact of 1923. The main provisions of the pact were as follows: "i). The number of members of the two communities will be decided by their respective strength in Bengal's population, and the two communities will vote separately to elect their members. ii). The Muslims will have 60% and the Hindus 40% of the seats in local self-government institutions. iii). Fifty-five percent of the government appointees will be Muslims, but 80% of the vacancies will be filled up by them until the overall percentage of 55 was reached. iv). Music before mosques, usually a standard excuse for Hindu-Muslim riots, was to be banned. v). Killing of cows for religious purposes on the Bakr-Id day, a standard pretext for starting communal violence, was to be permitted and nobody will be allowed to object to it. vi). A committee with equal members of Muslims and Hindus will be appointed in every subdivision to supervise the implementation of the above terms." see Nitish Sengupta, *Land of Two Rivers - A History of Bengal from the Mahabharata to Mujib* (henceforth *Land of Two Rivers...),* Penguin Books, New Delhi, 2011, pp. 338-339.
2. Mr. Saroj Chakrabarty who acted long days with the Chief Ministers of West Bengal as their personal assistant, used to attend Legislative Council of Bengal from the year of 1933 as a part-time reporter of two daily papers, namely 'The Mussalman' and 'Muhammadi' owned by Maulana Akram Khan and would get an allowance of Rs. 25/- per month. See, Saroj Chakrabarty, *With West Bengal Chief Ministers* - Memoirs 1962 To 1977 (henceforth ... *Chief Ministers),* Orient Longman, New Delhi (Printed from Sree Saraswati Press Ltd., 32 Acharya Prafulla Chandra Road, Calcutta) 1978, p. 324.
3. Daily News, London, 17.6.1925
4. Aparna Devi, *Manush Chittaranjan* (in Bengali), Paschim Banga Bangla Academy, 2010, p. 223

5. See name list of the Presidents of Bengal Provincial Congress committee, ascribed on the wall of Bidhan Bhavan, highest centre of West Bengal Pradesh Congress Committee, Philips More, Kolkata (henceforth Bidhan Bhavan...).
6. Nitish Sengupta, *Land of Two Rivers...,* pp. 339 and 347.
7. In the Krishnanagar Session of Bengal Provincial Congress Committee, the common platform of anti-colonial struggle, held in 1926, where the rebel poet Kazi Nazrul Islam (who later on earned the epithet of the national poet of Bangladesh), sang one of the most famous songs he ever composed *'Kandari Hushiar'* ('Helmsman Beware'). He gave the warning to the leaders of the country with the words: "In this dark night, O sentries of Motherland, be alert', 'this helpless nation is drowning-it does not know how to swim', helmsman, tell those who are drowning that they are no Hindus or Muslims, for they are drowning as human beings. See *Kandari Hushiar,* Sanchita, D.M. Library, Kolkata 06, p. 60)
8. Nitish Sengupta, *Land of Two Rivers...,* pp.347-348.
9. Aparna Devi, *op. cit.* p. 272.
10. Sachchidananda Banerjee, *Fazlul Huq Jibon O Rajniti* (in Bengali), Progressive Publishers, Calcutta, 2001, p.12
11. Partha Chatterjee, *Bengal 1920 -1947, The Land Question,* Vol. 1, Calcutta, 1984. p.94.
12. Amalendu Dey, *Pakistan Prastab O Fazlul Huq* (in Bengali, henceforth *Pakistan Prastab...*), Parul, Kolkata, 2015, p. 28.
13. Presidential address delivered by A.K. Fazlul Huq, on 30th December 1918, at the All India Muslim League, 1918 Session, Delhi. See in the Home Department Political, March, 1919, A., NOS. 251-259, National Archives of India, New Delhi.
14. Kalipada Biswas, *Jukta Banglar Sesh Adhyay* (in Bengali), Naya Uddyag, Kolkata, 2012, p.18.
15. P. Acharya, *Education and Communal Politics in Bengal* - A Case Study, IIM, Calcutta Working Paper Series, September, 1998.
16. Dilip Banerjee, *Election Recorder-An Analytical Reference, Bengal, West Bengal, 1862-2012,* Star Publishing house, Kolkata, 2012, pp. 70-71.
17. Bidyut Chakrabarty, *The Communal Award of 1932 and Its Implications in Bengal,* Modern Asian Studies, Vol. XXIII, No. 3 (1989), pp. 493 -523.
18. Nitish Sengupta, *Land of Two Rivers...,* p.370.
19. A. K. Fazlul Huq's reply to critics, see Amrita Bazar Patrika, 24th September, 1936.
20. Statement issued by A. K. Fazlul Huq, see Amrita Bazar Patrika, 1st September, 1936.
21. Amalendu Dey, *Pakistan Prastab...,* p. 29.

22. Fortnightly Report on the political situation in Bengal, 1st half of September 1936, Government of Bengal (Home political).

23. Bengal Legislative Assembly Proceedings. Thirteenth Session, 1942, vol. LXII - No. 2, pp. 34 and 36.

24. Amalendu Dey, *Pakistan Prastab...*, p.39.

25. *Krishak Andolaner Itihasa O Samasya* (In Bengali), Published by the West Bengal Unit, C.P.I, Calcutta, August, 1959, pp.13-23.

26. Muhammad Abdullah Rasul, *Krishak Sabhar Itihasa* (in Bengali), Calcutta, 1969, pp. 59-61.

27. Amalendu Dey, *Pakistan Prastab...*, p.39.

28. Nitish Sengupta, *Land of Two Rivers...*, p. 378.

29. Dilip Banerjee, *op.cit.* p.50.

30. *Ibid.*, p. 70

31. Humayun Kabir, *Muslim Politics 1906-1947 and other Essays*, Calcutta, 1969, pp. 25-26.

32. *"Eker par Ek Dheou"* a Bengali article by Amalesh Tripathy in *Saat Dashak-Samakal O Ananda Bazar*, Ananda Publishers, Kolkata, 2013, p. 54.

33. Report on the political situation in Bengal, 1937, 1st half of March, 1937, Government of Bengal, file No. 10/37.

34. *Ibid.*

35. See *Azad Patrika*, mouthpiece of the Indian Muslim League on 18th March, 1937.

36. M. A Rahim, *Bangler Mussalmander Itihas* 1757 -1947 (in Bengali), Dhaka, 1976, p. 254.

37. Shila Sen, *Muslim Politics in Bengal* (1937-1947), Viswakos Parisad, Kolkata, 2001, pp.102-103.

38. Humayun Kabir, *op.cit.* p.43.

39. *Amrita Bazar Patrika,* October 17, 1937.

40. *Ibid.*

41. Amalendu Dey, *Pakistan Prastab...*, p.43.

42. Humayun Kabir, *op.cit.* p.32.

43. Shila Sen, *op.cit.* p.103.

44. Bengal Legislative Assembly Proceedings, 1940, vol. LVII, No.5, p.114.

45. *Ibid.*, p.113.

46. Bengal Legislative Assembly Proceedings, 1939, Vol. LIV, No.2, p.14.

47. Bengal Legislative Assembly Proceedings-Vol. LIII, No. 4, p. 297.

48. Bengal Legislative Assembly Proceedings Vol. LII, No.4, 1938, p.360; also see Mohammad H. R. Talukdar, *Memoyors of Huseyn Shaheed Suhrawardy- with a brief account of his life and work*, The University Press Limited, Dhaka, 1987.p.5.

49. *Rabindra Rachanabali,* 4th Volume (Katha o Kahini Kabyagrantha),p.74.

50. *Rabindra Rachanabali, op.cit,* p. 29.

51. Bengal Legislative Assembly Proceedings Vol. LI, No.3, pp.606-607.

52. Amalendu Dey, *Pakistan Prastab...,* p.49.

53. Resolution on Pakistan, File No. F. 163/40-R, National Archives of India, New Delhi. Also see Amalendu Dey, *Pakistan Prostab...,* p.53.)

54. Speech delivered by A. K. Fazlul Huq on 8th January, 1942. For details see *Hindusthan Standard*, 9th January, 1942.

55. Amalendu Dey, *Islam in Modern India* (henceforth, *Islam....*), Calcutta, November, 1982, p.165.

56. Letters of Mahatma Gandhi to Subhas Chandra Bose, cited in, Gordon A. Leonard in his *'Bengal in the Nationalist Movement'* 1876-1940, New Delhi, p. 283.

57. S Bandopadhyaya, *Abibhakta Banglar Sesh Adhyaya*, 1937-47 (in Bengali), in Chaturanya, 5th September and 6th October, 1990.

58. Letter of Fazlul Huq to Liaquat Ali Khan, 8th September, 1941, see *Amrita Bazar Patrika,* 11th September, 1941.

59. *Amrita Bazar Patrika,* July 31, 1941.

60. *Amrita Bazar Patrika,* August 26, 1941.

61. *Amrita Bazar Patrika,* 7th December, 1941; Also see Nitish Sengupta, *Land of Two Rivers...,* p.409.

62. Kalipada Biswas, *op.cit.*p.209.

63. *Ibid.*

64. After the resignation of Fazlul Huq on 1st December 1941, the anti-Huq group of Muslim League leaders assembled in the Legislative Assembly and formed a new party known as 'Bengal Legislative Muslim League Party'. It is interesting to note that Nawab Khwaja Habibullah of Dhaka was the claimant of the leadership of the new party from its inception. But, his desire was not fulfilled and eventually Khwaja Najimuddin was elected as the leader of the 'Bengal Legislative Muslim League Party' then Nawab Khwaja Habibullah discarded his relation with Nazimuddin group and subsequently joined his hand with Fazlul Huq and became the Minister of the second ministry of Huq. See Sachchidananda Banerjee, *op.cit.*p.68.

65. The Bengal Legislative Assembly Proceedings, Thirteenth Session, 1942, Vol. LXII, No. 3, p. 403; also see Amlendu Dey, *Pakistan Prostab...,*p. 109.

66. Dilip Banerjee, *op.cit.*p.113. After Subhas Bose's ouster from the Congress in 1939, the Congress Party in Bengal was divided into two faction i.e. Official Congress led by Kiran Shankar Roy and Congress (Bose Group) led by Sarat Chandra Bose.
67. *Ibid.,* p.113.
68. *Ibid.,* p.111.
69. Sachchidananda Banerjee, *op.cit.*p.72.
70. R. C. Majumdar, *History of Bengal*, Vol. 4, cited in Nitish Sengupta, *Land of Two Rivers...,* p.408.
71. Statements by Ex-Ministers, Bengal Legislalive Assembly Proceedings, Vol. LXI, 6th Session, 1943.
72. Nitish Sengupta, *Land of Two Rivers...,* p.415.
73. Letter of Fazlul Huq to M. A. Jinnah, 13th November, 1942; see *Amrita Bazar Patrika,* 17th February, 1943.
74. Telegram of M.A. Jinnah to A.K. Fazlul Huq, 11th February, 1943; see *Amrita Bazar Patrika,* 17th February, 1943.
75. Nitish Sengupta, *Land of Two Rivers...,* p.416.
76. Statements by ex-ministers, Bengal Legislative Assembly Proceedings, Vol. LXV, 1943, pp, 39 -61; Also see Nitish Sengupta, *Land of Two Rivers...,* pp.416-417.
77. Statements by ex-ministers, Bengal Legislative Assembly Proceedings, Vol. LXV, 1943, pp. 39-61.
78. Nitish Sengupta, *Land of Two Rivers...,* p. 418.
79. Dilip Banerjee, *op.cit.*p.114.
80. *Ibid.,* pp. 111-112.
81. Nitish Sengupta, *Land of Two Rivers...,* pp. 419-420.
82. *Ibid.*
83. Amartya Sen, *Poverty and Famine - An Essay on Entitlement and Deprivation*, Oxford, 1981, pp.52-53.
84. Ashok Mitra, *Teenkuri Dash* (in Bengali), Vol. II (1403 BS), pp. 113-117; and his two articles in *Chaturangaa,* 11th March and 12th April, 1992.
85. Nitish Sengupta, *Land of Two Rivers...,* p.424.
86. Bengal Legislative Assembly Proceedings, Vol. LXIX, No. 2, 1945, p. 458.
87. Nicholas Mansergh, ed. *Transfer of Power,* Vol. III, p. 1055.
88. Nitish Sengupta, *Land of Two Rivers...,* p.425.
89. *Amrita Bazar Patrika*, 29th March, 1945.
90. Dilip Banerjee, *op.cit.*p.1010, Annexure-II,. Ruling Delivered by Shri Nausher Ali, Speaker, Bengal Legislative Assembly on 29th March, 1945.

91. *Ibid.*, p.114.
92. Syed Sharifuddin Pirzada, ed., *Quid - e - Azam Jinnah's Correspondence,* (Indian Edition), New Delhi, 1981, p. 290.
93. Dilip Banerjee, *op.cit.*p.114.
94. Humayun Kabir's Article *"Bengal Election"* 1946 : A Mockery; see *Amrita Bazar Patrika,* 14th April, 1946.
95. Maulana Abul Kalam Azad's Report on Bengal Election, see *Amrita Bazar Patrika,* 5th April, 1946.
96. Amalendu Dey, *Islam* ..., p. 221.
97. Sachchidananda Banerjee, *op.cit.*p.93.
98. Shila Sen, *op.cit.*p.279.
99. Dilip Banerjee, *op.cit.*p.115.
100. Nitish Sengupta, *Land of Two Rivers...,* p.454.
101. Indian Annual Register 1946, Vol. I, p. 227; see Dilip Banerjee, *op.cit.*p.127.
102. For details see Gene D. Overstreet and Marshal Wind Miller, *Communism in India,* Bombay, 1960, p. 183.
103. Tarun Kumar Banerjee and Debesh Roychowdhury, ed. *Colonial India – Ideas and Movments,* Progressive Publishers, Calcutta, 2001, p.258.
104. Suniti Kumar Ghosh, *India and the Raj,* 1919-1947, Research Unit for Political Economy, Bombay, 1995, p. 337.
105. Amalendu Dey, *Pakistan Prastab...*, p. 207.
106. H.S. Suhrawardy could have easily formed the ministry with the support of 25 European members along with 115 Muslim League members. But he felt that it would be improper to have a council of ministers in which there would be no representation of a large part of the population. So, H. S. Suharawardy did his best to form a coalition Government with the Congress. In spite of invitation from His Excellency the Governor, Frederick Burrows on 2nd April, he took a long time i.e. 24th April, 1946 to make the Council of Ministers. In that case he felt the necessity to work in a united manner of both the Hindus and Muslims community for the development of the Bengal. It is a fact that his attempt of the formation of joint Hindu-Muslim Ministry was not materialized initially and on 24th April Suharawardy Ministry was formed with Jogendra Nath Mondal, the lone Hindu Minister and other seven members of the Muslim League. But, in the meantime, after 'Direct Action Day' on 16th August 1946, the Muslim League's joined in the interim Government at the Centre on 15th October, 1946. In the Central interim Government, no Muslim representative from Bengal was taken by M.A. Jinnah. Only Jogendra Nath Mondal was selected to represent Bengal by the Muslim League as well as M.A. Jinnah. Naturally Jogendra Nath Mondal had to resign from the Bengal Cabinet and thereby H. S. Suharawardy reconstituted his Cabinet on 15th November, 1946 inducting one Muslim Member namely Mr. Fazlur Rahaman in place of Jogendra

Nath Mondal. At the same time, H. S. Suharawardy inducted three other Hindu members of whom one represented the upper caste. The names of the three Hindu Ministers were Tarak Nath Mukherjee, Nagendra Narayan Roy and Dwarikanath Barori respectively. The Council of Minister of Bengal and Portfolios headed by H. S. Suharawardy were as follows: 1. Huseyan Shaheed Suhrawardy – Prime Minister, Home (Except Jail), 2. Mohammad Ali – Finance, Health, Local Self-Government, 3. Saiyed Muazzamuddin Hossain – Education, 4. Ahmed Hossain – Agriculture, Forest, Fisheries, 5. Abdul Gofran – Civil supplies, 6. Abul Fazal Md. Abdur Rahaman - Co-operation, Credit and Relief, 7. Shamsuddin Ahhmed – Commerce, Labour and Industries, 8. Tarak Nath Mukherjee – Irrigation and Water-ways, 9. Nagendra Narayan Roy – Judicial and Legislative, 10. Fazlur Rahaman- Land, Land Revenue and Jail, 11. Dwarikanath Barori – Works and Buildings. However, the Government did not last longer than 15 months owing to partition of the country. The last Cabinet meeting was held on 11th August 1947 just 3 days before the Independence. For details see Dilip Banerjee, *op.cit.* pp. 116-118; and also see Nitish Sengupta, *Land of Two Rivers...,* pp. 470-471.

107. Nitish Sengupta, *Land of Two Rivers...,* p.455.

108. *Ibid.,* pp. 456-457; and also see Stanley Wolpert, *Jinnah of Pakistan,* p. 267.

109. Nitish Sengupta, *op. cit.* pp. 457-458; also see, H. M. Seervai, *op. cit.* pp. 66; also see, Sumit Sarkar, *Modern India 1885-19470,* Macmillan, New Delhi, 2001, p.430, in which it has been mentioned that "existing provincial assemblies being grouped into three sections while electing the constituent assembly: Section A for the Hindu majority provinces, Section B and C for the Muslim – majority provinces of the north-west and north-east (including Assam); Also see, Bipan Chandra, et. al, *India After Independence 1947-2000,* Penguin Books, New Delhi, 2000, p.38, in which it has been mentioned that important provisions of the Cabinet Mission were relating to grouping of provinces into sections A, B, and C. Section A consisted of Madras, Bombay, U. P., Bihar, the Central Provinces and Orissa – the 'Hindu majority' provinces. Section B and C similarly consisted of the 'Muslim-majority' provinces of Punjab, NWFP and Sind in the west and Assam and Bengal in the east.

110. Maulana Abul Kalam Azad, *India Wins Freedom-The Complete Version,* Orient Black Swan, New Delhi, 2014, pp. 158- 164.

111. *Ibid.,* pp.164-165; also see-Leonard Mosley, *The Last Days of the British Raj* (1961), pp.21-23.

112. Maulana Abul Kalam Azad, *op.cit.* p.170.

113. *Ibid.,* p.165.

114. Nitish Sengupta, *Land of Two Rivers...,* p.460.

115. *Ibid.,* p.461.

116. Maulana Abul Kalam Azad, *op.cit.* p.168.

117. *Ibid.,* p.169.

118. Amrita Bazar Patrika, 20th October, 1946.

119. Nitish Sengupta, *Land of Two Rivers...*, pp.472-473.

120. Ibid., p.474.

121. Ibid., p. 478.

122. Fortnightly Report on the Political Situation in Bengal, 2nd half of April, 1947. Govt. of Bengal.

123. Nitish Sengupta, *Land of Two Rivers...*, p.475.

124. Penderel Moon, ed. Wavell - The Viceroy's Journal, 1973, p.423.

125. Amrita Bazar Patrika, 12th April 1947.

126. Amrita Bazar Patrika, 28th April 1947.

127. Fortnightly Report, 2nd half of May, 1947, Government of Bengal.

128. Amrita Bazar Patrika, 17th May, 1947.

129. Sachchidananda Banerjee, op.cit.p.106.

130. Record of the Viceroy's meeting with Nehru, 11th May, 1947. TP vol. IX, No. 405. Also see, Joya Chatterji, *Bengal divided – Hindu Communalism and Partition,* 1932-1947, Foundation Books, New Delhi, 1996, p. 260.

131. Nitish Sengupta, *Land of Two Rivers...*, p. 483.

132. For details see "*Politics of Partition and Warning of the Time*" an Article by Ichhamuddin Sarker in *Dalit Lives and Dalit Visions in Eastern India,* Centre for Ambedkar studies, Jadavpur University, 2007, pp. 133-139.

133. Ichhamuddin Sarker, *op.cit.* p. 139.

CHAPTER

2

Tasks and Goals of the Indian National Congress in West Bengal after Independence (1947-1948)

The demand of the Bengali Hindus for a separate province inside India in which they would be the majority was intended to lead them secured through the disaster of partition to a bright future. After take-over of the office of the Government of West Bengal as a separate state in August 1947, it soon became clear that these plans were going badly wrong. Partition transformed Bengal's political landscape. Having lost two-thirds of its territory to East Pakistan, West Bengal was left with only 89 of the 250 constituencies in the Assembly of undivided Bengal.[1]

Position of the Congress Party and the Muslim League in West Bengal after Partition

The Partition of Bengal virtually overturned all the previous balances and changed the position of every political party in the new province. Before partition, the provincial wings of two all-India parties namely the All India Muslim League (henceforth AIML) and the Indian National Congress (henceforth INC) had dominated Bengal's politics. In West Bengal, the most obvious disaster of partition fell on the Muslim League. It may be recalled here that after the domination over Bengal Government since 1937, the Muslim League in West Bengal virtually collapsed. Those Muslim notables who stayed on in West Bengal, they had no other alternative but to join other parties particularly in the congress. After independence, the ruling power in the other provinces automatically devolved to the hands of the leaders of existing provincial congress committees and most of which had the opportunities to run the respective provincial governments between 1937 and 1939. But, in West Bengal, the situation was quite different because as a political party the congress did not get the opportunity to rule over Bengal like other provinces. So, at the critical juncture when India won independence and subsequently was partitioned, the leaders of the Bengal's congress had no clear mandate in their province. Factional hostilities broke out at every level of the Bengal congress for controlling power of the new state. In that connection, the name of the 'Hooghly Group' deserved special mention. It was the 'Hooghly Group' whose front ranking leaders were a handful of Gandhian camp and latter-day belonged to 'no-changers'[2] who, as followers of Mahatma, had taken up spinning, weaving, good works and village welfare in the mid-1920s. Their main working centres were situated in the Arambagh subdivision of the Hooghly district and in Bankura. In these rural areas of Bengal, the congress had put down strong roots during non-cooperation and the anti-*chaukadari* tax campaigns of the 1920s.[3] It was also able to win adequate support from the middle castes of Bengal particularly the *Mahishyas*, once lowly fisher-men who were pushing at the gates of the twice-born.[4] In the 1930's Prafulla Chandra Sen, one of the leading figures of the Bengal Provincial Congress stood against the Bose brothers[5] and build up a considerable network of supporters in this south-western region of Bengal. He now emerged as a leader of the Hooghly faction and his protégé, Atulya Ghosh, another notable congress leader became the faction's most effective organizer and fixer. But, even after the defenestration of the Bose bloc from the congress, the Hooghly Group was not in a position to control the Bengal politics. It had to come across huge difficulties due to its influence over a narrow geographical limits and control over only 10 seats of 250 in the Bengal Assembly, was far from the dominating position in the politics of the province. It was only after partition that its stock began to rise.

The Hooghly faction[6] had to device and weave for its solicitation of power after independence. It is important to note that despite partition, the Bengal congress was still an organization dominated by the members from Eastern Bengal. According to the constitution of the congress party, the Provincial Congress Committee consisted of the provincial delegates to the All-India Congress Committee. The old rules laid down that the number of delegates from each province were determined by the district's population, not by the size of its congress membership. Since they had the largest populations, the eastern districts of Bengal would send many more delegates to the AICC than the western part of Bengal. The East Bengal sent 344 delegates which were many more in comparison of West Bengal's delegate 200 in numbers, even though congress members were almost as numerous in the Hindu-dominated west as in the much more populous Muslim east[7].

In July 1947, the Congress Working Committee decided that Provincial Committees in the partitioned provinces of Bengal and the Punjab should continue to function as before until such time as the congress came to rewrite its constitution.[8] In this way the decision of the Congress Working Committee allowed delegates from East Bengal and its continuous control over the Bengal Provincial Congress Committee. In August 1947, Dr. Prafulla Chandra Ghosh (henceforth P. C. Ghosh), an ardent disciple of Gandhiji from the *Abhay Ashram* in Comilla, East Bengal and a protégé of Acharya J. B. Kripalini, the then All-India Congress President, took charge of the state government of West Bengal with the blessings of the central congress leadership. Surendra Mohan Ghosh, a key man in the erstwhile terrorist organization, named Jugantar from Mymensingh, East Bengal, was allowed to continue, to be the president of the West Bengal Congress for the time being,

Background of Prafulla Chandra Ghosh

Prafulla Chandra Ghosh was a remarkable character in Indian politics. He was born on 24th day of December, 1891 in the Malikanda village of Dhaka district in East Bengal. His father Purna Chandra Ghosh was a village primary school teacher and mother Binodini Devi was a pious and generous woman. He was all along a very bright student and as a result of that he became the first class first in Chemistry from Dhaka College in 1913, and in 1916 he was not only the first class first in M.A but also became the toper among the pass out students of M.A, M. Sc in Chemistry. He did his Ph. D. from Calcutta University in 1920.[9] As a mark of extraordinary scholar, his some 'Research Papers' were published in the Journal of 'London Chemical Society'. Not only that, as a first Indian, even before getting Ph. D. Degree, he was appointed in the post of "Deputy Assay Master" in Calcutta Mint with the monthly salary of worth Rs-500.[10]

Abhaya Ashram

In personal life as well as spiritual life, P. C. Ghosh was very much influenced by Swami Vivekananda and Sree Aurobindo. Later, when he came into the contact with M. K. Gandhi, became an ardent disciple of Gandhiji. After the meeting with Gandhiji in 1920 and deeply inspired by him about non-violence as well as fearlessness; P. C. Ghosh decided to join in the freedom movement in India under the guidance of Gandhiji, and thereupon he resigned from the service accordingly in order to engage himself in freedom movement in all respect. After leaving service to join non-cooperation movement and for self realization through the service of the country, P. C. Ghosh along with Suresh Chandra Bandopadhyay, and consultation with Desh Bandhu Chittaranjan Das and Gandhiji established *'Abhay Ashram'* in 1922, whose main centre was Comilla in Eastern Bengal.[11] Remaining in the path of truth, non-violence and adoration to God P. C. Ghosh devoted his life for the sake of his motherland on the path of Mathma Gandhi and that is why he was in favor of Council boycott against Deshbandhu's move to Council entry. Due to lack of unanimity, there was an election for the post of 'secretary' in Bengal Provincial Congress Committee. In that election Deshpran Birendranath Saahmal from Midnapore was the candidate of the followers of Council entry i,e, the group of Deshbandhu Chittaranjan Das , and Prafulla Chandra Ghosh was the candidate of Council boycott group as well as Gandian Group. At last, P. C. Ghosh won the election by a margin of 10 votes. [12]

Role of Prafulla Chandra Ghosh in Tripuri Congress

As a strong believer of Gandhian Philosophy as well as thought, Prafulla Chandra Ghosh along with 80 (eighty) delegates of Bengal used their voting right in the historic Tripuri Congress in 1938 in favor of Pattravi Sitarammaia. Incidentally, Pattravi Sitarammaia was supported by Gandhiji against Subash Chandra Bose in the presidential election of the congress party. After the resignation of Subash Chandra Bose, as a Congress President in April 1939, Babu Rajendra Prosad was elected the Congress President and P. C. Ghosh was one of the members of the Working Committee, formed by the Congress President.[13] Though, there were differences of opinion in politics, in spite of that P. C. Ghosh had good personal relation with Bose brothers. Before partition, especially after the declaration of 'Direct Action Day' on 16th August,1946 by the Muslim League, severe communal violence took place in Calcutta and thereupon same communal brutality had broken out at Noakhali in Eastern Bengal in the month of October, 1946 and the almost same thing happened through Bihar holocaust. In that situation Mahatma Gandhi, the 77 years old man, rushed to Noakhali in order to restore communal harmony and tranquility and avoided to attend the celebration of Independence Day on 26th January, 1947 and expressed unhappiness for communal intolerance.

Way to Partition

In the meantime, after the election of 1946, it was found that within the 11 provinces the Congress Party had got the thumping majority in 8 provinces where Muslim League only 3 provinces. In the Bengal Assembly election

(1946, March) there was a resounding success both for the Muslim League and the Congress party. The Muslim League got 115 seats out of 121 Muslims seats, and the Congress got 87 out of 90 general seats wiping out the Hindu Mahasabha, excepting the University seat won by Dr. Shyama Prasad Mookherjee.[14] Naturally, after election Muslim League formed Ministry in Bengal province. As per the instruction of Viceroy, Pundit Jawaharlal Nehru formed central Ministry on 2nd September, 1946. Though at the beginning, Muslim League did not join with the Nehru's Central Ministry, but in the month of October without any consultation with Prime Minister Jawaharlal Nehru, League joined the Central Ministry according to the advice of Viceroy.[15]

Due to increasing communal violence and mass killing in different parts of the country especially after the Muslims to adopt the slogan of 'Lar ke lenge Pakistan'or 'no cause is dearer or nobler than Pakistan' or Nehru's controversial faux pas after the acceptance of Cabinet Mission Plan, whether the Congress would follow the Cabinet Mission Plan in to-to or not, Nehru answered that his party was 'completely unfettered by any agreement and free to meet all situation as they arise',[16] (10th July 1946) – thus it makes clear that India was going to divide. But Ghandiji was dead against the partition and expressed his view that if the communal violence would continue then the destruction of the country was inevitable. Pundit Nehru and Sarder Ballav Bhai Pattel boldly stated that it was not possible to work with the League. They also said that if the partition happened, then the League members would engage themselves into their developmental work, and they (Nehru & Patel) also did for the betterment of their part and thus peace might restore.[17]

Stand of *Abhaya Ashram* and the Selection of P.C. Ghosh as the Leader of the West Bengal Legislative Assembly

Keeping in mind the above situation, when the partition of India as well as Bengal was inevitable, the activists of the *'Abhoy Ashram'* (Coomilla, now in Bangladesh) decided that they would not change their working place whether it was east or west Bengal, but one might be allowed to work in his birth place. Though the birth place of P. C. Ghosh was East Bengal, but he was deeply associated with the work of West Bengal. In that situation, due to the desire of his associates of West Bengal, P. C. Ghosh inclined to become the leader of the West Bengal Legislative Assembly. The president of the Bengal Provincial Congress Committee (henceforth BPCC), Surendra Mohan Ghosh also expressed his desire to become the leader of the Legislative Assembly. J. B. Kripalini, the then All

India Congress President decided that he personally would talk to the M.L.As of the congress party and also cleared that most acceptable between the two would be elected as the leader of the Legislative party, but there would be no open opposition. Both Surendra Mohan Ghosh and Prafulla Chandra Ghosh were agreed with the proposal and lastly majority of the congress M.L.As expressed their confidence on P. C. Ghosh and that is why he was elected the leader of the Legislative Assembly. After becoming the leader P. C. Ghosh at first proposed Surendra Mohan Ghosh to become a member of his Ministry but he declined.[18]

Shadow Ministry - (New Bengal Ministry Prior to 15th August, 1947)

The year 1947, experienced not only the birth of Independent India but also witnessed the 'Partition of Bengal'. Indeed, West Bengal suffered most due to the partition; it was a blow to the economy, culture and identity of the Bengali people. It was an overall crisis of the Bengali nationality during the first phase of the post-independence days that left permanent socio- cultural impact in the psyche of the Bengali people.[19] Before the partition of Bengal, it was decided among the Congress, Muslim League and the Government of India that the leader of the West Bengal Legislative Assembly along with his colleagues would join with the Muslim League Ministry headed by Khwaja Nazimuddin- as a 'Shadow Ministry'. No work would be done in West Bengal without the approval of the shadow Ministry. Though, in all affairs i.e. work order and implementation of any project would be exercised by the League Ministry of United Bengal. In case of any disputes as well as differences of opinion between League Ministry and Shadow Ministry, Governor had the right to resolve, if necessary the Government of India would interfere to solve the problem. Actually on and from 3rd July, 1947, i.e. the day of oath taking of the 'Shadow Ministry' of P. C. Ghosh to 15th August, 1947 were very crucial day in the life of P. C. Ghosh.[20] The first biggest challenge came before the Shadow Ministry with the Government Employees'. Government of India given the rights of all the Govt. Employees' of united Bengal to work either in East Bengal or India as well as West Bengal. As most of the employees' were Hindus, so almost all of them wanted to work in West Bengal. The Ministry unanimously decided to absorb them.[21]

Steps taken by P.C. Ghosh as head of the Shadow Ministry

Prafulla Chandra Ghosh had no earlier experience in the field of administration. He thought that if he would go ahead with the development of common people, honesty and hard work, in spite of some mistake the country would progress. His second impression was that if the recruitment of Chief Secretary and other Secretaries were up to the mark then the implementation of the policy of the council of ministry would be easier. Keeping in mind the above thinking, P. C. Ghosh went through all the secret reports of the higher officials of administrative and judicial. He recruited Sukumar Sen (I. C. S) as the Chief Secretary, Karuna Kumar Hazra (I.C.S.) as personal secretary, Ranajit Gupta (I.C.S.) as Home Secretary and Shaibal Kumar Gupta (I.C.S) as Education Secretary. These recruitments were no-doubt very good because the devotion and sincerities they showed in their working place was noteworthy. At the time of the 'Shadow Ministry' one day, after noon a letter from Mahatma Gandhi came in the hands of P. C. Ghosh by somebody. In that letter Ghandhiji wrote (30th June, 1947), "Sardar Vallabhbhai Patel sent a message that there should be a Marwari in your Cabinet – Badridas Goenka or Khaitan. It appears to me that it is proper to do it and improper not to do it."[22] P.C. Ghosh was very much astonished after getting the letter from Gandhi, as because a few days ago he (Ghosh) approved the name of the ministers from Centre. Sarder Patel was one of the approval bodies, but at that time he personally did not say anything regarding that matter. It was fully illogical that a minister from Marwari community must be inducted. Thereafter, as Gandhiji was not able to hear the telephonic conversation, P. C. Ghosh narrated the whole matter to Kripaliniji, so that he could inform Gandhiji. After knowing fully well, Gndhiji told Kripaliniji, 'If Prafulla thought that the proposal was unjustified, he might think that I had not written him that letter'.[23] It was worthy of mention that P. C. Ghosh had no grudge against any Marwari, as because according to his will Iswardas Jalan, a man of Marwari community became the first Speaker of the West Bengal Legislative Assembly and Ashutosh Mullick became his Deputy.[24] Iswardas Jalan became the Speaker by dint of his worthiness, not because as a Marwari. In the Shadow Ministry, and the first Ministry of P. C. Ghosh there was no Muslim and for that reason nobody told him anything. Prafulla Chandra Ghosh all along deeply believed that one able and honest Hindu Minister could do justice to all communities and at the same time a Muslim Minister vice-versa. Worthy men should be given the opportunity to perform in the appropriate places irrespective of caste, class and religion. Ministers should be inducted from each and every community – this policy is nothing but to perpetuate the communal ailment.

Pakistan Flag Hoisted in Maldah – Murshidabad and Indian Flag in Khulna

When Gandhiji was doing his best to restore the peace and communal harmony in Calcutta, even at the day of independence i.e. on 15th August, 1947, in the meantime, P. C. Ghosh Ministry had to face a severe problem. On 14th August 1947, Pakistani flag was hoisted in the district town of Murshidabad and Maldah. On 15th August, 1947, Indian flag was hoisted in Khulna. The report of the boundary commission of two Bengal as well as Radcliffe Award was published on 17th August. In that report, it was found that the entire Khulna district was within the part of East Pakistan, on the other hand some part of Murshidabad and Maldah districts along with the main city of Maldah and Murshidabad had become the part of West Bengal. Naturally, there was an overcast environment in two Bengal. In that situation, P. C. Ghosh along with Khwaza Nazimuddin made a joint statement. The essence of the joint statement was that if there was a necessity regarding the change of the Radcliffe Award, it must be done with the consultation of the government of two Bengal, and until and unless it had not done, the people of both side had to obey the boundary line. Gandhiji welcomed the joint statement as statesmanlike and sagacious. Though, Sarder Ballav Bhai Pattel, the first Home Minister of India did not like the joint statement. Later Government of India formed a five men committee in order to consider the demands of the people, but the result was meaningless. [25]

Problems Faced by P. C. Ghosh

As the first Premier of West Bengal, Prafulla Chandra Ghosh had to take the responsibility of the administration at a very critical moment. At that time there were main three problems before him, such as: i). Food Crisis, ii). Communal Problem and iii). Corruption. In the Government store room there were food grains for only some days. So, with the import of the food grain by the steamer and without any delay it was transferred to the necessary places. In order to meet up the food problem, in spite of huge hardship, P. C. Ghosh was able to collect almost one lakhs maund food grains for his own province (West Bengal). But, another danger came from Maitriyee Basu, leader of the congress trade union. Maitriyee Basu came to P. C. Ghosh only few days before the Durga Puja and demanded that one month's salary had to be given as advance to the driver of the food supply department. P. C. Ghosh informed her that if she would come to him at least two weeks ago, then an arrangement might be done for giving an advance to all the equal salary holders. So, it was not possible by any means to give the salary of one month as advance only to the drivers of the food supply departments. After that without giving any notice as well as intimation, all of a sudden, one day morning the drivers of the food supply departments started ceasing work. In that circumstances, in order to meet the crisis, Premier Ghosh with the help of Charu Chandra Bhandari, the then supply Minister, appealed to the non government transport owner to help the government by giving car drivers. In that way P. C. Ghosh showed his capacity that he was not a man to bend his head to the illegal and unjustified demands.[26]

It is a fact that the restoration of communal harmony was not an easy task. In order to make the proper atmosphere regarding the peaceful living of the Muslim community in West Bengal, P. C. Ghosh did his best. According to the consultation with Khaza Nazimuddin, and the President of both the Congress and the Muslim League the decision regarding the Puja, Korbani, Tajia and processions, P. C. Ghosh decided that all the religious practices would be performed according to the arrangement of the previous British administration.

Fasting of Gandhiji to end Communalism

At the day of independence i.e. on 15th August, 1947, Mahatma Gandhi was in Calcutta. In order to restore peace and communal harmony in Calcutta where Hindus did not have the courage to go to the locality of the Muslims and the Muslims had no capacity to go to the Hindu areas. In that context, Gandhiji gave a proposal to Hussain Shahid Suharawardy to stay with him. It is found that on and from 13th August, 1947 Gandhiji managed to live in Calcutta at 150 Beleghata Main Road near – Haidari Match Factory and incidentally Suharawardy also had to pass a few days along with Gandhiji in the same house which was in fact an abandoned house of a Muslim gentleman.[27] Though, at the initial stage some people were not ready to tolerate Suharawardy and raised the slogan ‘Go back Gandhi’, but after one or two days the situation started becoming normal. In the meanwhile, after receiving the news of communal violence at Thatta in Punjab the situation of Hindu–Muslim relations in Calcutta was becoming out of control. As a follow up of the above mentioned Punjab incident a sizeable percentage of Hindus of Calcutta had determined to take revenge and they found no way out but to humiliate Gandhiji at any cost because for Gandhi only they were not supposed to take actions as per their plan and challenging mind. In that situation, the house where Gandhiji was living along with Suharawardy was attacked on 31st August, 1947[28]. Premier P. C. Ghosh after receiving that news, rushed to the place forthwith along with police commissioner at midnight. On the next day i.e. 1st September, 1947, at 9.15 p.m. Gandhiji started his fasting for indefinite period and declared he would end his fasting only when communal harmony would restore. It was just a miracle, after starting the fasting of Gandhiji, those people who were involved in the incident of the attack on Gandhiji's residence they repented and requested Gandhiji time and again to stop his fasting. Not only that, they started handing over their arms to Gandhiji. On the other hand, it was declared on behalf of the Government of West Bengal that those who would hand over the arms and other weapons within the limited days, no action would be taken against them.[29] At last, with the written commitment made by Nirmal Chatturjya, Niranjan Sing Tali and Suharawardy on behalf of the Hindus, Sikhs and Muslims community respectively, Gandhi decided to end his fasting on 4th September at 9.15 p.m. Before the discontinuing his fasting Gandhiji reiterated, "see, I am ending my fasting on the basis of your commitment, if the communal violence recurs, you must not come back to me with your life on the pretext of the violence, rather if you sacrificed your life to stop the communal violence, I will be happy."[30]

Shanti Sena

During this time a group of youth and Students being inspired by the nobility of Gandhiji, they formed 'Shanti Sena' in order to restore communal harmony. Mahatmaji advised the activists of the *Shanti Sena* to work in the trouble prone areas defying the question of safety and security of their own lives. In that peace restoring campaign on 3rd September, 1947, a highly educated youth named Sachin Mitra sacrificed his life. Later on, more three educated youths namely Smritish Bondopadhyay, Bireshwar Ghosh and Sushil Dasgupta sacrificed their lives for the restoration of law and order and communal understanding. Such type of life sacrifice of a few patriots of Bengal set an example of love for motherland for the days to come. [31]

P. C. Ghosh's Attempt to Eradicate Corruptions

For the sake of eradication of corruption P. C. Ghosh, the Premier of West Bengal gave his special attention. He strongly believed that the main obstacle for the cause of nation building was no other than corruption. In this respect P. C. Ghosh was fortunate enough to enjoy full support and sympathy from J. B. Kripalini, the then All India Congress President and Chakrabarty Raja Gopalachari, the then Governor of West Bengal. Sukumar Sen, the then Chief Secretary of the state was also very much enthusiastic regarding this matter. Besides these, P. C. Ghosh had received help from many official and non official personalities of the Government, both from the provincial and Central Governments. Premier Ghosh thought that the primary safe-guards of democracy were-i). equitable Public Service Commission and ii) entirely Free, Honest and Efficient Judicial system. It is ethically in-correct for a person to become a member of Public Service Commission, if once he or she became the Secretary of any one department there. In the case of judiciary also, no person should be inducted who once became the M. L. A. or M. P. According to the suggestions of the Premier P. C. Ghosh regarding the recruitment of the Public Service Commission, a three man Service Commission headed by a retired District Judge B. K. Basu was appointed by Chakrabarty Raja Gopalachari, the Governor of the state . The other two members were – Scientist Sudhamay Ghosh and Jitendra Prasad Neogi, Professor of Economics. The question regarding the appointment of the Judges in High Court was not arisen, but how many Judges were needed, was the vital question came to the fore front to meet the demand of the day. In the undivided Bengal, the total numbers of Judges were 22. Premier Ghosh realized that 13 Judges would be sufficient for West Bengal, 7 for Calcutta and 6 for rest of the part of West Bengal.[32]

Election of P. C. Ghosh as the Member of the Legislative Assembly

It may be mentioned here that when Prafulla Chandra Ghosh was elected as the leader of the West Bengal Legislative Party, he was not the Member of the Legislative Assembly. But, after becoming leader of the Legislative Party as well as Premier or Chief Minister of West Bengal, it was mandatory for him to become an M.L.A. In that context, Khagendra Nath Bandopadhyay, a Congress M.L.A. from Birbhum District left his Suri Assembly seat for P. C. Ghosh who later on won the by-election due to the whole hearted efforts of Khagendra Nath Bandopadhyay.[33] In that election, being aware of his weak position, P. C. Ghosh sought help from the central congress leadership and Acharya Kripalani, the then All India Congress President responded positively and in his election campaign he appealed "... the new province of Bengal was created under difficult conditions and needed its ablest leader to steer through the initial stages of independence, Sri Prafulla Chandra Ghosh has justified the choice... Bengal is fortunate in having at its helm of affairs one who can be truly described as the first servant of the people. I hope the people of Birbhum will be proud to elect him as their representative in the Assembly. Knowing as I do the work and worth of Sri Prafulla Chandra Ghosh I feel that to oppose him in this election would be doing a distinct disservice not only to West Bengal but to united Bengal"[34].That by-election was won by Dr. Prafulla Chandra

Ghosh defeating his nearest rival, a Hindu Mahasabha candidate by a margin of 22,480 to 13,492 votes..[35]

Unexpected Problems faced by P. C. Ghosh

During the period of Shadow Ministry, P. C. Ghosh was quite aware regarding the impending problems of his Ministry. The very first of all, was the desire of Sarder Ballav Bhai Patel through the letter of Gandhiji, which had already been mentioned. The Second problem came from his close circle. Ghosh became the Premier of West Bengal for the earnest desire of somebody, now one of them came to him (Ghosh) and asked him to form a committee consisting of some special personalities, who were obviously the outsiders and insisted him to consult with them before doing any work. But, P. C. Ghosh literally expressed his inability for the simple reason that if it would happen, the outsiders would be able to get inform about all the secret matters of the Government and that committee would be transformed into a Supper Cabinet. Though, there was no answer from that person, but he was not satisfied.[36] The third problem for P. C. Ghosh had come with the discharge of Radhanath Das, Supply Minister of his Ministry in the charge of corruption in collaboration with League Ministers. But, as a consequence of that 'Hooghly Group' the most influential group in Provincial Congress Committee became very angry against Premier P. C. Ghosh.

Security Bill

In the meantime, as an inevitable consequence of the Partition of Bengal huge Refugee influx, communal environmental situation along with sabotaging activities of the communists gradually led to the degradation of the law and order of the province. In order to tackle this situation, P. C. Ghosh brought 'Security Bill' in Cabinet in December, 1947. When Prafulla Chandra Ghosh introduced the Security Bill in the Assembly of the West Bengal Legislature, the Communist Party of India jointly with the Socialist Republican Party started agitating against the proposed Bill and described it as 'Black Bill'. Without joining with the CPI and SRP, the other Left parties also opposed the Security Bill.[37] As Premier Ghosh explained, "No patriotic citizen who stands for the safety and integrity of the state need have any fear of the provisions of the bill. Saboteurs, communal mischief mongers, gun runners and foreign agents and spies would have every reason for fear. No right thinking citizen would want to feel otherwise"[38]. The communists were deadly against the Security Bill, and the anti Ghosh group within the congress party started using the grievances against P. C. Ghosh secretly. When the Security Bill was being discussed in the cabinet then one day a group of people came in a jeep and began to throw stones in the Assembly compound. In that situation to disperse the mob, police had no other alternatives but to fire and as a result one innocent namely Sishir Mandal, an employee of the Relief and Welfare Ambulance Corps died on the spot on 10th December, 1947. Speaking on the floor of the Assembly, P. C. Ghosh denounced the agitation as a "well-laid conspiracy" designed to discredit the Government and to capture power by violence.[39] In the midst of controversy and huge excitement, the Security Bill was passed, but with this the days of the Ghosh Ministry began to lose its spirit and solidarity. [40]

Move to Oust P. C. Ghosh from the Seat of Premiership

In the meanwhile, Ghanashyam Das Birla came to no. 8 Theatre Road i.e. Government resident of the Primer P. C. Ghosh in the Month of December 1947, with a paper signed by the majority of the congress M.L.A.s. and gave it to P. C. Ghosh. In that paper, though there was no specific allegation against the Premier, but it was mentioned that in order to run the administration more effectively there should be a change of leadership of the Congress Legislative Party. In place of P. C. Ghosh they wanted Dr. Bidhan Chandra Roy (henceforth B.C. Roy) as their leader. Having read over all ongoing politics and situation he realized that he would better leave the Ministry rather than to continue it for the greater interest of the country. In spite of being aware of the ultimate result he was determined to pass the security bill and in the long run it was passed on 4th January, 1948. As the situation was followed Prafulla Chandra Ghosh, a true follower of Gandhiji and a man of high moral values, realized that he had lost the confidence of the majority of the congress M.L.As. So, he resigned from the post of the leader of the Congress Legislative Party on 14th January, 1948 and at a meeting on 15th January 1948, the Congress Legislative Party unanimously accepted the resignation of P. C. Ghosh. In the same meeting Bidhan Chandra Roy was elected leader of the Congress Legislative Assembly (on15th January, 1948).[41]However, P. C. Ghosh left the Secretariat on 22nd January, 1948. B. C. Roy, after becoming the leader of the Legislative party invited P. C. Ghosh, to become the Home Minister of his Cabinet, but he did not comply with the request of B. C. Roy. [42]

Activities and Achievements of P. C. Ghosh as the First Premier of West Bengal

Before leaving the Ministry on 22th January, 1947 what Prafulla Chandra Ghosh Ministry had done only within five (5) months were as follow:

1. Directives were issued to the Secretaries to give notes in files in Bengali language, which were implemented with enthusiastically by Sukumar Sen, the Chief Secretary of the state;
2. Directives were given to introduce English education after class five in lieu of class three;
3. Excepting Tols and Madrasas any School, College or Hospitals aided by the Government would not be reserved for any community;
4. Policies were taken to allow more financial aids to the collages of rural areas. It was decided that government grant would be given to 'Ramkrishna Mission Vidyapith, Belur, and Shantiniketan. Belur Vidyapith started taking Government grant from the month of October, 1947;
5. It was decided that the education of the first 8 (eight) years would be the '*Buniadi* i.e. Basic Education. The main features of the basic education were as under: i).the medium of conferring education would be vernacular as well as mother tongue. ii). knowledge of History, Geography, Literature, Mathematics and general Sciences would be imparted to the pupils through the productive works like- preparation of thread by spinner, agriculture etc. iii). it was 8 years compulsory education for the all children from the age of 6 to 14;[43]
6. Education must not be controlled by the State rather it should be in the hands of those who dedicated for the purpose and of high academic caliber. Ancient Indian education was not under the state controlled, yet India could enjoy the highest place in the field of the scientific activities. Government would allocate fund and only verify whether the allotted fund had been spent for the specific projects or not. The educationists would also not become MLAs or MPs. Governor Rajaji after convincing with that view, one day he had given a proposal to the authority of the 'Belur Math' for taking the responsibility of education. But due to lack of capacity they were not ready to take that responsibility;
7. In the field of the admission of the students merit was only the determining measure. In the case of medical admission the system of admitting the sons of the doctors and the Ministers quota was declared null and void;
8. Rupees two lakhs were sanctioned for the construction of the Atomic substances scientific laboratory. Rupees more one lakh

had been sanctioned for the development of scientific researches in Government Collages. It was planned that Chemistry laboratory of the Presidency College would be newly constructed;

9. Double shift had been introduced in Government colleges, Medical, School and Colleges for the accommodation of the advancing students from East Bengal;
10. Monthly salary of the primary school teachers had been enhanced rupees 10;
11. The ancestral house of poet Rabindranath Tagore was taken over officially and handed over to the hand of the 'Rabindra Smriti Raksha Committee' on 30th August, 1947. An arrangement had been made to give three 'Rabindra Award' yearly whose monetary value was Rupees 5000;
12. An arrangement had also been made to give Rupees 100 per month to ailing rebel poet Kazi Nazrul Islam;
13. A plan had been made to establish a University for the Science education outside Calcutta. A commitment had been received on behalf of the Jhargram Raj Estate that eight (8) hundred bigha land and 50 bigha wetlands along with rupees one lakh without any cost would be hand over to the West Bengal Government. But, before taking any initiatives for the fulfillments of the above planning, P. C. Ghosh had to leave the office of the Primer of West Bengal;
14. Prohibition of alcohol was taken as a policy and that policy was initiated in some districts at the beginning;
15. It was decided that the salary of the lower income group of employees would be enhanced rupees two crores per year with the expectation of rupees one crore would be assisted by the Central Government;
16. The residents of the devastated areas caused by the cyclone and sea flood of 1942, were giving *chaukidari* tax up to rupees one, their flood loan had been exempted. As huge employees came from East Bengal to West Bengal that is why it was decided that no employee would be allowed to continue his or her service after the age of 55;
17. It was executed with the agreement of the Government of India that all the I.M.S. officers would be excluded from the Government service of West Bengal;

18. As the numbers of Bengalese in Arms Police Brigade were very thin, therefore, 800 Bengalese youths were recruited in that department;
19. It was necessitated for the children to practice song in the school. But there was a scarcity of efficient teachers. So, with the consultation of Pankaj Mallick, the legendary singer some financial cooperation was conferred to a singing association for the preparation of singing teacher;
20. After taking the responsibility of the Premiership of West Bengal, P. C. Ghosh noticed, some wealthy people's concept was that in free country, Government would do everything for the development of education. So, P. C. Ghosh appealed to the peoples to donate money for the spread of education and medical facilities. After that, P. C. Ghosh started receiving money from the people and the last cheque what he received was rupees fifty thousands;
21. In order to provide more facilities to the patients Premier Ghosh wanted to stop horse riding at Maidan and construct hospital by the Government or Non-Government Organizations. For the implementation of the above plan discussion was going on with the Turf-Club, but before implementing it he had to leave the Ministry;
22. As the cow milk was imported to Calcutta from the rural areas, so it was very hard to collect some milk for the ailing persons in the village areas. It was planned that cow milk would be produced and supplied to Calcutta in a reasonable price. For the implementation of the above project it was decided to hand over four thousand acre land to the Government. But P. C. Ghosh had no scope to implement that plan as he had to quit the Ministry as well as Premiership on 22nd January, 1948;[44]

Background of P. C. Ghosh as an All India Leader

It has already been mentioned that at the time of the independence of India, Prafulla Chandra Ghosh, Member of the Congress Working Committee (CWC) was unanimously elected the leader of the Congress Assembly Party (CAP) of West Bengal on 22nd June, 1947. Subsequently he became the first Premier of West Bengal (3rd July, 1947) with the support of both Acharya Kripalani, the then All India Congress President and the Congress High Command. But that did not mean that he was a powerful political personality in West Bengal. He was not even a member of the state legislative assembly at the time of his sworn in as a head of the shadow Ministry on 3rd July, 1947. He won a bye-election from Birbhum in November, 1947.[45] However, it may be recalled that after joining non-cooperation movement in 1921 Prafulla Chandra Ghosh along with Suresh Chandra Banerjee organized *Abhay Ashram* as its founder secretary to work for the country. He toured the various districts of East Bengal in order to win mass support in favor of non-cooperation movement. He was sent to jail for three weeks on the ground of distributing leaflets which urged the people to join the Congress Volunteer Corps (CVC). He was then elected Secretary of the Bengal Provincial Congress Committee defeating his nearest contestant candidate Deshpran Birendranath Sashmal. He spent huge times for travelling throughout the country with Chakrabarty Raja Gopalachari, Jamunalal Bajaj, Ballabhbhai Patel and even also along with Gandhiji. He had accomplished many constructive works in the villages of pre-independent era including the spread of Charka. He also joined in the *Khadi Pratisthan* and introduced many new concept like-dyeing, printing, agriculture and fisheries as a genuine organizer of *Abhay Ashram*. Not only that, he attended the Lahore Congress in 1929 and in 1930. He was arrested on the charge of conducting the Satyagraha movement at Midnapore district in Bengal and having organization the Sayagraha Committee through the *'Abhay Ashram'*. Thereafter being released from jail in 1931 he attended the Congress Session of Karachi and again was arrested and released in 1932. He was also one of the delegates of the Calcutta Session of the Congress and in the Congress Workers' Conference of Poona (1933). Prafulla Chandra Ghosh got an opportunity to become the member of the All India Village Development Organization (AIVDO) in the Bombay Session of the Congress in 1934. As an ardent follower of Gandhiji, P. C. Ghosh performed his duties in the villages of Bengal and Orissa and organized volunteers for constructive work in the path shown by Mahatma Gandhi. It is interesting to note that between the year of 1935 and 1939, he attended the Haripura (1938) and Tripuri Session (1939) of the Congress and supported the candidature of Pattabhi Sitaramayya against Subhas Chandra Bose, and subsequently became a member of the Congress Working Committee.[46] However, again he was arrested in 1940 and released in 1941. In 1942, as a result of his involvement in the Quit India Movement once again he was arrested. He was however released in 1944. After releasing from jail he met Gandhiji at *Sevagram Ashram* and went to Balarampur in order to assist Labanyalata Chanda and Jamuna Ghosh (his sister) in their Basic Education centers. He had also an opportunity to become the President of the Kustarba Committee in Bengal in 1945. After wide scale communal disturbances following the great Calcutta Killing in 1946, Prafulla Chandra Ghosh visited the riot affected areas of Eastern Bengal.

Bangaal vs *Ghoti*

As a man, Prafulla Chandra Ghosh was liberal in outlook and against the prevailing caste system and untouchability in the society. He was always stood for women emancipation and was also in favour of modern scientific education. Moreover, he never wanted to neglect Indian Cultural Heritage and her rich languages. According to him an Indian Child should be educated in his mother tongue. P. C. Ghosh fully supported Gandhiji's Basic Education System and he was against the concept that education should be controlled by the state. But, most astonishing event was that in spite of the above background as well as complete devotion as a true Gandhian in the field of congress sponsored activities all over India as and when necessities, after the selection of his name as leader of the Congress Legislative Party and thereafter the first Premier of West Bengal, the factional hostilities broke out in West Bengal politics and he was branded as a '*Bangaal*' or East Bengalee.[47] In fact during the time of the independence, in West Bengal there were major three faction within the Congress Party- namely the Gandhian Group, the Jugantar Group and the Hooghly Group. Among these three factions none was powerful enough to control the party within the state legislature. In that situation, when P. C. Ghosh, leader of the Gandhian Group became the first Premier of West Bengal and thereby the domination of the Gandhian Group automatically established over West Bengal politics which provoked to determine the Jugantar and the Hooghly Groups to break their dominance at the aim of establishing their own authority in West Bengal politics. Surendra Mohan Ghosh, the leader of the Jugantar group and the then President of the Pradesh Congress Committee was also the aspirant for the Premier post in West Bengal,[48]was unhappy because it had poor representation in the Ministry (only two minister out of total of eight). In another side, antipathy developed between P. C. Ghosh and Hooghly Group led by Atulya Ghosh when Premier Ghosh decided to reconstitute his Cabinet soon after its formation. On 23rd August, 1947, P. C. Ghosh left for Delhi being summoned by the All India Congress President. It was widely believed in West Bengal Congress circles that the mission of P. C. Ghosh was to confer with the Congress President regarding the reconstitution of the Ministry[49]. On his return from Delhi speculation was revived. It was believed that some of his Cabinet Ministers would resign because the party needed them in other fields of activities. The vacancies thereby would be filled up by P. C. Ghosh's close associates.[50]Another interesting factor which added fuel to animosity between Prafulla Chandra Ghosh and the Hooghly Group was cultural in essence. The Hooghly Group and its leaders those who were a band of West Bengal congressmen deliberately unleashed the sentiment of 'sons-of-the-soil' among *Ghotis* (leaders mostly of Calcutta origin) of West Bengal to destroy East Bengal's as well as the influence of *Bangaal* refugees in the congress and for that reason they were reluctant to accept Prafulla Chandra Ghosh, an East Bengalee, as leader of the party[51].

Meanwhile the District Congress Committee in Midnapore (a stronghold of the Hooghly Group) carried a resolution asking Nikunja Behari Maity, Minister for Waterways and Irrigation, to resign in protest against P. C. Ghosh's intention to reshuffle his Ministry.[52] Nikunja Behari Maity was a senior Midnapore congressman and a hard-core follower of the Hooghly Group, resigned from the Ghosh Ministry on 8th September, 1947 following the resolution of the Midnapore District Congress Committee.[53] Shortly thereafter, three other Ministers of P. C. Ghosh cabinet, namely- Radhanath Das who was charged in corruption with the collaboration of League Ministers[54], Bimal Chandra Sinha and Jadabendra Nath Panja who were also the followers of the Hooghly Group, resigned on 2nd September, 1947.[55] In its target to oust P. C. Ghosh from the seat of power of West Bengal, the Hooghly Group teamed up with the Jugantar Group, which remained unhappy about its power position within the Ministry. The Jugantar Group easily cooperated with the Hooghly group in the hope that the ouster of P. C. Ghosh might create an opportunity to strengthen its position.[56]

Interference of Central Leaders in West Bengal Politics

In that time the Ministry of Prafulla Chandra Ghosh confronted a real crisis. As P. C. Ghosh was not a powerful congressman in West Bengal, therefore, he needed central support and he appealed to Kripalaniji accordingly. The latter immediately came forward and condemned the course of action taken by the Midnapore District Congress Committee on the ground that it was 'unconstitutional' and 'destructive' of all discipline[57]. Kripalaniji's intervention pushed congress factionalism into the background for the time being. Premier Ghosh filled two of the three vacancies (and the third remained vacant for unknown reason) by appointing Annada Prasad Chowdhury and Charu Chandra Bhandari as Minister-in-Charge of Finance, Health and Local Self Govt. and Civil Supplies respectively on 2nd September, 1947.[58] It is needless to say that the newly appointed two ministers were close associates of P. C. Ghosh during the nationalist movement. It may not however be assumed that hereafter the internal conflict of the congress party was resolved. It reappeared before long.[59] In early September of 1947, a violent communal riot broke out in West Bengal between the Hindus and the Muslims. The city of Calcutta in particular became the scene of extreme violence and lawlessness.[60] On behalf of the state government, in a broadcast P. C. Ghosh announced that the majority of the people who had been longing for peace would try their best for the restoration and preservation of communal harmony by working in a spirit of brotherliness against a handful of miscreants.[61] However, in spite of very energetic efforts of Premier P. C. Ghosh, no noteworthy improvement of the situation was in sight.

Deterioration of Central Favour on P. C. Ghosh

In the light of the above it appears that Prafulla Chandra Ghosh was willing to rely more on Central leaders as a counterweight to his small mass base in west Bengal. Interestingly, the cordial familiarity between P. C. Ghosh and the Central Congress leadership started thinning when he declined to comply with Gandhiji's wish (which was conveyed to him through Patel) to induct a representative of Marwary Community into the Ministry of West Bengal[62]. It may be mentioned that Gandhiji received substantial financial assistance from the Marwari community, particularly from Ghanashyam Das Birla, at the time of carrying out several constructive social works as part of the nationalist movement[63]. May be Gandhi was inclined of acknowledging this by way of allowing the Marwari community to take part Governmental power after independence. But, P. C. Ghosh declined to allow Gandhiji's proposal on the ground of a 'narrow nationalism'.[64]

Selection of Bidhan Chandra Roy as the Premier of West Bengal

It may be noted that immediately after P. C. Ghosh's continuation to power in West Bengal Premier; the Hooghly Group and the Jugantar group were deeply engaged into an alliance with the aim of removing him (Ghosh) from the seat of power. It was very much clear that due to factional feud the congress party in West Bengal did not remain under the exclusive control of any of the three factions, but the combination or alliance of two against the third was unpreventable. So, taking advantage of this situation, the Hooghly Group was determined to pull down the dominance of the Gandhian Group. Actually, the logic of the partition was on their side because the leaders of the East Bengal had to leave their respective constituencies on the wrong side i.e. the then East Pakistan (now Bangladesh). Therefore, as a calculated move, first- the Hooghly Group joined hands with Jugantar Group to kick out Prafulla Chandra Ghosh from his office within six months after he had been sworn in as Premier of West Bengal. Then in a more enthusiastic move, the Hooghly faction extended its supporting hand to

Bidhan Chandra Roy for becoming next Premier of West Bengal. The reasons behind the selection of B. C Roy in place of P. C. Ghosh were something very special to the Hooghly faction. Dr. B. C. Roy was an eminent personality of Bengal without any factional affiliation. Besides these – in view of the cultural antipathy between East Bengal and West Bengal congressmen, it seems likely that B. C. Roy was acceptable to the Hooghly Group because he was a son of West Bengal itself.[65]

Keeping in mind the above facts, the king-makers i.e. Hooghly faction hoped to influence B. C. Roy by their control over the party, because Bidhan Chandra Roy had no organizational background at all of his own. Dr. Bidhan Chandra Roy was not only a successful physician from the time of the 1920s but also one of the so-called Big-Five in Calcutta city politics.[66] Not only that he was a former Mayor of Calcutta Corporation (1931-1933) and ex- Vice Chancellor of the Calcutta University (13th March, 1942 to 12th March 1944). He had also served as an Alderman of the Calcutta Corporation since 1938 to 1944. Naturally, in these different roles through a few decades B. C. Roy was able to put his feel the pulse not only of the city's middle-class literate but also of its moneyed men.[67] Besides the possessing of above mentioned high qualities, Dr. Bidhan Chandra Roy was an appropriate person to make a bridge between small town district leaders i.e. the Hooghly faction and the influential person of the Metropolis. More importantly B. C. Roy had the close connections with the top most political personalities in the central congress leadership including Prime Minister. It may be recalled that since 1932, when the congress high command's ambiguous reaction against the Communal Award and as a result, that particular year split the Bengal Party down the middle. In that time Bidhan Chandra Roy was considered as one of the centre's key men in Bengal politics.[68] Moreover, Bidhan Chandra Roy was personal physician both of Gandhiji and Nehruji. Therefore, considering the above facts the very shrewd politicians of Hooghly Group realized that they needed a link up to Delhi and that necessity might provide some help in this respect i.e. controlling power of West Bengal. Thereafter, they decided to select B. C. Roy for the top job of West Bengal calculating the hope that he (Roy) would be an effective detector at the centre on their behalf.[69]

In spite of the above facts - behind the screen, there was also a background as to the choice of Bidhan Chandra Roy as Premier of West Bengal. In this regard let us see what Saroj Chakrabarty, the personal assistant of B. C. Roy informs us about the decision in favour of Dr. Roy. In his words,- "Lord Mountbatten as independent India's first Governor General was specially invited by Prime Minister Nehru at a dinner party in his house. Lady Mountbatten was there with her husband. Only those who were close to the Prime Minister were invited at the dinner. Dr. B. C. Roy who had just returned from America stopped at Delhi on his way back to Calcutta. Nehru had invited him to the dinner party specially to introduce him to Lord and Lady Mountbatten. Dr. Roy had a very animated discussion with the Governor-General and told him of the stupendous problems that the leaders would have to surmount flowing from the partition of the country. Bengal and Punjab were reeling under refugee influx. Lord Mountbatten and his gifted wife were so attracted by Dr. Roy's dynamic personality and political foresight that they discovered in him a person who could not only face the problems that came in the wake of partition followed by onrush of millions of refugees into West Bengal and the eastern states but was also capable of occupying the highest position in the country. The Governor General urged Nehru to send him to the problem – ridden States of Bengal instead of wasting his talent as Governor of Uttar Pradesh. The Prime Minister heeded to his advice and requested Dr. Roy to go to Calcutta for taking over the reins of the province. That night's dinner party and Dr. Roy's chance Meeting with Mountbatten proved to be a fateful, not only for West Bengal but also for the country".[70]

Formation of Ministry headed by Bidhan Chandra Roy

When the birth anniversary of Netaji Subhas Chandra Bose was celebrating in Calcutta on the 23rd day of January 1948, then Bidhan Chandra Roy formed his cabinet after a short swearing-in-ceremony by Governor Chakrabarty Rajagopalachari in Government House at 9.15 a.m. Incidentally the story of Bidhan Chandra Roy at the helm of West Bengal from 9.15 a. m of the 23rd day of January, 1948 to 12 noon of the 1st of July 1962, was the development of West Bengal in all its sphere of activities. It was a fascinating era of transformation of the vivisected province named West Bengal into a vibrant progressive and industrially advanced state of the country, from darkness to light, frustration to hope and confidence.[71]

On the question of Ministry formation, Bidhan Chandra Roy consulted with Gandhiji and received his blessings. With the hope of a dynamic administration B. C. Roy formed his Ministry by the following personalities - i). Nalini Ranjan Sarkar, a big business magnate of Calcutta and a former Minister of the A. K. Fazlul Huqe Ministry in 1937 and later a member of the Viceroy's Executive Council. ii). Harendra Nath Chaudhury iii). Nikunja Bihari Maity, 4). Bimal Chandra Sinha, 5). Bhupati Mazumdar, 6). Prafulla Chandra Sen,7). Niharendu Dutta Majumdar, 8). Mohini Mohan Burman, 9). Kalipada Mukherjee, 10). Jadavendra Nath Panja and 11). Hem Chandra

Naskar. Of these, four, including B. C. Roy were not members of the Legislative Assembly. It is noteworthy that Kiran Sankar Roy, the then Leader of the Congress Legislative Party of the East Bengal Legislative Assembly and the leader of the Congress Party of Pakistan was appointed as Home Minister of B. C. Roy Ministry on 4th March, 1948.[72] B. C. Roy wanted to include Prafulla Chandra Ghosh, the retiring Chief Minister, in his cabinet, but P. C. Ghosh expressed his unwillingness on the ground that B. C. Roy declined the same invitation of Prafulla Chandra Ghosh to join his cabinet. Not only that supporters of P. C. Ghosh sometimes charged B. C. Roy with having his hand in the removal of Prafulla Chandra Ghosh from leadership of the party while the supporters of B. C. Roy accused P. C. Ghosh of having carried on systematic vilification against B. C. Roy's Ministry in his capacity as a member of the Congress Working Committee so as to bring it in the bad books of the congress high command. The problems between B. C. Roy and P. C. Ghosh came to such a situation that ultimately P. C. Ghosh with his group (Gandhian Group) including Suresh Chandra Banerjee and some senior congressmen like Charu Chandra Bhandari, Pramatha Nath Banerjee, Ananda Prasad Chowdhury, Kanailal De, Deben Sen, Haripada Chatterjee, Bimal Ghosh etc. seceded from the congress and formed a new party known as 'Krishak Majdoor Praja Party (KMPP) at the end of February, 1951 and started functioning as an opposition bloc.[73]

Announcement of B. C. Roy as an Impartial Leader of West Bengal

It has already been mentioned that Prafulla Chandra Ghosh was the leader of the Gandhian group and became the first Primer of West Bengal. At the same time the Jugantar group and the Hooghly group were also very much eager to handle the political power of the state. As a consequence of the lure of power, the stage was created for the removal of P. C. Ghosh and advent of B. C. Roy at the helm of West Bengal. Under the circumstances, Bidhan Chandra Roy made it clear that he did not belong to any group as because he had been unanimously elected the leader. He tried his best to keep up his commitments and in case of discharge his duties as the Chief Minister of the state. He not only could go beyond from narrow barriers of party politics but always ready to enroll co-operation and suggestion of his opponent and critics for the benefit of West Bengal. In order to keep the government machineries above group politics, once B. C. Roy expressed his ultimate goal of administration in the following manner, "The policy of my Ministry would be generally to satisfy the needs of the people of the province. The Ministry's immediate task was to tackle the Food and Clothing problem. The second task was to utilize the people who had come from East Bengal (nearly 1 million refugees had by then crossed the border) to West Bengal and lastly- to remove panic among the border population and if possible, to help in the restoration of confidence among the minorities in East Bengal,"[74].

Attempts of Bidhan Chandra Roy to solve Unemployment Problem

Bidhan Chandra Roy was very much well-regulated in his work. The office of the Chief Minister i.e. Writers' Buildings where he was the first to reach and the last to leave. After becoming the Chief Minister of West Bengal Bidhan Chandra Roy would not addressed any public assemblage at least for the next few months, instead, he was deeply engaged regarding the problems of the province and setting their priorities. Among the various problems of West Bengal, the most important was unemployment. It was difficult to provide employment to hundreds of unemployed youths who came to his residence. He advised them to start business to earn their living. The most of the refugees unemployed youth had no money at all even for their day to day existence. In that circumstances, the Premier would provide them some small funds either from his own resource or from the Department of Industries or Refugee-Relief Department and asked them to go to the whole – sale markets for buying articles that could sell together with their prices. In that way Bidhan Chandra Roy not only solved the daily needs of the unemployed moneyless youths but also instilled in them a spirit of self- reliance and hope.[75]

Many fair-price shops had been opened by the Government of West Bengal and B. C. Roy encouraged peoples to come forward and take advantage of them. He inspired Bengali young men for transport business, though taxi and bus permits were particularly reserved for the freedom fighters as a measure of relief. The Civil Supplies Department, Government of West Bengal issued a huge number of permits from time to time for importing pulses, rice, mustered oil etc. As huge amount of capital were required in case of the dealing of food grain business, but the political sufferers who had spent their most of the precious time in jail, had no such capital. In that situation, some cunning traders taking advantage of the economic weakness of the political sufferers known to the Ministers to sponsor their cases. As a result of the above situation, though Government had the best intention, but the issues of licenses and permits led to corruption and *Benami* (pseudo) transactions. This way corruption spread not only among a section of the public but among employees of the government departments who had dealings in licenses and permits.[76]

Attitude of B.C. Roy towards the Communists of West Bengal

After partition, Communist Party of India was first heaping strength and their violent activities becoming a threat to the law and order situation in West Bengal. In order to curb the excessiveness of the communists and maintain the law and order situation strictly, Bidhan Chandra Roy, the Premier of West Bengal searching a shrewd as well as tactful politician and a strong Man, and in that case his automatic choice fell on his life-long friend Mr. Kiran Shankar Roy, Zamindar of Teota in Eastern Bengal and leader of the Congress Assembly Party in Dhaka. It has also mentioned that B. C. Roy invited Kiran Shankar Roy to join his government as home minister and accordingly he (Kiran Shankar Roy) sworn in as Home Minister on 4th March, 1948. Thereafter, within few months, Kiran Shankar Roy took the initiative in banning the communist party in West Bengal. At the allegation of capturing power following the path of violent activities and creating a situation of anarchy the Communist Party of India was declared illegal on 27th March, 1948.[77] However, in order to justify behind the banning of the communist party by the Government, Kiran Shankar Roy made allegations against that party in the Assembly. He informed that the communist party attempted to generate a state of anarchy with the object of seizing power by violent means, agitating villagers to ignore the forces of law and order, exciting labour to act of violence against administration and to sabotage all outcome and finally attaining arms and making West Bengal as the first base of operation. On the question of banning of the communist party i.e. whether the party should be banned or not, Jawaharlal Nehru, the then Prime Minister of India gave his reaction[78] after consulting in central cabinet that any step in the nature of banning of Communist Party in India should be avoided at present. Not only that, he also realized the swiftly pushed through the West Bengal Security Act that was even more draconian than the one it replaced.[79]

Concern and Initiatives of Dr. B. C. Roy to Deal with the Refugee Problems of West Bengal

The most important task before the Ministry of Dr. Bidhan Chandra Roy was to face with refugee problem at the very beginning of the partition of India as well as Bengal. The inflow of refugees from East Pakistan throughout the year of 1948 was the most critical problem that B. C. Roy had to face and a series of correspondence passed between him and the

Prime Minister of which both the leaders made their own appraisals. Bidhan Chandra Roy informed the Prime Minister regarding a misleading propaganda made by a Minister of East Pakistan named Hamidul Huq Chowdhury that 20,000 people from there had migrated to West Bengal while 30,000 Muslims had gone to East Pakistan from West Bengal. B. C. Roy apprised Prime Minister Nehru that though it was impossible to give any exact figure, but as per information, it appears that approximately 10 lakhs of people in most cases belonging to middle class Hindus had migrated to West Bengal.[80] In a letter dated 22nd March 1948, Prime Minister Nehru communicated to Bidhan Chandra Roy that some news from East Bengal were so alarming that some of the followers were turned upset. Furthermore, it was also stated that he could presume the entire situation of that part of Bengal and decided to take some cautious policy to minimize the tension out of that unwanted situation. As the situation prevailed in view of maintaining a cordial relation with any neighboring country it was decided that there should not be any miscalculated steps so that the migration of the people of East Bengal might get inspired to cross the border and to settle in India particularly in West Bengal and a few other provinces of India. In fact Nehru had a mind to extend help to them and side by side to find out mechanism to heel up the wounded minds of the Hindus of the then East Pakistan.[81] In another letter regarding the disgusted refugee influx question dated August 16, 1948, the Prime Minister again wrote to B. C. Roy that, "I still think that every efforts should be made to prevent it. I think it was a very wrong thing for some of the Hindu leaders of East Bengal to come to West Bengal. In spite of our efforts, it is difficult to induce most provinces to absorb more refugees. We have been pressing them to do so for a long time. I think that in spite of every difficulty in East Bengal it is far better for our people to face the situation there than to come away".[82] Not only that in another letter addressed to Bidhan Chandra Roy, dated 25th August, 1948, Pundit Nehru again wrote that " ... running away is never a solution to a problem. ... To the last I would try to check migration even if there is war". [83]

Bidhan Chandra Roy in a press conference held on 6th November, 1948, announced "It was the view of both Central and West Bengal Government that able bodied men should arrange for their own source of subsistence because help could not be doled out indefinitely and continuance of such gratuitous relief would be demoralizing to the individual concerned."[84] He advised the refugees who were presented a cross section of East Bengal Hindus i.e. peasants, artisans and lower middle classes to form registered co-operative societies so that Government could provide loan on the basis of proper scheme. Besides these, in order to check migration B. C. Roy tried to create a pressure on Nehru for appointment of a Deputy High Commissioner in Pakistan to represent the grievances of the Hindus to East Bengal Government to check migration. As a consequences of that Santosh Kumar Basu, a veteran congressman and ex-Mayor of Calcutta Corporation was selected for the said post.[85] In order to sort out the refugee problem as well as regarding the settling of the refugees, B. C. Roy sent a 11 member team headed by Nikunja Bihari Maity, Relief and Rehabilitation Minister of West Bengal in the Andaman on 16th November, 1948 with the object of exploring the probabilities of agriculture, forest, fisheries and development of industries. The report of West Bengal Government regarding the settling of the Bengalese refugees in the Andaman was placed before the Prime Minister and other concerned central Ministers in the first week of December 1948, at the time of B. C. Roy's attending the Inter- Dominion Conference. [86]

When Bidhan Chandra Roy became the Chief Minister of West Bengal then democracy was in its first stage of gestation. The fall of the 1st Ministry of West Bengal headed by Prafulla Chandra Ghosh within six months of its assumption and the threat to replace of B. C. Roy's Ministry only within a period of three months due to devastating as well as dangerous factional politics within the congress party in West Bengal gave rise to speculations that any Ministry of Bengal was a matter of months only. In that situation, Bidhan Chandra Roy acknowledged that the greatest safeguard of the parliamentary democracy was a durable government formed by the elected people representatives and chief gossips and rumor - mongering had to be prevented, if government wanted its progress. He also visualized that if once a government was formed by the majority members of a party it was expected to stick to materialize plans to achieve the desired goals of the respective government. It was however the credit of Bidhan Chandra Roy to defeat any kind of conspiracy regarding the destabilization of the government and left no stone unturned to push up the trend and measures of development. He ultimately showed his worth of able leadership to lead the government and also the victory in three successive general elections and to form Congress Ministry in the province of West Bengal. [87]

Notes and References

1. Joya Chatterji, *The Spoils of Partition - Bengal and India, 1947-1967* (henceforth- *The Spoils...),* Cambridge University Press, New York, 2007, p. 211.
2. No-changers were those congressmen who, after 1923, stuck to non-cooperation, while the 'pro-changers' were those who wanted to enter the councils. See Tanika Sarkar, *Bengal 1928-1934. The politics of Protest,* Delhi, 1987, pp.26-33.
3. Rajat Kanta Ray, *Social Conflict and Political Unrest in Bengal, 1875-1927*, Oxford, 1984, pp.290-292, The *choukidari* tax was levied on a locality to pay for its *choukidar* (village tax collecter).
4. Hitesranjan Sanyal, *'Congress Movements in the Villages of Eastern Midnapore, 1921-1931,* in Marc Gaborieu (ed.), *Asia du sud. Traditions et changement,* Paris, 1979, Sanyal, '*Arambager Jatiotabadi Andolan*' (The nationalist movement in Arambagh), *Anya Artha,* 6 (September 1974), Sanyal, '*Bankura Jelay Jatiabadi Andolan', Anya Artha,* 10 (January 1977), and Partha Chatterjee, '*Caste and Politics in West Bengal, in His Present History of West Bengal*, Delhi, 1997.
5. In the 1930's during the internecine struggles inside the Bengal Congress between Sarat and Subhas Bose and their rivals, the Hooghly faction did their bit by leading the attack on the ' Krishak Samitis (peasant committees), which the Boses had tried to set up, see Joya Chatterji, *Bengal divided – Hindu Communalism and Partition, 1932-1947* (henceforth *Bengal Divided...*), Foundation Books, New Delhi, 1996, p. 117.
6. During the time of the independence in West Bengal there were three major factions within the Congress Party- namely the Gandhian Group led by Prafulla Chandra Ghosh, the *Jugantar* Group and the Hooghly Group led by Surendra Mohan Ghosh and Atulya Ghosh respectively. Among these three factions none was powerful enough to control the party within the state legislature. Ginger Group: Several Congressmen too felt resentment against the Congress Government influenced by the Hooghly Group. The most reactive among them were: Prafulla Banerjee, Naren Sen, Ramlochan Mukherjee, Jehangir Kabir, Jagannath Kolay, Maitreyee Bose, Shyamapada Bhattacharya, Aurobindo Ghosh, Haren Majumdar, Kanailal Goswami, Pratap Chandra Chunder— these congressmen were collectively known as Ginger Group. They wanted to revitalize the congress party and save it from the corruption through weakening the dominance of the Hooghly Group. No doubt the leaders of the Ginger Group were prominent, but certainly they were not of Atulya Ghosh's stature. Due to lack of (1). Sufficient organizational strength and internal cohesion along with (2) absence of leaders like Atulya Ghosh - gradually disintegrated and failed to reach the goal. See Prasanta Sen Gupta, *The Congress Party in West Bengal- A Study of Factionalism1947-86,* Minerva Associates (Publications) Pvt. Ltd. Calcutta, 1988, pp.41-45. Also see Dr. Prafulla Chandra Ghosh, *Jiban Smritir Bhumika* (in Bengali), Titas , Kolkata, 2014, p. 94.

7. Hence Mymensingh in the east, with its large population but with only 29,500 or so congress members, had fifty–five delegates to the Provincial Congress Committee. In contrast, Midnapore in the west, with almost 35,000 members, had only thirty-two delegates: see Kamini Kumar Banerjee, *Why West Bengal has no respect for the Congress*, 15 July 1949, AICC-II, PB-3 (ii)/1949.
8. Summary of the Proceedings of the Working Committee, AICC-I, G-30/1945-46.
9. Dr. Prafulla Chandra Ghosh, *op.cit.* pp. 24-25.
10. Atulya Ghosh, *Kasta Kalpita* (henceforth- *Kasta...),* Ananda Publishers, Calcutta, 1980, p-62; also see, Dr. Prafulla Chandra Ghosh, *op.cit.* p. 26. Dr. Ghosh in his '*Jiban Smritir Bhumika'* mentioned that he would draw the salary of Rs 500 per month as a first Indian Deputy Assay Master, though Atulya Ghosh in his ' *Kasta Kalpita'* mentioned that the salary of Dr. Ghosh as a Deputy Assay Master was Rs 1000 to 1200.
11. Dr. Prafulla Chandra Ghosh, *op.cit.* p.46; also see Atulya Ghosh, *Kasta...* pp. 65-66.
12. Dr. Prafulla Chandra Ghosh, *op.cit.* p.46,
13. *Ibid.,* pp. 79-80.
14. Nitish Sengupta, *Land of Two Rivers...,* p.454.
15. Dr. Prafulla Chandra Ghosh, *op.cit.* p.93.
16. Nitish Sengupta, *Land of Two Rivers...,* pp.459-461.
17. Dr. Prafulla Chandra Ghosh, *op.cit.* p.94.
18. *Ibid.*
19. Chandan Basu, *The Making of the Left Ideology in West Bengal - Culture, Political, Economy, Revolution 1947-1970,* Abhijeet Publications, Delhi-110094, 2009, p.4.
20. Dilip Banerjee, *op.cit.* p. 953.
21. Dr. Prafulla Chandra Ghosh, *op.cit.* 95-96.
22. Letter from Gandhiji to Dr. Prafulla Chandra Ghosh, see Annexure -1, cited in Dilip Banerjee, *op. cit.* p. 953.
23. Dr. Prafulla Chandra Ghosh, *op.cit.* pp. 97-98.
24. Dilip Banerjee, *op. cit.* p. 121.
25. Dr. Prafulla Chandra Ghosh, *op.cit.* p.99.
26. *Ibid.,* p. 100.
27. Nirmal Kumar Basu, *Satchallisher Dairy*, 1947, ed. by Abhik Kumar Dey, Punachha, Kolkata, January-2014, pp. 315-319.
28. *Ibid.,* p.350.
29. Dr. Prafulla Chandra Ghosh, *op.cit.* p.101.
30. Nirmal Kumar Basu, *op.cit.* p.353.

31. Dr. Prafulla Chandra Ghosh, *op.cit.* p.102.
32. *Ibid.,* p.103.
33. Nitish Sengupta, *Dr. Bidhan Chandra Roy Jiban O Samaykal* (in Bengali, henceforth Dr. Bidhan Chandra...), Dey's, Kolkata, 3rd edition-2009, pp.75-76.
34. *Amrita Bazar Patrika,* November, 14, 1947.
35. *The Statesman,* November, 21, 1947.
36. Dr. Prafulla Chandra Ghosh, *op.cit.* p.108.
37. Prafulla Kumar Chakrabarty, *The Marginal Men,* Naya Udyog, Calcutta, 1999, pp.45-46.
38. *The Statesman,* December, 9, 1947.
39. Saroj Chakrabarty, *My Years With Dr. B. C. Roy* (henceforth ... With Dr. B.C. Roy), A Centenary Volume, Saraswaty Press Limited, Calcutta, 1982. P. 69.
40. Nitish Sengupta, *Dr. Bidhan Chandra...,* pp.75-76.
41. *The Statesman,* January, 16, 1948. Also see Dilip Banerjee, *op. cit.* p. 122).
42. Dr. Prafulla Chandra Ghosh, *op.cit.* p. 110.
43. *Ibid.,* pp. 78-79.
44. *Ibid.,* pp. 103-107.
45. Dilip Banerjee, *op. cit.* p. 119.
46. Dr. Prafulla Chandra Ghosh, *op.cit.* pp. 79-80.
47. Joya Chatterji, *The Spoils...,* p. 221.
48. Dr. Prafulla Chandra Ghosh, *op.cit.* p. 94.
49. *The Statesman,* August, 23, 1947.
50. *The Statesman,* August, 27, 1947.
51. Joya Chatterji, *The Spoils...,* p. 221.
52. *The Statesman,* September, 5, 1947.
53. Dilip Banerjee, *op. cit.* p. 121).
54. Dr. Prafulla Chandra Ghosh, *op.cit.* pp. 108-109.
55. Dilip Banerjee, *op. cit.* p. 121.
56. Prasanta Sen Gupta, *op.cit.* p.22.
57. *The Statesman,* September, 6, 1947.
58. Dilip Banerjee, *op. cit.* p. 121).
59. Prasanta Sen Gupta, *op.cit.* p.22.
60. Government press note placed the casualty list as 291 dead and 292 injured. For details, see *The Statesman,* September 3, 1947.
61. *Ibid.*

62. *Ananda Bazar Patrika,* February 17, 1957.

63. On 1 October, 1927, Gandhi wrote to Virla, "My thirst for money is simply unquenchable. I need at least Rs 200,000 for Khadi, Untouchability and Education. Then there is the Ashram expenditure. No work remains unfinished for want of funds, but God gives after severe trials. This alone satisfied me. You can give as much as you can for whatever you have faith in," In a reply Birla wrote, "Whenever you find any particular kind of work impeded for lack of funds, you have only to write to me". See G. D. Birla, *In the Shadow of Mahatma,* Calcutta, Orient Longman, 1953.

64. Dr. Prafulla Chandra Ghosh, *op.cit.* p. 99.

65. Prasanta Sen Gupta, *op.cit.* p.24.

66. Saroj Chakrabarty, ... *With Dr. B. C. Roy*, p.4. Tulshi Charan Goswami, Nalini Ranjan Sarkar, Sarat Chandra Bose, Bidhan Chandra Roy and Nirmal Chandra Chunder were known as so-called Big-Five in Calcutta city politics.

67. *Ibid.,* p.12.

68. Joya Chatterji, *Bengal Divided...,* pp. 47-48.

69. Joya Chatterji, *The Spoils...,* p.217.

70. Saroj Chakrabarty, ... *With Dr. B.C. Roy*, pp.6-7.

71. *Ibid.,* p.1; Also see, Dilip Banerjee, *op.cit.* p. 123.

72. Dilip Banerjee, *op.cit.* pp. 123-124.

73. Saroj Chakrabarty, ... *With Dr. B.C. Roy*, pp.7-8. Also see, Dilip Banerjee, *op. cit.* p.124)

74. Saroj Chakrabarty, ... *With Dr. B.C. Roy*, pp.8-9.

75. *Ibid.,* p. 11.

76. *Ibid.,* p. 12.

77. By an order of Calcutta High Court on 27th March, 1950 the Communist Party of India was declared legal. Also see "*Bidhan Chandra Karnadhar - Tabu Khandita Banglar Nabhishvas*" A Bengali Article by Amalendu Dey in *Saat Dashak Samokal O Ananda Bazar* (in Bengali), Ananda Publishers, Kolkata, 2013, p. 100.

78. Nehru expressed his disapproval in his fortnightly letter to chief ministers dated 1st April 1948, telling them that 'the West Bengal government as you know has banned the Communist Party...without reference to us...this procedure is undesirable because any such action leads to repercussions', see G. Parthasarathi (ed.), *Jawaharlal Nehru. Letters to Chief Ministers 1947-1964,* Government of India, Delhi, 1985, vol. I, p. 99.

79. The West Bengal Security (Amendment) Bill, with its harsh provisions, was put to the Assembly in September 1948. It was explicitly designed to 'extend the existing power of controlling processions to case affecting the safety and stability of the province'. It gave the police greater powers than they had

previously possessed to search without warrant and to detain 'under- trials' in custody for up to thirty days, doubling the previous limit of fifteen days, a move that was justified 'in order to facilitate the collection of materials and preparation of necessary papers for consideration of the provincial government': 'West Bengal Security (Amendment) Bill, 1948, With Statement of Objects and Reasons' (issued by the Government of West Bengal Judicial and Legislative Department), 15th September 1948, Kiran Sankar Roy's Private Papers (by kind permission of Sri Surjya Sankar Roy).

80. Saroj Chakrabarty, ... *With Dr. B.C. Roy*, p. 24.

81. *Ibid.*, pp. 29-30.

82. *Ibid.*, pp. 30-31.

83. Nehru's letter addressed to B. C. Roy, dated 25th August, 1848 cited in Saroj Chakrabarty, ... *With Dr. B.C. Roy*, p.32.

84. *Ibid.*, p. 33.

85. *Ibid.*, pp. 33-34.

86. *Ibid.*, p. 34.

87. *Ibid.*, p.35.

CHAPTER

3

State Entrepreneurship and the Congress Party in the Era of Dr. Bidhan Chandra Roy Ideology verses Necessity and Reconstruction

Dr. Bidhan Chandra Roy was never a politician by profession, but he entered into the arena of politics only when he was called for the interest of the state of West Bengal; otherwise, he was engaged himself to his own medical profession. It appears to Bidhan Chandra Roy (henceforth B. C. Roy) that politics was nothing but doing something for the welfare as well as improvement of the people as a whole. As a reputed medical practitioner throughout the country and abroad, he was always against any kind of group politics.[1] Incidentally, factional conflict within the congress party in West Bengal started among the Gandhian, Jugantar and Hooghly groups. As a result of the said conflict along with the advantage of the partition of Bengal, the Hooghly group and its leader Atulya Ghosh was able to side line the former two groups. After that, Atulya Ghosh, the indisputable leader of the Hooghly Group emerged as the most influential political figure in the West Bengal congress politics and subsequently became the President of the Pradesh Congress Committee.[2] In the meantime, as an outcome of the factional hostilities over the question of supremacy in West Bengal politics, the Congress Legislative Party (henceforth CLP) expressed its no confidence against Prafulla Chandra Ghosh (henceforth P.C. Ghosh), the first Premier of West Bengal and decided to select Bidhan Chandra Roy as their leader.[3] (Though, there were many factors behind the over through of the Ministry headed by Prafulla Chandra Ghosh, which has already been discussed in the previous chapter). In that context, after taking the advice of Gandhiji, B. C. Roy was determined to accept the decision of the Congress Legislative Party of West Bengal provided if there would be no party interference regarding the choice of his cabinet colleagues as well as control of the administration. Eventually, with the consent of the Congress Legislative Party along with the Pradesh Congress Committee (henceforth PCC) as per his pre-condition, B. C. Roy agreed to become the Chief Minister of West Bengal after P. C. Ghosh.[4]

Physician Chief Minister - Bidhan Chandra Roy

It is noteworthy that at the time of the transfer of power as well as partition of India B. C. Roy was in abroad for his eye treatment. He returned back to India on 1st November, 1947, with no intention to participate in the active politics.[5] He then went to Delhi towards the middle of December, 1947 in order to meet ailing Shyama Prasad Mookherjee who was then suffering from gall-bladder trouble. In course of their meeting, Shyama Prasad Mookherjee expressed his desire to resign from the Membership of the Bengal Legislative Assembly and instead of his place i.e. registered graduates of the Calcutta University's constituency he proposed B. C. Roy to be elected. As per the proposal of Shyama Prasad Mookherjee, B. C. Roy was elected accordingly from that constituency with no opposition towards the end of December, 1947.[6]

However, On 23rd January, 1948, (Birth day of Netaji Subhas Chandra Bose) Bidhan Chandra Roy was sworn-in as the second Chief Minister of West Bengal which had then earned the epithet as the 'problematic state of India'.[7] Actually, the problems of the state were diverse, some strange to itself and mostly persisting the heritage or legacy of the past. The severe famine, bloody war, out-bursts of communal furiousness, inter-district shifting of panicky population, irreparable loss of territory due to partition, large-scale movements of the dispossessed as well as uprooted people which were collectively created a lot of problems in the state. Frustration was everywhere as because land was insufficient and industries were chiefly in the hands of the non-Bengali people and thereupon production ran at low ebb. The prices of the essential commodities were so high that the basic necessaries of life were not available within the purchasing limits of common men and moreover unemployment within the middle class educated population altogether collectively developed West Bengal into a chaotic situation at the time of oath taking ceremony of Bidhan Chandra Roy as the second Chief Minister of West Bengal.[8]

Dispassionate Chief Minister

It is noteworthy that Bidhan Chandra Roy all along his career occupied distinction as because whatever duties as well as responsibilities were entrusted to him, his sole objective was to do his best. The key words of his activities were- 'Do your best and leave to God the rest.' At that time, the chair of the Chief Minister of West Bengal was not a bed of roses. Almost all the problems what Prafulla Chandra Ghosh had to face still remained the same. Additional problems were also flourished. But after taken up the ribbons of the West Bengal Ministry in his hand, B. C. Roy was not a man of fleeing character or to be frightened by adversities rather devoted his heart and soul into the work to solve any problems. While the general condition of the state administration was very much confusing, the internal condition of the party was also in a way of depressing. Not only that, there were many groups and sections in the congress party organization in West Bengal, what have already been mentioned. Moreover, there were many aspirants to grab the power and position in that changing set up, but Bidhan Chandra Roy, the man at the steering wheel in the state showed his courage and strength of character and a desire of determination to continue his responsibilities in the midst of chaos, disorder and opposition of the party maneuver.[9] In the field of the overcome of all that adverse situations, the main advantage of B. C. Roy was that he became the Chief Minister at the request of the West Bengal Congress Legislature Party, not out of his own desire. Therefore, he could stand above party and side by side exercised it in the case of inducting his Cabinet Ministers and in many cases they did not belong to the congress party as well as member of the Legislature also.[10]

Beside the above relevant expectations of the common people, various experiences of Bidhan Chandra Roy gave him many lessons how to manage the inharmonious demands of rival groups. As a result of the partition and the inrush of huge refugees continuously from East Pakistan and considerable labour unrest collectively created as if an unstable situation in West Bengal. Most of the days of the months there was a demonstration for various demands. Not only that the agitating forces were aimed to discredit the Government and at the same time shake the stability of the administration. In that context, after assuming the chair of the Chief-Minister of West Bengal, initially B. C. Roy had to face a huge number of emergent crucial situations. Almost every day, demonstrations for this or that were held just opposite his residence and people would give slogans generally against the congress party and the government runs by the congressmen. Even in some cases the demonstrators surrounded the house of Bidhan Chandra Roy, the then Chief Minister of West Bengal and the Writers' Buildings, the chief administrative buildings of the State Government. But by dint of his indomitable spirit to conquer every difficulty, Bidhan Chandra Roy would remain calm and dispassionate. Keeping in mind the dignity and status, as the head of the administration of the state he would meet the representatives of the demonstrators and discuss about their demands. In many occasions it was found that the demonstrators would convince about the sincerity of the Chief Minister and at the same time realized the difficulties of the government. But one thing was noticed that Bidhan Chandra Roy was never succumbed to any threats and indiscipline whatever it might be.[11]

Understanding Basic Requirements of the State

Bidhan Chandra Roy's profound knowledge of facts and practical commonsense, firmness as well as sympathetic understanding of every critical situation along with humanistic approach urged him to handle the 'Ship of State' strictly forward without allowing it to make a mistake in the troubled water of Bengal. The most remarkable features of his character was that he had a tireless temper that even in the midst of troublous conditions never showed any sign of irritation or mental agitation. Actually his inner power had lied in his tremendous intelligence, depth of knowledge and his passion for exactness as well as the miraculous orderliness of his mind.[12] He had the remarkable capacity and a clear conception of the difficulties faced by him as the head of the administrator of the state. As like as rest of the India, West Bengal was under a system of administrative control of the British for about two centuries, wherein state enterprises as well as state trading were almost unknown. During the time of the British administration the trade system in West Bengal was in the control of their cousin – the industrialists. But after independence present administration was supposed to be controlled and guided by the choice of the people who were virtually the voters and would form the government. Their basic requirements of the post independent India particularly in West Bengal were adequate food, clothes and shelter. They also felt the necessities of more education along with higher economic status and better health care facilities.[13]

Be and Make

It is noteworthy that as a man of strict principle, Bidhan Chandra Roy with becoming the Chief Minister of West Bengal, he gave up his highly lucrative medical practice, though he would give free medical treatment in the every morning at least two or three hours to the people those who would come to him. In this way his days were used to start generally with a free service to the ailing humanity and there after the Chief Minister would reach the secretariat of the state i.e. Writers Buildings by 8.30 - 9 a.m. That practice of the Chief Minister Bidhan Chandra Roy entirely changed the whole routine of attendance and activities in the Writers' Buildings where previously officers and others staff used to come normally not before 10.30 or 11a.m. in the morning. Thus without issuing any kind of order as well as making any suggestions, the early attendance of the officers and others staff in the Writers' Building came into practice. It was not unexpected that when the Chief Minister was at his office desk within 9 a.m. others officers could not be late. In that manner, first of all performing his own duty perfectly, as the Chief Minister, Bidhan Chandra Roy successfully revolutionized office attendance in the Writers' Building without applying any obligation.[14]

It is a fact that Bidhan Chandra Roy was not a demagogue or orator, but as a debater he showed his outstanding efficiency in the old Legislative Council during the British regime. Moreover, as the Vice-Chancellor of the Calcutta University (13th March, 1942 to 12th March 1944), as a Mayor of Calcutta Corporation (1931-1933), as an Alderman of the Calcutta Corporation since 1938 to 1944 and above all as a Chief Minister (23rd January, 1948 to 1st July, 1962) in the Legislative Assembly he proved his extraordinary talent and efficacy. Facts and logic were his main component behind any kind of arguments and by dint of his infallible logic he was able to silence the opposition in the West Bengal Legislative Assembly and Council. In the early days of the Chief Ministership of Bidhan Chandra Roy, the opposition parties in the two houses were very strong as well as powerful and it was only because of his undeniable and logical illustration from the administrative point of view led to win over the issues raised by the critics. He was actually the citadel of strength to the Treasury Benches and always came forward to the help of his colleagues. As Bidhan Chandra Roy had the rare capacity to soothe a storm, and as a result of that tremendous capacity or his mesmeric personality and technique saved many awkward situations in the West Bengal Legislature. In spite of becoming a born fighter, Bidhan Chandra Roy would acknowledge the reasonable demands of the opposition only when he was convinced that was the benefit of the people.[15]

For the all round development of West Bengal and for the well- being of its people, Bidhan Chandra Roy, the Chief Minister accomplished numerous measures as per the demands of the situation, which has been discussed below:

Food Crisis

The year 1950 was a critical year for West Bengal not only from the refugees point of view but also in respect of the shortage of food also. At that time the overall condition of food was acute throughout the country.

Bihar was in almost a famine condition and stories of mass starvation would publish through newspapers regularly. One of the main causes behind the shortage of food was the partition of the country which gave almost 20 million acres of excellent rice-growing paddy fields to the East Pakistan[16] and thereby rice became comparatively unavailable and more expensive in West Bengal. In addition the influx of lakhs of refugees from East Pakistan to West Bengal, diversion of 200,000 acres of *aus* rice growing lands to jute cultivation[17] and damage of crops due to natural calamities - collectively resulted in a yearly deficit of 200,000 tons[18] food grain in the state. Naturally in order to fulfill the need, West Bengal government had no any other alternative but to depend on supplies from other parts of India as well as more allocation of central government. The partition of Bengal actually broke the economic backbone of Bengal particularly the West Bengal because the partitioned hardened the main sources of raw materials; while the big jute industries were located in West Bengal but jute was basically grown in East Bengal. Not only that East Bengal was the main source of the production of paddy and fish for the headless province of West Bengal. At that time the government of West Bengal held only six weeks food stock but the requirement of refugees came to about 24,000 tons of rice. In that situation, Bidhan Chandra Roy, the chief minister felt that once there was a breakdown in the rationing system its explosion would rock his government and there would be food riots in the troubled city.[19] During 1950's in the midst of acute food crisis in West Bengal the number of mouths to feed increased rapidly as a result of the influx of millions of refugees from East Pakistan. Along with it there was extraordinary increase of birth rate widened the state's food-gap continued.[20] At the aim of controlling the situation Bidhan Chandra Roy and Prafulla Chandra Sen (henceforth P.C. Sen), the Food Minister of West Bengal made a number of trips to Delhi to restock the serious low food stocks of the province.

First Food Movement

In the month of April 1951, two women named Bandana Talukdar and Kabita Basu raised their voice for food and as a consequence of that they were shoot dead by police in Cooch Bihar.[21]In the summer of the year of 1952, the members of the opposition group in the Assembly launched their first food movement demanding increase of the quantum of rice and wheat in ration for the people, particularly for manual workers of West Bengal. Processions were daily taken out for the demand of more food at a cheaper rate. Rafi Ahmed Kidwai, the then Union Food Minister rushed to Calcutta and met the chief minister and opposition leaders including Jyoti Basu for discussion about the food situation in the state of West Bengal.[22] In a letter dated 25th July, 1952 B. C. Roy apprised Jawaharlal Nehru, the Prime Minister of India that "actually the whole movement was political. It was not against the Food Minister Prafulla Chandra Sen (Nehru apprehended this) and his food policy at all, because he does nothing without consulting every detail with me." [23]

Food Movement of 1959

The most important issue that was discussed in the National Development Council (NDC) in the presence of the Chief Ministers of different States of India about state trading in food. Bidhan Chandra Roy was an enthusiastic supporter of that issue and initiator of the planning of gradual take-over of the trade of food grains from private traders. No other Chief Minister had to face such strong food movements year after year as B. C. Roy had in his own state. He was determined that people's food could not be left into the hands of the trading community who were gradually confiscating the faith of the people and the government by their unashamed trade pactice.[24]

In the first week of June, 1959 the chief minister B. C. Roy was in Darjeeling along with his cabinet colleagues. He received there a telegram from the Howrah district Congress Committee to the following manner: "Rice position is hope less, please take immediate action before rice disappears completely from the market".[25] Scarcity of food was continued in West Bengal particularly in south Bengal due to heavy drought, late monsoon and lack of employment. Not only that in the same year following unprecedented rains more than half of Bengal was in the grip of devastating floods that overflowed nine districts including Purulia, Burdwan, Murshidabad, Birbhum and Nadia. It was as if a repetition of natural calamities what occurred in West Bengal in 1956 and from that destruction the people were not fully recovered. According to official estimates, at least one million acres of paddy lands were affected.[26] Reports reached Darjeeling that the hungry villagers from the border district of 24 Pargana were coming daily almost 3,000 to Calcutta for searching of food which indicates the creation of near famine situation.[27] As the Food Minister, Prafulla Chandra Sen was failed to tackle the food crisis in West Bengal, that is why *'Swadhinata Patrika'* had given the name of Food Minister, as 'famine minister' on 27th August, 1959. In that context B. C. Roy wrote a long letter to the Union Food Minister regarding the alarming food crisis in his State. Although, in the meantime, the central government agreed to meet the entire food deficit of West Bengal, estimated at about 9.5 lakh tons.[28]

B. C. Roy's Effort to Meet the Food Crisis

The chief minister returned to Calcutta on 11th June, 1959 in order to review the alarming food crisis with food minister P. C. Sen and Join Secretary B. R. Gupta. Binoy Bhusan Ghosh, the then Unoin Food Secretary, came to Calcutta on the spot verification about the acute food crisis in West Bengal. After on the spot study, the central government decided to allot extra 10,000 tons of rice in addition to the monthly quota of the state 75,000 tones. About ten million people representing one-third of the entire population of the state were under the purview of modified rationing in which rice was to be sold at Rs.17.5 per mound, though in open market rice was then being sold at Rs. 40 per mound. In Calcutta about 4.2 million people were drawing ration of 1.5 *seers* of rice and 1 *seer* of wheat per week.[29]

On the 22nd of June, 1959 B. C. Roy executed a major change in food policy and announced it at a quickly summoned press conference in the evening at his residence. Earlier he had discussed food crisis in a meeting of the Congress Parliamentary Party at Writers' Buildings. As an ardent disciple of Gandhi, B. C. Roy, the chief minister of West Bengal instead of leaving the responsibility on food minister P. C. Sen, he himself took upon the whole responsibility for the failure of the food policy of his Government. Explaining the basic cause of West Bengal's difficulties he remarked, 'less production in the current year because of draught'. B. C. Roy felt the necessity of a more vigorous programme for production of food to meet the challenge of the scarcity of food grain. At that point of time he expressed his view to intensive 'grow more food campaign' on 8thJuly, 1959 at the event of rearrangement and reallocation of the Agriculture portfolio. It was well known to B. C. Roy that there was a little possibility for extension of paddy farming land through the reclamation of lands in his state. The only option was open for the state to take the special drive towards increasing the growth of agricultural product per acre. Keeping in mind that view B. C. Roy upgraded Tarun Kanti Ghosh, a 34 years young member of the Assembly to the rank of a full Cabinet Minister with in charge of Agriculture and Food Production Department.[30]

Measures for the Production of More Food

In the first few years after independence the annual production of rice increased in the year of 1953-1954 from about three and one-third million tons to five million 220 thousand tons. Actually, the annual production during that time exceeded than the annual requirement in the state. The surplus production of rice in West Bengal was possible due to the adoption of thoughtful planning and extraordinary activities in the agricultural front on behalf of the state government. For the improvement of the agricultural production Rs.10.49 crores were estimated to cost under agriculture and rural development scheme. Not only that in order to facilitate agricultural activities huge number of tons of improved seeds, fertilizers and manures were distributed by the state Government among the cultivators. Moreover, 38,000 acres of waste lands were reclaimed and transferred into cultivable land for the expansion of agricultural area by the end of the March, 1954. In addition to this, in order to provide irrigation facilities to the cultivators for more production a good number of irrigation tanks were executed. Major projects for irrigation along with drainage including the Mayurakshi Project were calculated to benefit 10 lakhs acres of land in different stages of execution. There was also a gigantic multi-purpose Damodar Valley Project and the Sonarpur-Arapanch Scheme Project also designed for the reclamation of wasteland in 24-parganas by draining out the cumulated water and thereupon as many as 17000 acres lands were reclaimed of which 1,200 acres of land were brought directly under cultivation during the year 1953-1954.[31]

Role of the Communists

The Communists and their companions were not sitting idle after the failure of the state government to execute state trading in food grains. During that time the communist government in Kerela, headed by E.M.S. Namboodripad faced a state-wide agitation due to adopting 'repressive' measures that led to a near collapse situation. In that context, to prevent the dismissal of the communist government in Kerala, as a diversionary tactics, the Bengal communist party was prepared and submitted a long 52-page memorandum to Rajendra Prasad, the then President of India. In that memorandum, many charges against the state government was brought by the Bengal communists such as 'blatant misrule' like- colossal waste of public funds, rank corruption and nepotism, appeasement of vested interests, misuse of administrative machinery and suppression of fundamental rights.[32]

Due to the price hike of food grain and open confession of the chief minister B. C. Roy about the failure of his government over state control trade of food grain,[33]the opposition parties specially the communists planned to stage one of their fiercest attacks against the government. In one of his writings, Jyoti Basu showed with various statistics that West Bengal need 40 lakh tons rich per year but, after independence the state government utterly failed to reach that target except the year of 1953-1954.[34] Moreover there was a tremendous pressure of lakhs of refugees from East Bengal. It was found that up to the year of 1956 almost 40 lakhs refugees came from East Bengal as well as East Pakistan to India and among them 31 lakhs were staying in West Bengal.[35] Towards the end of the year, 1958 'Price Increase and Famine Resistance Committee (henceforth PIFRC)' was formed with Suresh Chandra Bandopadhyay and Hemanta Kumar Basu as President and Secretary respectively. A hungry procession was also held as per the decision of the PIFRC.[36] It is important to note that the main target of the opposition parties was not so much B. C. Roy, the Chief Minister, but Prafulla Chandra Sen, the Food Minister of the state. Actually the Food Minister P. C. Sen was next to Chief Minister in the cabinet and would control the party machinery in West Bengal in combination with Atulya Ghosh. The opposition felt that if once he would remove then not only the congress party in the state but the cabinet would also be rudely shaken. However, in the meantime, the Price Increase and Famine Resistance Committee (PIFRC) earlier announced their programmes of mass action on and from 20th August, 1959 unless necessary steps were taken to improve the food situation.[37]

Preparation of the Government to Tackle Food Movement

Meanwhile, on the evening of the 14th and 15th August, 1959 the Chief Minister B. C. Roy convened a secret meetings at his residence with all the heads of the police department and officials of the Home Department. After elaborate discussion, the Chief Minister issued a note of warning for giving point by point reply to the demands of the PIFRC which had threatened to launch 'mass action' programme against the hoarding of rice stocks, mass defiance of law, squatting and picketing. The Chief Minister also warned that law breakers must take the consequences for their action.[38]

Two days after the secret meeting i.e. on the 17th August 1959, police started searching in the early hours of the morning in Calcutta and the districts for political leaders who were involved in the threatening of mass violation of law. Simultaneously searching was also carried out in the offices of the communist party in Calcutta. Altogether 63 arrests were made of whom14 MLAs those who were the chief elements of the PIFRC belonged to the Communist Party, Revolutionary Socialist Party, the Socialist Unity Centre and Forward Bloc. As a protest against that arrest and for the demand of adequate supply of food, movement started in the different districts throughout the state but the police of the government tried to restrain the same by any means. In order to quell the food movement police resorted *lathi* charge and tear gas at Seerampur (Hoogly) and Dimondharbar (24

Parganas) on 26th August, 1959.[39] At the time of the police searching, Jyoti Basu, the then leader of the opposition was not traceable. Not only Jyoti Basu but also many workers of the communist party were in the underground to evade arrest.[40]

Both sides' i. e. the state government and the oppositions prepared for a showdown. By this time PIFRC took decision to launch their campaign towards Writers' Buildings on 19th August, 1959. In order to resist the move and to avoid any kind of untoward situation, Kalipada Mukherjee, the then police Minister issued a very strict order that those law-breakers would come to demonstrate in front of the house of Food Minister P. C. Sen, they must be checked before the prohibited zone and be dealt with severe punishment. The cabinet convened an urgent meeting on the 27th August, 1959 to finalize measures to be adopted to tackle the proposed massive demonstration of the left parties in Calcutta on 31st August 1959.[41] In the meanwhile, in Delhi on 23rd August, 1959 Ajit Prasad Jain, the then Food Minister, Government of India announced his decision of resignation in the Lok Sabha on the last day of the Food debate. He took the responsibility of his failure to tackle the food situation, particularly in West Bengal and thereafter S. K. Patil was inducted in the Central Cabinet as the next Food Minister.[42]

The 31st August, 1959 – Day of Massive Demonstration and Police Action

At last the 'D' day arrived. According to the estimate of various news papers at least 25,000-30,000, demonstrator arrived in Calcutta on 31st August, 1959. The Communist Party demanded lakhs people but Jyoti Basu claimed 3 lakhs demonstrators including many women - children and peasants from distant villages marched in procession towards Writers' Buildings after the *Maidan* meeting which was addressed by leftist leaders Manikuntala Sen and Makhan Pal.[43]Their programme was to surround the Writers' Buildings' until they could get the promise for food. The procession was lead by a row of volunteers who were followed by the leaders. The shouting slogan of the defiant processionists were : "Give us rice at cheap prices or resign, ' let Prafulla Sen resign', 'March to Writers' Buildings".[44]

Several Deputy Commissioner of police were deployed there to control the situation. Mr. Saroj Chakrabarty, P.A. to the then Chief Minister in his memoirs 'My Years With Dr. B. C. Roy' vividly described the happening of that fateful day of 31st August, 1959 in the following manner: "The jostling mob could only be checked by baton charges which were made.

Simultaneously tear gas shells were fired. Baton and lathi charges were intensified. After withstanding the police attacks for some time the demonstrators took to their heels. The fleeing demonstrators were pursued by several thousand policemen. The battle ended in the victory of guardians of law and order. The food minister was safe and so was Writers' Buildings, the seat of the state Government. This was an example of the theory that 'violence is suppressed by greater violence'. The day's round up included 300 arrests. The Calcutta Medical College, city's principal hospital, was filled with injured. All meetings and processions throughout the city were banned by the police chief."[45] As a result of the brutal lathi charge and firing of tear gas shells by the police at least 130 agitators were severely injured and a considerable percentage of the participants were found death.[46]

On the following day (on 1st September, 1959) as a protest against the police atrocities of 31st August, 1959 student strike was called on. On that day, as many as five police stations were attacked by the angry masses. In that context, the Commissioner of Police along with some of his officers came to Writers' Buildings to apprise the Chief Minister regarding their incapability to bring the situation under control with mere lathis, batons and tear-gas shells. After his talk to the police chief, the Chief Minister communicated to Govind Ballav Pant, the then Union Home Minister, over the secraphone and sought his permission to use firearms in order to quell the serious disturbances. However, the permission to use firearms came from Delhi in the afternoon.[47]As students were playing predominant role in food movement; necessarily the students became the soft target of the state police. On that point a student of Surendranath College, named Bibhuti Roychowdhury was first shoot dead by the police on 1st September, 1959. Among the arrested students leaders most notable were Gurudas Dasgupta, Protul Lahiri etc.[48] Not only that in order to disperse the agitators police fired 50-60 round on that 1st September, 1959 and thereby at least 7 demonstrators were shot death and more than 100 people sustained bullet injury.[49]

On the previous night i.e. on 31st August, 1959 in a statement Jyoti Basu declared that "despite all brutalities of the Government our movement will go on according to the programme". On the 2nd day of September again after police firing, in the evening, the Chief Minister B. C. Roy expressed his unhappiness about the previous day's riotous behavior made by the agitators. In his statement B. C. Roy denounced the attacks on ambulances. The cruelty of police firing turned most brutal on 3rd September, 1959. As a result of police firing in that 3 days - altogether 27 people died and next day the number of death reached in 37.[50] After 3rd September,

1959 the main centre of battle for food movement became the town place of Howra, Hooghly and 24 Pargana. Not only that the movement was also spread in Nadia, Murshidabad and even Jalpaiguri of North Bengal. On 10th September, 1959 the Martyrs day was observed by the students, wearing black badge and walking in the procession in Calcutta. The most remarkable event on that day was that 'black flag' was hoisted by Dr. Triguna Sen, the Hon'ble Vice-Chancellor of Jadavpur University. On the other hand, in order to save life and property and to stop chaos a 'Peace Committee' was formed by the one section of Professors-intellectuals and most important personalities among them were Nihar Ranjan Roy and Kalidas Nag.[51] As per the estimate of the 'The Statesman' 39 people including a police man lost their lives and 200 were untraced in that seven days disturbances.[52] However, as per the statement of Saroj Chakrabartay, P.A. to the Chief Minister B. C. Roy, "Calcutta was quieter on the day following with fewer incidents. The PSP announced its decision to postpone for a fortnight the food demonstration to enable its leader (Dr. Ghosh) to complete the unfinished negotiations with the State Government. The five day disturbances in Calcutta took a toll of 31 lives and injuries to 3,000 besides damage to property."[53]

Small Industry

In the industrial front particularly on the sphere of cottage industries - various schemes were taken by B. C Roy, the Chief Minister of West Bengal for the revival as well as encouragement of the beekeeping industry, khadi industry, mat industry, handmade paper industry, brass and bell metal industry, silk industry, handloom industry etc. Large scale schemes were also initiated for the enhancement of the supply of fish and milk for the people of the state.

Fish

For the improvement of fish farming numerous measures were taken by the state government under the stewardship of Bidhan Chandra Roy. For example, as many as 14,200 acres area of wetlands were reclaimed and prepared for fish farming. A lot of nursery units for fish farming were opened and thereby fingerlings were being raised for distribution among the pisciculturists at the prices of possible low cost. A number of measures for the development of *beel* fisheries were also taken on behalf of the Government of West Bengal. The Government started giving advance loan to the private owners of abandoned *beels* for dredging and making these convenient for pisciculture. Besides, the state government with the help of

Danish and Japanese fleet directly took the initiative to explore the possibilities of Deep-Sea Fishing in the Bay of Bengal.[54]

Milk

The planning for the extension of supply of milk in Calcutta was carried out with the removal of *khatals* from the city of Calcutta and resettlement of the displaced cattle in the various milk colonies situated in the rural areas or the outskirts of the main city on the pattern of Aarey Colony of Bombay. With a team of officers headed by Rafiuddin Ahmed, Minister-in-Charge of Agriculture, Animal Husbandry and Forests[55] worked silently for the materialization of this scheme and establishment of the first unit of a Milk Colony along with the accommodation of 1,272 milch animals including their offsprings at Haringhata in the district of Nadia, about 34 miles away from Calcutta.[56] The reason behind the selection of Haringhata as the site for the first milk colony was that, there were over 3,000 acres of land for growing fodder for providing feeding to the displaced cattle along with modern breeding facilities and for a modern dairy factory equipped with up-to-date machinery pasteurization, bottling and chilling plants. While laying the foundation stone on 3rd January, 1954 Chief Minister B. C. Roy addressed, "It would not merely benefit the city and at the same time ensure supply of pure milk but would also help restoring economic balance in village, opening up new avenues of employment. The problem of removal of '*Khatals*' from Calcutta had been engaging their attention since the days of Deshbandhu Chittaranjan Das, who was the first Mayor of Calcutta, had thought of it. The State Government had therefore been making unremitting efforts to solve the twin problem of removing the '*khatal*' and developing a huge milk colony at Haringhata."[57]As a result of the distance of Haringhata from Calcutta, it was very important to start another dairy at Calcutta in order to smooth handling the supply of milk requirements for the city. The Central Dairy at Belgachia in Calcutta was established with the most modern design on 23 acres of land in September, 1962. The daily output of milk together from Haringhata and Belgachia Dairy reached up to 2,15,000 litres per day in 1982.[58] The various finished products from that modern dairy farms guaranteed their purity and consequently within a very short days a good reputation were spread out in the Calcutta markets which influenced the quantity of supply and the prices of these commodities.[59]

Road and Transport

Considerable development perpetrated in the field of communication and transport in the state of West Bengal. Actually, road connection in the state something was crippled in the wake of the partition of Bengal. Moreover, the density of population in West Bengal was nearly three times in comparison with the rest of India as a whole. At the beginning of the planning for developing communication in the state it had only 0.57 miles of road in all categories for per thousand of her people while the figure of the rest of India was o.75 miles per thousands. However, it was estimated that approximately Rs. 200 crores would be spent for the completion of road construction in West Bengal. But very insufficient amount of money i.e. only Rs. 30 crores had been allocated for the expenditure regarding the road development works in West Bengal up to the end of the year of 1955-1956. In spite of scarcity of the allocation of funds, 1450 miles of new roads were constructed in addition to about 300 miles of national highways within the state. The aggregate length of 23 bridges which were also been constructed at that time were 6,090 feet. Simultaneously, with the development of roads the Government of West Bengal carried out a programme for the development of transport. Remaining the operations of the private transport service intact, the state transport service of West Bengal was brought into being in Calcutta. At the beginning of 1955, altogether 286 State Transport buses including 36 double-deckers started operating on 12 routes in the city and provided employment to about 3,300 persons.[60]

Education

During the Chief Ministership of Bidhan Chandra Roy, particularly the decade of 1950s are still considered to be 'era of nation building' as because the budget figures for the development purpose under any head was impressive. It is an example that the expenditure for Education Department was increased by the State Government from Rs.2.55 crores in the year of 1948-49 to Rs. 6.59 crores in 1954-55. It is noteworthy that, though the concept of the Basic School was developed in 1937, but up to the year of 1947, there was not a single Basic School throughout the state of West Bengal. As a result of giving the proper attention to the development of education as many as 275 Basic Schools were set up by the State Government within the year of 1954. Not only that during the year of 1947 to 1954, the number of primary schools was increased from 13,772 to 16,689, the Junior High Schools from 985 to 1,407, the High Schools from 761 to 1,402, the Colleges from 54 to 89 and the Technical Schools and Colleges from 90 to 144 respectively.[61]Another remarkable achievement of B. C. Roy was to the establishment of a Marine Engineering College in Calcutta, 1950.[62]

Birth of Kalyani University

Birla College of Agriculture at Kalyani, the biggest Agricultural College in West Bengal was opened by Pundit Jawaharlal Nehru, the then Prime Minister of India in 1954. Actually B. C. Roy, the Chief Minister of West Bengal earlier persuaded his friend G. D. Birla for the construction of that college and urged him to pay the total amount for running the institution. This institution was developed later on as the nucleus of a University, named Kalyani University with agriculture and animal husbandry as its base. This was also another example of B. C. Roy's diverse activities for the development of West Bengal.[63]

Birth of IIT, Kharagpur

Maulana Abul Kalam Azad, the first Education Minister of free India, was also the personal friend of Bidhan Chandra Roy, the Chief Minister of West Bengal. In course of discussion between the two the former approached the later to locate a site for setting up one of the five regional engineering colleges sometime in the year of 1950-51. The Chief Minister B. C. Roy accepted the offer at once and selected Hijli at Kharagpur in the district of Midnapur which is a distance of 100 miles from Calcutta for the purpose of setting up engineering college. Due to the insistence of Maulana Abul Kalam Azad prior to the approval of I.I.T. Kharagpur B. C. Roy agreed to take overall charge of the Institute as its Chairman in his personal capacity. With the help of his personal sagacity and indomitable spirit for doing something for the betterment of the state, B. C. Roy selected Jnan Chandra Ghosh, an eminent scholar and scientist as its first Director. B. C. Roy along with Jnan Chandra Ghosh jointly did the ground work to bring the life of the present day's well-known magnificent engineering college.[64]

Creation of Four New Universities

The meeting of the West Bengal Legislative Assembly was held on 22nd February, 1960 in order to listen the announcement of Governor Padmaja Naidu regarding the state venture towards the direction of education and employment opportunities by means of the process of industrialization. In previous session, the Legislative Assembly already passed the Burdwan University Bill and the University started its functioning from the next academic session. Proposal for the setting up of a new University in North Bengal was then already under way, and a new Bill providing for the establishment of another University for study in Humanities and Science in particular at Kalyani, not very far from Calcutta was already in due consideration in that session of the legislature assembly.[65]

Moreover, B. C. Roy was a great planner for the improvement of education and culture of West Bengal. Due to the efforts of B. C. Roy Viswa Bharati, established by Rabindra Nath Tagore in 1921 was elevated as Viswa Bharati University under the Governance of the Government of India in 1951. It may be noted here that the planning for the establishing of the above mentioned Kalyani University was initiated by B. C. Roy in 1954. It was B. C. Roy who took the special drive for passing the Jadavpur University Bill in the Legislative Assembly in 1955. As a President of the National Education Council, B. C. Roy himself moved the Jadavpur University Bill in the month of September 1955. Jadavpur University was occasionally opened by Dr. Sarvapally Radhakrishan, the then Vice-President of India on 18th March, 1956 for opening up a new era in the history of the higher education in India particularly in West Bengal. 'Academy of Dance, Drama and Music' was established in 1955. As a result of B. C. Roy's vision for commemorating to Gurudev Rabindra Nath Tagore a plan was formulated for establishing Rabindra Bharati University in 1959. He was also the founder President of Indian Institute of Social Welfare and Business Management in Calcutta.[66]

Medical and Public Health

It may be mentioned that notable development took place in the field of Medical and Public Health Services (MPHS) in West Bengal during the Chief Ministership of B. C. Roy. In the second year of Independence there were only less than 70 Health Centres all over the state. The number of Health Centres came into existence up to 166 at the beginning of the year of 1954. As a helmsman of West Bengal, with the help of his world-wide reputation of medical knowledge B. C. Roy chalked out a plan to raise the number of health centre within the years of 1955-56 further up to 271 with 2,762 beds. The number of beds in Sadar Hospital and Sub-divisional Hospitals were also increased to 2,469 and the tuberculosis beds to 2,353. As many as 16 National Malaria Control Units (NMCU) in West Bengal would function to minimize the disease of malaria in the state. Besides, the number of Maternity Centres was also increased to 96, the T.B. Clinics to 25, the Leprosy Clinics to 92 and of V.D. Clinics to 18. During that time in an average 82 hospital beds would ready for per 1000 population in West Bengal which was comparatively highest in number in India. An idea of taking the proper step for improvement of public health became so effective, it was found that the birth rate increased from 21.3 in 1948 to 22.7 per milla in 1953 and side by side death rate came down from 18.1 to 10.2.[67]

Calcutta's First Polio Clinic

The diseases named polio became a kind of epidemic in the city of Calcutta. As a Doctor, B. C. Roy had to treat a large number of crippled children suffering from polio and thereby he felt the necessity of establishing a polio hospital as well as clinic in Calcutta. Out of that feeling B. C. Roy asked Dr. Santosh Bose, one of his former students to go ahead with the plan for a polio hospital at Beliaghata in north-eastern suburbs of Calcutta. In the very outset it was completely a non-official venture and he himself by dint of his personal capacity started collecting necessary equipment for the polio clinic from within the country and abroad. After necessary arrangements about to start treatment of patients, B. C. Roy invited Jawaharlal Nehru, the then Prime Minister of India in the occasion to inaugurate the hospital which was named after him as "B. C. Roy Polio Clinic" by the promoters. However, after formally opening up the polio clinic and hospital Jawaharlal Nehru addressed, "I did not generally approve the naming of institutions after living persons but in that particular instance I have no objection to it because Dr. Roy is a great personality and the association of his name with the institution might benefit it immensely".[68]

Institutions

Bidhan Chandra Roy was closely connected with the introduction as well as management of various institutions throughout the country particularly in West Bengal. From his early age he was interested for the betterment of the people and intended in helping and working for various institutions. His activities in this field were numerous and varied. Incidentally, B. C. Roy was the first President of All India Medical Council (AIMC) and continued to be its President for several years.[69] There was hardly a meeting of the Council which he did not attend. He was closely associated with the Kamala Nehru Hospital, started by Mahatma Gandhi in memory of the wife of Pundit Jawaharlal Nehru. He played a very active part in the work of this hospital at Allahabad.

It is noteworthy that, the Jadavpur Tuberculosis Hospital, the first of its kind in Bengal was started by B. C. Roy.[70] Not only that, he was instrumental of the initiation of Kancharapara Hospital for Tuberculosis and Chittaranjan Seva Sadan (CSS). Chittaranjan Seva Sadan may be considered as one of the biggest maternity hospitals in India having sister institutions like Sishu Sadan, Hydro- Radiological Institute, and lately Cancer Hospital within its vast campus.[71]

Bidhan Chandra Roy was also the guiding spirit behind the Victoria Institution in Calcutta and the development of Engineering and Technical education in the State of West Bengal. The Jadavpur Engineering College and Technological Institute at Kharagpur reached its present position due to the tireless effort of B. C. Roy. Even Nirmal Hriday Home (NHH), started by Mother Teresa was also received every possible cooperation from B. C. Roy.[72]

New Township and Minor Scheme

The Government of West Bengal chalked out a very ambitious and feasible programme for the foundation of new townships. The Kalyani Township Scheme was the finest example of this planning of state Government. In order to implement the proposed Kalyani Township Scheme, 10,000 acres of land were acquired by the state Government at the adjacent area of Kanchrapara of which over 3,000 acres of lands fully developed. A perfectly modern town with concrete roads along with pipe water, electric light, underground drainage system, public parks, educational institutions and all other amenities were arranged for sprung up the township quickly of being executed fit for human dwelling. In addition to that a large number of minor schemes for the economic development of West Bengal were started operating and ultimately executed under the extremely momentous Community Development Projects and National Extension Service. The major schemes which were initiated by the State Government and received the sanction from the Indian Planning Commission were-Ganga Barrage Scheme, Durgapur Coke Oven Plant Scheme, Tharmal Plant, Coal Tar Distillation, Gas Grid, Calcutta Sewage Gas Scheme and Chittaranjan Locomotives. It is noteworthy that with the completion of these schemes jointly with the Damodar Vally Project and the Mayurakshi Project changed the face of West Bengal.[73] In spite of above mentioned schemes two other significant measures relating to the establishment of a modern salt-factory at Contai, Midnapore and expansion of deep-sea-fishing scheme by acquisition of five more trawlers were also initiated by the West Bengal Government just after the general election of 1952.[74] After his successful eye operation in the month of August- September, 1952 in Europe and America B. C. Roy started working out plans for development of better Sewage disposal system of Calcutta, production of Sewage gas, production of anti-biotics with experts in Switzerland, Germany, France, U.S.A. and England.[75]

Refugees and the Government of West Bengal during the Regime of B. C. Roy

As a result of the partition of Bengal at the cost of gaining independence, West Bengal started suffering from huge as well as continuous refugee problem as a matter of fact. With the bifurcation of Bengal and creation of new state in the union of India i.e. West Bengal which was started its journey with the unlimited liability of the refugees from East Pakistan. Actually aftermath the events of the great Calcutta Killing, Noakhali and Bihar holocaust just on the eve of the partition of the country, the communal situation became so embittered that a large section of the Hindus from East Pakistan and a section of Muslims from West Bengal started leaving their ancestral property and were forced to become refugees for the sake of life security and honour in both the countries.[76]Actually, as consequence of Noakhali riots of 1946 the Hindus started coming to West Bengal and that processes increased in many more after partition. The inflow of the Hindu refugees to West Bengal was accelerated at the event of the police action in Hyderabad in September 1949. It was estimated that as much as a million of Hindus migrated from East Pakistan to West Bengal by March 1948.[77] By June 1948 the number of refugees reached up to 1.1 million. Of these number of refugees – 350,000 belonged to the urban middle classes, 550,000 to the rural middle classes, something more than 100,000 were agriculturists and something less than 100,000 artisans. The number of refugees varied from district to district.[78]

The second phase of the influx of the refugees began with the communal violence of February 1950 in East Pakistan. This time the refugees had come to West Bengal as if glacier. The entire administrative machinery of the state of West Bengal was virtually cracked down under the tremendous stress and strains of the huge influx from East Pakistan. The February riots of 1950 started a chain reaction of organized communal violence in both East Pakistan and West Bengal and instead of one way traffic it assumed the character of two-way traffic. During the communal disturbances of 1950 not only the Hindus came from East Pakistan to West Bengal but also a large section of panicky Muslims left West Bengal and took shelter in East Pakistan as well as other side of the border. However, the Census report of 1951 shows that there were at least 3.5 million refugees came into the state of West Bengal after independence.[79]

Since the beginning of the independence the influx of refugees was a constant problem for the state of West Bengal. In order to tackle the extensive refugee problem initially relief and rehabilitation were provided by the

Government of West Bengal for giving minimum support to the huge displaced as well as destitute persons. They were given shelter in the various camps namely Cuparse camp, relief camp of Dhubulia, Kashipur camp and others. Some children and girls those who had lost their guardians during communal violence and at the time of coming to West Bengal were also temporarily rehabilitated at the suburban areas of Calcutta namely Belur, Baburghat and Bansberia relief camps. Some relief camps for providing shelter of the refugees were set up even outside of West Bengal and measures were adopted to send the refugees there. Moreover, shelter less as well as homeless large number of refugees jointly started setting up colonies for their accommodation in Calcutta and outskirts of Calcutta. At that time an organization named 'Nikhil Banga Bastuhara Karma Parishad' (NBBKP) was established under the influence of some leaders of the Congress party in order to protect the interest of the refugees. Some more colonies for them were also set up under the efforts of 'Nikhil Banga Bastuhara Karma Parishad'. The left parties also did not lag behind for asserting their influence over the refugees. Some colonies were established for the tireless efforts of the left parties namely CPI, RSP, RCPI, Forward Block etc. In the meantime another organization named 'South Calcutta Shahartali (suburb) Bastuhara Samhati' was also established. Many more refugee colonies came into existence between Kanchara Para to Jadavpur within the month of August in 1950. These refugee colonies sprang up in the virgin land of state Government and in some cases the lands were owned by individual personalities.[80]

Administrative Steps

In the midst of hue and cry of the influx of refugees from East Bengal as an alternative measures in some cases government facilities in the form of loans were provided to the refugees so that they could purchase land, build houses, start business or any other profession for their livelihood. On behalf of the government of West Bengal some steps were taken for continuing education of the children of the refugee families in schools or colleges or to take any other activities to start their life anew.[81]However, in the wake of huge refugee influx and communal violence, some measures were taken on the administrative level to minimize the refugee problem in both East and West Bengal. In that context, the two Chief Secretaries of West and East Bengal namely Sukumar Sen and Aziz Ahmed used to meet frequently with a view for implementing decisions regarding the refugee problem through the Inter- Dominion Conferences at administrative level. On 9thApril, 1949, at the conclusion of one such conference which was known as the Chief Secretaries' Conference an optimistic note was sounded for the first time regarding the relationship between East and West Bengal.[82]

The Government of West Bengal headed by Bidhan Chandra Roy desperately tried to boost up the depleted financial situation in terms of the relief and rehabilitation of 16 lakhs uprooted people from East Pakistan. Bidhan Chandra Roy was worried about the collection of financial assistance from the Central Government as well as from the Prime Minister to every concerned ministry about relief and rehabilitation as and when he found that the state of West Bengal was not getting the similar treatment like the other States having refugees from West Pakistan.[83]Under the circumstances, on 1st December, 1949, Bidhan Chandra Roy wrote a letter to Jawaharlal Nehru. In that letter accusing Jawaharlal Nehru, Bidhan Chandra Roy categorically mentioned that "You are under the impression that your government gave us a 'large grant' for the purpose of relief and rehabilitation. Do you realize that the total grant received for this purpose from your government in the two years, 1948-49 and 1949-50, was a little over 3 crores, the rest about 5 crores was given in the form of loan? Do you realize that this sum is 'insignificant' compared to what has been spent for refugees from West Pakistan?"[84]

In the meantime, as a reaction of large scale exodus from East Bengal in the month of February, 1950, widespread counter of communal violence started in different districts of West Bengal that was about to crack the law and order as well as the administrative machinery of the state government. At that moment of disturbances, B. C. Roy urged the leaders of the Government of India to take some measures regarding the communication with the Pakistan Government in order to take up appropriate security measures in disturbed areas and nab the guilty persons who were responsible for occurring violence and also visit the leaders of the Pakistan Government in the riot affected areas. As a responsible administrator, B. C. Roy then convened a meeting of leaders of the political parties and appealed them to maintain law and order as well as communal harmony.[85]

Question of Exchange of Population

The Government of India was fully aware about the gravity of the situation. The Prime Minister Jawaharlal Nehru in one of his statements before parliament on the 23rd of February, 1950, referred to the tragedies in the district of Khulna, Rajshahi and Barishal of East Bengal which was followed by the incidents in the district of Murshidabad and Calcutta of West Bengal and then subsequently in Dhaka. It is mention-worthy that the question of exchange of Hindu-Muslim population between West Bengal and East Pakistan was raised by Dr. Shyama Prasad Mookherjee during the debate session of the parliament on 27th February 1950. Prime Minister Jawaharlal Nehru ruled out the proposal of the exchange of Hindu-Muslim population on the ground of totally unrealistic and the vague conception. Moreover, he said that "The proposal for an exchange of population was completely antagonistic to India's political, economic, social and spiritual principles. It was a question of breach of trust." In response to the statement of Prime Minister Nehru, Shyama Prasad Mookherjee in his reply said, "When Pandit Nehru himself had arranged the exchange of population in Punjab, he had kept this question of breach of trust in cold storage. At the present moment it would be proper for him to keep the question of breach of trust in cold storage again and face the reality like an experienced politician."[86]

Nehru-Liaquat Ali Pact (8th April, 1950)

Under the pressure of above circumstances, the leaders of both the countries started thinking that if the ongoing atrocities on Hindus were not checked immediately then there were only two alternatives i.e. Exchange of population or War. After realizing the seriousness of the situation these leaders felt the need for dealing with the burning problem on the highest political level with utmost priority. As a follow up of the ongoing incidents, Liaquat Ali Khan, the then Prime Minister of Pakistan was invited in Delhi by the Government of India for a discussion over minorities problems of both the countries particularly the refugee problem. However, giving response to the invitation of the Government of India, Liaquat Ali Khan arrived in Delhi on 2nd April, 1950. Bidhan Chandra Roy, the chief minister of West Bengal was communicated earlier to arrive in Delhi for consultation. It is interesting to note that in spite of becoming the main sufferer as a head of the administrator of the state, B. C. Roy did not take part in the negotiations between India and Pakistan regarding refugee problem. However, the much talked agreement, known as 'Nehru-Liaquat Ali Pact' or 'Delhi Pact' was signed at the end of four days long discussion on 8th April, 1950 regarding the minority problems of India and Pakistan with special reference to the situation in East Bengal, West Bengal, Tripura and Assam.[87]

Resignation of Shyama Prasad Mookherjee from Central Ministry

It is a fact the 'Nehru-Liaquat Ali Pact' was hailed by many from different corner and peoples started thinking that there would be an end of diminishing of human misery in the name of communal violence in both the countries. Although, there were some intellectuals and political personalities in India as well as West Bengal who straightly expressed their unwillingness to accept the agreement as an appropriate method for the solution of the Hindu–Muslim Problem. The most important among them were Shyama Prasad Mookherjee, the then Industry and Supply Minister, Government of India[88] and Kshitish Chandra Neogy, Commerce Secretary, Government of India. Both of them resigned from their respective position as a mark of protest against the weak, puzzled and disproportionate policies adopted by the Government of India towards Pakistan. Moreover, they did not agree with the provisions of the 'Nehru-Liaquat Ali Pact' by which Government of India wanted to solve the Hindu-Muslim problem of both the countries especially in two Bengals.[89]In one of his speeches in Parliament on 19th April, 1950, Shyama Prasad Mookherjee emphatically declared that "When we have no power to force the Pakistan Government to follow the provisions of the Nehru-Liaquat Ali Pact, naturally no problems will be solved by it. Therefore, this Pact will be failed to give adequate security to the Hindus of the Pakistan and they will be compelled to come over India in a large scale."[90]As a member of the Indian Central Government, at that time Shyama Prasad Mookherjee felt that firmer action should have taken against Pakistan and it was supposition of some contemporary political thinkers that probably inside the Cabinet he was backed by the proposal of Sarder Ballavbhai Patel for a hard line with Pakistan and an exchange of populations.[91]

Prime Minister Nehru and his Government was severely criticized by Shyama Prasad Mookherjee both on the floor of the Parliament and outside on refugee problems. In one of his hard-hitting speeches in Delhi on 30th July, in 1950, Shyama Prasad Mookherjee warned the Government for its failure to handle the refugee problem. As millions of Hindus were migrated to West Bengal and the exodus was still continuing even after signing the 'Nehru-Liaquat Ali Pact'; so, in order to solve the refugee problem permanently, Shyama Prosad Mookherjee prescribed some items which were as under: " (i). Unification of the two countries; (ii). Planned exchange of population and (iii). Sufficient territories yielded by Pakistan to accommodate the displaced minorities of East Bengal." Referring to the three suggestions given by Shyama Prasad Mookherjee, Jawaharlal Nehru, the Prime Minister in one of his speeches in the Parliament on 9th August, 1950, ruled out straightly on the ground of embarrassing international relations, a violence of the constitution and the high ideals of the congress party, nursing since long back. Referring the compulsory exchange of population, Jawaharlal Nehru considered that it would be as like as 'uncivilised, brutal and barbarous'.[92]

However, Bidhan Chandra Roy tried his best and he worked tirelessly for planned settlement of refugees both within and outside of West Bengal during the entire period of his Chief Ministership. But, somehow in this field, he did not get whole hearted support to the desired extend from some of his party colleagues who were the West Bengalese.[93]

Dandakaranya

It has already been mentioned that the Government of West Bengal, headed by Bidhan Chandra Roy took various measures to rehabilitate the refugees from East Bengal and in this regard the government set up many refugee camps throughout the state. The Government also worked out for setting up Dandakaranya Project, which was known as A.MP.O. i. e. Dandakaranya Project constituted with some portion of Andhra, Madhya Pradesh and Orissa. The development programme of Dandakaranya included reclamation of land and its distribution among the displaced persons along with necessary equipments for agriculture. But, the refugees found there a hostile settlement considering their background of cultivation in the fertile as well as soft soil of East Pakistan. The output from lands of Dandakarnya was hardly coequal with the efforts put in so, the refugees were more attached towards the government subsidy than to the output of their allocated lands.[94] Naturally, a huge gap was observed between the promises and performance on behalf of the government. At the initial stage of the Dandakarnya Project, it was expected that as many as 35,000 families would be rehabilitated, but in practice it was found that the number of families settled there till 1963 were about 6,500 only.[95]Actually, in view of the refugee rehabilitation, the Dandakaranya Project was more of a dream than a reality. Discontent among the refugees started growing and intensified. As a result of the above circumstances, the refugees led by different political parties voiced their grievances through staged demonstration and processions.[96]The disturbing reports started reaching in Writers' Buildings, the State Government's headquarter about the suitability of Dandakaranya Project. The virgin soil of Dandakaranya was being reclaimed and thereafter distributed among the refugee families for their settlement under a centrally sponsored scheme headed by an officer named Fletcher. The hope of the ambitious project was going to be dashed when the representatives of the refugees started urging the Bengal Ministers repeatedly regarding the necessity of the radical changes of the Dandakaranya Development Authority (DDA), otherwise, the entire scheme might be omitted. Irrigation facilities were lacking and as a result of that almost the entire refugee population of Dandakarnya started living in camps. The blame was basically laid on the administration which was undoubtedly moving in a lackadaisical manner.[97]

Under that circumstances, Bidhan Chandra Roy, the Chief Minister of West Bengal decided to go over there with a team of Ministers for an on the spot study of the situation and hear the grievances of refugees personally. A ministerial team comprised of the Chief Minister B. C. Roy himself, P. C. Sen, the then State Rehabilitation Minister; Tarun Kanti Ghosh, Food Production Minister; two ladies Deputy Ministers, Departmental Secretaries and Meher Chand Khanna, the then Union Rehabilitation Minister left for Dandakarnya by a special plane on 24th April, 1960. After returning to Calcutta, the Chief Minister B. C. Roy prepared a note in which he gave some concrete suggestions to make Dandakaranya scheme a viable one. He wrote in strong terms to the Prime Minister about the Dandakaranya issue. At the invitation of Jawaharlal Nehru, the Prime Minister of India, the Chief Minister accompanied by his Rehabilitation Minister, P. C. Sen flew to the Capital on 16th June, 1960. Following top level discussions about the pros and cons of Dandakaranya scheme between the Prime Minister and the Chief Minister a press note was issued by the Secretariat of the Prime Minister on 17th June, 1960 and announced the reconstitution of Dandakaranya Development Authority with a whole time Chairman. It is mention worthy that Sukumar Sen, ex-Chief Secretary of West Bengal and later India's first Election Commissioner became the Chairman of the DDA, who would enjoy his power of autonomy to expedite the scheme of rehabilitation of displaced persons from East Bengal in Dandakaranya.[98]

In spite of taking the above said measures, the condition of the refugees almost remained gloomy. As per the survey report which was conducted by the State Statistical Bureau, it was revealed that among the 2,31,000 urban families 1,42,000 families were not 'properly' resettled. In rural areas, only 83,000 families were 'properly' rehabilitated while the target was expected to reach 2,83,000. The report concluded that less than 50 percent of the total refugees were 'properly' rehabilitated, that means more than 50 percent refugees were not given the proper rehabilitation.[99]

Bidhan Chandra Roy as a Chief Minister and his burden of responsibilities

From the very outset of his Chief Ministership, Bidhan Chandra Roy had carried out the responsibility of the Home Department including Police, Publicity, Transport and Jail department. In addition to this, he had to handle the responsibility of Finance Department due to the illness of Nalini Ranjan

Sarkar, the Finance Minister and after his (Nalini Ranjan Sarkar) sad demise on 25th January, 1953; B. C. Roy had to take the charge of the Finance Department as a full-fledged Finance Minister. He was also the Minister-in-charge of Development and planning of the state. Moreover, B. C. Roy held the responsibility of the Miniter-in-Charge of the Industry and Commerce, Medical and Public Health, Port and Pilot-age, Printing Press and several others miscellaneous departments. These departments collectively constituted nearly three- fourths of the total burden of the Government of West Bengal. He had to look into the pros and cons of the administration of some of these departments and the policies as well as future course of action was also formulated by him. In that case he was assisted by Ministers of State and Deputy Ministers. From the given facts it would be a rational conclusion in terms of the allocation of the portfolios of the Government of West Bengal that the major share of the burden of the administration was carried out by Bidhan Chandra Roy alone. He was legitimately entitled to the credit for whatever successes were achieved.[100]

In that connection it may be noted here that due to the untimely demise of his two able colleagues, namely Kiran Shankar Roy and Nalini Ranjan Sarkar, the administrative burden of Bidhan Chandra Roy increased many fold. In that context, there was only Prafulla Chandra Sen who was hardly a mature politician to handle the crisis of the state administration or consultation in any serious matter. Naturally, it was obvious that Bidhan Chandra Roy had to carry on the entire burden of the administrative machineries and side by side the task of guiding his party in the floor of the Assembly House fell almost absolutely on his shoulder.[101]

Reaction to Chinese Aggression

A serious repercussion was reflected on the floor of the West Bengal Legislative Assembly following the Chinese aggression at Ladakh on 21st October, 1959 which took a toll of 17 Indian Army men. In that atmosphere of foreign aggression, the Government of India adopted the policy to check anti-Indian and pro-Chinese propaganda. Bidhan Chandra Roy, the leader of the House raised his fingers towards the communist bloc and remarked, "Any one supporting Chinese policy unpatriotic. Indian main weapon was unity and whoever went against that unity was a traitor."[102]

Assam Holocaust

In the first week of July, 1960 a telegram was received by B. C. Roy at Ranikhet, a hill resort in Uttar Pradesh - from P. C. Sen regarding the large scale violence in the wake of language agitation in certain districts of Assam and thereupon a huge numbers of Bengalese had to flee from that state. The entire Brahmaputra valley was converted into an area of large-scale violence and thereupon a considerable number of Bengalese had to flee from Assam. Incidentally, the *'Bangal Kheda'* i.e. remove Bengali movement in Assam was not nothing new. It may be noted that the office of the Anandabazar Patrika in Guahati, capital city of Assam was attacked as because the Anandabazar Patrika through its writings protested against anti Bengali agitation in Assam in 1955. Not only that the Hindusthan Standard and Anandabazar Patrika were also burned for the same reason.[103] Naturally, as an inevitable outcome of the Assam holocaust disturbances broke-out in some important places of North Bengal namely Siliguri, Alipurduar and Jalpaiguri towns. That violent reaction took a tool of six human lives. Taking advantage of that situation the opposition parties of West Bengal started their activities in the form of demonstration and strike. In that hour of disturbances, Bidhan Chandra Roy wrote two letters - one to Dr. Rajendra Prasad, President of the country and another to Jawaharlal Nehru, Prime Minister of India. In his letters, B. C. Roy urged both the highest administrative stakeholder of the country to impose Presidential rule on account of failure of the Government of Assam to check lawlessness and protect the life and property of the language minorities' under the special power laid down in the constitution. But the Prime Minister ruled out the proposal of B. C. Roy and pleaded for time to bring about normalcy. However, it was for the first time in the history of West Bengal that the Independence Day (15th August, 1960) was observed as a day of mourning and protest. Black flags were hoisted in the afternoon and silent processions was taken on the streets.[104]

The Assam situation was debated in Lok Sabha for three days from 1st day of September, 1960. The Prime Minister's speech however, disappointed the Bengal MP's. The 90 minutes speech of the Prime Minister was frequently interrupted and could not give any satisfactory explanation how and why the Central Intelligence was failed in Assam. At the conclusion of the three days debate, the Lok Sabha adopted an amended resolution moved by Atulya Ghosh (he was hailed as the star speaker in the Assam debate) which was accepted by the Prime Minister on behalf of the Government. The resolution inter-alia stated: "In view of the tragic happenings which have taken place in Assam and have created a sense of fear and insecurity in the minds of the minorities in Assam a comprehensive enquiry by one or more Supreme Court Judges be instituted to enquire into the disturbances and the circumstances leading up to them and suggest remedies for ensuring adequate protection and full enjoyment of their rights guaranteed under the constitution to the citizens and prevent recurrence of such incidents in future".[105]

Movement for Bengali Language

In the midst of the atrocities on Bengali speaking population in Assam, there started a language movement also. Some Assam Cabinet members hailed from the five hill districts of the state took a drastic decision to resign from the cabinet in view of the government's stand on the state language issue and demanded separation of hill districts from Assam.[106]The Assam disturbances along with language issues reached its climax on 19th May, 1961, when 11 satyagrahis were killed at Silchar out of police firing. The Bengalese of the said region was carrying on a continuous agitation for recognition of Bengali as one of the state languages even after the visit of all India leaders including Pundit Nehru. Following the incident, on 21st May, in a chartered plane some Bengali leaders of Assam arrived in Calcutta along with the ashes of the victim satyagrah is of police firing. As a mark of protest against the brutalities on Bengalese in Assam, a spontaneous strike was observed in Calcutta. In the afternoon silent processions were taken up in the city in a peaceful manner.[107]

Innovative Measures of B. C. Roy to Solve the Problem of over population in Calcutta

It was nothing unknown to Bidhan Chandra Roy that the city of Calcutta which earned the epithet "the city of processions" from Jawaharlal Nehru was facing serious problem due to over concentration of population.[108] Keeping in mind the above situation of Calcutta, one scholar came into the decision that after partition, Calcutta i, e, once-fabled capital city of the British Indian empire had to face appalling problems of overflowed population exponentially. It was overburdened far beyond the capacity of its infrastructure.[109] At the aim of tackling the trends of increasing population in the city, B. C. Roy therefore, took some calculated programmes of development of the rural areas as well as creation of new townships so that he could expand it by mingling with the small towns. By the late 1960s, the 270 miles of surfaced roads of the city that once the envy of urban India frequently waterlogged and traffic was usually at a stalemate due to endless lines of cycles, rickshaws over crowded buses and trams - collectively created over burden of the city of Calcutta.[110] In that context, Government of West Bengal under the able leadership of its visionary chief minister, B. C. Roy took some bold steps under 'Dispersal Scheme' which included setting up a numerous colleges outside of Calcutta with adequate infrastructure along with full equipments and good staff. The main idea was mooted by B. C. Roy to provide higher educational facilities at the door-step of mofussil students so that, they would not come to Calcutta unnecessarily. Another effective and positive step taken by the chief minister was the scheme for the reclamation of land nearing Calcutta for the distribution among the middle class people who could not afford to buy lands in proper Calcutta for the construction of houses. The concept of the term 'Greater Calcutta' as if became a reality due to endless fighting of B. C. Roy and in this regard he had achieved a degree of success.[111] In addition to this it may be noted here that the possibility of construction a sub-way as well as over head way for the solution of overcrowded traffic problem in Calcutta, the circular railway around the city and the necessity of linking up the three parts of West Bengal by constructing a barrage across the Ganga River at Farakka in the district of Murshidabad were some of the groundbreaking thinking as well as visionary programmes of B. C. Roy. Moreover, Bidhan Chandra Roy dreamed for the augmentation of the state's power resources by utilizing Calcutta's Sewage for generation of Gas.[112] The heavily congested transport system in Calcutta is at present bursting due to his vision and taking adequate steps regarding transport of Calcutta and the introduction of Metro service.[113]

Birth of Himalayan Mountaineering Institute

A spirit of enthusiasm was swept over the country following the news of the conquering of the hitherto un-conquered Mt. Everest, the highest peak of the world by two men i.e. Sir Edmund Hillary, a Newzealander and Tenzing Norgey, an Indian on 29th May, 1953. Sir John Hunt, Edmunt Hillary, Tenzing Norgey and Gregory came to Writers' Buildings to meet the Chief Minister on 25th June 1953. B. C. Roy discussed with them regarding the possibilities of a scheme to establish Mountaineering Institute and in this regard he sought help of Tenzing Norgey. In that context, the Government of West Bengal decided to establish Mountaineering Institute in Darjeeling in order to teach the youth about the technique of high altitude climbing. However, Tenzing Norgey accepted the proposal of the government and agreed to take charge of the Institute as its first Director. In the meantime, Jawaharlal Nehru, the Prime Minister of India in a letter to B. C. Roy, dated 26th December, 1953, suggested for establishment of the Himalayan Mountaineering Institute with Tenzing Norgey as the chief instructor from the 1st January,1954, with a salary of Rs- 500/- and an allowance of Rs-250/-. Thus the Himalayan Mountaineering Institute was born which played an eventful role in the subsequent years.[114]

Sports Bill and Stadium for Calcutta

There was no central body to regulate the affairs related to sports. Therefore, in order to control the sports affairs Bidhan Chandra Roy introduced "The Calcutta Sports Bill" on 24th August, 1955, for the constitute a board which would be responsible for the construction and management of a stadium in the city. The proposed Bill recommended setting up three bodies i.e. i). the Sports Association, which would be the parent body to exercise general supervision, ii). the Sports Control Committee for organizing sports and games, and iii). the Sports Board which would be in charge of the finance and properties of the Association along with power to raise loan with the consent of the government. Bidhan Chandra Roy received general support from the opposition in favour of the Bill. It was estimated that Rs. 50 lakhs would be the cost for the construction of a Stadium for accommodating 1, 25,000 people.[115]

Academy of Dance, Drama and Music

It is a fact that before the merger of the Princely States and abolition of Zamindari system the Rajas as well as the Zamindars were the chief patrons of all kinds of arts not only in Bengal but other parts of the country also. On that point, considering the above reality B. C. Roy felt that the responsibilities for people's cultural development had to be taken up by the State Government. In that context, Bidhan Chandra Roy sought help from reputed personalities like Pankaj Kumar Mallick, a well known singer; Ahindra Chowdhury who shined for decades in Bengal's theatrical art for the patronization of Bengal's traditional music, dance and drama. B. C. Roy selected Jorasanko House of poet Rabindranath Tagore for the development of his said mission and thereby he inaugurated by lighting a lamp the new four-stored building of the West Bengal Academy of Dance, Drama and Music there on 15th April, 1959 at the day of Bengali New Year. The 9,300 sq, ft. new building providing class rooms for the academy's three faculties of dance, drama and music with an auditorium of 300 seats which was helped by the State Government in maintaining the high standard of that pioneer institution in the country.[116]

Ministerial Crisis

Bidhan Chandra Roy had to pass many rigorous times during his long 14.5 years (23rd January 1948- 1st July 1962) of chief-ministership of West Bengal, but the most critical period what he had to face following the defeat of the congress candidate in South Calcutta by election held in June, 1949.[117]

A vacancy was created due to the sudden death of Satish Chandra Bose, elder brother of Sarat Chandra Bose. Incidentally, Sarat Chandra Bose was exit from the congress party and filed his nomination paper for that seat as a candidate of the 'Republican Socialist Party' which was founded by him. On the other side, Suresh Das, the then President of the South Calcutta District Congress Committee, was the contesting candidate for the same. However, with the help of his own supporter along with entire anti-government as well as anti-congress forces, Sarat Chandra Bose polled 19,300 votes as against 5,750 secured by Suresh Das.[118] This defeat shook the very foundation of the ministry as well as the congress organization in West Bengal. The impact of the defeat of that by election was so grave that the morning newspaper of Calcutta on 20th June, 1949, reported a speech of the Prime Minister, in which he expressed the view that the 'West Bengal Ministry should resign'.[119] Bidhan Chandra Roy, the chief minister of West Bengal, after knowing the view of the Prime Minister expressed his readiness to quit office following the situation created by the by-election debacle.

In that circumstances, putting his loyal friend, Nalini Ranjan Sarkar, as the acting Premier of West Bengal, Bidhan Chandra Roy left for Switzerland on 23rd June, 1949. In absence of B. C. Roy an emergency session of the Congress Working Committee meeting was to be held at Delhi on 13th July where Nalini Ranjan Sarkar, Kalipada Mukherjee and Prafulla Chandra Sen were advised to attend the same on behalf of the West Bengal Ministry. A storm of roar was raised in the congress circle in Delhi following the defeat of the congress candidate in South Calcutta by-election and thereby executive committee of the Congress Working Committee (henceforth CWC) took a resolution about the West Bengal situation on 28th July, 1949. The principal recommendations of the CWC were as under: i). interim general election for West Bengal within six months or as early as possible, b).formation of a new interim ministry and c).reconstitution of the executive committee of the PCC.[120] So far as an interim ministry was concerned, it was also, however, decided that details were to be postponed till the arrival of B. C. Roy, the leader of the Congress Assembly Party.

Under the above circumstances, B. C. Roy arrived in Bombay on the 2nd September and went straight to his friend Sardar Patel in Birla House for a medical check-up and to know his mind on the ministerial tangle and secure his support. Thereafter, Bidhan Chandra Roy returned to Calcutta and resuming his office and summoned a meeting of the West Bengal Congress Legislative Party on 10th September, 1949 for the discussion of the resolution regarding a new interim Ministry, taken by the CWC in its meeting held on 28th July, 1949. The Hooghly Group under the leadership of Atulya Ghosh was the sincere followers of B. C. Roy Ministry, tabled a resolution thus "Whereas the Congress Assembly Party have full confidence in its leader (Dr. Roy) and the present ministry, they respectfully request the Congress Working Committee to reconsider their decision regarding the necessity of forming an Interim Ministrey".[121] It is noteworthy that 50 members among the 55 attended the meeting of the Congress Legislative Party of which 34 members belonged to the Hooghly Group and voted in favour of the resolution while only 14 members opposed it.[122] As a consequent of such a development, the Congress Working Committee met again in Delhi on 4th and 5th October, 1949, over the issues of West Bengal Ministry where B. C. Roy put the case on behalf of his Ministry before the 21 member committee. Thereafter, being convinced by his hour long masterly exposition of the predominant condition in West Bengal during the transmigration period the CWC decided to postpone its previous stand and permitted the Ministry under B. C. Roy to continue subject to any change which he thought fit to make.[123] As to the reconstitution of the Provincial Congress Committee (PCC), the CWC also decided to resile from its earlier decision but, the decision of holding a general election in West Bengal remained unchanged.[124]

Postponement of Interim Election

At that point of time, after gaining vote of confidence from Congress Legislative Party, comparatively strong from his previous position, Bidhan Chandra Roy wrote a letter to Pundit Jawaharlal Nehru, the Prime Minister of India regarding the holding of the interim general election in West Bengal on 30th December, 1949.[125] Thereafter, B. C. Roy called on several central congress leaders and the party President to dissuade Working Committee from executing its resolution regarding the interim general election in West Bengal.[126] However, as a result of the skillful diplomatic efforts of Bidhan Chandra Roy the Prime Minister announced on 8th January, 1950, in a lengthy statement that "no interim election would be held in West Bengal under the restricted franchise of Government of India Act, 1935, on the basis of old electoral rolls, as previously announced by the Government, but that a general election would be held along with other states within a period of 8 or 9 months on the basis of adult franchise."[127]

Groupism in the Congress Party in West Bengal

The power struggle within the West Bengal Provincial Congress Committee between the ministerial group and the Gandhin Group or Khadi

Group led by Prafulla Chandra Ghosh and Jugantar group of Surendra Mohan Ghosh reached its climax in August-September, 1950 over the election of delegates for the Nasik Congress. Meanwhile, the Gandhian and the Jugantar Groups were frustrated as their hope to oust the B. C. Roy ministry was dashed to the ground. The Gandhian Group was further upset as because Kripaliniji was defeated in the Presidential election of the All India Congress Party.[128] It is mentionable that after that incident the Gandhian Group decided to defect from the congress party and accordingly it refrained from the elections of the PCC that was to be held on September, 1950. As the Jugantar Group had no enough capacity to fight against the Hooghly Group, naturally, the Hooghly Group led by Atulya Ghosh and the whole hearted backing from B. C. Roy, the Chief Minister, P. C. Sen, the Food Minister, Kalipada Mukherjee and some other Ministers easily managed to take control over the PCC. On September 17, 1950 Atulya Ghosh and Bijay Singh Nahar of Hooghly Group were elected President and Secretary respectively of the West Bengal Provincial Congress Committee by an overwhelming majority.[129]After that Atulya Ghosh's supremacy in the Provincial Congress Continued for a decade and a half until the congress itself divided into two camps as Congress (O) and Congress (R). One of the most important sources behind the strength of the Hooghly Group was the harmonious relationship between B. C. Roy, the Chief Minister and its leader Atulya Ghosh. As one observer had rightly pointed out, "These two men (Dr. Roy and Atulya GHosh) cooperated and collaborated on a simple principle: division of powers. While Dr. Roy was in full charge of the ministerial and governmental affairs, Ghosh was in complete control of the party machine".[130]

Birth of Krishak Majdoor Praja Party (KMPP)

In November 1950, the followers of the Gandhian Group under the leadership of Prafulla Chandra Ghosh and Suresh Chandra Banerjee along with another 100 congressmen organized a conference in Calcutta and resolved to form a separate political party. In May 1951, Prafulla Chandra Ghosh and his followers teamed up with several congressmen those who in the meantime defected from the congress party at the national level under the leadership of Kripaliniji and Rafi Ahmed Kidwai which led to the emergence of a new party known as the Krishak Majdoor Praja Party (KMPP).[131] The object of the establishment of the KMPP was a 'classless non-exploiting democracy'. Naturally, following the development when on 8th February, 1952, the budget session of the West Bengal Assembly was opened then for the first time the Ministry had to face a strong opposition.

It is noteworthy that though, the nine Muslim League members and two Communist Members namely Jyoti Basu and Ratanlal Brahman had played the role of the opposition in a comparatively weak manner, but, opposition benches thereafter occupied by men who were stalwarts in the congress with outstanding records of sacrifice.[132.]

One Pice War - Resistance to Tram Fare

The Calcutta Tramway Company made an upward revision of the second class fare by one pice and decided to execute it from 1st July 1953, though at that time the second class fare was three pice.[133] As the government of West Bengal gave the approval of the fare hike to the British Tram Company, therefore, before leaving for Europe on 5th July, 1953, B. C. Roy issued a statement defending the Tramway Company's enhancement of the second class fare by one pice on the ground that the fares in Calcutta were the lowest in the country.[134] A 'Tram Fare Resistance Committee' was formed by the combined opposition parties with Suresh Chandra Banerjee as the Chairman. They demanded not to pay the enhanced fare and started picketing from 1st July. After the arrest of Jyoti Basu, Ganesh Ghosh, Subodh Bandopadhyay and Jyotish Joarder in the early hours of 3rd July the agitation took a violent turn and police was asked to prepare at lalbazar to meet the situation.[135] In all 588 arrests were made in connection with the day's incidents for picketing, inciting people to acts of violence, non-payments of tram fare, throwing crackers and for setting fire to terms.[136]

Incidentally, in absence of B. C. Roy, food minister P.C. Sen was in charge as the care taker chief Minister and the 'Tram Fare Resistance Committee' took the fullest advantage of that situation. They declared a strike on 9th July, 1953. The law and order situation began to deteriorate day by day. After a Cabinet Meeting on that day Kalipada Mukherjee, the Police Minister told press correspondents that "Government is determined to meet force with force". This statement added fuel to the fire. On the 17th of July the mob seized control over a large area in South Calcutta. Police fired six rounds and one person died due to police firing.[137] In the meantime, following the instruction of the 'Tram Fare Resistance Committee' passengers refused to pay enhanced fare and thereby the tram company was forced to stop the running of trams. But, with the initiation of the agitation of the tram employees against the decision of the tram company the movement got a momentum. A spontaneous strike and procession throughout the Calcutta was held defying the 144 Cr. P.c. naturally, scuffle broke out between the agitators and the police. Under the circumstances, in order to quell the agitators the police had to resort *lathi* charge, tear gas cells and fire which led to large scale arrest and injuries. [138]

Assault on Press Reporters

Following the above circumstances, defying the Section 144 Cr. P.c. the 'Tram Fare Resistance Committee' arranged a mammoth public meeting at Calcutta Maidan on 22nd July, 1953. It seems that both the groups were preparing for showdown. However, immediately after the beginning of the meeting a truckload police man arrived there under the leadership of a Deputy Commissioner. The police men ran towards the meeting and started beating the people and herded into police vans. The most astonishing event of the police atrocities of that day was the assault of as many as 18 press reporters and photographers those who were there to cover the meeting. Two of the injured were admitted in hospital, six pressmen were also arrested. Among the assaulted press reporters, most prominent were- Anil Bhattacharya and Tarak Das of 'Jugantar'; Sunil Sengupta of 'Swadhinata', Shyamadas Basu of 'Times of India', Bidya Munshi of 'Blitzs', Ajit Some of 'Ananda Bazar', Sudin Roy of 'The Statesman', etc.[139] On the next day i.e. on 23rd July, 1953 all the news papers gave horrible pictures of assault on pressmen and followed it up with thundering editorials of police 'barbarity'. One Satyendranath Majumder, editor of 'Satyayug' commented its editorial regarding police as the 'shame of mothers' womb'. As an aftermath of that event the government of West Bengal as if became isolated from the people of the state.[140]

In that critical juncture, postponing his eye operation, B. C. Roy returned to Calcutta to control the situation on 30th July, 1953. After his arrival in Calcutta, within 12 hours holding a cabinet meeting B. C. Roy constituted a one man commission headed by Mr. Justice Prasanta Behari Mookerjee to look for the question of the entire tramway fare structure and the economic bearing of the proposed increase in the second class fare.[141] Thereafter, on 2nd August, 1953, Bidhan Chandra Roy met the leaders of the movement including Suresh Chandra Banerjee and Hemanta Kumar Bose at Writers' Buildings. On the following day i.e. on 3rd August, B. C. Roy appointed a tribunal and adopted comfortable policy to grant bail to all persons who were detained on charges of violent activities. The leaders of the movement also decided to suspend their direct action and the movement thus came to an end.[142] Actually, pursuing the unique policy of 'discussion, adjustment and compromise' Bidhan Chandra Roy was able to thwart the anti-Government programme of the opposition.

Hunger Strike by West Bengal Policemen

During the Chief Ministership of Prafullya Chandra Ghosh the Government of West Bengal had to face a several threat of a call for strike by some policemen for the fulfillment of their some economic demands. Though, P. C. Ghosh somehow was able to manage the agitating temper of the policemen but the discontent among policemen came into the forefront with the commencement of hunger strike by 5,000 armed and other branches of the Calcutta police on 10th December, 1954.[143] At that moment in order to maintain basic law and order the state administration had to call for the Army and the National Volunteer Force (NVF) in the morning of 11th December, 1954. In order to avoid any untoward situation and put down the agitation as many as 54 leaders of the agitating policemen were arrested under the Protective Detention Act (PDA) and the Defence of India Rules (DIR). But instead of overcome the crisis the movement soon spread into several districts of West Bengal. In that critical hour of the administration high level conferences were held regularly at Chief Minister's room and the police chiefs were to wait for directions from the chief minister. At last, on the 7th day of strike, the Government of West Bengal decided to take action against the agitating policemen and accordingly it was circulated that stringent measures would be taken if they failed to join their respective duty. However, a large number of strikers returned to their duties on 17th December, 1954 and gradually the situation turned into normal. It may be noted that B. C. Roy, the chief minister of West Bengal was very much worried for the sign of rebellious mood of the disciplined police. Moreover, the Government had the information that a section of the police force came under the influence of the extremist group of politicians. There might become danger for any government at the time of a crisis. Following the stress of the police strike B. C. Roy was so perplexed that his sleeping was disturbed and suffered a heart attack which was his second attack after the first in 1930.[144]

Movement of All Bengal Teachers' Association (ABTA)

The Secondary School Teachers' started strike for indefinite period on and from 10th February 1954 for the fulfillment of their various demands, among them most important were- enhancement of the monthly salary from Rs-73 to 180 and dearness allowance of Rs. 35 as recommended by the Madhyamick Education Board. It is noteworthy that Secondary School Teachers under the banner of the All Bengal Teachers' Association (ABTA) submitted their charter of demands to the chief minister few months ago. But, as and when the government was not willing to accept the demands of the teachers' then altogether 18,000 secondary school teachers' went for 'direct action' to gain their demands. A large procession of the agitating teachers' under the leadership of Manoranjan Sengupta, Satyapriya Roy,

Anila Devi etc. marched towards Mahakaran on 11th February, 1954, but the police created barricade and did not allow the procession to proceed towards the Mahakaran. Thereafter, the agitating teachers' started sit on demonstration in front of the Raj Bhavan. A strike was observed throughout the West Bengal on 12th February, in favour of the demands of the teachers'.[145] When the sit on demonstration of the teachers' were going on then at midnight of 14th February the police broke the demonstration camp and arrested many agitating teachers'. In order to show sympathy or solidarity huge number of students, labour and co-citizens of the city join with the teachers' on 15th February. On 16th February as many as 400 teachers' along with activists of different democratic movements were arrested by the police. On the same day i.e. on 16th February, 1954, Calcutta witnessed one of the worst disturbances as a result of the teachers' strike. As if, whole Calcutta City came forward with monetary help in favour of the teachers. Even the rickshaw pullers were not taking fare from the lady teachers. Some police officers were found to take blessing from teachers by touching their feet.[146]

Near about 40,000 people came into the street and marched towards assembly house to compel the Government to accept the demands of the Secondary School Teachers'. That was one of the biggest ever movement launched by the teachers under the umbrella of the All Bengal Teachers Association dominated by the communists. But, due to the obstruction of the police personnel a scuffle broke out and police resorted lathi charge, teargas cell and firing thereby 6 people lost their lives and 157 got serious injuries. Forty four persons were arrested. They included Suresh Chandra Banerjee and six other MLAs.[147]After the incident of 16th February, Government imposed 144 Cr. P.c. all over Calcutta to suppress any kind of agitation. As a result of the lathi charge of the police along with Military, one Rabindra Sarkar, student of Rani Bhavani School, North Calcutta, lost his life. Aged teacher of Naktala School, named Jannchandra Roy also died due to police atrocities. In a large gathering on Wellington Square that was held on 17th February against the barbaric police action. In the Assembly House, Jyoti Basu described Dr. Bidhan Chandra Roy as 'tyrannous Niro'.[148] In the meanwhile, when such fight was going on between police and processionists, in the Assembly Chief Minister Bidhan Chandra Roy accepted most of the demands of the teachers'. But, by that time, the situation was beyond control. However, due to the severe criticism of the opposition MLAs that resulted the acceptance of the major demands of the teachers' by the government and thereby the teachers' movement at last came to an end on 21st February. The arrested teachers' were being released from 22nd February as per the condition imposed by the agitating teachers' prior to withdrawal of the strike on 21st February, 1954.[149]

No Confidence against the Government in 1958

The year 1958, was a challenging year for the government headed by Bidhan Chandra Roy. Siddhartha Shankar Ray, the then Judicial Minister of B. C. Roy Ministry resigned from the Ministry on 10th March, 1958 following the disagreement with the various government policies. In a statement, Siddhartha Shankar Ray criticized the food policy of the government on the ground that it was 'diabolical', 'irresponsible', 'dangerous', and 'devastating'. The "base and inefficient" nature of the administration was a reflection of the "base and inefficient nature of the leadership of the party", the minister remarked.[150] In the resignation of Ray, the opposition parties found a good opportunity to strike at the congress government. Prafulla Chandra Ghosh of KMPP, remarked that the congress government was being run by the sheer force of majority and its policy was nothing but that of living a life of living death.[151] However, in the pretext of the resignation of Siddhartha Shankar Ray, at last on 27th March, 1958, the Assembly met at 2.30 p.m. and after more than eight and half hours of heated debate the no-confidence motion was moved by Jyoti Basu, the Leader of the Opposition, accusing the congress ministry of indulging in deliberate and systematic 'corrupt practices'.[152] From Government side only Bijay Singh Nahar and the Chief Minister participated in the debate. At 11.15 p.m. the Speaker put the no-confidence motion before the house which was defeated by voice-vote due to the congress members standing solidly behind their leader.[153]

In the by-election of Bhowanipur Assembly Constituency, Siddhartha Shankar Ray with the support of the left parties defeating the congress candidate Bijay Kumar Banerjee came into victorious. In that election, Siddhartha Shankar Ray secured 23,222 votes against 12, 684 polled by his congress rival Bijay Kumar Banerjee. Though, in the year of 1957 general election as a congress candidate Ray had a majority of 7, 000 votes.[154]

Demand for Inclusion of Some Portion of Bihar into West Bengal

Following the appointment of a high power commission by the Government of India in 1953 to consider the question of redistribution of provinces, the West Bengal Government submitted its memorandum to the commission in the first week of June, 1954. In this memorandum Government of West Bengal demanded integration of Purnia, Manbhum, Singhbhum and the Santhal Pargana districts of Bihar and Goalpara district of Assam into West Bengal. Dr. Bidhan Chandra Roy, the Chief Minister of West Bengal argued before the State Reorganization Commission (SRC) in Calcutta on 12th February 1955, that the boundaries of West Bengal with Bihar and Assam needed to be reconstructed so that the state could function as a compact unit of the Indian administration. Not only that in comparison with the others states in India the density of population was the highest in West Bengal and was needed to be relieved.[155]

On 30th September, 1955, the long expected report of the State Reorganization Commission (S.R.C.) was signed by its Chairman Fazl Ali, Mr. K. M. Pannikar and Pundit Kunzru. According to the recommendation of the commission providing a link with disconnected northern part, a portion of Purnia district along with a portion of the Manbhum district of Bihar was proposed to be transferred to West Bengal. No doubt it was an unexpected recommendation to the leaders of the West Bengal Pradesh Congress Committee and state administration as well.[156]

Bengal- Behar Merger Scheme

Following the above circumstances Bidhan Chandra Roy, Chief Minister of the state along with Atulya Ghosh, state congress chief, left for Delhi to meet the S.R.C. In course of discussion during that meeting was to be held on 15th January 1956, Srikrishna Sinha, Chief Minister of Bihar gave the proposal about 'Merger of Bengal and Bihar' which was accepted by Bidhan Chandra Roy. As a result of that meeting a historic joint statement was issued from Delhi on 23rd January, 1956 by the Chief Minister of West Bengal and Bihar proposing merger of their states that was likely to be called "Purva Pradesh". The Prime minister of India and Congress Working Committee also welcomed the 'wisdom and foresight' of the two leaders.[157]

Anti-Merger Movement

But in West Bengal, the opposition parties specially the leftists raised their strong voice against the merger scheme. Though, Executive Council of the West Bengal Pradesh Congress Committee in its meeting held on 1st February, 1956, welcomed the broad outlook of the Chief Minister. However, the Anti-Merger Committee declared *bundh* on 24th February. On the following day, i, e, on 25th February, Bihar Assembly approved its Chief Minister's resolution on union of Bengal and Bihar by 157 votes against 25.[158]

Meanwhile, Bidhan Chandra Roy had to face violent demonstration while he was addressing public meetings to mobilize public opinion in support of his merger plan. In that context, B. C. Roy informed the Assembly on the 17th of March that if the merger proposal which was before the people was rejected, the question regarding the implementation of the State Reorganization Commission's recommendations about West Bengal would arise. [159]

During that time two Parliamentary by-elections i.e. one in Midnapore and the other in North Calcutta were held. B. C. Roy put the merger issue before the voters and at the same time his opponents i.e. the anti –merger group took up the challenge. In the circumstances, Asoke Sen, a Barrister of the Calcutta High Court, was chosen as the congress candidate for the Parliamentary seat of North Calcutta by-election and the opposition group nominated Mohit Moitra, Secretary of the anti-merger committee for the same. During the campaign period of that high voltage by election, the opposition approached the voters with attractive slogans such as "Bengal is being sold to Bihar, Bengali as a community is going to die, save Bengal defeat Congress". But it was very difficult for the congress party and its leaders to convince the voters about the benefits of merger scheme. However, in the result of the by-election Mohit Moitra, candidate of anti-merger group as well as leftist defeated his congress rival Asoke Sen by 84,953 votes against 51,880. Thereafter, accepting the verdict of the people, Bidhan Chandra Roy through the Director of Publicity, Government of West Bengal withdrew the proposal of Union of Bengal and Bihar. At last, according to the recommendation the State Reorganization Commission (SRC) Purulia Sub-Division of Manbhum district and some portion of Kishenganj Sub-Division of Purnia district were transferred from Bihar to West Bengal.[160]

The result was that an additional area and population of 2,900 sq. miles and 1.7 million respectively incorporated with West Bengal. Therefore, the number of West Bengal's seat in Lok Sabha was raised from 34 to 36 and that in the Assembly from 242 to 252.[161]

Berubari Union

Following a statement of the Prime Minister of India in the Lok Sabha on 9th December, 1958, over the decision of transfer a small part (amounting to more than four squire miles among the total area of 8.75 sq. miles where 12,000 people lived among them Muslims were 100) of West Bengal territories (Berubari Union of Jalpaiguri district) to Pakistan, the political situation of West Bengal became so explosive that as many as four adjournment motions were moved by the opposition members on 15th December, 1958. At the time of his statement the Prime Minister gave a reference of the "opinion of Revenue officers of West Bengal" which compelled the chief minister giving his explanation to the Assembly house. Though, the chief minister informed the house that the West Bengal Revenue officers neither give any opinion nor they were authorized to do so i.e. transfer of parts of Berubari to Pakistan. In that context, B. C. Roy placed the matter before the House and on the basis of unanimous decision an emphatic protest was communicated to the central government against the re-adjustment of boundary between the two Prime Ministers of India and Pakistan.[162]

However, ignoring the protest of the Chief Minister as well as feeling of the people of West Bengal, a small portion of the state under the district of Jalpaiguri i.e. Berubari was transferred to Pakistan as per the terms of the Nehru-Noon Agreement. It was finally passed by the Lok Sabha and later by the Rajya Sabha on 22nd December, 1960 without any change. Though, as a mark of protest Asok Sen, Union Law Minister and Congress M.Ps from West Bengal were absent from the said meeting of both the Lok Sabha and the Rajya Sabha. [163]

Economic Reconstruction during the Era of B. C. Roy

Planning for Metro Railway Project

At the very beginning of his Chief-Ministership, Bidhan Chandra Roy, ignoring every possible odd circumstance, caused by the partition and instead of that he always thought about positive side i. e. the economic reconstruction as well as development of the province. Even in the midst of most depressing environment he continued his tireless efforts silently for the planning and uplifting the livelihood of the people of West Bengal. As and when he would go abroad for his eye treatment then he used to visit some European countries simultaneously for exploring the possibilities of establishment of a salt-factory with German collaboration. He used to go Paris for on the spot study and to discuss with experts who constructed the under-ground railway there. It is noteworthy that when the central government felt the necessity for such an investigation for an underground railway for Calcutta and expert from USSR had done the same accordingly, but due to the initiative of B. C. Roy a French team came before 23 years and after investigation submitted its report to the State Government. Therefore, one may recall that the background for the introduction of Metro Rail in Calcutta, initiated by Dr. Bidhan Chandra Roy. Besides, B. C. Roy would visit Birmingham to see manufacturers of double-decker diesel engine buses for Calcutta State Transport Service (CSTS) and contacted a Swedish firm for chief wooden house as well as cheap houses of concrete structure for the urban population and refugees. The visionary chief minister firmly believed that if West Bengal or India was to progress with the fast changing world then his visit to the West in quest of knowledge and on-the-spot study of various developmental works was essentially inevitable.[164]

Mayurakshi Project

In the midst of the troubled political situation and huge refugee influx, the Government of West Bengal had done its first big achievement by formally opening an important phase of the multi-purpose Mayurakshi Project on 30th July, 1951. It was an irrigation canals and Tilpara Barrage situated near the town of Suri in Birbhum district. The purpose of the project was irrigation, flood control and generation of hydro-electric power which was to be followed by many more such schemes for the development of West Bengal during his tenure.[165]

Durgapur Project

The building up of Durgapur industrial base on the stands on Damodor River always is considered as one of the greatest achievements of Bidhan Chandra Roy. With the completion of the Durgapur Dam in the month of August, 1955, the industrial development started in Durgapur. Durgapur Steel Plant (1959), Coke Oven Plant (1959), Thermal Power, Coal Tar Distillation, Gas Grid and Alloy Plant along with Pig Iron Plant were constructed one by one. On 29th December, 1959 was a remarkable day in the history of the industrial development in India because on that day the melting furnace of metal was introduced and as an industrial base Durgapur entered into the arena of world industrial atlas.[166] In that connection it may be recalled that in order to implementation of the Durgapur industrial project an extensive area of land was acquired by the state government on proper compensation. In that case 20,000 inhabitants were displaced. The Revenue officers were instructed by B. C. Roy, the Chief Minister to acquire suitable alternative lands for the displaced persons. It was a remarkable task of peaceful rehabilitation of the huge people which was completed very peaceful manner. In that connection, besides, B. C. Roy, the name of Ananda Gopal Mukherjee, the local MLA deserved special mention. Ananda Gopal Mukherjee played very vital role in building up of Durgapur industrial hub by efficiently executing the order of the chief minister and even declined a ministerial offer after the election of 1957 for the sake of Durgapur project.[167]

India's First Express Highway-Durgapur

With the development of Durgapur as the most important industrial base in West Bengal, B. C. Roy started thinking if Durgapur one day was to become the 'Ruhr of India' then it must have an Express Highway. The Chief Minister also felt the necessity for a shorter trunk-route to connect Calcutta with this industrial complex. However, according to the direction of the chief minister a blue print was prepared accordingly and he went to Delhi to obtain necessary approval and sanction of money. As a result of skilful persuasion of B. C. Roy, the Union Minister for Transport and Communications announced on 7th October, 1958, an allotment of Rs. 5 crores for the construction of a new 'National Expressway' from Calcutta to Durgapur. That 'National Expressway' is now serving as life-line between Calcutta and Durgapur.[168]

Oil Refinery

It is interesting to note that for the establishment of a third oil refinery in the eastern region of the country, when the government of India was negotiating with Messrs. Caltex & Co. then the idea of setting up of the same in west Bengal draw the attention of Bidhan Chandra Roy. In a letter dated 22nd April, 1952 addressed to the Prime Minister, B. C. Roy urged him to establish the third one million ton refinery near Calcutta. However, after years long negotiations, the oil refinery at Haldia came into the realization. It is needless to say that the establishment of an oil refinery would lead to the growth of numerous subsidiary chemical industries which provided a large scale employment of technically qualified middle-class youth of the West Bengal.[169]

India's Plastic Industry Comes to Age

As a result of the tireless effort of Bidhan Chandra Roy, the far-sighted Chief Minister of the West Bengal a congenial climate for the establishment of big and small industries was created in the state. Mr. D. L. Majumdar, the Law Secretary of the Company Affairs Ministry of India disclosed to the Chief Minister that as many as 848 and 961 companies were registered in the year of 1956-57 and 1957-58 respectively in West Bengal which were leading in the number of new companies registered in the country. Though, it is a fact that the total number of companies registered in Bombay was more than that in West Bengal. It may be mention worthy that the West Bengal's first three five year plans were mainly the outcome of the creation and implementation of B. C. Roy and the fourth plan was implemented by Prafulla Chandra Sen.[170] However, being attracted by the industrial-friendly environment of West Bengal the representatives of the Imperial Chemical Industries (ICI) met the Chief Minister for establishing a big project for the manufacture of polythene at Rishra near Calcutta. Thereafter the completion of the negotiations with the Central and State Governments for three years the setting up plant of the Imperial Chemical Industries (ICI) that opened the new chapter of potentialities of the industry as a foreign exchange savior, provider of employment, supplier of the basic material manufactured from abundantly available local resources for the first time to a large group of small-scale and cottage industries.[171]

Others Developmental Projects

It is noteworthy that on 5th March, 1960 the Chief Minister apprised the Assembly House about seven big projects which were received the sanction by the planning commission. They included-(i). Salt-Lake Reclamation Scheme (Rs.19 crores),(ii). Jaldhaka Hydro-electric Scheme (Rs.4.5 crores), (iii). Bandel Thermal Power Station with a capacity of 750 MW, (iv). Durgapur Thermal Power Station,(v). Durgapur Fertilizer Project (Rs.20 crores) (vi). Tar Distillation Plant at Durgapur and (vii). Calcutta - Durgapur Gas Grid Project. Total expenditure in all these schemes amounted of Rs.82 crores including Rs. 32 crores in foreign exchange. On the previous day i, e, March 4th, 1960 the Chief Minister met a three-man International Economic Mission of the World Bank and pleaded for a loan of Rs. 32 crores to be repaid in rupee payment, if necessary. [172]

Zamindari Abolition Bill

There were some important Bills relating to the land system passed during the chief ministership of B. C. Roy. In the '*Bargaders* Acts' of 1950 some provisions were there to protect the share croppers. According to the Acts a 'share croppers conflict –removal board' was set up. Not only that 'Zamindari Accusation Acts, and 'Land Reforms Acts' were passed in 1953 and 1955 respectively. According to the 'Zamindari Accusation Acts of 1953, the permanent settlement and Zamindari systems were declared null and void. There were provisions to give compensations to the Zamindars. However, on and from 1st *Baishak*, 1362 (Bengali Calendar) i.e.1955 the accusation of Zamindari was started by the Government of West Bengal. The shares of the share-croppers were fixed 60% instead of tebhaga i.e. 2/3. It was circulated that the owner of the vested lands would be allowed to retain 25 acres of cultivable lands and 15 acres of housing as well as garden lands. Measures were taken to distribute the surplus lands among the share croppers and landless peasants. The abolition of Zamindari system by the

West Bengal Government in 1953, marked the beginning of one of the most revolutionary measures in the history of the land reforms in the country to stop exploitation of peasantry by the landlords.[173] With the passage of the Bill the power and prestige of the landed aristocracy began to decline steadily. The Zamindars started selling their palatial buildings which they could no longer maintain. In that connection, the State Government was advised by the Central Government to examine the cases and purchase such properties for utilization of nation- building purpose.[174]

Merger of Cooch Behar and Chandannagar

The merger of Cooch Behar Princely State to West Bengal was a memorable event in the history of West Bengal. The merger of Cooch Behar took place on 1st January, 1950. Bidhan Chandra Roy, the chief minister of West Bengal received the Instrument of Accession from Nanjappa, an emissary of Sardar Ballavbhai Patel, Union Home Minister and presided over the public function of the merger ceremony. On that ceremonial occasion, B. C. Roy officially announced that "the princely State of Cooch Behar would be maintained as a separate district with headquarter at Cooch Behar for historical as well as sentimental reasons and that all the State servants would be absorbed in West Bengal Government services." The accession of Cooch Behar meant an additional of 1918 square miles of territory with a population of eight lakhs into West Bengal.[175]In that connection it may be noted that once French occupied Chandannagar was merged with West Bengal on 2nd October, 1954.[176]

Bengali as official language

One of the most important steps taken by the Government of West Bengal was passing the 'West Bengal Official Language Bill'-1961. This Bill was passed on 25th September, 1961 without any difficulties by voice vote. This Bill adopted the Bengali language as the official language of the state. In this connection it may be noted here that the Bill accommodated the scope of 'Nepali' as official language along with Bengali for the three subdivision of Darjeeling district, namely-Darjeeling, Kalimpong (Now – separate district) and Kurseong.[177]

First General Election - 1952

The year 1952 was a turning point in the political history of India as because for the first time the country had gone to polls on the basis of adult franchise under the constitution and occupied the honored position as one of the 'biggest democratic countries in the world'. Before going for first general election, the congress party in the centre and the provinces made all necessary preparation for fighting the election battle. It is noteworthy that United Socialist Organization (USO) comprised of the Communist party along with Forward Bloc, Socialist Republican Party, Bolshevik Party, INA, Peoples' Movement etc. which came to be known as anti-congress United Front. Though, Krishak Majdur Praja Party (KMPP) under the leadership of Prafulla Chandra Ghosh, Praja Socialist Party and Jana Sangha fought the election separately.[178]The first general election in the State of West Bengal was held on and from January 3-22 and 25, altogether 21 days along with Lok Sabha.[179]

However, in the first general election B. C. Roy won by a majority of 4,111 votes against his rival candidate Satyapriya Banerjee of Forward Block (Marxist) from Bowbazar constituency. The congress party returned to power with a comfortable majority of 143 in a house of 238 of which General Seats were 186, Scheduled Castes 40 and Scheduled Tribes 12.[180] But, in the midst of resounding victory, most of the senior ministers like Prafulla Chandra Sen, Kalipada Mukherjee, Bimal Chandra Sinha, Bhupati Majumder, Nikunja Behari Maity, Niharendu Dutta Majumdar were defeated by the candidates of the Leftist parties. Rai Harendra Nath Chowdhury was defeated by Jyoti Basu in Baranagore constituency.[181] Only four Ministers i.e. Hem Chandra Naskar, J. N. Panja, S. P. Burman and B. C. Roy, the Chief Minister were elected by the voters. The Hooghly-Midnapore group - the main dominating faction of the congress organization and the cabinet in West Bengal was simply wiped out. Naturally, Bidhan Chandra Roy began to handle power simultaneously over the party organization and the government.[182]

Cabinet Formation

In spite of winning the West Bengal congress party with a comfortable majority, Bidhan Chandra Roy formed his cabinet almost three months later. We have already mentioned that most of the important Cabinet Ministers of the previous government were defeated. Moreover, the President of the All India Congress Committee directed that 'no defeated minister was to be taken back into the Cabinet either through a by-election or by becoming a member of the Upper House'. West Bengal had a bicameral legislature. In that circumstances, after three months skillful negotiation, Bidhan Chandra Roy was able to obtain approval from the Congress High Command regarding the formation of his new Cabinet on 11th June, 1952 including defeated Prafulla Chandra Sen and Kalipada Mukherjee[183] who were to return to the Upper House from local bodies' constituencies. Bidhan Chandra

Roy inducted in his Cabinet a lady, named Renuka Ray[183].a,(wife of Chief Secretary S. N. Ray) who was also defeated in the Lok Sabha election and the portfolio of Refugee and Relief was given to her.[184]The style of formation of the Cabinet of Bidhan Chandra Roy became a matter of controversy and created uproar in the Lok Sabha for selecting the wife of the Chief Secretary. The opposition parties particularly the communists did not lag behind in seizing this opportunity. They started attacking as well as criticizing the ministry through wall posters and placard along with public meeting and on the floor of the House.[185]

General Election of 1957

The second general election in the State of West Bengal was held on and from March 1-14; altogether 14 days along with Lok Sabha.[186] Prior to the commencement of the said election the political scene in West Bengal was tilted to the congress party due mainly to the rapid development programmes in the field of social service, establishment of the industries in public and private sectors, creating jobs for educated unemployed youths and benefits achieved from the two Five Years Plans.[187] Moreover, Nehru's popularity as well as acceptability as a leader of the Indian National Congress with the masses remained incontestable as ever. It may be noted here that the Chhatra Parishad, Students wing of the Indian National Congress, was formed on 28th August 1954,[188] for the first time in 1957 election, addressed street corner meeting which were the monopoly of the left parties since long days. The activists of the Chhatra Parishad were able to draw the attention of the press and the public by their activities and they were given charge of a difficult area of Bow Bazar constituency of B. C. Roy, over which communist influence was ever dominant. One of the notable incidents of that election was the Chief Minister B. C. Roy's contesting with Md. Ismail, the communist candidate.[189]

After campaign all over the state along with state congress chief-Atulya Ghosh, Bidhan Chandra Roy lastly begun to tour his constituency on foot. He entered every bustee, met every shop-keeper and small trader, particularly Muslims, who were the balancing factor by virtue of their number. Two days prior to the date of polling, he went to the Nakhoda Mosque, located in a predominantly Muslim locality. The Imam came to receive him and escorted him upstairs. But unfortunately in his team there was a person named Gopal Mukhopadhyay [190] who had earned notoriety in the Calcutta Killings. His presence in the Mosque was a great tactical blunder which displeased Muslim voters in general.[191]

It is important to note here that the situation during the general election of 1957 was so exciting that with the end of the polling, there was a big victory procession (even before the votes were counted) of Md. Ismail came out and the same was passed in front of the house of Bidhan Chandra Roy. At that time, one of the Chhatra Parishad leaders told to Mr. Saroj Chakraborty, P. A. to the chief minister in confidentially that the communalism and violence became so predominant that "If Mohammad Ismail becomes elected he would automatically be the Chief Minister, and if he becomes Chief Minister Calcutta would go to Pakistan as half of Kashmir had already gone." [192] Secret police report revealed that Pakistani agents were active in Chief Minister's constituency and foreign currency on a large scale was spent to bring about his defeat. This was repeated by the Chief Minister on the floor of the Assembly on the 18th of March, 1957. Though, Dr. Roy was elected after strong fight only by 440 votes.[193] After the win of B. C. Roy, one of the leftist trade union leaders named Biren Roy, remarked that "Md. Ismail defeated, but Calcutta saved". There was news to them that with the defeat of Bidhan Chandra Roy communal riot again would start, as because the notorious Gopal Mukhopadhyay and his team were ready to do so.[194] However, in 1957 general election congress was voted to power in West Bengal. In a house of 252 elective seats, including 11 from Purulia of which General Seats were 194, Scheduled Castes 43 and Scheduled Tribes 15; Congress captured 152 seats. Side by side after a strong fight the opposition parties increased their representation from 88 to 100.[195]

Formation of Ministry

On the morning of April 26, 1957 West Bengal's third Ministry headed by Bidhan Chandra Roy came into being at Darjeeling.[196]The Cabinet consisted of 14 Cabinet members including the Chief Minister. Other members were, P. C. Sen, Kalipada Mookherjee, Khagendra Nath Dasgupta, Ajay Kumar Mukherjee, Hem Chandra Naskar, Shyama Prasad Barman, Rafiuddin Ahmed, Iswar Das Jalan, Bhupati Majumdar, Bimal Chandra Sinha, Siddhartha Shankar Ray, Rai Harendra Nath Chaudhury and Janab Abdus Sattar. The five Minister of State were-Mrs. Purabi Mukherjee, Tarun Kanti Ghosh, Anath Bandhu Roy, Ardhendu Sekhar Naskar and Asutosh Ghosh. Among the 12 Deputy Ministers, there was a young lady-Maya Banerjee who was given the Refugee, Relief and Rehabilitation portfolio.[197]

General Election of 1962

As like as previous two general elections the central theme of election campaign of Bidhan Chandra Roy was economic development made by the state under two Five Year Plans. The United Front of six leftist parties (CPI, RSP, SUC, Forward Bloc, Forward Bloc (M) and RCPI) started their election campaign on 16th November 1961 in Calcutta Maidan, from where their leaders raised the slogan of an alternative government in West Bengal.[198]

In the 3rd general election of 1962 which was also the last electoral fight of B. C. Roy who contested from two constituency i.e. (i). Chowranghee in Calcutta and (ii). Saltora in Bankura district. However, B. C. Roy was declared elected from Saltora Constituency by 9,929 to 4,512 votes against his nearest rival Biswanath Bandopadhyay of CPI. In Chowringhee he also won by 22,556 votes against 7,390 secured by his opponent, CPI candidate, Biswanath Mukherjee.[199]The Calcutta papers came out with banner headlines- "Dr. Roy performs double".[200]

In that election the congress found itself in absolute majority with a total of 157 seats out of 252 member State Assembly of which General Seats were 194, Scheduled Castes 43 and Scheduled Tribes 15. But, in Calcutta party was able to bag 14 out of 26 seats. In the Lok Sabha, Congress secured 22 out of 36 seats in West Bengal.[201] In all India level the congress party secured its absolute majority in 14 of the 15 states.[202]

Cabinet formation

The swearing-in-ceremony of the members of the fourth cabinet headed by Bidhan Chandra Roy was held at Raj Bhavan on 11th March, 1962. After B. C. Roy taking his oath of office and Secrecy from Governor Miss Padmaja Naidu, he was followed by Prafulla Chandra Sen, Kalipada Mukherjee, Khagendra Nath Dasgupta, Ajay Kumar Mukherji, Iswar Das Jalan, Rai Harendra Nath Chowdhury, Tarun Kanti Ghosh, Shrimati Purabi Mukherjee, Shyamadas Bhattacharjee, Jagannath Koley, Jiban Ratan Dhar, Saila Kumar Mukherjee, Shrimati Ava Maiti, Janab S. M. Fazlur Rahaman and Bijay Sing Nahar. All of them held Cabinet ranks. Of these, five were new comers, three upgraded from State Ministership and eight were Ministers of the outgoing cabinet. The Council of Ministers was expanded later on by addition of 11 Ministers of State and 10 Deputy Minister.[203]

Notes and References

1. K. P. Thomas, *Dr. Bidhan Chandra Roy*, West Bengal Pradesh Congress Committee, Calcutta, 1955, p. 213.
2. *The Statesman, September 14, 1960.*
3. *The Statesman, January 16, 1948*

4. K.P. Thomas, *op.cit.* pp. 224-225.
5. Atulya Ghosh, *Kasta...,* p. 49.
6. K.P. Thomas, *op.cit.* pp.223.
7. Atulya Ghosh, *Kasta...,* p. 50.
8. K. P. Thomas, *op.cit.* p.236.
9. *Ibid.,* p. 227.
10. Atulya Ghosh, *Kasta...,* p.50.
11. K. P. Thomas, *op.cit.* pp. 227-228.
12. *Ibide.,* pp. 228-229.
13. *Ibide.,* p. 231.
14. *Ibide.,* p. 233.
15. *Ibide.,* pp. 234-235.
16. C. N. Vakil, *Economic Consequences of Divided India. A Study of the Economy of India and Pakistan,* Bombay, 1950. p.15.
17. Vir Virender Singh Tyagi, *The Economic Impact of Partition on Indian Agriculture and Related Industries,* American University, Washington, DC, doctoral dissertation, 1958, p.117.
18. Saroj Chakrabarty, ... *With Dr. B.C. Roy,* p. 85.
19. *Ibid.*
20. J. K. Boyce, *Agrarian Impasse in Bengal - Institutional Constrains to Technological Change,* Oxford, 1987, pp.141-142.
21. Sandip Bandyopadhyay, *Bikshubdha Bangla - Pashimbanger Birodhi Rajniti* 1947-2007, (in Bengali), Radical Impression Kolkata,2014, p.36; Also see *"Bidhan Chandra Karnadhar Tabu Khandita Banglar Nabhishvas"* a Bengali article by Amalendu Dey in *Sat Dashak Samakal O Ananda Bazar,* Ananda Publishers, Kolkata, 2013. p.102.
22. Saroj Chakrabarty, ... *With Dr. B.C. Roy,* p. 110.
23. *Ibide.,* p. 111.
24. *Ibide.,* p. 269.
25. *Ibide.,* p.273.
26. *Ibide.,* pp. 284-285.
27. Prafulla Kumar Chakrabarty, *op.cit.* pp. 354-357.
28. Saroj Chakrabarty, ... *With Dr. B.C. Roy,* p. 274.
29. *Ibid.*
30. *Ibid.,* pp. 274-275.
31. K. P. Thomas, *op.cit.*pp.237-238 .

32. Saroj Chakrabarty, ... *With Dr. B. C. Roy,* pp. 275-276.
33. *The Statesman,* 13th September, 1953.
34. Jyoti Basu, *"Pashimbange Congressi Shashaner Koekti Dik "*(in Bengali), Swadhinata, Sharadiya, 1955.
35. Gayan Bikash Moitra, *Dandakaranya, Swadhinata, Shardiya,*(in Bengali) 1957.
36. Sandip Bandyopadhyay, *op.cit.*p.46.
37. Saroj Chakrabarty, ... *With Dr. B.C. Roy,* p.276.
38. *Ibid.,* p.277.
39. *Swadhinata,* August 27, 195.
40. Saroj Chakrabarty, ... *With Dr. B.C. Roy,* p.278.
41. *Ananda Bazar Patrika,* 28th August, 1959.
42. Saroj Chakrabarty, ... *With Dr. B.C. Roy,* p.278.
43. Jyoti Basu had gone underground and Bhabani Sen, Biswanath Mukhopadhyay, Hemanta Basu, Binay Chaudhury, Ganesh Ghosh, Shibdas Ghosh, Indrajit Gupta were arrested. See Manikuntala Sen, *Sediner Katha* (in Bengali), 1982, pp.284-285.
44. Saroj Chakrabarty, ... *With Dr. B.C. Roy,* p. 279; *Also see* Sandip Bandyopadhyay, op.cit. pp. 47-48.
45. *Ibid.,* p. 280.
46. *Swadhinata,* 1st September, 1959. Amalendu Dey, a noted historian has given a lively description of the incident as under: On that 31st August, 1959 almost one lakhs peasants assembled at Esplanade East in Calcutta to March towards Writers' Buildings for demand of food. When the hungry people started marching towards Writers' Buildings, head quarter of state administration, then police made barricade to stop the moving of the agitators towards Writers' Buildings. But as and when the hungry people moved towards their destination breaking police barricade, then police fired on the demonstrators and as a result of that 80 person were shot dead and many were sustained injury. As a protest of that huge killing by police firing, next day i.e. on 1st September 1959 a general strike and hartal was observed all over West Bengal. In that context, Atulya Ghosh, the then President of West Bengal Pradesh Congress Committee remarked, "The towns of the West Bengal were captured by the leftists. But in coming election Congress party will win from the rural areas and form the Government." see *"Bidhan Chandra Karnadhar Tabu Khandita Banglar Nabhishvas"*a Bengali article by Amalendu Dey in *Sat Dashak Samakal O Ananda Bazar,*Ananda Publishers, Kolkata, 2013. p.104.
47. Saroj Chakrabarty, ... *With Dr. B.C. Roy,* p. 280.
48. *Swadhinata,* 2nd September,1959.
49. *Ananda Bazar Patrika,* 2nd September, 1959.

50. *Swadhinata,* September, 4-5, 1959.
51. *Swadhinata,* September, 11, 1959; *Also see The Statesman,* September, 7, 1959.
52. *The Statesman,* September, 9, 1959.
53. Saroj Chakrabarty, ... *With Dr. B.C. Roy,* p. 281.
54. K. P. Thomas, *op.cit.* p.238.
55. Dilip Banerjee, *op.cit.* p. 916.
56. K. P. Thomas, *op.cit.* p.239.
57. Saroj Chakrabarty, ... *With Dr. B.C. Roy,* p. 141.
58. *Ibide.,* p. *142.*
59. K. P. Thomas, *op.cit.* pp. *238-239.*
60. *Ibide.,* p. *239.*
61. *Ibide.,* pp. *239-340.*
62. Saroj Chakrabarty, ... *With Dr. B.C. Roy,* p. *85.*
63. *Ibide.,* p. *158.*
64. *Ibide.,* pp. *201-202.*
65. *Ibide.,* p. *298.*
66. *"Bidhan Chandra Karnadhar Tabu Khandita Banglar Nabhishvas"* A Bengali Article by Amalendu Dey in *Saat Dashak Samokal O Ananda Bazar,* Ananda Publishers, Kolkata, 2013, p. 97.
67. K. P. Thomas, *op.cit.* p.*240.*
68. Saroj Chakrabarty, ... *With Dr. B.C. Roy,* pp. *157-158.*
69. K. P. Thomas, *op.cit.* p.*26.*
70. *Ibid.,* p. *258.*
71. *Ibid.,* p. *264.*
72. *Ibid.,* pp. *266-267.*
73. *Ibid.,* pp. *240-241.also see"Bidhan Chandra Karnadhar Tabu Khandita Banglar Nabhishvas"* A Bengali Article by Amalendu Dey in *Saat Dashak Samokal O Ananda Bazar,* Ananda Publishers, Kolkata, 2013, p. 97.
74. Saroj Chakrabarty, ... *With Dr. B.C. Roy,* p. *107.*
75. *Ibid.,* p..*114.*
76. *"Bidhan Chandra Karnadhar Tabu Khandita Banglar Nabhishvas"* A Bengali Article by Amalendu Dey in *Saat Dashak Samokal O Ananda Bazar,* Ananda Publishers, Kolkata, 2013, p. 92.
77. Statement of the Central Rehabilitation Minister on 11 March, 1948; see *Amrita Bazar Patrika,* March 12, 1948.

78. Information supplied by the Relief and Rehabilitation Commissioner of West Bengal on 5th June 1948; see *Amrita Bazar Patrika,* June 6, 1948.

79. Prafulla Kumar Chakrabarty, *op.cit.* pp. 2-3.

80. *"Bidhan Chandra Karnadhar Tabu Khandita Banglar Nabhishvas"* A Bengali Article by Amalendu Dey in *Saat Dashak Samokal O Ananda Bazar*, Ananda Publishers, Kolkata, 2013, p. 93.

81. K. P. Thomas, *op.cit.* pp. *241-242.*

82. Saroj Chakrabarty, ... *With Dr. B.C. Roy,* p. 39; Also see, Dinesh Chandra Singha, 1950: *Raktaranjito Dhaka- Barishal Abang* (in Bengali), Kodex, Kolkata,2012, p.22.

83. Saroj Chakrabarty, ... *With Dr. B. C. Roy,* p. *56.*

84. *Ibid.,*pp. 57-58. In the same letter, accusing Nehru for taking his step motherly attitude, B. C. Roy further remarked that "the exodus of 1.5 millions of people who belong to upper and middle class Hindu families, who came here hungry and starved, having lost all including their hope of finding subsistence in the new place. For months, the Government of India would not recognize the existence of refugee problems from East Pakistan, and therefore, would not accept the liabilities on their account. The provincial Government had to carry on as best as they could. And for these refugees, a magnificent sum of Rs.20/ - per capita has been granted by the Centre in two years".

85. *Ibid.,* pp. 71-72 .

86. Debate in Lok Sabha, 27th February, 1950. See Prafulla Kumar Chakrabarty, *op.cit.* pp. 30-31; *Also see "Bidhan Chandra Karnadhar Tabu Khandita Banglar Nabhishvas"* A Bengali Article by Amalendu Dey in *Saat Dashak Samokal O Ananda Bazar*, Ananda Publishers, Kolkata, 2013, p. 94.

87. Saroj Chakrabarty, ... *With Dr. B. C. Roy,* p. 78. Also see *"Bidhan Chandra KarnadharTabu Khaaaandita Banglar Nabhishvas"* A Bengali Article by Amalendu Dey in *Saat Dashak Samokal O Ananda Bazar*, Ananda Publishers, Kolkata, 2013, pp. 93-94.The much talked 'Nehru-Liaquat Ali Pact' or 'Delhi Pact' incorporated provisions regarding the equality of citizenship irrespective of religion, provide equal opportunity to serve in the country's civil service and military forces, adequate facilities for migrants from the two Bengals, Tripura and Assam and resorting appropriate steps to safeguard the interests of minorities by the Government of both the countries. It was also decided in the 'Nehru-Liaquat Ali Pact' that a Minority Commission would be appointment in order to look after the conditions of the minorities of East Bengal, West Bengal and third for Assam with a Minister as Chairman. According to the pact further decision was taken regarding the appointment of two Central Ministers of each Government with the designation as Minority Affairs Ministers to visit the riot-prone areas at the aim of protecting the victims as well as restoring confidence into the minds of the minorities.

88. Rita Basu, *Dr. Shyamaprasad Mookherjee and an Alternate Politics in Bengal,* Progressive, Kolkata, 2002, p.95.

89. Saroj Chakrabarty, ... *With Dr. B. C. Roy,* p. *79.*
90. *"Bidhan Chandra Karnadhar Tabu Khandita Banglar Nabhishvas"* A Bengali Article by Amalendu Dey in *Saat Dashak Samokal O Ananda Bazar,* Ananda Publishers, Kolkata, 2013, p. 94.
91. Balraj Madhok, *Portrait of a Martyr: Biography of Dr. Shyama Prasad Mookherjee,* Bombay, 1969, p.28.
92. Saroj Chakrabarty, ... *With Dr. B.C. Roy,* p. 84.
93. *Ibid.,* p. 90.
94. Dandakaranya, comprised the districts of Koraput and Kalahandi of Orissa and Baster of Madhya Pradesh, was essentially a forest area with more than 40 percent of the land covered by thick forests. The area under cultivation was obviously small. See S. D. Thaper, *The Dandakaranya Project: Failure of an ambitious Scheme, Economic Weekly,* Vol.XV(9), March, 1963, P.402.
95. *Ibid.*
96. On 17th March 1958, a large number of refugees arrived in Calcutta from different districts and held a mass rally. Addressing the gathering several leaders of the opposition parties spoke against the decision of the Congress Government to rehabilitate the refugees outside West Bengal. Expressing their unwillingness to settle in Dandakaranya the refugees shouted slogans: *"Jeeban debo, tabuo Bangla Charbana"* (We shall give our life and blood, yet we shall not leave Bengal. See *The Statesman,* March 18,1958.
97. Saroj Chakrabarty, ... *With Dr. B. C. Roy,* p. 302.
98. *Ibid.,* p. 303.
99. *The Statesman,* June 11, 1958.
100. K. P. Thomas, *op. cit.* p. 244.
101. Saroj Chakrabarty, ... *With Dr. B. C. Roy,* p. 91.
102. *Ibid.,* pp. 287-288.
103. *"Bidhan Chandra Karnadhar Tabu Khandita Banglar Nabhishvas"* A Bengali Article by Amalendu Dey in *Saat Dashak Samokal O Ananda Bazar,* Ananda Publishers, Kolkata, 2013, p. 103.
104. Saroj Chakrabarty, ... *With Dr. B. C. Roy,* pp. *307-308.*
105. *Ibid.,* p. *308.*
106. *Ibid.,* p. *309.*
107. *Ibid.,* p. *335.*
108. *Ibid.,* p. *36.*
109. Joya Chatterji, *The Spoils...,* p.252.
110. *Ibid.,* p.253.
111. K. P. Thomas, *op. cit.* p. 247.

112. *Ibid.,* p. 248.
113. Saroj Chakrabarty, ... *With Dr. B. C. Roy,* p. *56.*
114. *Ibid.,* p. 129.
115. *Ibid.,* p. 176.
116. *Ibid.,* pp. 271-272.
117. *Amrita Bazar Patrika,* June 15, 1949.
118. Saroj Chakrabarty, ... *With Dr. B. C. Roy, p.41.*
119. *Amrita Bazar Patrika,* June 20, 1949.
120. *Amrita Bazar Patrika,* July 29, 1949.
121. *Amrita Bazar Patrika,* September 11, 1949.
122. *Ibid.*
123. Stanley A. Kochanek, *The Congress Party in India,* Princeton University Press, 1968, p.254.
124. Saroj Chakrabarty, ... *With Dr. B. C. Roy, pp.* 55-56.
125. *Ibid.,* pp. 59-60. On 30th December 1949, B. C. Roy wrote to Nehru that –" you felt that the success of Sarat Bose at the South Calcutta by-election showed that people had lost faith in the Congress, as was exhibited by the election result. I have also heard that a large number of people who went to meet you in Calcutta expressed themselves as greatly dissatisfied with the Government both Provincial and Central, which showed that there was a tremendous feeling of frustration amongst them. Perhaps did not realize then that the whole trouble was not really political and that the sense of frustration was not due to the fact that the members of the Assembly or their representatives in the Ministry did not enjoy their confidence, but that it was a purely economic question. The main trouble with the people of West Bengal had been:

    (1). Want of food.

    (2). Want of employment.

    (3). Want of land in which they, particularly the refugees, could settle themselves. Such conditions could not possibly be removed by a general election and by putting in a new set of Assembly Members or Ministers".
126. Stanley A. Kochanek, *op.cit.p.254.*
127. *Amrita Bazar Patrika,* January 9, 1950. Also see Saroj Chakrabarty, ... *With Dr. B. C. Roy,* p. 68.
128. Kripaliniji was defeated by a margin of 214 votes. For details see *Ananda Bazar Patrika,* September 3, 1950.
129. *The Statesman,* September18, 1950.
130. Rakhahari Chatterji, *Politics of West Bengal: Mobilisation, Institutionalization and Rule, paper prepared for National Seminar on State Politics in India,* Kurukshetra University, March, 1981.

131. Sankar Ghosh, *Political Ideas and Movements in India*, Calcutta: Allied Publishers, 1975, p. 329.

132. Saroj Chakrabarty, ... *With Dr. B. C. Roy*, p. *87*.

133. Sandip Bandyopadhyay, *op.cit.* p. 30.

134. *"Bidhan Chandra Karnadhar Tabu Khandita Banglar Nabhishvas"* A Bengali Article by Amalendu Dey in *Saat Dashak Samokal O Ananda Bazar*, Ananda Publishers, Kolkata, 2013, p. 102.

135. *The Statesman,* 2-9th July 1953.

136. Saroj Chakrabarty, ... *With Dr. B. C. Roy*, pp. 131-132.

137. *Amrita Bazar Patrika,* 18th July, 1953.

138. *"Bidhan Chandra Karnadhar Tabu Khandita Banglar Nabhishvas"* A Bengali Article by Amalendu Dey in *Saat Dashak Samokal O Ananda Bazar*, Ananda Publishers, Kolkata, 2013, p. 102.

139. Sandip Bandyopadhyay, *op.cit.* p.34.

140. *"Bidhan Chandra Karnadhar Tabu Khandita Banglar Nabhishvas"* A Bengali Article by Amalendu Dey in *Saat Dashak Samokal O Ananda Bazar*, Ananda Publishers, Kolkata, 2013, p. 102.

141. See Saroj Chakrabarty, ... *With Dr. B. C. Roy*, pp. 134-135. B. C. Roy had his peculiar way of dealing with difficult situation. After getting an assessment of the situation from his cabinet colleagues he quietly sent for Suresh Chandra Majumdar of '*Ananda Bazar Patrika*' whose two influential papers *(Ananda Bazar Patrika and Hindusthan Standard)* were up against the Government. Next, he asked Tusher Kanti Ghosh of *'Amrita Bazar Patrika'* to see him and discussed matters with him. By doing so, he softened the heart of Majumdar and Ghosh and gradually the voice of the papers of Calcutta towards the Government improved.

142. *Ibid.*, p.135.

143. *"Bidhan Chandra Karnadhar Tabu Khandita Banglar Nabhishvas"* A Bengali Article by Amalendu Dey in *Saat Dashak Samokal O Ananda Bazar*, Ananda Publishers, Kolkata, 2013, p.103.

144. Saroj Chakrabarty, ... *With Dr. B. C. Roy*, pp. 158-160.

145. *"Bidhan Chandra Karnadhar Tabu Khandita Banglar Nabhishvas"* A Bengali Article by Amalendu Dey in *Saat Dashak Samokal O Ananda Bazar*, Ananda Publishers, Kolkata, 2013, p.103; also see Sandip Bandyopadhyay, *op.cit.* p.*38*.

146. Amal Dasgupta, *"Mastermasai – Shricharaneshu"* (in Bengali), *Parichay, Falgun,* 1360 (B.S).

147. Saroj Chakrabarty, ... *With Dr. B. C. Roy*, p.145; *Also see The Statesman,* 17th February,1954.

148. *Swadhinata,* 18th February, 1954.

149. Sandip Bandyopadhyay, *op.cit.* p.41.
150. *The Statesman,* March 19, 1958.
151. *The Statesman,* March 28, 1958.
152. *Ibid.*
153. Saroj Chakrabarty, ... *With Dr. B. C. Roy,* pp. 251-253.
154. *Ibid.,*pp. 256-260; Also see *"Bidhan Chandra Karnadhar Tabu Khandita Banglar Nabhishvas"* A Bengali Article by Amalendu Dey in *Saat Dashak Samokal O Ananda Bazar*, Ananda Publishers, Kolkata, 2013, p.104.
155. Saroj Chakrabarty, ... *With Dr. B. C. Roy,* pp. 167-168.
156. *Ibid.,* pp. 181-182.
157. *Ibid.,* pp. 190-192.
158. *Ibid.,* pp. 193-195.
159. *Ibid.,* p. 199.
160. *Ibid.,* pp.201-203; also see *"Bidhan Chandra Karnadhar Tabu Khandita Banglar Nabhishvas"* A Bengali Article by Amalendu Dey in *Saat Dashak Samokal O Ananda Bazar*, Ananda Publishers, Kolkata, 2013, p.96
161. Saroj Chakrabarty, ... *With Dr. B. C. Roy,* p. 213.
162. *Ibid.,* pp. 265-267.
163. *Ibid.,* pp. 321-322.
164. *Ibid.,* pp. 45-46.
165. Joya Chatterji, *The Spoils...,* p.255; Also see Saroj Chakrabarty, ... *With Dr. B. C. Roy,* pp. 95-96.
166. *"Bidhan Chandra Karnadhar Tabu Khandita Banglar Nabhishvas"* A Bengali Article by Amalendu Dey in *Saat Dashak Samokal O Ananda Bazar*, Ananda Publishers, Kolkata, 2013, p.104.
167. Saroj Chakrabarty, ... *With Dr. B. C. Roy,* p. 156.
168. *Ibid.,* p. 261.
169. *Ibid.,* p. 109.
170. *"Bidhan Chandra Karnadhar Tabu Khandita Banglar Nabhishvas"* A Bengali Article by Amalendu Dey in *Saat Dashak Samokal O Ananda Bazar*, Ananda Publishers, Kolkata, 2013, p.96.
171. Saroj Chakrabarty, ... *With Dr. B.C. Roy,* pp. 272-273.
172. *Ibid.,* p. 299.
173. *"Bidhan Chandra Karnadhar Tabu Khandita Banglar Nabhishvas"* A Bengali Article by Amalendu Dey in *Saat Dashak Samokal O Ananda Bazar*, Ananda Publishers, Kolkata, 2013, p. p.97.
174. Saroj Chakrabarty, ... *With Dr. B. C. Roy,* p. 128.

175. Ibid., pp. 67-68.

176. "Bidhan Chandra Karnadhar Tabu Khandita Banglar Nabhishvas" A Bengali Article by Amalendu Dey in *Saat Dashak Samokal O Ananda Bazar*, Ananda Publishers, Kolkata, 2013, p.96.

177. Saroj Chakrabarty, ... *With Dr. B. C. Roy,* p. 348.

178. "Bidhan Chandra Karnadhar Tabu Khandita Banglar Nabhishvas" A Bengali Article by Amalendu Dey in *Saat Dashak Samokal O Ananda Bazar*, Ananda Publishers, Kolkata, 2013, p.101.

179. Dilip Banerjee, *op.cit.* p. 884.

180. Ibid., p. 885.

181. Ibid., p. 334.

182. Saroj Chakrabarty, ... *With Dr. B. C. Roy,* p. 103.

183. *Ibid.,* p. 104. In a letter dated 5th May, 1952, addressed to Nehru, B. C. Roy wrote: "Seven of my Ministers have been defeated in the election. While I am not bothering about the other five, P. C. Sen of the Food Department and K. P. Mukherjee of the Labour Department have not only been very useful members of my Cabinet but they possess extraordinary knowledge of their own departments and in making selections for the next Assembly I have the impression that these two will certainly be returned even if the others fail to be returned."

183. a. For details see Renuka Ray, *My Reminiscences, Social Development During the Gandhian Era and After,* Allied Publishers Private Limited, Calcutta, 1982, pp.190-207.

184. Dilip Banerjee, *op.cit.* pp. 915-916.

185. Saroj Chakrabarty, ... *With Dr. B. C. Roy,* pp. 103-106.

186. Dilip Banerjee, *op.cit.* p.884.

187. Saroj Chakrabarty, ... *With Dr. B. C. Roy,* pp. 118-119.

188. Atulya Ghosh, *Kasta...,* p.329.

189. "Bidhan Chandra Karnadhar Tabu Khandita Banglar Nabhishvas" A Bengali Article by Amalendu Dey in *Saat Dashak Samokal O Ananda Bazar*, Ananda Publishers, Kolkata, 2013, p.101. Bow Bazar is situated in the heart of the city, the Chief Minister's constituency and it had a cosmopolitan character. It is basically a Muslim influential area because out of 63,229 votes about 29,000 were Muslims. Besides, there were Englishmen, French, a good number of Chinese and people from many other countries of the world in this constituency. Excepting B. C. Roy, four other persons filed nomination papers for the Bow Bazar constituency including Md. Ismail, the communist candidate, a Hindu Mahasabha candidate and two independent. See Saroj Chakrabarty, ... *With Dr. B. C. Roy,* pp. 227-228.

190. Sandip Bandyopadhyay, *op.cit.* p.54.

191. Saroj Chakrabarty, ... *With Dr. B. C. Roy,* pp. 231-232.
192. *Ibid.,* pp. 232-235.
193. *"Bidhan Chandra Karnadhar Tabu Khandita Banglar Nabhishvas"* A Bengali Article by Amalendu Dey in *Saat Dashak Samokal O Ananda Bazar*, Ananda Publishers, Kolkata, 2013, p.101.
194. Sandip Bandyopadhyay, *op.cit.* p.54.
195. Dilip Banerjee, *op.cit.* pp. 972-973.
196. *Ibid.,* p. 884.
197. *Ibid.,* pp. 238-239.
198. Saroj Chakrabarty, ... *With Dr. B. C. Roy,* p.349.
199. Dilip Banerjee, *op. cit.* pp. 374, 384.
200. Saroj Chakrabarty, ... *With Dr. B. C. Roy,* p. 374.
201. Dilip Banerjee, *op.cit.* pp.974, 885, 373-76, 295.
202. Saroj Chakrabarty, ... *With Dr. B. C. Roy,* p. 375.
203. Dilip Banerjee, *op.cit.* pp. 884, 917-918; Also see *Ibid.,* p. 377.

CHAPTER

4

Dominance with a Difference: Strains and Challenges (1962-1967)

During the severe food movement of 1959 led by the communists, the congress party in West Bengal did not try to face the problem politically as if the political stage of the congress as a party did not exist. At that time, the communists were always in the limelight as because they were holding processions, meetings, demonstrations and courting arrest. But, on behalf of the congress party there was no meetings and processions to counter opposition propaganda excepting a few press statements made by Atulya Ghosh. It would come out from the activities of the congress party that it had more or less accepted the leftist hegemony over Calcutta and the urban areas around it.[1] In that situation, Atulya Ghosh, the then all powerful congress leader of West Bengal, remarked, "Calcutta has become Communist, but in coming election after winning from rural Bengal we will form the Ministry."[2] However, after the 3rd general elections (1962) it was found that the words of Atulya Ghosh became true and with the help of rural vote-bank the congress party again had returned in power. Bidhan Chandra Roy became the Chief Minister along with previous set up and Prafulla Chandra Sen took the charge of his former Food and others departments in addition to agriculture.

Vacuum Created Due to Sudden Death of B. C. Roy

But that set up was not continuing for a long time due to the sudden death of B. C. Roy, the sitting Chief-Minister of West Bengal, dated 1st July, 1962. In that context, an automatic question raised who would replace B. C. Roy. Under the circumstances, Smt. Padmaja Naidu, the then Governor of West Bengal convened a conference with legal experts of the State Government at Raj Bhavan to resolve the ongoing constitutional crisis. The Governor had the privilege to take the valuable advice regarding the complicated constitutional matter from Dr. Sarvapalli Radhakrishan, the then President of India. Dr. Radhakrishan was then present at Raj Bhavan to attend the 80th Birth-anniversary of B. C. Roy. After a comprehensive discussion a brief press note was issued from Governor's Secretariat on the same night and announced: "On account of the sudden demise of Dr. B. C. Roy, Chief Minister of West Bengal, on July 1, 1962, the Governor of West Bengal has been pleased to order that Prafulla Chandra Sen, a Minister of the Council of Ministers, West Bengal, will temporarily discharge the functions of the Chief Minister."[3]

Background of Prafulla Chandra Sen

Prafulla Chandra Sen who during the days of the freedom struggle as well as nationalist movement was in the forefront and known in his working place as well as his home town, Arambagh, as the 'Gandhi of Arambagh' (in Hooghly district).[4] Personally, he was entirely clean in so far as money matters are concerned. Throughout his entire carrier i. e. from Chairman of Union Board to Cabinet Minister for 20 years and Chief Minister for 5 years, he had not even possessed one katha of land, house or car, and there was no bank balance in his own name.[5] In many occasions it was found that a particular General Secretary who was entrusted for keeping the party fund, calling on him at his residence in the first week of every month in order to collect his salary cheque amounting Rs. 1400/- for crediting the sum to the account of the West Bengal Pradesh Congress Committee. His household expenditure was very small and it was met out from party fund. In his earlier work place at Mayapur in Hooghly district, he had built a modest dwelling house as like as an *Ashram* of the Gandhian type with flower and kitchen garden.[6]

Causes behind the selection of P. C. Sen as Chief-Minister after B. C. Roy

All the important portfolios like Home and Finance along with his earlier departments i.e. Food and Agriculture were given to Prafulla Chandra Sen. Though, Prafulla Chandra Sen was not an all India figure as like as his predecessor but his political stature was very high in his state i.e. in West Bengal. His position in West Bengal Cabinet was so important that it was almost unwritten declaration on behalf of the cabinet as well as the congress party in West Bengal that after B. C. Roy Prafulla Chandra Sen would be the helm of affairs in the state. For example, in the general election of 1957, when B. C. Roy's chances of victory were black, then B. C. Roy was telling one of his congress friends, "Even if I am not elected, Congress will be returned to power, and Prafulla will be there".[7] Not only that, even at the time of the severe food movement in West Bengal, 1959, the main target of the opposition was to humiliate Prafulla Chandra Sen under any circumstances.[8] Keeping in mind his unique position both in party and in government it was common that Prafulla Chandra Sen used to enter into chief minister's room early in the morning and the two together would discuss numerous problems of the state over a cup of tea. But, the other colleagues of B. C. Roy had not enjoyed that privilege. Naturally, after B. C. Roy's death there were none to challenge him among the surviving senior congress leaders, both in the government and in the party organization.[9]

Prafulla Chandra Sen at Helm

As after the death of B. C. Roy, Prafulla Chandra Sen temporarily became the Chief Minister, but, later he was unanimously elected Leader of the Congress Parliamentary Party on 8th day of July 1962. The *Sradh* ceremony of B. C. Roy was being performed in the morning while in another part of the city Prafulla Chandra Sen, known as the "number two man" in the cabinet of B. C. Roy was crowneds as the leader of Congress Legislative Party (CLP) within 10 minutes.[10] The meeting was attended by 186 Congress MLAs and MLCs. The name of P. C. Sen was moved by Atulya Ghosh, the then State Congress President and was seconded by Kalipada Mukherji, the Home Minister of the state. It was also a rumour that some of the followers of Atulya Ghosh request the latter to become the Chief Minister of West Bengal. It was not materialized at the end. In the question of leadership, the third name which had come was Kalipada Mukherjee. Kali Babu had a very strong political base in Calcutta. Though, he had a good record as a political sufferer but his performance as Home Minister (Police) roused sharp criticism in the form of his use of police in order to suppress the various movement and assault of pressmen which alienated him from the intelligentsia and the press. Naturally, he stepped down from the race of leadership. However, in order to solve the question of leadership Prafulla Chandra Sen, Atulya Ghosh and Kalipada Mukherjee had to sit together and decided that Prafulla Chandra Sen would be the next Chief Minister.[11] Regarding the unanimous selection of Prafulla Chandra Sen as the next Chief Minister of West Bengal, Saroj Chakrabarty, personal assistant of the Chief Ministers observed, "He was perhaps the only fortunate politician in the sensitive State of West Bengal who did not encounter any opposition either from his partymen in the organization or Congress legislators. Analysing the events since 1947, it was found that every Chief

Minister beginning from Dr. Prafulla Chandra Ghosh, and even the great Dr. B. C. Roy and Ajoy Mukherjee had to face some form of contests within and outside the party. After 1972 general elections Siddhartha Sankar Ray's unanimous selection as the leader of the Congress Party was possible due largely to the Ajoy Mukherjee's decline to contest the election."[12] But the main reason for the smooth sailing of Prafulla Chandra Sen became possible due to the unequivocal support of Atulya Ghosh who had complete control over the party machinery in West Bengal. It is noteworthy that Atulya Ghosh had his grounding in politics under Prafulla Chandra Sen whom he would regard as his political Guru i. e. preceptor. Naturally, it was easy to think that after B. C. Roy, Prafulla Chandra Sen would be in the steering in wheel.[13]

Thereafter, Atulya Ghosh and P. C. Sen drove in to the Raj Bhavan. After an hour's meeting with Padmaja Naidu, the Governor of the state the personnel of the cabinet and their respective portfolios were announced. All the members of the Council of Ministers numbering 15 were retained while the vacancy caused by the death of B. C. Roy was not filled up. The new Chief Minister took charge in addition to his 'pet' portfolios of Food, Agriculture and Supplies along with some of the portfolios held by his predecessor. Among them were General Administration, Political, Anti-Corruption and Enforcement Branch of the Home Department, Finance and Development Department. Kalipada Mukherji was next in line and he was brought to Sen's adjacent room. He was given the additional charge of the Home (Transport) Department. Actually Prafulla Chandra Sen wanted to have him in close proximity for frequent consultation on administrative and organizational matters. In the beginning of July, 1962 an inner cabinet was formed with P. C. Sen, Atulya Ghosh and Kalipada Mukherji. They collectively took decisions on the state and party matters. Tarun Kanti Ghosh, a Cabinet Minister of the previous Ministry was raised to the rank of a Full Cabinet Minister and was given the important portfolio of Commerce and Industries.[14]

On assuming office Prafulla Chandra Sen made his first statement which reflected his mood at that time. The statement was as follows: "Today I have been elected Leader of the Congress Parliamentary Party and I seek the blessings of the departed soul. He was a great leader and it will be very difficult to fill the void created by his untimely demise. But I am sure if we can inspire team work amongst us both in the Congress and in the Government we shall be able to fulfill his dreams. The legacy that Dr. Roy has left will certainly show the illumine the path which we will tread with courage, devotion and wisdom so that West Bengal, known as a problematic

State, may steer clear of all obstacles through our united efforts". On the Morning of the following day i. e. on 9th July 1962, Governor Padmaja Naidu administered oath taking ceremony at Raj Bhavan in a brief function. The other members of Dr. Roy's cabinet retained their respective portfolio.[15] From Raj Bhavan Prafulla Chandra Sen went to the Assembly House to attend the second Budget session and later announced to a group of journalists that the "unfinished tasks undertaken by Dr. Roy would be carried on".[16]

Prafulla Chandra Sen's apparent modesty charmed anyone who came in contact with him, irrespective of their official status –whether they belonged to the ordinary run of people or to high society. In spite of that, Sen had more affinity for rural people with his long contacts at grass root level. He was out and out a staunch supporter of the congress party, a lifelong bachelor and free from the burden of a domestic life to devote his whole time and energy for the people. Though, he was very much aware about his limitation and used to say, "I cannot fill the void created by Dr. B. C. Roy and all that I shall endeavour to do is to follow his imprints".[17] In case of his comparison with Dr. Roy, a few months after of his Chief-Ministership one of his overly enthusiastic friends remarked that the administration was going on smoothly in the absence of B. C. Roy. Prafulla Chandra Sen reacted at once and said, "Do not compare me with Dr. Roy. Dr. Roy was Dr. Roy". [18]

Decentralization of power by P. C. Sen

In comparison with Bidhan Chandra Roy so far as cabinet colleagues were concerned, Prafulla Chandra Sen made a big departure regarding the essence of governmental power. During B. C. Roy's regime ministers would force to discharge their duties according to the will of the Chief Minister. As a head of the administration of the state though B. C. Roy always thought about the betterment of West Bengal but at the same time he did not like to make any question about his activities. As Saroj Chakrabarty stated, "During Dr. Roy's regime the essence of governmental power, though exercised by the Cabinet, reflected the policies of which he was the author, and often he was charged with over-centralisation."[19]As to the achievements of B. C. Roy no body other than Padmaja Naidu, the then Governor of West Bengal described him as 'Benevolent Patriarch'. So, everybody accepted the attitude of B. C. Roy and acknowledged that 'king can do no wrong'. Regarding the attitude of the over-centralisation of B. C. Roy's administration Hemchandra Naskar, Minister-in-Cgharge of Forest and Fisheries of B. C. Roy cabinet would jokingly said, "we are all tortoise minister, have to come to Writers Building with slow motion like tortoise and whenever we come Dr. Roy would overturn us and we started to through our hands and legs but could not move. Again at 5.p.m. Dr. Roy would converted us in our former position then we had to leave the Writers Buildings for our home by car in a tortoise motion."[20] But P. C. Sen did not accept the over-centralise attitude of his predecessor because he would believe in team work and spirit of comradeship. As a result of that differences of opinion occurred in several times and thereupon he had resigned from B. C. Roy's Ministry, though at last due to request of B. C Roy he had to withdraw his resignation. Naturally P. C. Sen was very much aware about the helplessness of the ministers. He himself was able to form a strong organization at Arambagh in the way of de-centralisation of power and cohesion with various groups which one might call it as 'team sprit'.[21] So, after becoming Chief Minister P. C. Sen from the very beginning made it clear to his cabinet colleagues that they were free to take decisions to run their departments according to the decision of the cabinet. In fact he separated himself from that extraordinary powers and distributed it to his colleagues. The ministers could approach him for suggessions but it depended on them to take final decision. In this way, he wanted to generate a 'spirit of comradeship' as well as 'team spirit' and joint responsibility in the cabinet. On 11th July, 1962, P. C. Sen delivered his first budget speech in the House where he firmly asserted steady progress of West Bengal in agricultural production that led the state a self-dependent one. P. C. Sen had brought a change in the use of language in the House. He had switched over to Bengali instead of English in making important statements on behalf of the government. He was really a fine speaker in Bengali and would cautious to place his argument with supporting data. From that time onward the practice of the delivering speeches on the floor of the Assembly House were started in the mother tongue.[22]

Aam Darbar

As a grass root politician it was very much clear to Prafulla Chandra Sen that the original strength of democracy was laid in the well understanding between the government and the common people. Actually, whatever we understand about the term "peoples' man" P. C. Sen was the finest example of that term. It was no need to mention that the common people had not the courage to go to B. C. Roy easily but peoples could go to P. C. Sen without any hesitation. So, in democracy as a representative of the masses, P. C. Sen started *'Aam Darbar"* from the month of August in 1962.[23] As per the decision announced by the chief minister P. C. Sen in the month of

August in 1962 arrangements were made to hear the complaints from the public in the afternoon of every Monday at his residence. Actually from the ancient times the kings of the Indian sub-continent used to maintain direct relationship with the masses through that practice and thereby they would aware about the error of the administration and take appropriate steps for the interest of the common people. That practices were continued in the Muslim period also. Even emperor Aurangzeb also had heard the problems of the masses through *'Aam Darbar'* and had taken appropriate measures and if necessary he personally would go to the place of occurrence. Not only that Dr. Sarvapally Radha Krishnan also introduced the same technique to hear the miseries as well as complaints from the masses.[24]The first day of his '*Aam Darbar'* continued for two hours and any member of the public could come straightly and presents his petition directly to the Chief Minister. The first 'Meet the people' programme of P. C. Sen attracted headlines in various news papers and created a great awakening among the masses. People, particularly poorer section of the society stood in line in front of his Raj Bhavan residence. On the first day of his *Aam Darbar* i. e. on 20th August, the chief minister had talked to 500 men and women individually and taken appropriate steps to solve their petitions. He wanted to redress their grievances on the spot. In that benevolent approach to help the common people, he was assisted by his cabinet colleagues Jagannath Koley. Though, most of the complaints were related to minor matters such as delaying in government sanction in respect of tube wells, relief and individual help. So, after hearing the petitioners' complaints P. C. Sen would give appropriate orders to solve them as early as possible. In that way, P. C. Sen with the help of his couple of personal staff categorized the problems and sent them to the concerned departments for enquiry and report without delay. As a result of taking such type of measures in some cases quick action was taken to relieve the common people. Gradually the number of visitors increased and it touched 1600 and on that occasion the Chief Minister was assisted by his 11 cabinet colleagues. But, a section of the bureaucracy somewhat did not support the *'Aam Darbar'* arrangement of P. C. Sen. It was also reported in the news paper that if *'Aaam Darbar'* would continue then the Chief Minister's relief fund would dry up very soon. In spite of that the chief minister did not stop the *'Aam Darbar'*. However that *'Aam Darbars'* were abandoned after a couple of months as the chief minister became preoccupied when a national emergency arose in October-November of that year in the pretext of the Chinese aggression against India.[25]

The Cabinet of West Bengal Ministry moved to Darjeeling in the last week of May, 1963 and Government's step 'to meet people' was started in both Darjeeling and Kalimpong. Representatives of Gorkha League, Darjeeling Municipality and Indian Tea Association came in groups and discussed about their various problems with the cabinet team. This was a changing approach of the government which raised hopes as well as aspiration in the minds of the long neglected hill people. This was repeated in Kalimpong. [26]

Cabinet Meeting in the Districts

Chief Minister P. C. Sen had taken another important step i. e. holding of the cabinet meetings in an every district of West Bengal. There were some minister in his cabinet who had no personal conception about all over West Bengal. Besides that they were not well acquainted regarding the special problems of some districts. As a result of that where no need of tube wells or repairing of road but the money would sanction for that area as a part of average assistance for development, but where there was no infrastructure at all from beginning in order to solve that problem no special allocation were made instead of average assistance. So, first of all, P. C. Sen, the Chief Minister of the state wanted that the ministers should understand the problems of all the districts and after that according to the decision of the çabinet they should discharge duties in connection with their own department. Whenever the cabinet meeting was held in the particular district it would help the ministers to get acquainted the nature of problems of that district and accordingly they would take appropriate measures to solve the problem. That type of cabinet meeting in the districts was arranged first at *Arambagh,* the home town of Prafulla Chandra Sen. Naturally after taking those steps a direct communication took place in between the government and the stakeholders. The opposition smelled their space for politics in West Bengal was going to be crunched. Due to the unhappiness of the bureaucracy and their influence on some ministers however, P. C. Sen had to stop the cabinet meeting in the districts later on.[27]

First Encounter with Lawlessness

In response to the citizens' ovation of Prafulla Chandra Sen on 9th September , 1962 at Calcutta Maidan Chief Minister Sen said, "If I could heartly feel the various complicated problems of West Bengal then it would be easier to solve them. Though I knew that there were so many hindrances in that path but I strongly believe that we must overcome any type of difficulty and would be able to solve the hundreds problems of Bengal." Chief Minister Sen also promised that they must maintain law and order of the city of Calcutta as well as West Bengal even if at the cost of his life.

He was well aware about the excitement of Bengal politics and that is why as a "peoples' man" P. C. Sen always wanted cooperation from the people.[28]After long observation of P. C. Sen's connection with the people Pratap Chandra Chaunder, one of the influential leaders as well as former president of WBPCC, has rightly written, "So far as my knowledge about the politicians and administrator of India and among them Prafulla Chandra was the leader of the people. He was really very much sympathetic towards the common people irrespective of caste and creed. He had born for people and sacrificed his life also for the people."[29]

As a head of the administration of the state of West Bengal, P. C. Sen was very adamant in the field of maintenance of law and order of the state as well as to encounter any kind of lawlessness. For example, on 4th September 1962, a student was arrested by the Railway Police at Sealdah for his travelling in a higher class without proper ticket of that class only ignoring the established norms of the Indian Railways that led to a major challenge to law and order. As a consequence of that incidence plundering were held at least 17 places, 13 trams were burned and property of lakhs of rupees were destroyed. Before the news reached in Writers' Buildings at 11 O'clock i. e. in the Chief Minister's office, 200 people were arrested and 90 people injured. After hearing the news the Chief Minister promptly sent his Chief Secretary, R. Gupta, to the disturbed area for an assessment of the situation. R. Gupta returned to Chief Minister's room and after apprising him about the situation a new instruction was issued to the Police Chief, S. M. Ghosh, to arrest the ring leaders of the disturbances by plain-clothes police from the backside. That was the first time i. e. the use of plain cloth police was started to nab the anti socials in order to establish law and order.[30]

First Delhi Visit of P. C. Sen as the Chief Minister

Prafulla Chandra Sen went to Delhi nine weeks after his assumption of office as the Chief Minister. After reaching New Delhi on 7th September he went straight to 19 Canning Lane residence of Atulya Ghosh,[31] which then had become the hub of Delhi's political activities. After B. C. Roy's death and Pundit Nehru's trouble in health, Atulya Ghosh gradually became prominence in all India congress organization which at a time had come under his grip. His influence was so vast that the congress chief ministers of many other states were frequently seen to come to his house in Delhi for renewal of acquaintance. Some of the journalists of metropolitan used to come regularly to his residence at any times of day and night. The West Bengal Chief Minister, P. C. Sen's metting with Prime Minister Nehru was held in the morning of 8th September for half an hour. Meanwhile at the indication of Atulya Ghosh a felicitation ceremony was organized by the West Bengal M.Ps. in honour of Prafulla Chandra Sen. Most of the Delhi dignitaries were invited to renew the contact with new Chief Minister. In the evening Prafulla Chandra Sen met Dr. S. Radhakrishnan, the President of India. Later, a press conference was held for the introduction of the new Chief Minister to Delhi journalists.[32]

Cabinet Expansion

After his return to Calcutta the Chief Minister, P. C. Sen expanded his cabinet by inclusion of Sankar Das Banerji, a very well known Barrister and former speaker of the State Legislative Assembly. The decision of the inclusion of Sankar Das Banerji in the cabinet was taken in Delhi with the willingness of Atulya Ghosh. In all cabinet reshuffles during his 4.5 year tenure of Chief Ministership, Atulya Ghosh was the person who had a dominant voice. The portfolios of Finance and Home (Transport) Departments were given to Sankar Das Banerji. At the time of formation of B. C. Roy's cabinet after 1962 general election, its strength was 16, but after his demise and Kalipada Mukherji's death[33] the number was reduced by two. The strength of the cabinet became again 16 owing to inclusion of Samarjit Banerji of Nadia, as a Minister of State followed by the inclusion of Sankar Das Banerji.[34]

Reaction of Chinese intrusion

The political scenario of India was undergoing a vast change, as the people in general had been ascertained into a sense of security specially after the signing of 'Pancha Sheel Pact' between India and China in 1954, due to a vague feeling that her neighbor country China would never engage herself into any major conflict over the boundary issue. A wave of sensation swept over Calcutta when citizens had read reports about Chinese attacking Indian teritory in Thag-La-pass near Dhola on 20th September, 1962. When China was attacking India, the people of Bengal were celebrating their biggest national festival Durga puja. On that occasion, 'Chinese Aggression Resistance Organisation' (CARO) was formed for the first time in Calcutta under the leadership of a leftist leader, Soumendra Nath Tagore. In a meeting, held on 16th October where on behalf of the 'Chinese Aggression Resistance Organisation' Tagore charged Nehru for following a weak-kneed policy which threatened India in the face of its sovereignty. At the same time he criticized the CPI for playing down the Chinese injurious role and observed that it would not be astonishing if China one day tried to attack the whole of

India, taking the opportunities of the disintegrating forces within the country. A day ahead of China's extensive attack on NEFA front on 19th October, S. A. Dange, the then Chairman of the Communist Party of India, in a statement in Bombay supported the Government of India's stand that the Chinese had encroached south of the Mac-Mahon Line and they should be thrown out. Dange also criticized the Chinese anti-Indian policy and remarked: "India was neither aggressive nor expansionist and Mr. Nehru's foreign policy is not made either by dollar aid or rouble aid. We the (CPI) are neither Peking patriots nor Washington patriots. We the citizens of India are neither aggressive nor expansionist. Anyone who attacks such a country of ours must be rebuffed".[35]

When fighting broke out in between Indian and Chinese soldiers in NEFA then the Indian soldiers were hurriedly air-lifted without adequate warm clothing to fight in cold, not only that they were not habituated to fight in that atmosphere. In that context, P. C. Sen came to office one morning and expressed that he had been enlightened at midnight by Lal Bahadur Shastri, the then Home Minister of India from Delhi and seeking his help to collect warm clothings, woolen jersy, boots etc. from Calcutta market as much as quantities possible for the Jawans in NEFA. As a result of the direct intervention of Chief Minister P. C. Sen whatever necessaries for the Army were available in Calcutta market were collected as soon as possible and then rushed to Army authorities. On 22nd October 1962, in a broadcast over the All-India Radio network the people of India heard the sound of the voice of Nehru which was overloaded with emotion. The Prime Minister denounced the Chinese treachery against a country which had befriended it and worked with sincerity for its admission into the U. N. West Germany and Canada branded China as the aggressor and denounced Chinese attack on India.[36]

State of Emergency and Role of the West Bengal Government

As a consequence of the Chinese attack against India a State of Emergency in the country was proclaimed by the President of India on 26th October, 1962.[37] In that hour of distress the West Bengal Government announced its decision to raise Home Guards and a resolution in that respect was adopted by the State Defence Committee (SDC) accordingly on 30th October, 1962. Though, the Chief Minister could not attend office on account of his illness during that crucial time for two days in spite of that he issued an appeal to the people to come forward for the necessity of the nation and requested to report to the Commissioner of Police and District Magistrates for their enlistment as Home Guards. There was a remarkable national emersion in the country. The recruiting centres were crowded by willing men. The mood of the people was revealed when a middle aged man while waiting at the Delhi recruiting centre remarked: "I may not walk fast but I can sit down and shoot". [38]

The West Bengal Assembly unanimously adopted the 'West Bengal Home Guards Bill-1962' and the 'National Defence Fund (West Bengal) Bill-1962' on 21st November, 1962, before it was adjourned sine die to facilitate the members to go back to their own constituencies to enthuse people in defence efforts. Siddhartha Shankar Ray (S. S. Ray), an Independent member of the Assembly strongly supported the two measures induced by the Chief Minister and said that it was for the Union Government to consider Chinese cease-fire proposal.[39] But considering the Chinese 'barbarous attack' the country should be ready for worse. As a step to thrive people's morale he suggested foundation of a wing of the Defence Ministry in Calcutta. "India", he said, "should take as much help as possible from USA and UK who were the country's genuine friends".[40] S. S. Ray also thanked the Chief Minister for arresting China's 'friends'. In that connection it should be mentionable that in view of the Chinese attack in India a massive country wide operation went on 21st November 1962, which brought under the purview in jail custody of 350 members of the Communist Party of India along with some of the leading workers of the Party on various States. Amongst the arrested persons - some were members of Parliament, 30 of the Members of the Legislative Assembles and Councils, 5 Ministers of the first Communist Government of Kerala and a Nepali woman of Darjeeling. Madras province headed the list with 100 arrests which followed by West Bengal's 60. In that connection Shri Jyoti Basu, the Leader of the Opposition in West Bengal Legislative Assembly; Ganesh Ghosh, the Chief Whip of the Communist Party in the Assembly; Promode Dasgupta, the State Sercretary of CPI along with Harekrishna Konar, Mr. Muzaffar Ahmed and the Editor of the Communist organ, 'Swadhinata', were also arrested. Secret police reports exposed that most of the arrested persons were beloning to the pro-Chinese wing of the C. P. I. in West Bengal. Though, Somnath Lahiri, the then acting spokesman of the C. P. I. in the Assembly lamented that the arrests were made at a time when his party was trying its best to help defence efforts. Notwithstanding, Somnath Lahiri had come one morning along with a number of his party men to meet Chief Minister in Writers' Buildings and handed over several thousand rupees for the National Defence Fund.[41]

Internal Chaos of the C.P.I. and its Impact on the Politics of West Bengal

In the meanwhile, secret police reports received in Chief Minister's office about the forthcoming split in the Communist Party of the State. According to the reports the West Bengal CPI Secretariat urged its Central Secretariat to take quick disciplinary actions against Promode Dasgupta and Muzaffar Ahmed (they were in jail) and oust them from the party. The main charges against them were that they liquidated 'Swadhinata', the party organ in Calcutta, and as a consequence of that the communist party of West Bengal could not implement the resolution of National Council on Indo-China conflict.[42] As a result of the difference of opinions among the leaders of the Communist Party of India specially after the Chinese attack in India, lastly at midnight of April 14-15, 1964 the National Executive Council of the Communist Party of India under the Chairmanship of S. A. Dange took the necessary step to expel seven members and suspend 25 others including Jyoti Basu of the West Bengal. In that context, the 32 rebel members walked out of the Council meeting at once on 11th April, 1964 and declared, "We represent the Communist Party of India, we are confident that the vast majority of the party members and the public will support our principled stand and rally to uphold the honour and prestige and the revolutionary traditions of the Communist movement in India".[43]

Achievements of P. C. Sen

(i). Resounding Victory in the bye-elections

Prafulla Chandra Sen was possessed with an element of fortune during the first year of his office as the Chief Minister. Successive events proved that the Chinese invasion helped him to raise his dignity as one of the efficient Chief Ministers of the country. The way he organized the State had lighted patriotic feelings in the face of the prime influence of the communists. Compulsion of events helped in bringing about a lasting cleavage amongst his chief political opponents, the communists on the pretext of Chinese aggression. As a result of the division within the communist party, the results of the five bye-elections to the State Assembly on 8th April, 1963, showed that congress had captured all the five seats. Actually, that was a 'day of victory' for Prafulla Chandra Sen. The Prime Minister's credence about the performance of West Bengal Government as well as congress organisation in the state one year after the death of B. C. Roy was steadily rising and as a result of that he made several visits to the state and consented to inaugurate the political convention of the Pradesh Congress Committee (henceforth PCC) at Digha on 28th April, 1963. It was really a credit for a State Chief Minister to make the Prime Minister available to visit his state. Digha, a small and sea resort in Midnapore district founded by B.C. Roy and inhabited by a few hundred people, but a large crowed of many thousands were assembled to hear Nehru who reached there with Lal Bahadur Shastri, the then Union Home Minister and Shrimati Indira Gandhi to participate in the conference. Nehru's speech was mainly concentrated to India's attitude towards China and acceptance of the Colombo proposals.[44]

(ii). Bidhan Chandra Children Hospital

Prime Minister Nehru came to Calcutta on 1st July, 1963 to attend the occasion of the first death anniversary of Bidhan Chandra Roy. His programme included laying the foundation-stone ceremony of a Children Hospital in the north-eastern side of Calcutta after the name of Dr. Bidhan Chandra Roy. The primary focus of his seven minute speech was concentrated mainly to the various problems of the children and to pay his tributes to great B. C. Roy. Padmaja Naidu, the then Governor of West Bengal, Vijay Luxmi Pundit, Governor of Maharashtra, Dr. Sushila Nayar, Union Health Minister and P. C. Sen, Chief Minister of West Bengal were present in the occasion. The 82nd birthday as well as first death anniversary of B. C. Roy was attracted a large convention at the prayer meeting in the park, opposite to his house. Tushar Kanti Ghosh, President of the B. C. Roy Memorial Committee communicated in the prayer meeting that Rs. 50 lakhs had already been collected and the same was invested in the National Defence Certificates (NDC).[45]

(iii). Durgapur Gas Grid project

Prafulla Chandra Sen, the Chief Minister of the state went to Durgapur on 31st August, 1963 along with Atulya Ghosh and Sir D. N. Mitra, Chairman of the Durgapur Project Ltd. for the purpose of the inauguration of the gas grid project of the Government of West Bengal. The 180 miles long gas pipe line in Durgapur was perhaps the longest gas pipe line in the country.[46]

iv). First Indian Electric Locomotive

The Prime Minister Nehru went to Durgapur and Assansol for the fulfillment of his two pre-schedule important engagements there. Nehru arrived at Durgapur, the 'dream city' of Bidhan Chandra Roy, to open the Indo-Soviet Coal Mining Machinery Project of Rs. 35-crore on 16th November, 1963. Bidhan Chandra Roy, the creator of 'Rhur' of West Bengal was respectfully remembered by Nehru in the assembled gathering. It was expected that as per the requirement the coal mining industry in India it would produce coal cutters, conveyors and other necessary types of basic machinery. Considering the Coal utmost importance was given by B. C. Roy to meterialise the scheme two years prior to his death. Incidentally, at Chittaranjan, the first Indian built electric locomotive was given the name 'Bidhan' by the Prime Minister Nehru. The Prime Minister then got into the locomotive and drove the engine. The workshop of Chittaranjan was turning out steam engines and passenger coaches in a very large scale that it would soon enabled India to enter into the export market. The A. C. locomotive which was turned out from a design that was supplied by a Continental Consortium a few weeks after the imported locomotive introduced on Indian tracks.[47]

(v). Haldia Port in the Making

P. C. Sen, the Chief Minister of the state had taken special attempt for the fulfillment of Haldia Project. When Union Shipping Minister Raj Bahadur came to Calcutta for an on the spot study regarding the feasibility of the Haldia port, then P. C. Sen along with Humayun Kabir, the then Union Oil and Natural Gas Minister and a group of M.P.s and M.L.As also went there by a special steamer on 28th December, 1963. The making of Haldia was really a thrilling experience. The first phase of the project was then almost towards the completion. As a result of the efficient pursuance of the Chief Minister P. C. Sen, Raj Bahadur was convinced to declare that the new port would be prepared with five berths for skillful handling of coal, iron and general commodities and for that Rs. 30 crores including Rs. 14 crores from the World Bank as the foreign exchange component would be allocated on behalf of the central government. Thereafter, Haldia port gained new life and planned to handle 11 million tons of cargo annually without affecting the cargo movement of Calcutta port.

In the initial stage of the project there were some genuine difficulties regarding the acquisition of land that connected the question of displacement of many families and rehabilitation. It was estimated that approximately about 10,000 people of 54 villages were to be displaced. In that connection due to the very positive approach and adequate measures taken by the Chief Minister P. C. Sen the displaced persons were however, provided lands for their rehabilitation within a few miles distance of the project. In case of the rehabilitation of the displaced persons from the project area a public meeting was organized by the congress workers where the visiting ministers addressed about the future of the project and necessity of the rehabilitation. In that meeting Humayun Kabir for the first time announced that "Government of India was considering for the establishment of an oil refinery that was likely to be cost of Rs. 30 crores, thereby opening up the probabilities of establishing new petrochemical industries."[48]

(vi). Model of the Second Hooghly Bridge

On 6th July, 1964, a gigantic model of the Second Hooghly Bridge and details of the design were displayed on the corridor in Writers' Buildings facing Chief Minister's room. This model was prepared by the British firm named Rendell Palmer & Triton which was appointed by the State Government for a feasibility study of the proposed bridge at the point of Princep Ghat. To find out the feasibility of its construction the firm had taken two years to prepare the same and the West Bengal Government paid then Rs. 17 lakhs as its remuneration. The firm's representative, J. R. Otter explained to the Chief Minister that according to the model, the bridge was designed to be of tied arch type, much simpler but longer, than the Howrah Bridge (now Rabindra Setu) which had also been designed by the same firm. The proposed Second Hooghly Bridge would be 75 ft. wide and about a mile long and the tentative expenditure would be the amount of Rs. 12 crores. Though, the proposed work of the Bridge started eight years later during Siddhartha Sankar Ray's Ministry and the foundation was laid by Prime Minister Indira Gandhi, but the credit has to go to P. C. Sen who is said to have done the ground work for the said Bridge during his regime.[49]

Problems Faced by P. C. Sen

(i) Angry Opposition and No-Confidence Motion

P. C. Sen, the Chief Minister of the state had to face such a situation in the Assembly for the first time of his chief ministership for which he was not mentally ready at all. It was on 16th day of July, 1963 that a war of words at one point tended to deteriorate into a physical clash. The excitement started over a statement of the Chief Minister that he did not believe in the correctness of the statement made by Hemanta Kumar Bose, the Forward Bloc leader about the deaths on account of starvation in Purulia, the drought-prone district in West Bengal. Though, the Chief Minister admitted that the food situation was not up to the mark and at the same time he accused the surplus growers for the store of food grain for more profit which was the main cause behind the rise in food prices. The Chief Minister also expressed his helplessness regarding the taking any drastic action against the said profiteers owing to the changed policy of the Union Government in connection with Defence of India Rules (DIR) against profiteers. As the Chief Minister did not accept the statement of Hemanta kumar Basu as correct, so, in protest the opposition stopped the business of the House for that day. Not only that the opposition members of the Assembly resorted to a token three-day hunger-strike in the Assembly House in order to draw the public attention towards the demand for a 'radical change' of the food-policy of the Government of West Bengal.[50]

At last, at the end of the three day food debate as well as token hunger -strike the Chief Minister defended his Government's policy and firmly stated that there could not be any basic change in the food policy of the government as because it was formulated on the basis of long experience and numerous trials. Finally, the opposition group brought a notice of no-confidence motion against the P. C. Sen's Ministry.[51] Naturally, the Assembly Hall was resounded with exciting speeches on 22nd July, 1963 both from Treasury and Opposition Benches regarding the question of no–confidence motion. But, surprisingly the Chief Minister remained unperturbed entirely the long eight-hour debate. Chief Minister gave suitable answer against any kind of questions and queries of the opposition. Thereafter, when the Chief Minister sought the confidence of the House, the House again showed its confidence on the Ministry of P. C. Sen, by rejecting the no-confidence motion of the opposition with overwhelming majority. But, the most significant event of the motion was that the Independent Member of the House, Siddhartha Shankar Ray's efficient summing up of the P. C. Sen Ministry's achievements which had done the Chief Minister's task very easy. Introduction of adult franchise in municipal elections, release of political prisoners and the setting up of the Estimates Committee of the Assembly were mentioned by S. S. Ray as the instances of the Sen Ministry's remarkable achievements. Before ending his speech Siddhartha Shankar Ray pointed his finger to the Forward Bloc and other non-communist groups and threw a straight question: "Supposing your non-confidence motions are carried, would you be prepared to co-operate with the Communists in forming a Government?" But, the oppositions were not in a position to give a suitable reply to the question of S. S. Ray because the Communists were still unacceptable to the other opposition parties also.[52]

(ii). No Confidence Motion in Assembly

P. C. Sen, the Chief Minister, had to face another no-confidence motion tabled by the opposition parties on 11th August, 1964. The visitors' galleries were filled up to hear the debate about no confidence motion. A storm had burst in the House over a remark of the Chief Minister P. C. Sen that opposition members "had come down on their knees and begged him to drop the adjournment motion on food". K. C. Basu, the speaker of the House had already accepted the motion. By centering no confidence motion disorderly scenes were manifested for the first time in the House and thereby the visitors' saw hanging of shoes by a member of the Forward Bloc. From the very beginning of the session it was the Forward Bloc party which spearheaded the attack on the Chief Minister as well as his government. At last the no-confidence motion of the opposition was defeated by a voice vote.[53]

(iii). Food Crisis

West Bengal experienced one of the lowest positions during the year of 1952-65 so far as the growth of agricultural production is concerned. In the field of food grains the rate of growth was much lower. The growth rate of productivity in case of rice was 0.03 per cent in West Bengal as against 1.40 per cent of the country. The scarcity of food grain also added fuel following the partition of British India in the name of independence, 1947 and thereupon a large number of refugees migrated to West Bengal. According to one estimate that more than 3 million refugees crossed the border of East Pakistan during the year of 1947-67.[54] On 7th February, 1964 Chief Minister P. C. Sen apprised Pundit Jawaharlal Nehru regarding the impending food crisis of West Bengal. Chief Minister, Prafulla Chandra Sen communicated to Nehru that due to partition of the country as well as Bengal already 31 lakhs people had migrated from East Pakistan to West Bengal and at the beginning of the year of 1964 as a result of the fresh communal violence in East Pakistan more 11 lakhs people had come in West Bengal. Therefore, it was very difficult for the state of West Bengal to give shelter as well as provide adequate food grains to all (31+11) = 44 lakhs people along with West Bengal's own population without the help of the entral government. Pundit Nehru, however, assured P. C. Sen about giving adequate financial help from central government and remarked, "Prafullababu, West Bengal is perhaps the only state in India which can claim to be secular." The reason behind the statement of Nehru was that as 42 lakhs Hindus came toWest Bengal after partition and in response to it only 2 lakhs Muslim had to go to East Pakistan from West Bengal.[55]

Actually, when Prafulla Chandra Sen was taking the charge of the Chief Ministership of West Bengal then there was no sufficient stock of food grains for feeding the people of the state. At that time mustered oil would import from Uttar-Pradesh, fish from East Bengal i. e. West Bengal had to depend on import in the field of food grains.[56] Naturally, the Chief Minister who was also the Food Minister from 1948 was very much worried over the rice position owing to unexpected reversal of policy by the Orissa Government. Biju Patnaik, the Chief Minister of Orissa declared imposition of ban on rice export from his State to West Bengal. Though Nehru personally took the initiatives to solve the food problem of West Bengal by the discussion with Biju Patnaik, but it was seen that Orissa herself was suffering from acute drought. In that situation the rationing system of West

Bengal was almost going to collapse. Chief Minister was always keeping contact with the central government for sending food grains. So, as a result of that the Union Cabinet decided to supply 20,000 tons of rice to West Bengal immediately. In that way the acute food problem of West Bengal was settled for the time being.[57]

Dum Dum Dawai

Due to scarcity of food grains the price of rice started increasing and as a result of that in the month of September and October in 1963 the price of rice hiked up to the level of amounting Rs. 42 and Rs. 47 per maund. That time some big cultivators and profiteers would stock the food grains for gaining more profit which undoubtedly created artificial crisis in the market. Government supplies in the fair prices shops were inadequate. In that chaotic situation, some young men of Dum Dum region raised their voice of protest against some profiteers and forced them to distribute the commodities among the people as per the rate of fair price shops. That action of the Dum Dum youths popularly came to be known as Dum Dum Dawai.[58] Following the example of the *Dum Dum dawai* the people in a point of their desperation took law into their own hands and forced rice traders to sell commodities in below the prevailing prices. Groups of young men started raiding shops and demanded sale of rice at the minimum price. So, frightened shop owners downed their shutters. In that context, on 15th October, 1963 an emergent cabinet meeting was called by the Chief Minister to review the situation. The situation was very confusing. Union Deputy Minister along with the Food Secretary had to come to Calcutta from Delhi to measure the food crisis. The Chief Minister summoned delegates of rice traders and after long discourse a consensus was reached between the traders and the government. As per that agreement as well as consensus it was decided that the dealers were to sell Bengal medium and fine varieties of rice at the rate of Rs. 35 per maund and imported Orissa and Andhra Pradesh rice Rs. 32 at retail price. It was found that whenever government tried to control over the prices of consumer goods like rice, wheat, cloth, edible oil, sugar, fish etc, excepting controlling the sources of supply the attempt in those cases was foiled by cunning tradesmen. Nearly 8,000 licensed fish merchants were affected and among them there were 374 wholesalers in Calcutta, Howrah and the suburbs areas. Towards the end of the November a kind of price war in Calcutta continued between shopkeepers and consumers. In respect of fish, more than half of Calcutta fish market stalls had become empty leaving the consumers in the lurch.[59]

(iv). Crackdown on Rice Millers

Despite opposition the West Bengal Government strongly enforced anti-profiteering and food grains licensing orders relating to the distribution of rice in January and February, 1964. Government recruited 1,000 more employees in order to materialize it in the food department. Although, enactment of that orders meant the deviation from the previous policy of the Government in the rice trade because previously it was decided that Government would not interfere into the trade of food grains. Naturally, when the traders of the food grains communicated their grievances to Mr. Swaran Singh, Union Food Minister, but considering the situation the Minister also supported the steps taken by the Chief Minister of West Bengal. The Government would think that the crisis was created by 'unholy combination of a section of *Jotedars* and rice mill owners who wanted to defeat the government policy through the methods of coercion'.[60]

(v). Fair Price Shops and Statutory Rationing System

Prime Minister Lal Bahadur Shastri was also very much aware about the acute food problem of West Bengal which was manifested in a comment made by him to the reporters at Raj Bhavan in Calcutta on 20th September, 1964 in the form of 'food is my greatest worry'. Even in a letter addressed to Chief Minister Prafulla Chandra Sen from Cairo, dated 10th October, 1964 Prime Minister Shahtriji expressed his great concern regarding food situation. Not only that with the consultation with the Prime Minister P. C. Sen introduced the system of selling of necessary commodities through fair-price shops and consumer co-operative.[61] Considering the urgency of the situation, statutory rationing in the city of Calcutta was introduced by the state government. In order to tackle the food crisis as well as protect people from hoarders-profiteers and save the state from a disaster as similar to the Bengal Famine of 1943; P. C. Sen introduced cordoning system in the state.[62]

Intelligence Report on Food Movement

About that time the Intelligence Branch of the State Government submitted a report to Home Secretary about a brief profile of six pages of the food movement in West Bengal during the years 1950 to 1963. As per the report, it was stated that agitation over food was an annual device of the opposition i. e. the communists in West Bengal politics. The real reason behind the food movement organized by the communists was not economic but political. The report stated, "The consideration is really political and not economic, as the organizers loudly proclaim. Shortage due to occasional crop failure and the natural rise in the price of rice and other foodstuff in September-October every year and exploited by the leftist political parties to work up a movement and to turn the people against the Government with vain hope of dislodging the Congress from power. Attempts are made to capture the sentiments of the people by stories of deaths due to starvation (unreal)."[63] The Intelligence report also mentioned, "The Food Minister (P. C. Sen) has sometimes been personally the target of attacks (particularly in 1959) as the political parties feel that he is the life-wire of the Congress Organiation in this State and his removal from the Ministry may hasten the fall of the Government."[64] The main aim of the movement was to create an atmosphere so that the Food Minister P. C. Sen would be bound to resign. According to the report, "The Leftist party hoped that if the food Minister could be removed, not only the Government but the Congress party itself would be substantially weakened." [65]

P. C. Sen's Food Policy and the Congress Party

Actually, Prafulla Chandra Sen wanted to contraband keeping rice collection and supply system in government's hand. Though, his intention was honest but in order to implement that system he did not get support even from others leaders of his party. The majority of his party men had reservations regarding monopoly procurement and cordoning. The cadres of the congress party even tried to dissuade him from the process in which he engaged himself. There was rising discontent within the congress party in West Bengal and organizationally the congress separated itself from that type of activities of its own Chief Minister. When food collection campaign was going on under government initiatives then Atulya Ghosh, all powerful man in West Bengal congress and one of the most influential All India Congress leaders wrote in a daily news paper that the monopoly collection of the food grain was not the only way to solve food problem. He pleaded for the introduction of whole rationing system and the peasants had to be encouraged for more production with giving fertilizer and seeds of rice.[66]

Police Firing at Basirhat and Lost of Two Lives

So, naturally, when food policy of P. C. Sen was going on as a failure then from several regions in mofussil areas the movement started in the month of February 1966 for the demand of food and kerosene oil. As the School Final and Higher Secondary examination were coming but due to lack of kerosene oil the students of the village areas were not able to make their studies. Therefore the demand for kerosene was incorporated with the demand of food. In that context, the food movement in Basirhat started on 16th February, 1966 from a public gathering at Sub-Divisional office. When the Sub-Divisional officer refused to meet with the aggrieved people as well as youth-students then they after being furious went to attack the Sub-Divisional office. In that situation police fired 11 rounds and thereby 6 persons received bullet injuries and next day one person named Ali Hafez was succumbed to death.[67] The tragic incident undoubtedly added fuel to the fire.

After reaching the news of police firing at Basirhat on 16th February, 1966 in Calcutta the Students Federation of India, declared that a protest day will be observed in the next day i. e. on 17th February. Naturally, protest-day was observed accordingly all over the state and a strike was called at Basirhat on that fateful day. The people of Basirhat particularly School and College students were assembled in front of the B. D. O. office at Swarup Nagar. A scuffle was happened on that day also in between police and the students and as a result of that Nurul Islam, a student of class five of Tentulia Multipurpose School died due to police firing. Though the police claimed that the students went to attack Thana but the Headmaster of the school of departed Nurul Islam gave his statement in newspaper that the police was firing first.[68]

Impact of Basirhat Police Firing

However, after police firing at Basirhat and death of a school boy resulted a heavy public upsurge which gradually led to the situation out of control of the state government and lowered the image of its chief minister badly. As a consequence of Basirhat incident, the aggrieved people of the different regions of 24 parganas started showing their grievances. On 18th February, the people of Baduria demanded all the confiscated rice had to be distributed through rationing system in a cheap rate. On 19th February, the common people gheraod B.D.O. office of Habra. There was huge demonstration at Beldanga in the district of Murshidabad. But each and every field police had fired on the people. In Baduria, Kalu Mandal and Abdul Hamid had lost their lives due to police firings. In Beldanga Sushil Sen and Tapan Dey died due to same reason.[69] After the fateful incident the police firings became as if a day to day affairs. Upananda Mukhapadhyay, the then I. G. wrote that after being furious Prafulla Chandra Sen used to remark, 'Why the police personnel were not firing, they should do that'. But at the beginning the police were not agree to fire on the fasting people.[70]

Actually, in that time Prafulla Chandra Sen became unstable. He himself acknowledged that the collection of rice was not up to the expectation and if that situation would continue then the state might have to face the 'shadow of famine'.[71] Though, it was not officially declared about famine in West Bengal but actually the shadow of famine gradually swallowed the state as because the price rate of rice became Rs. 2 per k.g.[72] Most of the people would maintain their livelihood only consuming half-meal in a day and the demand for supply of rice at the rate of ten anna raised from the famish people. In that situation, when for the demand of food Krishnagar-Ranaghat and Shantipur of Nadia district became bloody on10th March, Prafulley Chandra Sen jockingly commented to the press men that *'Shantipur dubu-dubu, Nade bhese jay re'*(i.e. Shantipur on the point of drowning, it is floting in the river) which certainly tarnished the image of Chief Minister Sen who once was the freedom fighter and pro-Gandhian leader.[73] In that connection Prafulla Chakrabarty in his book 'The Marginal Men' wrote, "In the winter of 1966 Sen was perhaps the most unpopular man in West Bengal, there can be no doubt, the measures he took to mitigate the food shortage were well meaning."[74]

Joint Oppositions and 8-Points Charter of Demands

In that circumstances the leaders of the opposition parties, 'Rastriya Sangram Samiti' of the trade unions, the 'Council of Action' of SFI, AISF, PSU and DSO jointly decided to observe 22nd February, 1966 as Martyrs' Day. The day was observed by organizing rallies, meetings and demonstrations throughout the state. They also made it a grant success under the caption of 'All Bengal Demand Day' by holding street corner meetings in all the important road junctions in Calcutta on 21st February. So, Martyrs' Day was observed all over the state accordingly by organizing meetings and demonstrations. In Calcutta a meeting was organized at the Maidan on that day. In that meeting leaders like Somenath Lahiri, Jatin Chakrabarty and others condemned the food policy of the state government and demanded a judicial inquiry into the police firing of Basirhat. The leaders urged the government to accept the demand of 8-points charter of the Joint Opposition Front which included:-i). Supply of rations to all non- producer in rural areas, ii). Liberal issue of ration cards, iii). Stoppage of servicing of levy notices on landowners with less than seven acres of holdings, iv). Equitable distribution of kerosene and other essential commodities, v). Lifting of the emergency, vi). Withdrawal of D. I. Rules, vii). Unconditional release of political detainees those who arrested in connection with food movement and viii). Judicial inquiry into the recent police firings in 24-Parganas.[75]

Stormy Budget Session and Clash among the Legislatures

In the meantime, Saila Kumar Mukherjee, State Finance Minister had an extraordinary experience at the time of his budget speech on 21st February, in the financial year of 1966-67. When the Finance Minister had commenced his budget reading then it was forcibly snatched away by Kamal Guha, a Forward Bloc member, within four minutes. The reason behind that action of Kamal Guha was mainly as the government arrested three opposition members' in connection with food movement.[76] Not only that an untoward incident also happened in the assembly following the impact of the police excesses in 24 Pargana. A violent fight broke out in the assembly between the opposition members and the ruling party on 22nd February that never happened before. Two members were injured as a result of boxing, torn microphone rods, stools and portfolios. Due to the gravity of the situation the Houses was adjourned for 90 minutes. Battle cries and attacking mode were seen in the House on that day in lieu of the day's agenda of discussion on Governor's address. The Chief Minister was not present in the House on that day. For three days there were no business at all transacted in the House. As a consequence of all that the angry Chief Minister cancelled his dialogue with the Opposition Leaders regarding Basirhat happenings.[77]

Krishnagar Police Firing and Death of a Student-Ananda Hait

The initiation of the Krishnagar agitation started on 4th March, 1966 by centering a student processions. Actually the environment was so explosive that in the pretext of the student strike and the observance of the martyr day on 22nd February, all the Schools and Colleges were closed from 21st February, 1966. That time the opposition members would enter into the Assembly House wearing black badge. In that circumstances when police blocked the processions of the students in front of the Krishnagar Collegiate School and Post Office then the conflict started in between students and the police personnel. As a result of that conflict Ananda Hait, a youth of 17th years old died due to police firing. Besides more two persons named Anath Paul and Paresh Banerjee became injured due to the same reason. Police had used tear gas and lathi-charge along with bullet firing in order to disperse the processions. But the furious people had thrown stone on police personnel and thereupon the agitation gradually transferred from the hands of the students to the massas.[78] After being furious due to police atrocities and death of Ananda Hait, the common people then set on fire in Ration Office and Collectorate Office. Due to the gravity of the situation, even the lawyers also came out from the Court to show their protest. Not only that as the Government Bhawan bears the symbol of state power, therefore, the agitated people would set on fire even on School Board, Electricity office, Train compartment and Rail Station also. So, as a result of wide scale setting fire even the Fire Brigade was unable to extinguish the fire.[79]

On the other hand, after receiving the news of the police firing in Krishnagar demonstrations started at different places in Calcutta. The Cinema Halls were shutting down. Trams and Buses were setting fire. The tram line was uprooted by the youths at the corner of Hedua of North Calcutta. Scuffle started in between police personnel and the masses at Sealdah. As a result of that after promulgating 144 Cr.Pc.in Calcutta schools and colleges were declared closed for sine die. The Higher Secondary examination was also declared suspended.[80] After considering the depth of the situations of Nadia and Calcutta the Chief Minister was so worried that he started talking to General Manekshaw, Commander-in Chief of Eastern Army on 5th March, 1966. [81]

Bandh on 10th March, 1966

In the meanwhile, from the Maidan rally of 25th February, 1966, the opposition leaders declared that West Bengal Bandh would be observed on 10th March as a protest against the faulty food policy of the government and the police firing on the agitators as well as arrests of the opposition leaders in connection with food movement. The top congress leaders became afraid remembering the September disturbances of 1959, i. e. the mob had attacked houses of the congress leaders and ministers. So, instead of making elaborate preparation to face the storm which was about to outburst that *The Statesman* analyst called 'a surrender to the inevitable'.[82] So, a good number of police force deployed to protect the lives and houses of eminent ministers and congress leaders. On the day of Bandh Calcutta and most of the places in the districts were completely paralyzed. Railway property was mainly marked out for destruction. The government wanted to run the trains but the demonstrators in order to dislocate the train uprooted rail tracks, set fire to railway coaches and go-downs and ruined other railway installations. The skirmish started between the police and the demonstrators which resulting in two deaths in Calcutta and eleven in the districts due to police firing. Several policemen had also injured in mob-police clashes. At least 100 persons were injured only Calcutta and considering the situation Army had to call to maintain normalcy in all the disturbed areas.[83]

Attempts of the Central Leaderships to Normalize the Trouble-Prone Situation

When West Bengal was blazing in the wake of food movement in 1966 and the helplessness of the state government was closely watched by the central government. In that critical juncture, Prime Minister Indira Gandhi talked to the Chief Minister P. C. Sen over telephone and advised that the Home Minister, G. L. Nanda should visit Calcutta to help him in that trouble period. But the Chief Minister considered the suggestion of Prime Minister as an interference of central government in the matters which were solely concerned the state and he also took it as to undermine the prestige of the state government. But very efficiently the Prime Minister took that internal disputation by making a personal visit to Calcutta on her way to Guahati on 6th March, 1966. Worried Prime Minister discussed the whole matter with the Chief Minister and his colleagues throughout the day and made certain suggestions namely, release of opposition leaders and resumption of talk with them. But the proposals of Prime Minister were not acceptable to P. C. Sen and his colleagues. Naturally the events were permitted to take their own course of action for the time being.[84] But, after her return to Delhi she pursued an opposite course of action very wisely. She had the capability to feel the pulse of Bengal. So, Prime Minister herself convened a meeting of the Opposition M. Ps particularly from West Bengal. She discussed with Hiren Mukherjee, N. C. Chatterjee and others about the situation and boycotting the Budget session by the Opposition M.L.As. (All Opposition M.L.As had been arrested and put in prison.) Meanwhile, due to the state wide disturbances of 10th and 11th March, as many as 39 persons had to lose their lives and 5,500 persons were sent to jail. The losses of property in terms of national income at that time was amounting Rs. 6.5 crore.[85] It should be mentionable that some eminent personalities of West Bengal like- Dr. Triguna Sen, Satyajit Roy, Bivekananda Mukhopadhyay, Shaibal Gupta etc. apprised Prime Minister Indira Gandhi through telegram regarding the deplorable conditions of public life in the state.[86] As a direct impact of the said incidents as well as the outcry in Parliament prompted Indira Gandhi, the Prime Minister to adopt a strong line regarding the state of West Bengal. She sent a central team on 12th March, 1966, comprising of two Minister- G. L. Nanda, the Home Minister and Subramanium, Minister for Agriculture to investigate the situation and advice the state government for restoring normalcy. In spite of reservation of Chief Minister P. C. Sen it became impossible for him to resist the flying visit of Nanda and Subrahmanium as central government representatives. They came with indications from the Prime Minister to neutralize the abnormal situations continuing in the state. They discussed about the ongoing situation with the Council of Ministers and also with the Opposition M. Ps. (M.L.As of ULF were all behind prison bars), Vice-Chancellors of Universities (it was mainly a student movement), Newspaper Editors and some congress leaders. Their immediate intentions were to reopen the dialogue between the Chief Minister and the State Opposition M.L.As.[87]

P. C. Sen's Threat to Resign from the Chief-Ministership

During that disquieted period the Chief Minister was fighting alone the battle with the help of security forces. He was confused with the magnitude of the task. It has already been mentioned that the congress did not try to face with the problem politically as if the political stage of the congress as a party did not exist. Moreover, Atulya Ghosh also started criticizing the food policy adopted by the chief minister. In that circumstances the masterly persuasiveness of the central ministers and the criticism of a section of his colleagues, a sense of helplessness developed in P. C. Sen's mind. So, he took an unexpected resolution regarding his firm decision to resign from the post of the Chief Ministership. He sent a letter to the Secretary of the Parliamentary Party expressing his 'irrevocable' decision to resign accordingly on 19th March, 1966. The explanation behind his resignation was given by him was that he would be more capable to serve the poor people better by staying outside the government. The decision was taken by him personally. Considering the ongoing situation, P. C. Sen felt that it was the only way to end the political deadlock for restoring peace in the state. Following the incident the Home Minister Guljaril Nanda and Union Food Minister, C. Subrahmaniam both of them rushed to Calcutta at once after hearing the decision of the resignation of P. C. Sen. When the news of his decision to summon a party meeting and his wish to resign were known to them and to Atulya Ghosh, then all the three together drove to the Assembly buildings and entered into the Chief Minister's room. Even the Prime Minister Indira Gandhi was also sought to soothe him. However, all the four leaders were closeted for an hour. After a significant discussion they succeeded in changing his decision and withdraw the resignation letter as a face saving formula of the congress party in West Bengal.[88]

Chief Minister's Surrender to the Opposition Demands

The above mentioned developments had taken place before the Assembly House met on that day. As soon as the House commenced its function the Chief Minister with the permission of the Speaker proclaimed his decision to release of the Opposition legislators including Jyoti Basu, the Leader of the Opposition, held dialogues between the Government and the Opposition and thereby a commission was appointed for the enquiry of police firing. In another announcement in the House, P. C. Sen declared that all members of both Assembly and Council and 12 others belonged to the different political parties were held under D. I. Rule had been released. After the surrender to the opposition demands by the Chief Minister, the opposition i. e. ULF announced its decision to continue their food movement and boycott the legislature. They could not abandon the threat of the political movement that brought them huge dividends and unity in their ranks. Thereafter, Jyoti Basu went to Delhi to talk with the Prime Minister separately. As a pragmatic politician he understood that unless the centre made sufficient supply the State government would be powerless, although their main target of attack was the state government. As a result of the meeting with the Prime Minister, wheat quota was increased for West Bengal and issuing of ration cards started for kerosene supply.[89]

Food Movement in 1966 and Role of the Congress Party in West Bengal

The food movement of 1966 was different from similar movements what happened in the past in two respects: (i). The forthcoming general election in the early year of 1967 and (ii). Change in the character of the movement owing to massive mobilization of the people. It may be noted that the new food policy of Chief Minister P. C. Sen was supported by the all left parties on principle but only with the aim of a state-wide movement on various policies of the government such as food, D. I. Rules, release of detainees and so on - the left parties choose the month of March in 1966 for the inception of the food movement.[90] It would be justifiable to mention that before commencing the vigorous food movement the left parties had gained adequate strength and consolidated their political base among the various segments of the people in West Bengal. After the formal division of the Communist Party of India, meanwhile the CPI (M) had infiltrated into the different segments of the people and established its influence over them. For example- the ABTA (All Bengal Teachers' Association), the WBCUTA (the West Bengal College and University Teachers' Association), the Co-ordination Committee of the State Government Employees' Unions and Associations etc.- all these CPI(M) controlled organizations helped it to maintain its mighty presence in all the segment of the middle classes in all over West Bengal. Besides, the students front like SFI (CPM-controlled), AISF (CPI-controlled), PSU (RSP-controlled), DSO (SUCI-controlled) etc. came under the control of the left parties. But from the entire said front the congress party was almost disappeared. The congress party still then only maintained its presence within the working class through the INTUC (Indian National Trade Union Congress), though an important section of the working class already came under the banners of CITU (Centre of Indian Trade

Unions, controlled by CPM), AITUC (All India Trade Union Congress, controlled by CPI) and the UTUC (United Trade Union Congress, controlled by RSP). But, still then the CPI and the CPI (M) were not in a position to capture 'Kishan Sabhas', the authority of the congress vote bank in rural Bengal.[91] It became therefore possible for the left parties to bring their entire controlled organisation in the forefront of the state politics. On that point, it is clear that if all these segments were united in any massive onslaught against the government then it would be certainly very difficult for the government to resist the assault with the help of the inadequate police force as well as without the support of an organized political party. Needless to say that at that time there was as such no party behind the Government and the Congress as a political party which 'had gone behind the purdah' in 1953, not reappeared at least up to that period.[92]

So, in that context popular displeasure was also increased many fold against the government due to shameless police action who discharge their duties as per the instruction of the government i.e. led by the congress party.[93] In that critical circumstances congress as a ruling political party could organize the people and stand against the atrocities of the police personnel. Regarding the food policy of the government, at least, as a political party congress was supposed to explain to the people that the joteders, hoarders and profiteers were primarily responsible for the deplorable condition of the masses. Not only that, congress could easily explain the government's policy of equitable distribution of the available food stocks which was being scuttled by the big landholders for more profit. But the class composition of the followers of the congress in the state made it impossible for the party to play such role. As a result of that contradiction within the congress as a political party it could not persuade the Chief Minister P. C. Sen to lift the paddy levy order or support the strict implementation of that order. Therefore, as an organization, congress party became completely perplexed as well as paralyzed. Naturally, it was almost impossible for the government alone to face the problem politically.[94]

In the light of the said incidents one may recall that the people of West Bengal as if took the decision to remove the congress party from the power. It is noteworthy that the movement was not organized only for want of food but against the mal administration also. At that critical time of the governmemnt, the style of functioning of the congress party particularly its disappearance from the entire scenario cannot be out of question. The entire scenario convinced the people of West Bengal to bring about a political change in West Bengal.

Scenario of All India Politics and its Reflection on West Bengal Politics

It is noteworthy that 1960s were turning point in terms of a series of political crisis which expedited the political instability both in West Bengal as well as in India. The death of Jawaharlal Nehru (27th May, 1964) and subsequent passing away of Lalbhadur Shastri (on 11th January, 1966) both the Prime Minister of India created a vacuum to lead the country. In order to tackle the situation the so-called 'Syndicate Group'[95] was formed and the task of the group was to find out the way to overcome the chaotic situation. In the meanwhile, a leadership crisis was there in West Bengal politics after the death of B. C. Roy. Incidentally, the situation was successfully handle with the selection of P. C. Sen as Chief Minister of West Bengal and Indira Gandhi became the best alternative choice of the Syndicate group as Prime Minister of India.[96] In all these developments, Atulya Ghosh a prominent member of the 'Sundicate Group' played a significant role to scale down the crisis. But so far as West Bengal was concerned P. C. Sen could not tackle the situation as was expected. Moreover, some of the acute problems especially the food crisis was not solved rather it remained unheeded by the congress party in spite of its expected attention. The cumulative results of all these were exposed with the food movement. In fact, it was a climax of the cracks that became inherent in the organization level of the congress party. Neither the central government nor that of the West Bengal was able to ameliorate the crisis. It has already been mentioned above how did P. C. Sen and his cabinet members take steps to handle these movement but his efforts ended in fiasco. On the other hand, the crisis within the organization invited misunderstanding among the members of the party and gradually the trend became so unbearable that some prominent members had to leave the party and eventually to form a new party. The case of Ajay Mukherjee and the emergence of a new political party named 'Bangla Congress' were the ultimate result of the ongoing political crisis of the then West Bengal. The subsequent development was to find out a political mechanism how to safe West Bengal and an alternative solution was found with the formation of United Front Government.

Bangla Congress and Ajay Kumar Mukherjee

It has already been mentioned that at the climax of the food movement (1966) and demand for kerosin oil, organized by the combined oppositions that ultimately led to the almost breakdown of the West Bengal administration and in other words it may be called that the administration as if went behind the curtain and oppositions virtually dominating the political affairs in West Bengal. In that circumstances, as a mark of protest against the corruption or highhandedness of some top leaders of the congress party in West Bengal, when 'Bangla Congress' a rival organization of ruling congress was going to originate under the leadership of Ajay Kumar Mukherjee and exposed the real nature of West Bengal Pradesh Congress before the common people which was considered a great setback for the congress party in the upcoming election in 1967. In that context, before going for in detail regarding the formation of 'Bangla Congress', we should look back at a glance some other subsequent development in the state which were as under:

Kamraj Plan vis-à-vis Reshuffle of the State Ministry

The endorsement of the Kamraj Plan by Congress Working Committee (CWC) and the All India Congress Committee (AICC) on 10th August, 1963 had its certain reactions in Calcutta and other state capitals. At that time the picture in West Bengal was quite different from that of some other states. The West Bengal congress organization and government administration were free from group hostility and thereby a harmonious relationship existed between them because the relation between Atulya Ghosh, supreme leader of the congress party in West Bengal and Prafulla Chandra Sen, the Chief Minister of West Bengal were very close. It was well-known to political circle that the voice of Atulya Ghosh would determine the various important issues or in another word it may be called that the politics as well as administration in West Bengal would function according to the instruction of Atulya Ghosh.[97]

Following the announcement of the Kamraj plan, on 18th August, 1963, P. C. Sen, the Chief Minister of West Bengal summoned a meeting of the State Ministers in the Assembly House. After almost one hour discussion with the ministers he announced that some ministers would resign from their office in accordance with the Kamraj Plan.[98] The Chief Minister himself expressed his desire to resign along with other ministers. All the ministers expressed their willingness in writing to the Chief Minister and offered their resignations.[99] In that context, some ministers were worried about the acceptance of their resignation from ministry. But, who would remain in the office of the ministry and whose resignation would be accepted that was only known to Chief Minister P. C. Sen and Atulya Ghosh.[100] Naturally, there was a flow of discussion in official and press circles regarding the names of the ministers who were going to be dropped from the cabinet. One Minister, however, expressed to his close circle that under the Kamraj Plan the congress chief (meaning Atulya Ghosh) would find out a plea to get cleanse him from the ministry. He was no other than, but Ajay Kumar Mukherjee whose unparallel position and hold in his own home district Midnapur, was looked upon with uneasiness and jealousy by some congress hierarchy of West Bengal. They wanted to displace him by a junior lady person namely Ava Maity who was very close to the party machinery. On 17th September, 1963, as per the Kamraj Plan the resignation of some ministers were accepted by the cabinet in its meeting which was held at Chief Minister's room in the Assembly House. Among the ministers most 'casualties' were Shri Ajay Kumar Mukherjee and the most skillful as well as capable minister, Shankar Das Banerji. The latter had to pay the cost for his impartiality and resistance party interference in the administration affairs of his departments. The Governor accepted the resignation of both the ministers on 1st October, 1963. But, people in general and particularly the political circles knew the motive behind the dropping of these two cabinet ministers.[101] It is noteworthy that if the Kamraj Plan could be viewed as a device at the hands of the party's ruling coterie to weaken its rivals, then the Hooghly Group was successful in case of utilizing it. Ajay Mukherjee's resignation of course drastically cut his power of patronage what was he enjoying as minister. The name of Sankar Das Banerjee was comprised probably to avoid the charge of discrimination.[102]

Bye-Election

However, in the midst of the discontent regarding the dropping some ministers in the pretext of Kamraj Plan, the congress party and the opposition groups were directly engaged in the bye-elections of two Parliamentary and two Assembly seats in the districts of Jalpaiguri and Cooch Behar. The date of the bye-elections in West Bengal was scheduled on 23rd December, 1963- that was exactly after a year of the Chinese aggression. We have already discussed that as consequence of the Chinese aggression a rapid political changes in the country particularly in West Bengal had been taken place. It has also been mentioned that in the previous bye-election results which were published on 8th April, 1963, the congress party won all the seats due to the impact of foreign aggression and thereby a spirit of nationalism swept over the country. Although the congress leaders claimed their credit for the victory, but actually the credit to a great range went to China for her devilish attack on a friendly country like India which brought about the electoral turn over that ultimately led to the total failure of the communist party in that previous bye-elections. But this time that was not repeated. In spite of large-scale arrests of the leaders and alienation of the communist party from the common people and not only that despite internal dissensions, the leaders of that party were trying whole-heartedly to build up a bridge with opposition groups like Forward Bloc, R.S.P. and P.S.P. for the purpose of electoral understanding in order to fight against the common enemy i.e. the congress.

However, on 23rd December, 1963 was fateful day to the congress party in the state of West Bengal. The congress candidate Narayan Chowdhury was defeated in the prestigious Burdwan Parliamentary seat by Hindu Mahasabhite candidate Nirmal Chandra Chatterjee with the support of the communist by 11,000 votes. The congress candidate for the other parliamentary seat in Cooch Behar became victorious defeating his Forward Bloc opponent B. K. Das Chowdhury by 60,000 votes. In the case of two Assembly seats i.e. Burdwan and Siliguri, the congress and the communists shared the victory. At Siliguri congress candidate Arun Moitra who later became the president of the PCC, defeated his rival communist candidate Charu Majumdar who subsequently became the famous theoretician of the party but in 1967 he founded the CPI-ML. Benoy Chowdhury, who was high rated leader in the communist party due to his profound knowledge in economics won the prestigious Burdwan Assembly seat. Therefore, the victory was shared 50-50 in between the congress and non-congress parties.[103]

The results of the bye-election was clearly indicates the come down of the support base of the congress party in West Bengal due to growing discontent against the leaders as well as administration. The encouragement and enthusiasm among the people which was seen in the initial years of Independence were somehow disappearing. A powerful group of West Bengal congress party as well as all India ruling hierarchy instead of following the path of sacrifice, were setting examples of luxurious living, dampening the spirit of common men and earnest followers of the congress. The faith in congress in West Bengal started diminishing because of erosion both in the administration and the congress organization which was moving towards corruption. The state congress organization and the rulers were in the hope that major opponent i. e. the communist party would not be able to show a serious threat afresh because of internal disagreement in view of the issue of China.[104]

Fact behind the Creation of Bangla Congress

Midnapore Congress Factionalism

Formerly undivided Midnapore was the southernmost district of Burdwan Division in West Bengal. At that time politics in Midnapore district was dominated by the congress party. Its internal cohesion was however begun to dilapidate due to the rise of two strong factions centering two eminent Midnapore congressmen, namely, Charu Chandra Mohanty and Ajay Kumar Mukherjee. Factionalism within the congress party in Midnapore started in the year of 1962 over the question of 'corruption and nepotism' in party organization. As a PCC chief, Ajay Kumar Mukherjee received some complaint from various sources that Shri Prabir Jana, the General Secretary of the Midnapore District Congress Committee (MDCC), who was not at all the member of Regional Transport Authority (RTA); in spite of that he was recommending the name of the applicants to the Regional Transport Authority (RTA) for route permits instead of taking bribes. It might be noted that Prabir Jana was nephew of an influential Midnapore congressman namely Nikunja Behari Maity and cousin brother of Ava Maity, the lady Minister of the state. It is noteworthy that Ava Maity was an ardent follower of the contemporary most powerful congress leaders in the state as well as centre i.e. Hooghly Group leaders like Atulya Ghosh and chief minister of West Bengal P. C. Sen.[105] However, in order to stop such 'corruption' Ajay Kumar Mukherjee and his followers like Sushil Kumar Dhara and Mrityunjay Jana (both were M.L.As) requested Charu Chandra Mahanty, the then president of the MDCC, to set up a new committee which would be consisted by the 'neutral and honest' congressmen and power would be given to them to recommend candidates for Bus route to the RTA.[106] But, when it was found that due to the opposition of Prabir Jana and Ava Maity no such committee was constituted, then Ajay Mukherjee remarked, "Charuda is soft on the nephew of Nikunjada. Ignoring our proposal he only tacitly allowed the General Secretary to indulge in corruption".[107]

Mohanty Group and the Mukherjee Group

At that stage the MDCC was divided into the Mohanty Group and the Mukherjee Group. Having failed to free the party from corruption, the Mukherjee Group determined to convince the public opinion against the corrupt leadership of the MDCC and a general campaign was launched accordingly. It is widely known to all that the accused Midnapore congress leaders were also belonged to the Hooghly Group. In other words, Ajay Mukherjee's bid to fight against the Mohanty Group means to hostile the Hooghly Group which was the operator of the congress party in West Bengal politics. Though, the Mohanty Group condemned the charges which were leveled against it as 'baseless and untrue' but it became difficult for the group to ignore Ajay Kumer Mukherjee as because he was after all a senior congressman and had a comparatively strong support base in

Midnapore. Ajay Mukherjee had also good rapport as well as huge acceptability among the old congressmen specially the freedom fighters for his devoting role in the freedom movement particularly as a one of the architects of 'Tamralipta Jatiya Sarkar' in the pretext of the 'Quit India Movement'.[108] However, the Mohanty Group wanted to undermine the strength of Ajay Mukherjee and that opportunity came in the form of the implementation of Kamraj Plan which was endorsed by CWC and AICC on 10th August, 1963.[109]

The Kamraj Plan was started to execute by the AICC throughout the country with the acceptance of the resignation of six central ministers by the Prime Minister Nehru on and from 24th August, 1963. Towards the end of the year i.e. on 9th October, 1963 Kamraj became the All India Congress president as per the recommendation of Atulya Ghosh who was also holding the portfolio of treasurer of the AICC and one of the influential members of the Syndicate Group. During that time Kamraj-Atulya were so powerful that nobody had anything to say against their activities - that mentality was prevailing into the mind of the people of whole country. In that context, Atulya Ghosh of his own told Ajay Mukherjee to resign from the ministership in accordance with Kamraj Plan and ultimately it was accepted.[110]

Rabindralal Sinha stepped down from the post of West Bengal Pradesh Congress Committee (WBPCC) after being inducted into the Cabinet of P. C. Sen as Education Minister in the month of June 1964. Since all others outgoing ministers were given some organizational responsibility in accordance with the aim of the Kamraj Plan. So, top congress leaders of West Bengal particularly Atulya Ghosh and Prafulla Chandra Sen were thinking to give a dignified organizational liability to Ajay Mukherjee as per his capability. In that context, considering the organizational skill as well as according to the wish of Atulya Ghosh and Preafulla Chandra Sen, Ajay Mukherjee was unanimously elected the President of the WBPCC in June 1964. Ajay Mukherjee gladly accepted the new responsibility with the hope that eradicating corruption he will restore the glory of the West Bengal Congress.[111] As the PCC President within few months it was very much clear to Ajay Mukherjee that some congress leaders who were misusing power and doing corruption for their selfish personal interest neglecting the common interest of the party and thereupon as an all India organization congress party was losing its reputation. The congress party which had gradually developed by the ideal as well as devotion and sacrifice of Deshbandhu, Gandhiji, Nehru, Pattel, but now it was rapidly losing its past heritage due to misuse of power, nepotism and selfish attitude of some leaders. After seeing such type of activities of the leaders many people in the meantime disillusioned to congress and were forced to cut off their relation with that glorious organization. So, taking into account the above fact as PCC chief, Ajay Mukherjee was determined to reform congress and make it free from corruption in order to bring back the lost glory of the party.[112]

Corruption within the Congress Party and Role of Nirmalendu Dey

It should be noted that as President of the West Bengal Pradesh Congress Committee, Ajoy Mukherjee's scope for free activities was limited because the various organizational component of PCC, particularly its executive committee remained under the direct control of the Hooghly Group as well as Atulya Ghosh. Ill-feeling began to intensify between the Mohanty Group and the Mukherjee Group by centering the question of the distribution of forms for the enrollment of new membership. Ajay Mukherjee received a number of complaints from various quarters regarding the fake membership as well as corruption about the distribution of membership forms by the General Secretary i.e. Prabir Jana who belonged to Mohanty Group, the ruling faction of the MDCC. On that point to minimize corruption in the field of the enrolment of new members, Ajay Mukherjee requested Nirmalendu Dey, the then General Secretary of the PCC to supply adequate number of membership forms at the Midnapore party office. At that time in case of the enrollment of membership the forms which would be used that must be signed by the General Secretary of the PCC. But the request of PCC chief, Ajay Mukherjee was unheeded time and again by his subordinate office bearer i. e. general secretary.[113]It was found that Prabir Jana and his group i.e. Mohanty group had a very close proximity with PCC general secretary Nirmalendu Dey alias Bodu Babu who would ultimately control West Bengal congress politics in the behest of Atulya Ghosh. It might be mentionable that as Bodu Babu was the nephew of Sukumar Dutta, a wealthy and influential congress MLA of undivided Bengal. As Sukumar Dutta was a very good orator and had a wide acceptability in the social as well as political circle of Bengal and had a friendly relationship with Atulya Ghosh, that's why Bodu Babu would call Atulya Babu as his *mama* (meternal uncle). Not only that though Bodu Babu came from a very well to do family in spite of that he had no good fame as well as honesty regarding the financial matters were concerned. But Ajay Babu's honesty relating to financial matters was always above question.[114] Therefore, it was not impossible to imagine that all the corruption committed by the Prabir Jana and his group regarding the enrollment of membership, collection of money in the name of the party, expenditure, bus root license permit through RTA, giving the job of primary teachers instead of getting Rs. 250-500 per candidate etc. were known to Bodu Babu and he would extent his supporting hand to protect them as because he himself enjoyed the brain trust of Atulya Ghosh.[115]

In that situation, it was very difficult for Ajay Mukherjee to continue his work without external help. So, he met All India Congress President Kamraj in the VIP lounge of the Calcutta air port along with Satish Chandra Samanta, M. P. and famous Sarbadhinayak of historical *Tamralipta Jatiya Sarkar* during the time of Quit India movement (1942) and Sushil Kumar Dhara, M.L.A. and August revolutionary as well as Commender-in-Chief of *'Bidyut Bahini'* of Tamralipta Jatiya Sarkar, and informed him about the Midnapore situation. After hearing all the events Kamraj strongly instructed PCC chief to print the membership form in his own name and distribute it according to his necessity. It was astonished that after getting Kamraj's approval to print the membership form and in the meantime Nirmalendu Dey agreed to supply the said form according to the instruction of PCC President Ajay Mukherjee.[116]

Ajay Mukherjee's Quit MDCC Office

Actually the internal displeasure between the two factions came into surface in the form of an open conflict on 23rd July, 1965. On that day, when Ajay Mukherjee and Charu Chandra Mohanty, both were President of the PCC and President of the MDCC respectively checking the enrolment of 'primary' and 'active' members in the party office, then a large crowd appeared and alleged that 'bogus' members had been enrolled.[117]Ajay Mukherjee then requested Charu Chandra Mohanty to make a joint statement asking the agitators to disperse. But unfortunately his appeal was undone by Mohanty and later Mukherjee said, "Charu-da left the room, held talks with some of his followers, and asked me to leave the party office. I departed in order to avoid any undesirable turn of events".[118]

Dismissal of Nirmalendu Dey by Ajay Mukherjee

Actually, the Mukherjee Group had no any kind of intention to capture the seat of power only to rid the party from 'corruption'. Therefore, after being driven out from the Midnapore District Congress (MDC) office on 23rd July, next day i.e. early morning of the 24th July, 1965, Ajay Mukherjee went to Calcutta in order to appraise the whole matter to Chief Minister P. C. Sen. After hearing everything P. C. Sen did not take any action rather he preferred to remain silent. Thereafter, Ajay Mukherjee came to a conclution that the leaders both from the District and also some from the State were jointly involved in hatching the conspiracy against him. But Ajay Mukherjee was not a man to surrender himself under pressure or illegal activities. He felt that in order to free the congress party from corruption the Pradesh Congress Committee had to be reformed. As general secretary of the PCC Nirmalendu Dey was involved with the illegal activities of the MDC leaders i.e. Mohanty groups, so, to eradicate corruption as well as conspiracy Ajay Mukherjee as President of the PCC served an order of dismissal to Nirmalendu Dey from the office of the general secretary of PCC on 1st September, 1965. He alleged in the order that the general secretary ignored his instructions to send membership forms to the MDCC office.[119]

Hunger Strike of Suhil Dhara in front of the Office of Midnapore District Congress Committee

On the other hand, as the Mukherjee Group was very much displeased over the driving away of its leader Ajay Mukherjee from the MDC office so, they resolved to draw public attention to it. Sushil Kumar Dhara, a close associate of Ajay Mukherjee and an MLA, staged a hunger strike, in front of the Midnapore District Congress party office accompanied by thirty congressmen at 5 p.m. on 25th July.[120] As a result of the propagation by the supporters of the Mukherjee group through microphone, within two hours after the commencement of the hunger strike the whole town of Midnapore came to know that 'revolutionary leader and M.L.A. Sushil Dhara started hunger strike in the office of the MDCC to remove corruption from the congress party.' After that the stream of people of the Midnapore city started coming to see Mr. Dhara. During the days of hunger strike each and every evening after offering prayer for half an hour, Mr. Dhara would address the public gathering for 10 to 15 minutes over the caption of 'why that hunger strike and sit on demonstration'?[121] Not only the common people but some M.L.A.s also came to the venue of hunger strike to show and prove their solidarity. Those M.L.A.s who joined with Suhalil Dhara were Mahendra Nath Mahato, Abdul Bari, Mrityunjay Jana and Mahatab Das. The incidents of hunger strike was published in the daily news papers and thereupon all over West Bengal the people particularly the congress activists were informed regarding the corruption of MDC party. Without assuring to solve the problem Chief Minister Prafulla Chandra Sen telegraphically requested Mr. Dhara to end his fast. He also wrote a letter to Dhara wherein he narrated that hunger strike would undermine the party's internal solidarity.[122] Later on with the request of many congress leaders of West Bengal specially Ajay Mukherjee after seven days of his fasting Mr. Dhara ended his fast.[123]

Ajay Mukherjee's Appeal for Kamraj's Intervention

In the meanwhile, when the hunger strike was going on against the corruption then Ajay Mukherjee felt the need for external help to control the situation. In a letter to AICC President Kamraj he accused the MDCC president and his supporters indulging in an 'unfair practices' with regard to the enrolment of new party members. He also sought to Kamraj's personal intervention in it.[124] Mukherjee's efforts to enlist external help invited reaction to the Mohanty Group. One of the spokesmen of that group remarked that the PCC president Ajay Mukherjee identified himself with a faction. He also refuted the charge of 'unfair practices' and blaming the hunger strikers said that they had "no other way to capture" the parry ogganisation.[125]Ajay Mukherjee sent a telegram to Kamraj again in which he stated, "Midnapore situation is fast deteriorating. Excitement was rapidly increasing. Your intervention is immediately solicited".[126] But, Mukherjee's hope of enlisting Kamraj's help had faded away in the ground when T. Manean, general secretary of the AICC, informed Mukherjee that the complaints regarding the enrolment of bogus members were vague. Only after getting the specific charges the Congress President "will look into them and take appropriate measures".[127]

Role of the Hooghly Group

When the possibility of Kamraj's intervention was diminishing then the Hooghly Group directly intervened into the Midnapore situation. Midnapore congress factionalism reached its climax in a meeting of the executive committee of the PCC at Arambag on 3rd August. Though, Ajay Mukherjee, the PCC President was also present there in spite of that the determining voice was of Atulya Ghosh. The committee carried a resolution denouncing "the anti-organizational activities of some Congressmen who were squatting before the district party office in Midnapore". Ajay Mukherjee had to give his consent to that resolution due to severe pressure created on him. Not only that, he had to listen some abuse language in that meeting. At last a three-man committee consisted by Atulya Ghosh (vice-president of PCC), Prafulla Chandra Sen (chief minister), and Rabindralal Sinha (minister-in-Charge of education) was set up and empowered it to inquire into the Midnapore happenings.[128]As per the recommendation of the three-man committee a meeting of the MDCC was summoned to resolve the factional dispute. The committee also requested its members to attend the meeting. For obvious reasons, the recommendation of the committee was not acceptable to the Mukherjee Group. Mukherjee's argument was that "The (Midnapore DCC) authorities who were the accused. So, how could they sit for judgement"? In spite of that the meeting was taken place on 3rd September, and it was not attended by Ajay Mukherjee. Charu Chandra Mohanty made a statement in that meeting regarding the happening of 23rd July and said "if he had addressed in a moment of excitement any improper words to Ajoy Mukherjee he was tendering "unqualified apology".[129] After the end of the meeting immediately Prafulla Chandra Sen informed Mukherjee about Mohanty's apology. In response to the information of P. C. Sen regarding Mohanty's apology Mukherjee replied its o. k, but the issue of question was "the unconstitutional and fraudulent methods adopted by the Mohanty Group regarding the enrolment of party members, and that was yet to be settled." In that situation, the factional conflict in the MDCC remained unsolved.[130]

Reaction of the Dismissal of Nirmalendu Dey

On the other hand, The Hooghly Group was so furious by centering the order of removal to general secretary of PCC Nirmalendu Dey, that as a counteracting it resolved to remove Ajay Mukherjee from the office of the PCC president. As a calculative measure regarding the removal of Ajay Mukherjee from the office of the PCC President a requisition meeting of the general committee of the PCC was convened by Suhrid Rudra, one of the three secretaries of PCC which was scheduled to be held on 11th September, 1965 at Kumar Singh Hall, Calcutta. It was signed by 111 members including Prafulla Chandra Sen and Atulya Ghosh. In a statement, Ajay Mukherjee remarked, "There is almost no democracy in West Bengal Congress and instead of that a 'Proto Fascist Dectatorship' has been established here. The meeting was not convened by general secretary and at the time of the convening the meeting I was not consulted as PCC President, therefore it is illegal." [131] However, the meeting was summoned on 11 September, 1965. For Ajay Mukherjee it was no doubt a serious threat to his position. Anticipating the outcome of the trial of strength in the PCC meeting, Ajay Mukherjee again drew the attention of Kamraj. In a telegram to Kamraj, Mukherjee wrote that the general secretary of the PCC had ignored his order of removal served on him, and as a consequence of that a move was under way to oust the PCC president.[132]

Meanwhile the Hooghly Group made another attempt to squeeze out Ajay Mukherjee. On 7 September, a meeting of the executive committee of the PCC was summoned by Suhrid Rudra to consider the order of removal served to the general secretary. But Ajay Mukherjee as the PCC president questioned regarding the validity of the meeting and commented that Rudra's action was ultra virus.[133] Ignoring the remarks of the PCC President the executive committee met on 7th September and condemned the action of PCC president considering the fact that he had "exceeded his powers" thereby the PCC president had ordered to remove the general secretary Nirmalendu Dey from his office without giving him any chance to explain his case.[134] The executive committee of the PCC, taking a resolution permitted Nirmalendu Dey, general secretary of the PCC to continue his work as usual. As the President of the PCC was unattended that is why Vice-President Labanyaprova Dutta conducted the meeting. [135]

On the other hand, the requisition meeting of the PCC, held on 11th September, carried a resolution expressing lack of confidence on the PCC President.[136] As the notice of the requisition meeting for the removal of Ajay Mukherjee was issued by Nirmalendu Dey and Suhrid Rudra on 2nd and 3rd September, so, the next day claiming the proposed meeting was unlawful and against any precedence, Binay Krishna Bag, one of the members of the PCC filed a suit in Calcutta High Court against Atulya Ghosh and Suhrid Rudra. Hon'ble Justice A. N. Roy in his ruling on 10th September, said that 'whatever resolution will adopt in the meeting on 11th September not be executed until the final verdict of the suit.'[137] It is needless to say that as Ajay Mukherjee earlier declared that the meeting was illegal, so he did not attend it but went to Delhi to meet Congress President Kamraj. The Delhi meeting ascertained fruitless and that ultimately paved the way for the emergence of a new party known as 'Bangla Congress'.[138] Ajay Mukherjee's attempts to gain help from central congress leaders thus futiled. The central congress leadership was either unconvinced by Mukherjee's course of action or reluctant to back Mukherjee going against the Hooghly Group led by Atulya Ghosh who was not only a very powerful congressman in the State of West Bengal but also an commanding party leader at the centre.[139]

Ajay Mukherjee's exit from the Chairmanship of the Medinipore Zilla Parishad

Whenever due to the ruling of the Hon'ble High Court a stalemate condition of the PCC was going on, in the meantime in an another requisition meeting held on 11th October, 1965 to oust Ajay Mukherjee from the post of the Chairman of the Medinipore Zilla Parishad. Rashbehari Paul, Vice-Chairman of the Zilla Parishad presided over the meeting. No-confidence proposal against Ajay Mukharjee mooted by Santosh Kumar Mukhopadhyay and seconded by Prodyut Kumar Mohanty and ultimately Ajay Mukherjee had to leave the Chairmanship of Zilla Parishad.[140]

Removal of Ajay Mukherjee from PCC Chief

During the unresolved situation of the suit and as per the ruling of the Hon'ble High Court Ajay Mukherjee remained PCC chief as usual but Nirmalendu Dey's function as general secretary was stopped. The suit was carried on for last five months. In the meantime, Ajay Mukherjee applead to all through a statement in a newspaper that who were considered to be thoughtful as well as old congressmen of West Bengal had to leave the congress party for various reason and ex-revolutionaries to help him in his efforts to reform congress from the corruption. During that time the Hon'ble High Court ordered to give penalty of Rs. 50 to Suhrid Rudra for showing his arrogance and instructed Atulya Ghosh to be present in the Court personally. However, on 6th January, 1966, Justice Shri G. K. Mitra and Shri Arun Kumar Mukherjee in their verdict clearly stated that the date of notice on 2nd and 3rd September 1965 regarding requisition meeting and the resolution of that meeting held on 11th September would not be executed. The Hon'ble Court also ordered that within 9th January, 1966 a fresh notice had to be issued through daily Ananda Bazar Patrika and Hindusthan Standards to resolve the question of the removing of the PCC president. The meeting would be held at Kumar Shing Hall of 46 no. Indian Mirror Street, Calcutta. The meeting would be presided over by a person nominated by the Indian National Congress and present members implement their voting right through secret ballots. In that context, on 10th January, 1966 Ajay Mukherjee again went to Delhi and met with Kamraj and after comprehensive discussion he requested Kamraj to help at the aim of ending anarchy in the PCC, but Kamraj was not agree with the proposal of Ajay Mukherjee. Therefore, as per the order of the Hon'ble High Court the meeting of the PCC was held on 20th January, at Kumar Shing Hall. Dr. Ram Suvag Singh presided over the meeting as central representative. In that meeting PCC passed a resolution over the no-confidence motion by a majority of 296 against 40 (they were adherents of Mukherjee) exposing lack of confidence in its President, Ajay Kumar Mukherjee, the 65 years old veteran congress leader and thereby he had automatically removed from his post.[141]

In response to a question asked by the press reporters Ajay Mukherjee remarked, "The offender did'nt know what was his offence, but judgment was over."[142] He furthermore stated that he didn't know what the reason behind that no-confidence motion was. In proposal there was no reason and even the proposer also didn't mention anything. If there was mention any reason then there was a question of answering. He narrated with an emotional voice that he was serving the congress party for 45 years but today without showing any reason why he had been deposed from the seat of the PCC president that would be deeply considered by the members he hoped. It is mention worthy that those members who had given their vote against Ajay Mukherjee showing their absolute loyalty to Atulya Ghosh and his coterie after coming out from the meeting room some of them expressed their original mental state of affairs by uttering 'whatever had done with Ajay Mukherjee was not only excessive but also unlawful.'[143] In that connection Sukharanjan Sengupta a press reporter is said to have asked Shankar Das Banerjee (one of the voting members of that day) almost secretly with a very low voice due to his personal intimacy, "whom did you cast your vote? Barrister Shankar Das Banerjee answered whisperingly and said that I had given my vote to the Judas"[144] It was the enough indication that though most of the members would believe that whatever Ajay Mukherjee had done, no doubly for the interest of the congress and whatever was doing by Atulya Ghosh and his coterie would damage the congress party in near future. The most unfortunate things was that in spite of knowing the fact the majority members had to cast their vote against Ajay Mukherjee as well as interest of the congress party because during that time Atulya Ghosh was so much powerful that most of the members had no courage as well as personality to go against the will of Atulya Ghosh.

Congress Workers Conference and Ajay Mukherjee

In spite of the happenings of all the above said matters, Ajay Mukherjee was not ready to surrender himself before the nexus without doing anything. Therefore, in order to alert the old and sincere congress activists about the upcoming crisis of the congress party in West Bengal a 'Congress Workers Conference' was convened on 5th and 6th February, in 1966 at Shyam Squire as well as Subash Bag in Calcutta. A reception committee for that conference was formed consisting Moitrayee Basu and Sushil Kumar Dhara as President and Secretary respectively. Almost six thousand and above congress activists attended the conference from the all districts of West Bengal. With the inaugural speech delivered by the old congress worker namely Ramnalini Chakrabarty, the functun of the conference was started. Most notable speakers of the conference were Ramnalini Chakrabarty, Surendranath Sarkar, Satish Chandra Samanta, Basanta Kumar Das etc. After the long discussion a chorus voice was raised from the conference i. e. "We are the Congress, not the corrupt Atulya-Prafulla coterie". A preparatory committee of 30-35 members were also formed which covered the representative of all the districts of West Bengal. Ajay Mukherjee and Sushil Dhara were selected President and General Secretary respectively and they were empowered to take any decision according to the necessity. But the most significant decision which was taken by the conference was to make a separate list of candidates, excepting the candidatures list made by the ruling faction of the party, for the coming forth general elections. In spite of the happenings of the above matters, Ajay Mukherjee and his adherents were not thinking about to quit congress with the hope that the central leadership would do something in order to end that deadlock in West Bengal congress.[145] In that Congress Workers Conference, Ajay Mukherjee also declared that his main aim was to free the country as well as congress party from corruption. In order to consider the matters relating to corruption and to take appropriate step a "Corruption Ressistance Society" was formed under the presidentship of Shri Ramnalini Chakrabarty and Shri Binay Jiban Ghosh was selected its Secretary.[146]

But, the decision to prepare a separate list of candidates for the ensuing 4th general election was not entertained by the central congress leadership. AICC President Kamraj told newsmen that only one list which would be forwarded by the PCC might be deserved consideration. He also added that the disappointed congressmen could make complaint separately and not in such a fashion.[147] In that circumstances, Ajay Mukherjee's tour of all over West Bengal and his open criticism of the congress government in the field of food crisis and the Subhas-Bag's conference in calcutta collectively provoked the state congress leadership to bring a charge against Ajay Mukherjee with having violating the party rules and acting in a manner that calculated to bring the party into disrepute. Ajay Mukherjee's answer was that "I am afraid I have nothing further to say in self-defence against your charges".[148]

Birth of Bangla Congress

However, within few days after the end of the Shyam Squire conference Ajay Mukherjee went to Jaypur in order to attend the annual conference of the AICC in 1966. But, in the meantime, the ruling faction of the WBPCC declared null and void of AICC membership of Ajay Mukherjee. However, in Jaypur Ajay Mukherjee tried his best to meet with congress President Kamraj again, but Mukherjee was not able to meet Kamraj after waiting for long time. Ajay Mukherjee also met with Prime Minister Indira Gandhi and narrated her about the happening in West Bengal congress politics. But it was difficult for the central leadership in that sensitive pre-election year to put down any decision which was against the pleasure of Atulya Ghosh and Prafulla Chandra Sen to satisfy Ajay Mukherjee and his group.[149] So, being neglected by the central leadership time and again Ajay Mukherjee had no other option but to come out from the congress fold and to form a new party at the earliest. Thereafter, with the consultation of some old congress leaders who had to leave the congress party due to the disagreement with Atulya Ghosh such as Nirmalendu Mukherjee, Indu Sengupta etc. Kamada Kinkar Mukherjee (father of Shri Pranab Mukherjee, former President of India), former MLC also inspired Ajay Babu and Sushil Dhara to proceed with their desired goal. As a result of that a preparatory meeting was held to take decision about the pros and cons regarding the formation of a new party.[150] In the second preparatory day of the formation of the new party it was unanimously resolved that a new party would be formed, but the final decision would have to be taken in the next extensive meeting. The last preparatory meeting was held on 1st May, 1966. In that meeting as the name of the new party 'Bangla Congress'[151]was accepted by all and a unanimous decision was also taken up as to the party flag, constitution and other preparatory programme of the party. It was also decided that the present preparatory committee would act as the executive committee of the party. Ajay Kumar Mukherejee, Sushil Kumar Dhara and Kanailal Bhattacharya were unanimously selected as its President, General Secretary and Treasurers respectively.[152] It may be noted that Pranab Mkherjee, son of Kamada Kinkar Mukherjee was attended one of the preparatory meeting in connection with the formation of Bangla Congress.[153] Though, Pranab Mukherjee himself claimed that he would attend the Shyam Squire meeting of the congress workers convened by Ajay Mukherjee on 5th to 6th February, 1966.[154]

It is noteworthy that the fact as it stands was in the subsequent days, the series of reverses at the hands of the left parties in the previous months on food movement, the split in the congress, the combination of all left forces, all these led to one result – the inevitable defeat of the congress party. However, what circumstances led to the decline of the congress party for the first time in West Bengal politics in the general election of 1967 were as under:

Making an Alliance against the Congress Party

In the midst of above said circumstances S. A. Dangey, CPI (R) leader came to Calcutta with the hope to make an alliance with the left communists and other left parties on the basis of a common programme to defeat congress party in West Bengal. Dange also considered the formation of the 'Bangla Congress' as a very good sign of 'healthy split'. It was an inevitable impact on people's movement at the aim of dethrones the congress party from the seat of power. [155]

Humayun Kabir Quits Congress

Actually the year of 1966 was an eventful year from the various points of view in West Bengal politics. As like as the case of Ajay Mukherjee; former Petroleum and Chemicals Minister, Humayun Kabir was also completely disillusioned about the congress leadership in West Bengal. It may be noted that when Moulana Abul Kalam Azad was in- charge of the Education Miniter of India, Humayun Kabir was the education secretary to the Ministry and later on he had to take up the portfolio of the Union State Minister- in- Charge of Education and Cultural Department. But, Humayun Kabir was not inducted in the Indira Gandhi's Ministry. As long as Humayun Kabir was the Minister of the Central Government he used to maintain a very close relation with the West Bengal Chief Minister Prafulla Chandra Sen and spent hours in his room whenever he came to Calcutta. He had exerted his influence for a petro-chemical complex in Haldia and for the development of metropolitan Calcutta. A tireless worker and a first rate intellectual Humayun Kabir had a very clean image and commanded respect from both Hindu and Muslim intelligentsia. When communalism usurped Bengal before Independence, he as a Member of the Upper House of West Bengal Assembly, fought for Hindu-Muslim unity and violently attacked Muslim League top leaders as well as Ministers like Nazimuddin, Suhrawardy and others leaders of the Treasury benches.[156]

It has already been mentioned that Humayun Kabir had good relation with Prafulla Chandra Sen but he was not in good terms with Atulya Ghosh. According to the opinion of some leaders that Humayun Kabir had a strong conviction as to a fact that he would never get a berth in Indira Gandhi's Cabinet and it was due to the conspiracy of Atulya Ghosh. From a source it is now clear that as Humayun Kabir was the selection of Pundit Nehru in his Ministry and a man of high caliber, a man like Atulya Ghosh could not comply with him. Naturally Humayun Kabir had also some negative impression about Atulya Ghosh.[157] However, after his exit from central cabinet, Humayun Kabir noticed the developments of West Bengal politics for a while and decided to quit congress and the congress parliamentary party on 8th September, 1966. In a letter to the congress president he said, "Congress in West Bengal is completely isolated" and being disgusted with "the discredited leadership and its hired supporters the people have lost all confidence on the Organisation".[158] Humayun Kabir had a forecast about the certain defeat for the congress party in West Bengal in the next election and taking into account the happenings he ultimately joined in Bangla Congress and tried his best to overthrow the congress party and its leaders namely Atulya Ghosh and Prafulla Chandra Sen from the seat of power in West Bengal.

Impact of Transport and Reserve Bank Strike

Apart from these very remarkable defections in the congress party i. e. the formation of Bangla Congress and Humayun Kabir's quit from the congress, the month of September, 1966 was noted for the transport strikes in the city of Calcutta. The transport strike continued for 44 days. During that time the employees' of Tramways and Calcutta State Transport Corporation (CSTC) and others transports were also a parties of that strike. Not only that 16 days long strike in the Reserve Bank also paralyzed the running of the State administration. The mass absenteeism of non-gazetted government employees due to the influence of the left-dominated coordination committee was a great blow to the smooth running of the state administration. Therefore, it was found that an unfavourable wave for the ruling congress party was blowing which after a while developed into a hurricane that revealed in the result of the crucial fourth general election.[159]

Political Stand of Bangla Congress

Amidst of every unfavourable atmosphere of the congress party, the most widely speculated question relating to the policies of the newly formed Bangla Congress in the upcoming fourth general election whether it would act as a rival of the Pradesh Congress as a iron hammer or a mild one. Though, both the Chief Minister and the leaders of the congress were not at all ready to entertain or give due importance to the Bangla Congress. Yet, some of the people within the government and the pro-congress mentalities were hoping about the some sort of reconciliation might happen between the congress and Bangla congress against the communists.

Following the circumstances, Ajay Mukherjee justified the formation of his party as a kind of crusade not against the congress party as such but against the 'corrupt and dictatorial' PCC leadership. Since the birth of Bangla Congress was endorsed by thousands of people all over the state and its object was to ensure so that the leaders who were then controlling the P.C.C. did not come back to power again. Moreover, after the formation of the Bangla Congress, it was found that a parallel congress was set up not only at the state level but its organization also at the district, subdivision and village levels. The office bearers of the various stages of the Bangla Congress were manned by the old and active congressmen who had detached from the parent organization. That is why Ajay Mukherjee then made a very meaningful statement. He said, "As it is impossible for his new party i.e. Bangla Congress alone to defeat the Congress party and restrain it from coming into power, for that reason his party would had to come into an understanding with the other opposition parties to avoid triangular contests in election and to ensure the defeat of Congress."[160]

Political Stand of the Congress Party to Counter the Oppositions

The West Bengal Pradesh Congress leaders felt the necessity for organizing "a counter display of strength". A large public meeting was organized by the Pradesh Congress in Calcutta Maidan on 31st July, 1966 but regarding the attending of number it could not thrash the recently held left communist assemblage in the same place. The principal speakers of that meeting were Atulya Ghosh and Prafulla Chandra Sen. Both leaders predicted a congress majority in the forthcoming general election in the state. They actually expected with a great hope that the opposition parties were not be able to set up candidates for the all 280 Assembly seats in the coming election of West Bengal. They also expected that the alliance of non-congress parties would not be effective as like as a chariot pulled by a heterogeneous group of animals. That was the technique of the West Bengal congress leadership to face the coming general election relying mostly on the divisions of the opposition instead of building up a potential and viable force within the congress party by enacting a bold and revolutionary policy to revitalize the congress workers.[161]

The Alliance - the story behind the emergence of PULF and ULF

In the last three general elections, as the opposition parties fought the election battle separately and division of the opposition votes undoubtedly helped congress party to come back power again and again. But it was first attempt to consolidate the all opposition votes against the common 'enemy' the congress party in the coming fourth general election. So, keeping in mind to resist the division of the opposition votes, the leaders of the 13 opposition in West Bengal conducted a series of negotiations to arrive at an electoral understanding between them. But only due to the dire animosity between the two sections of the communist party, C.P.I. and C.P.I. (M) the attempt of understanding was broken down. The two senior leaders who were not belonging to the communist fold i. e. Ajay Mukherjee of Bangla Congress and Hemanta Kumar Bose of the Forward Bloc took special initiative to settle the understandings by their personal contacts and appeals. Prafulla Chandra Ghosh, the first chief Minister of West Bengal and Humayun Kabir also volunteered their services with a view to achieve unity. At last there emerged two groupings i.e. ULF (United Left Front) and PULF (Peoples United Left Front) among the opposition parties. One i.e. ULF centered round the CPI (M) and the other i.e. PULF on Bangla Congress. The former group comprised of CPI (M), RSP, SSP, SUC, RCPI, Forward Bloc (Marxists) and the Workers' Party. The other group i. e. PULF comprised of Bangla Congress, CPI, Forward Bloc and Bolshevik Party. Humayun Kabir worked as like as bridge between the two fronts.[162]

Declaration of the Date of Election

On 12th January, 1967, the Election Commissioner of India announced the date of election of the West Bengal Legislative Assembly along with Loke Sabha which was scheduled to be held on 19th February, (one day) between 7-30 a.m. to 4-30 p.m. In that fourth general election in West Bengal there were 280 Legislative Assembly seats and 40 Parliamentary seats. According to the declaration of the election commission it was decided that the counting of votes would be held on 21st February, both all the Assembly and Lok Sabha seats.[163]

Country's Attention to Arambagh Poll

A few days letter when the possibility of the formation of a United Front between the ULF and the PULF was dashed then it was announced in the press that PULF (which comprised the Bangla Congress, CPI(R), Forward Bloc and the Bolshevik Party) would contest 190 Assembly and 25 Parliamentary seats. The CPI was given the permission to set up 57 candidates, Bangla Congress 80, Forward Bloc 47 and Bolshevic Party 4 Assembly seats respectively. Out of 25 Parliamentary seats the CPI fielded 10 candidates, Forward Bloc 6 and Bangla Congress 8. Prafulla Chandra Ghosh, the former Chief Minister, filed his nomination paper as an independent candidate from Jhargram Assembly Constituency in Midnapore district with the support of the PULF.[164] As the Bangla Congress was formed as protest against the corrupt leadership of Atulya Ghosh-Prafulla Chandra Sen and their coterie, so it was intended from the opposition bloc that a candidate must have to be filed against Prafulla Chandra Sen in Arambagh. In that case Jyoti Basu of CPI (M) and Hemanta Basu of Forward Bloc, the two famous leader were not agree to contest against Prafulla Chandra Sen for the supposed defeat in the hands of Prafulla Chandra Sen. But it was Ajay Mukherjee who first raised his voice against the corrupt leadership of PCC and decided to contest against Prafulla Chandra Sen. He also filed his nomination paper in his home constituency Tamluk.[165] Naturally, following Ajay Mukherjee's announcement to contest against Prafulla Chandra Sen reflected widespread interest in the political circle in West Bengal.[166]

Thereafter, the Chief Minister had to put forth his best efforts to effective his election machinery in Arambagh. On January 17, a month before of that polling the congress party organized a mammoth meeting at Arambagh which was to be addressed by Atulya Ghosh and Prafulla Chandra Sen. Union Finance Minister, Sachin Chowdhury was also contesting for the Parliamentary seat as a congress candidate from that area. The first meeting was disturbed due to the student demonstrations of the 'Netaji College' of Arambagh. At that crucial time a bulk of students under the leadership of very enthusiastic and joyous student leader Abdul Mannan joined Ajay Mukherjee's camp. Though, Bangla Congress had no as such strong organization in Arambagh, inspite of that by dint of extraordinary organizational capability of Sushil Dhara, general secretary of Bangla Congress, a strong support base in favour of Ajoy Mukherjee was established. In that case by centering Bibhuti Roy, a Madhyamick school teacher, Abani Hota, Nukul Pal along with student leader Mannan – a strong election campaigning group was organized which helped to create a crack in the stronghold of Prafulla Chandra Sen's Arambagh constituency and as a result of that the smooth sailing was not going in the Assembly election of Arambagh.[167]

As Prafulla Chandra Sen was the Chief Minister and doing his political work from pre-independence days that is why he had also diehard followers in Arambagh. Naturally there was a kind of phobia among the people to go against Prafulla Babu. But that phobia had gone away after the resistance of some atrocities of the congress party by the student-people joint effort and organized an ever biggest election meeting in Arambagh which was addressed by the famous press reporter Vivekananda Mukhopadhyay, Humayun Kabir, Satish Chandra Samanta, Hemanta Basu, Somenath Lahiri and others. Naturally, there was a tough election fight started between Ajay Mukherjee and Prafulla Chandra Sen in Arambagh. Therefore, according to the demand of the followers of Prafulla Chandra Sen, he had to give more attention towards his own constituency and as a result of that he had no enough time to address the election meeting throughout the West Bengal.[168]

Fourth General Election

However, in the light of above mentioned situations, the crucial Forth General Election[169] in West Bengal commenced on 19th February, 1969. On the whole the general pattern of the electoral fight all over the state was mainly triangular i. e. Congress, the Peoples United Left Front (PULF) and the United Left Front (ULF). The ruling party was in the mood to take advantages from the divisions of the two left fronts. The polling throughout the State of West Bengal was generally free from violence which many had feared. Obviously, it was indicated the growing political awareness among the voters who cast their votes. With the end of the polling in an almost a peaceful manner, the peoples as a whole were eagerly waiting for its results particularly the outcome of three constituencies i. e. Arambagh where Ajay Mukherjee and Prafulla Chandra Sen were the main contestants, Bankura Parliamentary constituency where Atulya Ghosh[170] and Jitendra Mohan Biswas were fighting their electoral battle against each other and Baranagar from where Jyoti Basu was contesting against congress candidate Amarendranath Bhattacharya.[171]

Results

On 22nd February, 1967 the results of 36 West Bengal Assembly constituencies including seven in Calcutta showed that the congress party captured 17 seats against 19 seats obtained by the opposition parties. Around 5 O' clock in the afternoon a message was spread that in the Bankura Parliamentary constituency Atulya Ghosh, the congress candidate was trailing behind his contestant Jitendra Mohan Biswas by several thousand votes. If Atulya Ghosh was defeated then what remains in the congress party of Bengal? After hearing that news the Chief Minister Prafulla Chandra Sen's prompt reaction was-"What, Atulya is suffering a reverse? I am going to Congress office".[172] The news spread as like as wild fire in the press room as well as from mouth to mouth and reached the ears of VIPs who were in writers' Buildings in the afternoon that Atulya Ghosh had been defeated by J. M. Biswas, CPI candidate with a margin of 29,770 votes. The number of votes cast in favour of J. M. Biswas was 1, 20,590 against 90,820 of Atulya Ghosh.[173]

On 23rd February was a very tragic day not only for the Chief Minister P. C. Sen but also for the ruling congress party. That day counting of votes decided the fate of many stalwarts which was a turning point in the political scenario of India. By about 8.30 a. m. it was almost clear that Chief Minister P. C. Sen was going down and expressed an opinion that he was going to defeat. With a low-spirited face the Chief Minister slowly said, "The Communists are coming. The prospects of Congress victory in this State are bleak".[174]However, after a neck to neck fight, at last defeating P. C. Sen with a margin of 881 votes, Ajay Mukherjee came into victorious in the prestigious Arambagh constituency.[175] Besides, the defeat of Atulya Ghosh and Prafulla Chandra Sen, the embarrassment of the congress party was not completed. More than half of the cabinet members such as Saila Kumar

Mukherjee, Jagannath Koley, Tarun Kanti Ghosh, Maya Banerjee, Shyamadas Bhattacharjee, Samarajit Banerjee and even Deputy Speaker Naren Sen were also rejected by the electorates.[176]

The Congress party secured 127 seats and the 14 non-Congress political parties and independents collectively captured 153 seats. The People's United Left Front (PULF) led by Ajay Mukherjee had secured 65 seats (Bangla Congress 35 of which Ajay Babu himself won from two constituency i.e. Tamluk and Arambagh, CPI- 16 and Forward Bloc- 14). The United Left Front (ULF) led by the left communist leader Jyoti Basu had captured 64 seats (CPI-M,- 43, SSP- 07, RSP- 07, Socialist Unity Centre- 04, Workers' Party- 02 and Marxist Forward Bloc- 01.)[177]

Peoples - the Last Word in Democracy

On the basis of the above said matters one may claim that the real architects of the victory against the congress party led by Atulya Ghosh were not mainly the political leaders, but the common people who had decided to farewell congress from power. The crucial role played by the Bangla Congress and its leader Ajay Mukherjee was also a very undeniable matter behind the defeat of the congress. In that connection, it may be mentioned that though the oppositions particularly the two left parties were not able to unite themselves against the congress party in order to oust from the power, but it was the people of West Bengal who had defeated congress. The entire matter had been reported in the contemporary Weekly news paper as the title of "People's Initiative" in the following way, "However, even as the rank and file was expressing regret at their leaders' refusal to confront the congress unitedly and debating which among them was more responsible for Left disunity, more results poured in which to the surprise of many people indicated that the Congress was on the point of overthrown despite all the circumstances favouring it. The common voter had evidently taken matters in their own hands. Soon the gloom was lifted and as the people had learnt of the defeat of Congress boss Atulya Ghosh at the hands of the CPI's J. M. Biswas and that of Chief Minister P. C. Sen by the Bangla Congress chief Ajoy Mukherjee, joyus crowds poured into the streets of Calcutta celebrating the two events." [178]

On 24th February the PULF and the ULF after meeting informally made a joint statement announcing in view of the serious obligation imposed on them by the electors to unite and form a non-congress Government.

Causes behind the fall of the Congress in Fourth General Election, 1967

In this respect let us look at the overall position of the congress and the symptoms of decline. The causes that led to the downfall of the congress party in West Bengal for the first time after Independence was a very significant question to the researchers. There were so many questions which had aroused behind the fall of the congress party in the fourth general election. There was popular displeasure against administration run by the congress leaders and gradual isolation of the party from the common people specially after the death of Jawaharlal Nehru in national level and B. C. Roy in West Bengal which ultimately led to the debacle in the poll. Not only that, when P. C. Sen Ministry was in a very odd position regarding the controlling of food movement and transport strike, almost at the same time misbehavior with veteran congress leader Ajay Mukherjee and as an inevitable consequence of that matter- the split among the congress as well as emergence of Bangla Congress also played vital role behind the fall of the congress in the election of 1967. In that context it is proper to mention that regarding the formation of Bangla Congress, Prafulla Chandra Sen himself acknowledged, "Ajoy Babu was dropped from the Cabinet in the plea of Kamraj Plan and he was dismissed from the Congress party for the interest of narrow group politics. West Bengal Congress had done great unjust and tried to defame Ajoy Baby without any reason and as a result of that he formed Bangla Congress with deep sorrow and sufferings."[179] In one of his writings entitled, "Atulya and Myself" Prafulla Chandra Sen confessed that at the time of dismissal of Ajay Mukherjee from congress he had committed a great mistake following the Atulya Ghosh's attitude.

There was another reason which crippled the vitality of the administration. Some important figures of the party machinery and their associates used some of the Ministers and their department as honeycomb to fulfill their personal ends. People's money instead of welfare activities were being drained into their pockets towards the end of the Ministry. However, the reputation of the congress government was submerged and people were losing faith gradually in the party and in the administration which reflected in the election of 1967. Apart from the above reasons—cordoning system during the time of severe food shortage, levy system as well as collection of food grain from the big cultivators instead of government prices, growing discontent among the business classes and common masses, inactive of the congress party before the fictitious propaganda of the opposition parties particularly the communists against many auspicious measures taken by the Chief Minister Prafulla Chandra Sen in order to soothe the people of over-crowded problem ridden state of West Bengal. Another most important factor which led to the fall of the congress party in that election was Muslim votes. As after the partition most of the Muslim League leaders had joined in the congress party with the hope that the congress would at least protect the interest of the Muslim community. But the communal riots in the year of 1964 had broken the hope of the Muslim community. Not only that during the India-Pakistan war in 1965, many Muslim leaders were arrested under D. I. Rule by West Bengal Government which enraged the Muslim people. That displeasure of the Muslim community people were consolidated mainly in the district of Nadia and 24-Parganas under the leadership of Kabir brothers i. e. Humayun Kabir and Jahangir Kabir and had given their verdict against the congress party in the election of 1967.[180]

Notes and References

1. Prafulla Kumar Chakrabarty, *op.cit.*p.361.
2. Dr. Binay Krishna Mukhopadhyay, *Nilkantha Prafulla Chandra* (in Bengalee), Janaswartha Barta, Kolkata, 2015, p. 291; Also see *"Bidhan Chandra Karnadhar Tabu Khandita Banglar Nabhishvas"* A Bengali Article by Amalendu Dey in *Saat Dashak Samokal O Ananda Bazar*, Ananda Publishers, Kolkata, 2013, p. 104.
3. Saroj Chakrabarty, ... *Chief Ministers,* p. 1.
4. *Ibid.,* p. 64.
5. Dr. Binay Krishna Mukhopadhyay, *op.cit.*p.7.
6. Saroj Chakrabarty, ... *Chief Ministers,* p. 05.
7. *Ibid.,* p.2.
8. Prafulla Kumar Chakrabarty, *op.cit.*p.359.
9. Saroj Chakrabarty, ... *Chief Ministers,* p.3.
10. Prasanta Sengupta, *op.cit.*p.46.
11. Dr. Binay Krishna Mukhopadhyay, *op.cit.*pp.295-296.
12. Saroj Chakrabarty, ... *Chief Ministers,* p. 2.
13. *Ibid.*
14. *Ibid.,* p. 8.
15. Prasanta Sengupta, *op.cit.*p.46.
16. Saroj Chakrabarty, ... *Chief Ministers,* p. 9.
17. *Ibid.,* p.6.

18. *Ibid.,* p.7.
19. *Ibid.,* p.10.
20. Dr. Binay Krishna Mukhopadhyay, *op.cit.*p.297.
21. *Ibid.,* pp.297-298.
22. *Ibid.,* pp.10- 11.
23. *Ibid.,* p.298.
24. *Ibid.,* p.299.
25. Saroj Chakrabarty, ... *Chief Ministers,* pp. 14-15; also see *Ibid.,* pp. 299-300.
26. Saroj Chakrabarty, ... *Chief Ministers,* p. 50.
27. Dr. Binay Krishna Mukhopadhyay, *op.cit.*p.300.
28. *Ibid.,* pp. 302-303.
29. Dr. Pratap Chandra Chaunder, *Amar Suhrid P.C. Sen, Janatar Katha* (in Bengali), p. 37, cited in Dr. Binay Krishna Mukhopadhyay, *op.cit.*p. 302.
30. Dr. Binay Krishna Mukhopadhyay, *op.cit.*p. 303; Also see, Saroj Chakrabarty, ... *Chief Ministers,* p. 15.
31. See Saroj Chakrabarty, ... *Chief Ministers,* pp. 16-17. In stead of 42 Ratendone Road, New Delhi where former Chief Minister Dr. B. C. Roy used to stay while at Delhi.
32. *Ibid.,* pp. 16-17.
33. *Ibid.,* pp. 17-18.
34. *Ibid.*
35. *Ibid.,* pp. 18-22.
36. *Ibid.,* pp. 27-28.
37. That was the first time since India became Independent that Government declared a State of Emergency. See, *Ibid.,* pp. 28-29.
38. *Ibid.,* pp. 28-29.
39. On November 21, a Chinese Govt. statement issued from Peking to foreign correspondents said: "Beginning from December 1, 1962, Chinese frontier guards will withdraw to positions 20 kilo miles (12.5 miles) behind the lines of actual control which existed between China and India on November 7, 1959". See *Ibid.,* p. 32.
40. *Ibid.,* p.34.
41. *Ibid.,* pp. 34-35.
42. *Ibid.,* p. 38.
43. *Ibid.,* pp. 84-85. The expelled members were P. Sundaryya, M. Basavapunniah, P. Rammurthi, A. K. Gopalan, Hare Krishna Konar, Promode Dasgupta and H. S. Surjeet. Amongst those suspended were Jyoti Basu and E. M. S.

Nambudripad. See Saroj Chakrabarty, ... *Chief Ministers,* pp. 84-85. On the other hand a nine member Secretariat was set up on 12th July, 1964 with Bhowani Sen as Secretary by the minority rightist section of the C.P.I.'s West Bengal Council. (Of the 96 members 23 were present at the meeting.) The deliberation was carried by Rajeswar Rao and P. C. Joshi of the Central Secretariat. The foundation of the parallel Secretariat was predicted in political circles as the first necessary step towards the formal recognition by the Party's top leadership that possibly the split in the C. P. I. was unbridgeable. It might be noted here that West Bengal was the only State Party Unit which was dominated by the leftists. See Saroj Chakrabarty, ... *Chief Ministers,* p. 102.

44. *Ibid.,* pp. 48-49. Actually, the Colombo Conference of six non-aligned nations, consisting of Indonesia, Burma, Cambodia, Ghana, U. A. R. and Ceylon, with the object of carrying on negotiations with Peking and Delhi about their proposal which was kept very secret at that time. See Saroj Chakrabarty, ... *Chief Ministers*, p. 38. The aim of the conference was to ensure a truce between the two warring countries. The Conference had given charge to the Prime Minister of Ceylone, Mrs. Bandarnaike to carry on discussion with the Chinese and Indian leaders and their recommendations in this respect. See, Saroj Chakrabarty, ... *Chief Ministers*, p.42.
45. *Ibid.,* p. 51.
46. *Ibid.,* p. 57.
47. *Ibid.,* p. 69.
48. *Ibid.,* pp.72-73; Also see Dr. Binay Krishna Mukhopadhyay, *op.cit.*p.312.
49. Saroj Chakrabarty, ... *Chief Ministers*, pp.104-105.
50. Proceedings of the West Bengal Legislative Assembly on 16th July 1963.
51. Saroj Chakrabarty, ... *Chief Ministers*, pp. 53-54; Also see Dr. Binay Krishna Mukhopadhyay, *op.cit.*p. 305.
52. Saroj Chakrabarty, ... *Chief Ministers*, pp. 54-55; Also see Dr. Binay Krishna Mukhopadhyay, *op.cit.*p. 304.
53. Saroj Chakrabarty, ... *Chief Ministers*, p. 104.
54. Prasanta Sen Gupta, op.cit. 88.
55. *Shatang Jibatu,* Durdarshan, *cited in,* Dr. Binay Krishna Mukhopadhyay, *op. cit.* p. 313.
56. Dr. Binay Krishna Mukhopadhyay, *op.cit.*p. 316.
57. *Ibid.,* pp.50, 308.
58. *Ibid.,*p. 309.
59. Saroj Chakrabarty, ... *Chief Ministers*, pp. 66-67.
60. Dr. Binay Krishna Mukhopadhyay, *op.cit.*p. 314. As per Government records, during that time there were 60 thousands stockiest in the state and each and every stockist had at least 100 maund of rice as stock. Besides, rice would

produce almost 1.3 million tons in 6 hundreds rice mill and in 7 thousands rice breaking machine in the state. Moreover, the agricultural production of that year was almost satisfactory. So, it was not possible for the state government to accept the price hike of the food grains and considered it as a men made crisis. The Government would think that if the stockists as well as growers remained under control then the gradual price hike of the food grain may be controlled. Considering the above fact 177 raids were carried out in Calcutta on rice shops and 206 fish stalls simultaneously and as a result of that 43 offenders were arrested. At the aim of the fixing of food market Government ordered fixing of prices of mustard oil at the rate of Rs. 3 and meat at Rs. 4 per kg. Despite vigorous attempts taken by the State Government it was found that in the month of May-June the prices of three essential commodities i.e. rice, fish and mustard oil again started rising. Therefore, every attempt in the field of the price fixation by the Government failed miserably to achieve its ultimate goal owing to conspiracy of the immodest profiteers. See Saroj Chakrabarty, ... *Chief Ministers*, pp. 87-88.

61. Saroj Chakrabarty, ... *Chief Ministers*, p.98; Also see Dr. Binay Krishna Mukhopadhyay, *op.cit.* p. 315.
62. Saroj Chakrabarty, ... *Chief Ministers*, pp. 112-113.
63. *Ibid.*, p. 82; Also see Dr. Binay Krishna Mukhopadhyay, *op.cit.* p. 318.
64. Saroj Chakrabarty, ... *Chief Ministers*, p.82.
65. *Ibid.*, p.83; Also see Dr. Binay Krishna Mukhopadhyay, *op.cit.* p. 319.
66. *"Bharater Khadyaniti"*, a Bengali article by Atulya Ghosh, in *Ananda Bazar Patrika,* 28th February, 1966; Also see, Prafulla Kumar Chakrabarty, *op.cit.* pp. 370-373.
67. *Ananda Bazar Patrika,* 17th February, 1966.
68. *Ananda Bazar Patrika,* 18th February, 1966. In the meanwhile, after reaching the news of the death of Ali Hafez (one of the six persons who received bullet injuries on 16th February) due to police firing on 16th February the people of Basirhat burst into anger and that grudge had extended in Bongaon, Barracpur and in Naihati. The death of Nurul Islam naturally lead to the observance of protest day on 17th February that turned into a field of direct conflict between police of the government and the common people. After that the movement gradually spread in Nadia, Murshidabad and Calcutta. However, on 17th February in the day of students-strike the students along with long procession from Calcutta University went to Assembly House in order to submit a memorandum to Chief Minister. Addressing the students Somenath Lahiri, Dr. Narayan Ray, Ila Mitra, Nikhil Das etc. delivered their speech in front of the entrance gate of the Assembly House. See *Ananda Bazar Patrika,* 18th February, 1966. Before reaching the procession of the students at Assembly House the opposition leaders demanded judicial enquiry of the police firing at Basirhat. But as soon as when the Chief Minister rejected the opposition demand for judicial enquiry Kamal Guha, a Forward Bloc leader had torn the

wire of microphone. After that the opposition walked out from the Assembly House and thereafter coming back when they were observing silences in the memory of the martyr then Dr. Maitryee Basu of congress party joined with them. Somenath Lahiri after congratulating to Dr. Maitree Basu stated in his speech that 'this Assembly Session started with police firing'. He also stated that the incident of Basirhat was only initiation and its protest just started now. See *Somenath Lahiri Rachana Sangraha,* vol. iv. (in Bengali), 1995, p.156.

69. *Ananda Bazar Patrika,* 20th February, 1966.
70. Upananda Mukhopadhyaya, *Ei Police Jiban* (in Bengali), 1987, p. 73.
71. *Ananda Bazar Patrika,* 19, 20 and 23th February, 1966.
72. *Ananda Bazar Patrika,* 20th February, 1966.
73. *Saat Dashak, Samakal O Ananda Bazar, Ananda Bazar Patrika Sankalon,* 1999, p.122; also see *Dainik Basumati,* 11th March, 1966.
74. Prafulla kumar Chakrabarty, *op.cit.*p.372.
75. *Ibid.,*.pp.383-384.
76. Saroj Chakrabarty, ... *Chief Ministers*, p. 151.
77. *Ibid.*, p. 152.
78. *Rakte Ranga Krishnagar* (in Bengali), Nadia Mukur Prakashana, April, 1966. pp. 21-22; Also see *Dainik Basumati,* 5th March, 1966.
79. *Rakte Ranga Krishnagar, op.cit.* p. 22-23. Following the death of Ananda Hait, the aggrieved people of Krishnagar ignoring the instruction of state administration organized a mourning procession with the dead body of Ananda Hait on 5th March, 1966. See *Rakte Ranga Krishnagar*, *op.cit.*p.7; Also see *Ananda Bazar Patrika, Dainik Basumati,* 6th March, 1966. The people of Krishnagar were so furious that the demonstrators started setting ablaze the Krishnagar railway station, police out post at Anandamayeetala, Bank, Settlement Office, Cooperative Office and more some Government Offices. Not only that the house of the Fazlur Rahaman, Minister-in-Charge of Fisheries and Khadi Bhawan were also attacked. On the same day the railway station of Madanpur and Payradanga in Nadia and at Birati and some other rail station in 24-Parganas were set on fire. Violent mobs burnt railway coaches, cut off telephone and telegraph wires and created barricades in the National Highway which leading to Krishnagar and adjoining areas isolated for a while from the rest of the country. The teen-age agitators also burnt the offices of the Life Insurance Corporation, District School Board and the Refugee Rehabilitation Ministry at Krishnagar. See, Prafulla Kumar Chakrabarty, *op.cit.*pp.384-85. In that situation whenever police intended to fire to disperse the agitated mobs then the youths instead of retreat they had opened the buttons of their shirt and welcomed the police in shouting voice to fire themselves as much as they could. As a result of the police firing in Krishnagar on 5th March two teenagers namely Hari Biswas and Arjun Ghosh were lost their lives. On the other side

two police personnel namely Jatin Dutta and Sudarshan Ghosh also had been died in the hands of the violent mobs. See, *Rakte Ranga Krishnagar, op.cit.* pp. 6-11 and 23-24. After considering the nature of the agitation of Krishnagar, Hiren Dasgupta thought that the student unrest of Krishnagar had converted into 'Student Revolt'. It was easy to assume that the demands of the movement were not confined for food, actually the agitators as if wanted to destroy the whole Government. See, Hiren Dasgupta O Harinarayan Adhikary, *Rajnaitik Patabhumite Bharatiya Upmahadesher Chhatra Aandalon* (in Bengali), Radical Impression, Calcutta, 1993, p.466.

80. *Ananda Bazar Patrika, Dainik Basumati,* 5th March, 1966.

81. *Ananda Bazar Patrika,* 6th March, 1966.

82. *The Statesman,* 29th March 1966.

83. *The Statesman,* 11th March 1966.The main disturbed centres in Calcutta on 11th March were Subodh Mallick Squire, Chittaranjan Avenue, Ahiritola, Bagbazar, Dum Dum, Entally, Bhwanipur, Behala, Metiaburuj etc. Barricades were made on the road by the dram, branches of trees and other general carriers. Severe scuffle broke out between police and demonstrators at Bidan Street in north Calcutta and Bowbazar-Wellington in Middle Calcutta. Besides, these two areas police firings were also broke out at Howrah, Kashipur, Agarpara, Sodepur, etc. The house of prominent Congress leader Pratap Chandra Chunder at Nirmal Chandra Street was attacked. Asit Gupta and Jiban Ghosh of Hidaram Banerjee Lane and Ashim Mitra, Bhanu Paul, Shanti Ghosh, Jagadish Thaper and Alok Majumder of Howrah were also lost their lives due to police firing on 11th March, 1966. See *Dainik Basumati,* 12th March, 1966. Not only that Post offices, Thanas, mobile police vehicles, trams, State bus goomties and milk distributions were also attacked. The most affected areas were mainly Barisa, Sarsuna, Thakurpukur, Jinjrapole and Sakherbazar. The Behala Thana was attacked three times and a teen ager was killed in police firing. Belghoria and Panihati Thanas were attacked with bombs and crackers. Police bullets killed a man at Beliaghata. Barricades were put up at Sealdah and other places to prevent the movement of police vehicles and fire engines. See, Prafulla kumar Chakrabarty, *op.cit.*p.387. In North Bengal at Alipurduar in the district of Jalpaiguri disturbances were broke out in several places. The railway station at Alipurduar was also set on fire. At Falakata the B.D.O.'s office was attacked and side by side telephone and telegraph wires were cut off. See Prafulla kumar Chakrabarty, *op.cit.*p.387.

84. *The Statesman,* 12th March, 1966; also see Prafulla kumar Chakrabarty, *op.cit.*p.388.

85. *The Statesman,* 28th March, 1966.

86. *Ajishnu Bhattacharya-r Rachana* (in Bengali), published in the *'Parichaya' Magh, 1372 (B.S.), cited in Bikshubdha Bangla, p.73.*

87. Saroj Chakrabarty, ... *Chief Ministers*, pp. 153-154.

88. *Ibid.,* pp.154-155. After emerging from Chief Ministers room Atulya Ghosh told the waiting Pressmen, "Nobody has said anything behind the Chief Minister's back. Whatever contrary views some of his fellow workers had held were placed before him and his final decisions have been accepted by all". P. C. Sen remarked that he had no allegation against the Centre as well as the party or the administration. His colleagues those who were present there expressed full confidence in the political judgment of P. C. Sen and hoped that as a loyal and devoted leader he (Sen) would be led by the counsel of his party men and friends apart from the organization.
89. *Ibid.,* pp. 155-156.
90. Prafulla kumar Chakrabarty, *op.cit.*p.381.
91. *Ibid.,* p.380.
92. *Ibid.*
93. It was the State food procurement policy and the cordoning system that had brought the West Bengal in such a position that the police could capitalize of the peoples adversity. Police created obstruction in the way of common people if they would carry a little amount of rice from one place to another place. Police would generally snatch the rice and torture them, whereas in lieu of getting money they silently allowed many Lorries which were filled with rice. So, the general anger of the common people was directed against the Government under whose control police would discharge their duties. See, Dr. Binay Krishna Mukhopadhyay, *op.cit.*p.340.
94. Prafulla kumar Chakrabarty, *op.cit.* p. 380; Also see Dr. Binay Krishna Mukhopadhyay, *op.cit.*p.340.
95. Bipan Chandra, et. al, *India After Independence-1947-2000,* Penguin Books, New Delhi, 2000, p. 261. As per the implementation of the Kamraj plan*, after the withdrawal of the six Union Minnister including Morarji Desai from the Central Cabinet - some senior Congress leaders from the South Indian States and Bengal included Neelam Sanjiva Reddy, the Andhra leader, Nijalingappa, the Chief Minister of Mysore, Kamraj, the then President of Tamilnadu Pradesh Congress Committee, Member of Congress Working Committee and Parliamentary Board of Indian National Congress, became famous throughout the country for his plan and Atulya Ghosh of Bengal met at Tirupathi outwardly to offer worship at the famous Vaishnavite shrine of South India in September 1963, but mainly to take consultation together about the problems facing the country. That was the beginning of what later entitled by a section of the Press as the 'Syndicate' which had been played a significant part in the election of K. Kamraj as the President of All India Congress party as well as Lal Bahadur Shastri as leader of succession to Nehru. They were also the mastermind behind the selection of Indira Gandhi as the next Prime Minister of the country after the death of Lalbahadur Shastri. S. K. Patil also became closely associated in that group from its inception. See V. K. Narasimhan, *Kamraj- A study*, National Book Trust, Publication Division, Ministry of Information and Broadcasting, Government of India, pp.104-105.

*Kamraj Plan: In the mid-1950s the cry of 'after Nehru, who?' was first heard. It became more pointed in the spring of 1962 when Nehru's serious illness was reported. Though he recovered in quick time but Nehru acquired a slight gravitate and 'probably he will never be the same again'. See *The Statesman,* August 3, 1962. Besides serious upset about India's military reverses in 1962 in India-China war, the most astonishing event for the Indian National Congress was the party's defeat in three crucial bye-elections to Lok Sabha in U. P. and Gujrat i. e. Amroha, Farukhabad and Rajkot in the spring of 1963. See Michael Brecher, *Succession in India: A study in Decision Making,* Oxford University Press, London, 1966, p.7. In that context, a 'simple but revolutionary plan' was presented to Nehru at Hyderabad in July 1963 by Kumaraswami Kamaraj Nadar, the then Chief Minister of Madras, (present Tamul Nadu) as well as topmost congress politician in South India. Kamraj apprised Nehru about his desire to leave the office of the Chief Minister for the necessity of party work. The plan, masterminded by Kamraj, demanded the resignation of senior congressmen in Government at the Centre as well as in the States on the ground it was not proper for the organization, if the top ranking congress leaders preferred to remain in Ministerial office for long and lost proximity with the masses. The idea was originated into the mind of K. Kamraj Nadar out of the feeling that he was getting out of contact with the mass people and that if he would give up the Chief Ministership and engaged himself to the organizational work then it would be very much effective to revitalize the party organization which will be better to face the next elections. Kamraj also worried after feeling over the factions and competitions for power in the congress party in many states and felt that in order to set up an example some top leaders should giving up office willfully and devoting themselves to the party work to keep touch with the common people. See V. K. Narasimhan, *op.cit,* pp. 97-98. The Prime Minister Nehru welcomed the idea and thought that if that practice would be applied on a large scale throughout the country then a new image of the congress party would be reflected in the public mind. Note: Though many commentators claimed that the whole 'Kamraj Plan' was developed with a very tactful move of the Prime Minister Nehru to get rid of the some Cabinet Ministers whom he wanted to give up and also revoke some of the Chief Ministers who were inventing problems in their States. See V. K. Narasimhan, *op.cit.* pp. 99-100. However, the Congress Working Committee and All India Congress Committee in its meeting held on 10th August, 1963, endorsed the 'Kamraj Plan' which was considered a great personal triumph for Kamraj. Not only that with the endorsement of Kamraj Plan, the AICC carried the 'party before post' resolution at the same time on 10th August, 1963. See Prasanta Sen Gupta, *op.cit.* pp. 48-49; Also see V. K. Narasimhan, *op.cit.* pp. 101-102.

96. Saroj Chakrabarty, ... *Chief Ministers,* pp. 147-149; Also see V. K. Narasimhan, *op.cit.* pp.132 -139.

97. Shree Radhakrishna Bari, (ed.), *Ajoyeo Purush- Ajoy Kumar* (in Bengali), on behalf of Tamralipta Swdhinata Sangram Itihas Committee, Parvatipur, Tamluk, Midnapore, Banirupa Press, Calcutta, 1990, p.139.

98. Prasanta Sen Gupta, *op.cit.*p.49.
99. Saroj Chakrabarty, ... *Chief Ministers*, p.56.
100. Shree Radhakrishna Bari, (ed.), *op.cit.*p.140.
101. Saroj Chakrabarty, ... *Chief Ministers*, p.59; also see Shree Radhakrishna Bari, (ed.), *op.cit.* pp. 140-141.
102. Prasanta Sen Gupta, *op.cit.*p 50.
103. Saroj Chakrabarty, ... *Chief Ministers*, pp.70-72.
104. *Ibid.*, p. 74.
105. Sushil Kumar Dhara, *Prabaha* -Vol. II, (in Bengali), Janakalyan Trust, Mahishadal, Midnapore, 1995, pp.104-105, 128.
106. *Ibid.*
107. Prasanta Sen Gupta, *op.cit.*pp.47-48.
108. Shree Radhakrishna Bari, (ed.), *op.cit.*p.110.
109. Prasanta Sen Gupta, *op.cit.* p.48.
110. Sushil Kumar Dhara, *op.cit.*p.101.
111. Shree Radhakrishna Bari, (ed.), *op.cit.*p.141.
112. *Ibid.*,.p.142.
113. Prasanta Sen Gupta, *op.cit.*p.50.
114. Personal interview with Sukharanjan Sengupta, a veteran journalist of West Bengal, on 5th February 2017.
115. Sushil Kumar Dhara, *op.cit.*pp.109, 121.
116. Sushil Kumar Dhara, *op.cit.* pp. 122-123.
117. *The Statesman*, July 27, 1965.
118. Prasanta Sen Gupta, *op.cit.* p.51. In other words- as alleged that the bogus membership form was pouring into the Medenipore District Congress party office, so, according to the allegation of Sushil Dhara after keeping the deposited form into a room until last date of submission the key of lock of that room was remained in the hands of MDCC President in presence of PCC president in order to stop the entry of the further bogus form. Though District Congress President, Charu Chandra Mohanty had extended three days one by one for the submission of membership form according to the need of Prabir Jana and his coterie. It was also menticnable that a kind of contest was going on between two factions of the Midnapore District Congress party over the question of enrolling highest number of active member. Therefore, before counting the actual figure of the both factions, the supporters of the factions and their leaders also remained in the office premises and above all Ajay Mukherjee and Charu Chandra Mohanty would remain in the party office to observe the situation. In that context, when Sushil Dhara went to the office of the District Magistrate to inquire over the question of the deployment of

police in the party office. In the meantime some followers of Prabir Jana and his group forced Ajay Mukherjee to leave the party office in presence of Charu Chandra Mohanty at 10 p.m. on 23rd July 1965. It is amazing! How dare they were to oust the PCC President from the district party office by his subordinate party leaders. It was clearly understood that those who had done that nefarious work their main source of strength was Bodu Babu and his closeness with Atulya Ghosh. See, Sushil Kumar Dhara, *op.cit.* pp.125.128.

119. Shree Radhakrishna Bari, (ed.), *op.cit.*p.143; Also see *The Statesman*, September 2, 1965; Saroj Chakrabarty, ... *Chief Ministers*, p.140.
120. *The Statesman*, July 27, 1965.
121. Sushil Kumar Dhara, *op.cit.* pp. 129-131.
122. *The Statesman,* August 1, 1965.
123. Sushil Kumar Dhara, *op.cit.*p.134.
124. *Amrita Bazar Patrika,* July 28, 1965.
125. *Ibid.*
126. *Amrita Bazar Patrika,* July 29, 1965.
127. *The Statesman,* August 1, 1965.
128. *The Statesman*, August 4, 1965; Also see, Sushil Kumar Dhara, *op.cit.*p.135.
129. *The Statesman*, *Ananda Bazar Patrika,* September 4, 1965.
130. Prasanta Sen Gupta, *op.cit.* p.53; Also see, Shree Radhakrishna Bari, (ed.), *op.cit.*p.144.
131. Shree Radhakrishna Bari, (ed.), *op.cit.*p.146.
132. *The Statesman*, September 3, 1965.
133. *The Statesman*, September 4, 1965.
134. *The Statesman*, September 8, 1965.
135. Shree Radhakrishna Bari, (ed.), *op. cit.* p. 147.
136. *The Statesman*, September 12, 1965.
137. Shree Radhakrishna Bari, (ed.), *op.cit.*p.148. Also see, Sushil Kumar Dhara, *op.cit.*p.139.
138. Saroj Chakrabarty, ... *Chief Ministers*, p. 140.
139. Prasanta Sen Gupta, *op.cit.*p.55.
140. Shree Radhakrishna Bari, (ed.), *op.cit.* p. 149; Also see, Sushil Kumar Dhara, *op.cit.*p.136.
141. Saroj Chakrabarty, ... *Chief Ministers*, p. 149; Also see. Shree Radhakrishna Bari, (ed.), *op.cit.* p.149, Sushil Kumar Dhara, *op.cit.*p.139.
142. Shree Radhakrishna Bari, (ed.), *op.cit.*p.150.
143. *Ibid.*

144. The word 'Judas' implies in case of treachery. Actually Judas was one of the disciples of Jesus Christ and due to his conspiracy Jesus had to suffer and was crucified to death. See, Personal interview with Sukharanjan Sengupta, a veteran journalist of West Bengal on 5th February, 2017.
145. *The Statesman*, February 6, 1966; Also see, Shree Radhakrishna Bari, (ed.), *op.cit.*p.153, Sushil Kumar Dhara, *op.cit.*p.144.
146. Shree Radhakrishna Bari, (ed.), *op.cit.*p.154.
147. *The Statesman*, February 8, 1966.
148. Prasanta Sen Gupta, *op.cit.*p.58.
149. Saroj Chakrabarty, ... *Chief Ministers*, pp. 160-161.
150. Shree Radhakrishna Bari, (ed.), *op.cit.* p.154; Also see, Sushil Kumar Dhara, *op. cit.* pp.137, 140.
151. Bangla Congress was formed on 1st May, 1966 by Ajay Kumar Mukherjee and his adherents, see Mihir Gangopadhyay, *Mati Theke Shikhare' Atulya Ghosh Smarane* (in Bengali), *Kheal Khushir Bisesh Sankhya,* Bidhan Sishu Uddyan, Kolkata, August, 2012, p.64; also see Pranab Mukherjee, *The Dramatic Decade - The Indira Gandhi Years,* Rupa, New Delhi, 2015, p.6.
152. Sushil Kumar Dhara, *op.cit.*p.150.
153. Personal interview with Sukharanjan Sengupta, a veteran journalist of West Bengal on 5th February, 2017.
154. Pranab Mukherjee, *op.cit.*p.6.
155. Saroj Chakrabarty, ... *Chief Ministers*, pp. 167-168.
156. *Ibid.,* pp. 172-173; also see Dr. Binay Krishna Mukhopadhyay, *op.cit.*p.346.
157. Personal interview with Sukharanjan Sengupta, a veteran journalist of West Bengal on 5th February, 2017.
158. Saroj Chakrabarty, ... *Chief Ministers*, pp. 172-173.
159. *Ibid.* Also see, Dr. Binay Krishna Mukhopadhyay, *op.cit.* pp. 346-347.
160. Saroj Chakrabarty, ... *Chief Ministers*, pp.168-169.
161. *Ibid.,* p.170.
162. Shree Radhakrishna Bari, (ed.), *op.cit.* p. 155; Also see, Sushil Kumar Dhara, *op.cit.* p. 153; Governor Padmaja Naidu's letter addressed to President Dr. S. Radha Krishnan, dated, 15th December 1966, cited in Saroj Chakrabarty, ... *Chief Ministers*, p. 183.
163. Saroj Chakrabarty, ... *Chief Ministers*,p. 185; Also see, Dilip Banerjee, *op.cit.* pp, 133, 884-885.
164. Saroj Chakrabarty, ... *Chief Ministers*,p.188.
165. The Arambagh Assembly Constituency in Hooghly District which was the home constituency of Prafulla Chandra Sen since Independence from where he was defeated in the first general election in 1952, by an independent

candidate, named Radha Krishna Pal by a margin of 29,000 votes. But after that due to the mediation of Bidhan Chandra Roy, Radha Krishna Pal had to leave Arambagh with an unhappy mind for Prafulla Chandra Sen and thereafter P. C. Sen elected from Arambagh in 1957, 1962 respectively. See, Sushil Kumar Dhara, *op.cit.* p. 154; Also see, Saroj Chakrabarty, ... *Chief Ministers*,pp.187-188.

166. Sushil Kumar Dhara, *op.cit.* p.154.

167. Sushil Kumar Dhara, *op. cit.* p.155. When Congress supporters would pull down Bangla Congress flags and attack its office then Bangla Congress supporters also had paid back their own coin. In a meeting of the election campaign, Atulya Ghosh in a choking voice thundered, "I do not regret Mr. Ajay Mukherjee's desertion of the Congress. But I am ashamed of having worked with him as a comrade." However the violence and counter-violence in Arambagh in between Congress and Bangla Congress became the day to day affairs which widely circulated in details through news papers in their front page columns. See, Saroj Chakrabarty, ... *Chief Ministers*,pp.187-188.

168. Sushil Kumar Dhara, *op.cit.* pp. 155-156.

169. On 15th February 1967 the Fourth General Election was started in the country when 50 million voters in eight States went to exercise their voting rights. The first day's polling was peaceful and smooth which commenced in Andhra, Bihar, Gujrat, Maharashtra, Madras, Mysore, Rajasthan, Uttar Pradesh and Manipur. At the same way no violent incidents were took place on the second day of polling also. Excepting certain isolated occurrences in some parts of Bihar, the third day of polling was generally peaceful. But the temperament of the people of the problem-ridden State of West Bengal was something difficult to predict when polling was commenced on 19th February. Actually the situation of West Bengal that created by acute food shortages, high prices of essential commodities and anarchy in educational institutions were collectively unfavorable for the ruling party. In that election total numbering of 2,02,36,424 electorates had decided the fate of 40 Lok Sabha members including 8 reserved for scheduled castes and two for scheduled tribes along with 280 Assembly members including 55 reserved seats for scheduled castes and 16 for scheduled tribes by exercising their voting rights. See, Dilip Banerjee, *op.cit.* pp, 885, 133.

170. It is appears that most colourful character of the West Bengal Congress as well as highest dominating voice of PCC, Atulya Ghosh contested for the Parliamentary seat in the first general election in 1952 from Burdwan. But in 2nd and 3rd general election which was held in 1957 and 1962 respectively he had filed his nomination paper for Parliamentary seat from Asansol and became victorious. But in the 4th general election which was held in 1967, Atulya Babu decided to contest from Bankura Parliamentary seat leaving his two time winning seat i.e. Asansol. See, Dilip Banerjee, *op.cit.*pp, 136, 141, 149, 154. It is noteworthy that Bankura Parliamentary constituency was comprised 3 Assembly Constituency of Purulia District along with 4 Assembly Constituiency of Bankura District. Actually due to the acute food movement

in the year of 1965-66 an anti establishment wave was blowing all over the State specially the labour class influential area of Asansol, so, that is way Atulya Babu probably decided to leave Asansol in order to avoid his supposed defeat and as a main face of the congress party in West Bengal he chooses Bankura, comparatively safe seat for his winning. But in order to counter Atulya Ghosh, the opposition selected Jitendra Mohan Biswas of CPI to file his nomination paper for Bankura Paliamentary seat. See, Sushil Kumar Dhara, *op.cit.* pp. 154-155.

171. Saroj Chakrabarty, ... *Chief Ministers*, pp. 191-192; Also see, Dilip Banerjee, *op.cit.* p.401.
172. Saroj Chakrabarty, ... *Chief Ministers*, pp. 193-194.
173. Dilip Banerjee, *op.cit,* p. 154.
174. Saroj Chakrabarty, ... *Chief Ministers*, p. 194.
175. There was some excitement in the afternoon at around 3 p.m. when the difference was brought down from 1000 votes to 300 and after sometime to nine votes only. One time it was found that P. C. Sen was ahead with 20,601 votes against 20,592 votes in favour of Ajay Mukherjee. But all possibilities of victory of Chief Minister P. C. Sen were dilapidated with the outcome of the final voting figures which had given Ajay Mukherjee a lead of 881 votes. Actually, the number of casting votes in favour of Ajay Mukherjee was 27,916 against Prafulla Chandra Sen's 27,035 votes. See, Dilip Banerjee, *op. cit.* p.406.
176. Saroj Chakrabarty, ... *Chief Ministers*, pp. 196-197.
177. Dilip Banerjee, *op.cit.* p. 882; also see *Weekly Link,* 26th February, 1967.
178. *Weekly Link,* 26th February, 1967.
179. Prafulla Chandra Sen's acknowlwdgement in his Bhumika (Preface) in *Ajoya Purush Ajy Kumar,* (ed). By Shree Radhakrishna Bari.
180. Dr. Binay Krishna Mukhopadhyay, *op.cit.* p.359.

CHAPTER

5

Period of Marginalization (1967-1971): A. Non-Congress Coalition Government and B. Presidential Rule

A political reconstruction throughout the country and the All India Congress Party started unfolding the strategies in the late 1960s. Prime Minister Indira Gandhi's various steps regarding economic stance were not appreciated by the senior congress leadership those who were popularly known as 'syndicate'. The so called 'syndicate' group had started asserting themselves in post Nehruvian era on the ground of their seniority and experience which was counted more than important that of the political novice of Indira Gandhi. The senior as well as prominent congress leaders like – K. Kamraj Nadar, S. Nijalingappa. S. K. Patil, Atulya Ghosh, C. Subramaniam, Neelam Sanjiva Reddy etc. collectively formed an unconventional group at the aim of pressurizing on Indira Gandhi to work on their advice.[1]

New Era- The All India Scenario

Before the election of 1967 the so-called syndicate group leaders were sometimes succeeded to compel Indira Gandhi to act according to their advice. In that context, it may be mentioned that in case of the removal of G. L. Nanda from the portfolio of Ministry of Home Affairs and Prime Minister had to resile regarding the keeping of Finance Minister Sachin Chowdhury and Commerce Minister Munabhai Shah in their respective portfolio due to the pressure of syndicate group.[2] But, the target of the syndicate group however, was not fulfilled as because most of these leaders were defeated in the election of 1967. The fourth general election was so detrimental for congress party in India that for the first time after independence congress as a party had failed to form governments in West Bengal, Bihar, Orissa, Tamil Nadu and Kerala due to lack of absolute majority.

Not only that many prominent congress leaders who had the reputation of huge sacrifice during the freedom movement had been dismissed from the congress before the proposed general election held in 1967 and encasing their popularity as well as strong support base they had formed regional party which had played a very crucial role in the field of the defeat of the congress party in that election. For example, as like as Ajay Mukherjee and his Bangla Congress in West Bengal, Mahamaya Prasad Sinha in Bihar, Pabitra Mohan Pradhan in Orissa, Chaudhury Charan Singh in Uttar Pradesh and Govinda Narayan Singh in Madhya Pradesh had become the main factor behind the defeat of the congress party and unable to form government in their respective states.[3] Out of sixteen, as many as eight states had detached from the congress hold. But the only glimpse of hope for the congress party was the outcome of the Parliamentary election. The Congress Party had won by a very thinner majority, because the congress had secured only 277 Lok Sabha seats out of 503 seats declared till 26th February, 1967. Though, in 1962 the strength of the congress party in Lok Sabha was 364.[4]

Excitement centering on Ajay Mukherjee

It may be noted that when the big bosses of the congress party were introspecting their root causes behind the electoral debacle in many states of India particularly in West Bengal then people of Calcutta had witnessed one of the biggest victory processions which was started with the arrival of Ajay Mukherjee at Howrah Station on 24th February,1967 after winning from Tamluk in the highest margin of vote in West Bengal and defeating 'Arambagh Gandhi' i. e. Prafulla Chandra Sen, the sitting Chief Minister of the state, from his home constituency in Arambagh.[5] In that procession the peoples were in so joyous mood that they walked miles after miles following Ajay Mukherjee with the temperament of dancing and jovial mood.[6] The peoples of Calcutta were as if turned into mad in joy due to the electoral debacle of the congress party specially the defeat of Atulya Ghosh and Prafulla Chandra Sen.[7] So, after the election of 1967 it was found that except on the floor of the Assembly House the congress was almost disappeared from the cities as well as districts across the state. Due to the wave of defeat of the congress party in West Bengal particularly its top boss Atulya Ghosh the 'Congress Empire' as if crumbled down.

New Leader- Ajay Mukherjee

Though after the come out of the election result many people had spoken many words regarding the debacle of the congress party, but before election only two persons i. e. Professor Humayun Kabir and Promode Dasgupta firmly uttered that congress would certainly defeat and not be able to form the Ministry. Humayun Kabir had strong conviction that 'congress would certainly defeat and Atulya Ghosh and Prafulla Sen have to take farewell'.[8] As from the beginning Humayun Kabir had the deep impression regarding the debacle of the congress in West Bengal, so it was he who first took initiative to form a non-congress coalition government. As a preparation of forming non-congress coalition government, in the very first day of election result i. e. 22nd February, 1967, Humayun Kabir first contacted with Ashok Ghosh, Forward Bloc leader and both of them tentatively decided that- Ajay Mukherjee should be the Chief Minister of West Bengal; C.P.I. (M) would be inducted in the government and in the first discussion of government formation parties like CPI (M), CPI, Bangla Congress, Forward Bloc and RSP would be invited. On the question of Chief Ministership, Humayun Kabir had expressed the view that as Dr. Prafulla Chandra Ghosh could not run the administration as the first Chief Minister of West Bengal, along with all, so, he should not be suitable for the Chief Minister.[9]

Keeping in mind the antipathy between CPI and CPI (M), whether CPI (M) would be agree or not to join with CPI in the proposed non-congress government, in that case Humayun Kabir took the help of Tridip Chowdhury of RSP who had intimacy with CPI (M) leader Jyoti Basu. On 24th February in presence of P. Sundariya, General Secretary of the party, CPI (M) State Committee decided that CPI (M) would support the non-congress government but would not show eagerness to join in the government. It was also decided that if the situation demands they would also join the government actively so that there would not be any impression among the masses that due to the non co-operation of CPI (M) the effort of the formation of non-congress government is facing problem. However, on 24th February at around 11 a.m. a meeting of five parties was held at Humayun Kabir's residence in Calcutta i. e. in room no. 4 of Central Government Hostel. Present leaders of that meeting were- Jyoti Basu and Niranjan Sen of CPI (M), apart from Humayun Kabir, Jahangir Kabir and Dr. Nalinakshya Sanyal of Bangla Congress (Ajay Mukherjee and Sushil Dhara - two main leaders of Bangla congress till not reached in Calcutta), Somenath Lahiri of CPI, Hemanta Basu, Ashok Ghosh and Amar Chakrabarty of Forward Bloc, Tridip Chowdhury and Jatin Chakrabarty of RSP. In that meeting it was almost decided that Ajay Mukherjee would be next Chief Minister and also decided to form Ministry by the seven persons from the big parties. The formulas of dividing the ministry portfolios were - each two from CPI (M) and Bangla Congress, and each one from CPI, Forward Bloc and RSP.[10]

On 25th February an all party meeting was held in Indian Association Hall at Bowbazar, Calcutta. In that meeting United Left front (ULF) consisting of seven parties namely CPI(M), RSP, SSP, SUC, Workers Party, Marxist Forward Bloc and RCPI; People United Left Front (PULF) being presented by four parties namely Bangla Congress, CPI, Forward Bloc and Balshevic Party; along with Praja Socialist Party i. e. 12 leaders of different political parties were present. Within a very short discussion it was decided instead of two fronts there would be only one front in the Assembly and Ajay Mukherjee would be the leader of that front. As per the suggestion of Humayun Kabir, the name of Ajay Kumar Mukherjee was officially proposed by the Forward Bloc leader Hemanta Basu and seconded by CPI (M) leader Jyoti Basu.[11] Amidst of huge clapping and the cry of joy the present peoples supported the move. But after that it was Biswanath Mukherjee of CPI and younger brother of Ajay Mukherjee suggested that since the name of Jyoti Basu as the leader of the front has the reservation of somebody in spite of becoming the leader of the largest party (43 MLAs) of the front, so he should be the 'Deputy leader' as well as deputy Chief Minister of the non congress coalition government. That move of Biswanath Mukherjee was supported by all except Samar Guha of PSP.[12] According to the proposal of Humayun Kabir in that meeting the leaders of the eleven parties separately sent letters to Governor Padmaja Naidu claiming that since they were majority, would be allowed to form the Ministry. On this issue they appeal to the Hon'ble Governor to invite Ajay Mukherjee as the leader of the majority group to take the responsibility as Chief Minister of West Bengal. Accordingly Padmaja Naidu is said to have gone to Delhi to consult with the President of India for a final decision.

At this hour there was a speculation among the non-congress leaders whether Delhi based central leaders would allow them to form a non-congress coalition government in West Bengal or not. But the non-congress leaders became astonished when on 27th February, Governor Naidu wanted to talk not only to Ajay Mukherjee but also to the leaders of different parties. Therefore, at first Ajay Mukherjee went to Raj Bhavan along with a list of 146 MLAs and after submitting to the Governor he claimed that the listed MLAs would extent support to him as leader of the Assembly. Then Jyoti Basu, Somenath Lahiri, Hemanta Basu, Dr. Prafulla Chandra Ghosh, Samar Guha, Makhan Pal and Arun Ghosh one by one went to meet the Governor and everybody expressed their opinion in favour of Ajay Mukherjee as their leader. The leaders had come back with an impression that central congress leadership accepted the verdict of West Bengal and would not create any hindrance in the way of the formation of first non-congress government. Only some cautions were given by Governor Naidu to the non-communist leaders in the form that "As West Bengal is a border State, so it has a great importance from various sides. You were going to form Government with the Communists, so countrymen expected special alertness from you".[13]

Birth of United Front

After the meeting with Governor Naidu on 27th February, 1967 when it was clear to all that non-congress government would be formed then the very next day i. e. on 28th February the leaders of the 14 parties (ULF-7, PULF-4, PSP, Gorkha League and Lok Sevak Sangha) along with many independent members again assembled in Indian Association Hall, Calcutta. In that meeting according to the proposal of Humayun Kabir, it was decided that the collective group of non-congress parties would be known as 'United Front' in the Assembly. In order to maintain coordination among the 14 parties and with the people of West Bengal a committee would be formed by the representatives, one from each party under the convenorship of two small party leaders namely Barada Mukutmani of Bolshevik Party and Sudhin Kumar of RCPI. Another very important decision was also taken up in that meeting regarding the number of Ministers those who would take the oath. The name of the proposed Ministers were Ajay Mukherjee and Jahangir Kabir of Bangla Congress, Jyoti Basu of CPI (M), Somenath Lahiri of CPI, Hemanta Basu of Forward Bloc and Dr. Prafulla Chandra Ghosh of Independent.[14]

Stands of the Congress Party in West Bengal

In the fourth general election of 1967, the congress party had lost its majority as because it had gotten only 127 seats out of 280 Assembly seats. Before the announcement of the result of all the Assembly seats on 23rd February it was clear that the congress party in West Bengal would not get the majority. On that day result of Arambagh was announced and Chief Minister Prafulla Chandra Sen himself was defeated by Ajay Mukherjee. After becoming sure of his own defeat along with the defeat of the congress party, the Chief Minister P. C. Sen communicated with Governor Padmaja Naidu and offered his resignation. On that fateful day of 23rd February the top congress leaders of West Bengal Pradesh Congress Committee (WBPCC) particularly Atulya Ghosh, Prafulla Chandra Sen, Bijayananda Chattopadhyay, Asoke Sen, Siddhartha Shankar Ray, Saila Kumar Mukherjee, Rabindralal Singha and Nirmalendu Dey were assembled in Congress Bhavan at night to discuss the future course of action of the

West Bengal Pradesh Congress. Prafulla Chandra Sen had communicated with Prime Minister Indira Gandhi and informed her in details about the position of West Bengal congress through telephone from the Congress Bhavan on that day. After prolonged discussion, it was found that as congress party had failed to become a majority one, therefore, it had three options such as: 1) accepting the verdict of the people they might sit on the opposition bloc, 2) defecting the MLAs from other parties congress could try to form government and 3) mixing with other parties to form a coalition government. But at last it was decided that as the congress party would not get majority, so it would not take any initiative to form the government. A draft statement was prepared regarding that matter which was approved by all along with Prafulla Chandra Sen. In the name of the General Secretary of PCC, Nirmalendu Dey alias Bodu Babu a statement on behalf of the WBPCC was published in news paper on 24th February in the following way-"West Bengal Pradesh Congress had accepted the verdict of the people. According to the procedure of the parliamentary democracy the leader of the Congress Legislative Party as leader of the single largest party might be invited to form the Government. But as congress did not get the majority therefore in order to give the appropriate honour of peoples' verdict it would sit on the opposition block and play the role of the responsible opposition party for the betterment of West Bengal."[15]

Though, Atulya Ghosh was confident in favour of sitting the congress party on the opposition bloc, but many congress leaders after enjoying the government power since 15th August 1947 did not want to remain far away from the power of the government. At this juncture, having been published the above statement by Nirmalendu Dey, general secretary of WBPCC in various news papers on 24th February; some local provincial congress leaders assembled at the residence of Prafulla Chandra Sen and decided that Ajay Mukherjee would be requested to form the Ministry with the support of the congress party. As congress party had 127 members, but in order to form Ministry it was needed only additional 14 members to prove majority to form the government. Ajay Mukherjee was an ex-congressman who was driven out from the congress party due to the interest of so called group politics; naturally there were many sympathizers within the congress party who were forced to side with the move against Ajay Mukherjee on 20th January 1966, in spite of the fact that they had some soft corner for Ajay Mukherjee. So, in that changing atmosphere one Byomkesh Majumdar was given the responsibility to manage Ajay Mukherjee who had 34 MLAs (actually, Bangla Congress won 35 seats, but as Ajay Mukherjee alone won from Tamluk and Arambag Constituency) and if he would agree to form Ministry then congress would support him. It was known to all that Ajay Mukherjee had formed Bangla Congress on 1st May, 1966 after suffering humiliation from the ruling faction of the congress protesting against their corruption. As Ajay Mukherjee protested against many corruption and illegal activities and as a result of that he became a victim of the political atmosphere of the state and in the long run he was expelled from the provincial congress party. So, Ajay Mukherjee's formation of Bangla Congress and his fight in the general election of 1967 may be considered as the crusade against the misuse of power and corruption of the top congress leaders for their own personal interest ignoring the corporate interest of the congress party. Needless to say that in that struggle for dignity Ajay Mukherjee became successful and as a bonus sitting Chief Minister Prafulla Chandra Sen who was popularly known as 'Arambagh Gandhi' in his home constituency Arambagh had been defeated by Ajay Mukherjee. Atulya Ghosh, another top boss of the then congress party in West Bengal was also defeated in Bankura Parliamentary Constituency by J. M. Biswas in a margin of 29,770 votes. [16] In that changing circumstances, when proposal came to Ajay Mukherjee as to the formation of ministry by the support of the congress party then that proposal was simply rejected by Ajay Mukherjee on the ground that he went to his "Supreme Court" i. e. *'Janatar Darbar'* against the corrupt leadership who were dominating the congress party in West Bengal.[17] Atulya Ghosh, the main dominating voice of WBPCC at that time mentioned in his Political Memoir- *"Kasta Kalpita"* that –'there was victory and defeat in democracy. In spite of speaking democracy in our language, we had some hesitation in our mind to accept defeat. He had differences of opinion with many at that time. He had also many supporters those who would think that if non-congress parties wanted to form Ministry, they should be obviously given that opportunity. In democracy the role of opposition was also very prestigious.'[18] But in later on Atulya Ghosh himself understood that the number of his supporters of his temperament was limited and naturally there was no whole hearted support in his line of thinking.

A. Non–Congress Coalition Government

First United Front Ministry - (2nd March, 1967 to 21st November, 1967)

Ajay Kumar Mukherjee was officially selected leader of the non-congress alliance parties along with independent MLAs on 25th February, 1967. Ajay Mukherjee had his first meeting with Governor Padmaja Naidu on 27th February, when he handed over to Governor a list of 146 MLAs who supported him as their leader and claimed to form the Ministry. The second and final meeting between Ajay Mukherjee and the Governor was held on 1st March and in an hour long discussion he presented a list of six names including him for inducting as Minister in his proposed Ministry. Apart from Ajay Mukherjee himself the other names were- Jyoti Basu, Somnath Lahiri, Hemanta Basu, Jehangir Kabir and Dr. P. C. Ghosh. It would be appropriate to mention here that Dr. Prafulla Chandra Ghosh was the College teacher of Ajay Mukherjee and the first Chief Minister of West Bengal. The Governor of West Bengal after accepting the recommendation of Ajay Mukherjee i. e. leader of the United Front communicated the proposed date of the swearing-in ceremony of the new Ministry on 2nd March, 1967.

Maidan Meeting of United Front

In the afternoon of that 1st March a gigantic gatherings of 12 lakhs people were held in Maidan of Calcutta which as if given the final shape of United Front. In the huge gathering the leaders of each and every party had delivered their valuable speeches from the well decorated rostrum. The meeting continued for four hours with the scenes of enthusiasm. When the would be Chief Minister and Deputy Chief Minister along with other four Ministers were garlanded the people were exulted by clapping and shouting 'Vande Mataram' and 'Leftist Unity Zindabad'. The principal tone of the speech from all the leaders was to work unitedly avoiding dissentions for the interest of the people of the state. Giving a suitable example Somenath Lahiri, CPI leader said, 'As mother had given lesson to her son by catching ear, the people in the same way had given the lesson - you be united and take the administrative responsibility unitedly. We had accepted the lesson lowering our heads given by mothers.'[19]

Swear-in Ceremony

The Oath taking ceremony of six Ministers along with Chief Minister Ajay Mukherjee was administered by Governor Padmaja Naidu on 2nd March, 1967 at Raj Bhavan. There was a huge crowd in front of the Raj Bhavan gate and Writers Buildings at the time of swear-in-ceremony. Thousands of people had come only to see the new Ministers of the United Front Government. The crowd was so dense in front of the gate of the Raj Bhavan that the cars of would be ministers could hardly move inside the Raj Bhavan campus. Some of them came in cars but others had to come on foot. The great hope and expectations were felt among the people on the spot in such a way that every sort of political crisis would be over and a new era of political atmosphere would come for the welfare of the people.[20] Their entrance into Raj Bhavan was marked by joyous shouting. Calcutta had never seen such astonishing outburst of popular enthusiasm and energy. After the end of the ceremony six Ministers of the new ministry, they at first went to three selected places of the city to offer wreaths at the martyrs' columns which were constructed in memory of the people who were killed in the time of food and other movements during the period of the congress regime.

An equally big crowd had congested before the main entrance gate of the Writers' Buildings at the aim of becoming witness of the entry of the new Ministers there. Ajay Mukherjee's arrival was responded by overwhelming shouts of 'Vande Mataram' and 'Leftist Unity Zindabad'. Ajay Mukherjee had responded to the cheering crowd with his natural smile on his lips by raising his hands. As a devotee of Gandhian philosophy he used to wear a white *khaddar Panjabi* and *dhoti* so as to show his simplicity as a leader of the people. Incidentally, he was an ardent follower of Gandhiji from the days of Non-Cooperation movement. As a freedom fighter Ajay Mukherjee was behind the British prison for many years and went under-ground for a long time during quit India movement. He was inducted as an Irrigation Minister in the Cabinet of Dr. B. C. Roy's Government. The 66-year old bachelor Chief Minister when entered into his official room, then again he was welcomed by a cheering crowd of government employees.[21]

However after entering into the office of the Chief Minister, the first and delicate task before Ajay Mukherjee was to settle the question of distribution of portfolios and to fix up as well as to induct the number of ministers from United Front partners as per their respective strength in the Assembly. According to the earlier decision of United Front meeting the distribution of portfolios were as follows:- 1) Shri Ajay Kumar Mukherjee of Bangla Congress—Chief Minister and Home, 2) Shri Jyoti Basu of CPI(M)—Deputy Chief Minister, Finance and Home (Transport), 3) Shri Somenath Lahiri of CPI—Parliamentary Affairs, Information and Public Relations and Local Self Government. 4) Shri Hemanta Kumar Basu of Forward Bloc—Public Works and Housing, 5) Dr. Prafulla Chandra Ghosh of Independent— Food and Supplies and Agriculture and 6) Shri Jehangir Kabir of Bangla Congress— Development, Planning and Forest.[22] As the United Front was formed by 14 non-congress parties along with independent parties, so according to the demand of all parties it was decided in the Front regarding the incorporation of more ministers in the first United Front Ministry. On 4th March Ajay Mukherjee had prepared a list of 10 names of prospective ministers accordingly. In case of the expansion of the ministry in the second phase, the number of ministers became 16 and the party-wise distribution of ministerial portfolios in the cabinet were: Bangla Congress and CPI (M) three each, CPI and Forward Bloc two each, R.S.P., S.S.P., P.S.P., S.U.C., Progressive Party and Gorkha League, one each, and one to an Independent.[23] However, more 10 ministers were taken their oath on 4th March. The name and portfolios of that ministers were- 7) Shri Hare Krishna Konar of CPI(M)—Land and Land Revenue, 8) Shri Niranjan Sengupta of CPI(M)—Refugee Relief and Rehabilitation and Home (Jails), 9) Shri Sushil Kumar Dhara of Bangla Congress—Commerce and Industries and Community Development, 10) Shri Biswanath Mukherjee of CPI—Irrigation and Waterways, 11) Shri Amar Prasad Chakrovorty of Forward Bloc—Excise, Judicial and Legislative and Press and Passport, 12) Shri Nani Bhattacharya of RSP—Health, 13) Shri Subodh Banerjee of SUC—Labour, 14) Shri Kashi Kanta Moitra of SSP—Animal Husbandry and Veterinary Services, Fisheries & Cottage & Small Scale Industries, 15) Shri Nishith Nath Kunda of PSP—Co-operation and Relief, 16) Shri Deoprakash Rai of Gorkha League—Tribal Welfare. The other ministers of the First United Front government headed by Ajay Mukherjee were- 17) Shri Jyoti Bhusan Bhattacharya of WPI—Education, 18) Shri Bibhuti Bhusan Dasgupta of LSS—Panchayet, Relief and Social Welfare and 19) Shri Charu Mihir Sarkar of Bangla Congress—Civil Defence and others.[24]

It was noteworthy that at the time of the selection of the third Minister of Bangla Congress some sort of crisis was created over that question in the party. Three persons i. e. Dr. Nalinakshya Sanyal, Shri Haridas Mitra and Shri Sushil Kumar Dhara were the claimant for the third minister of Bangla Congress. At last the contest was going on in between Dr. Nalinakshya Sanyal and Sushil Dhara. CPI and Forward Bloc had supported Sushil Dhara. Besides, President and Secretaries of various district committees had sent letters to the President of Bangla Congress, Ajay Mukherjee demanding the inclusion of Sushil Dhara as the minister for the interest of the organization. As Ajay Mukherjee had no problem to take up Sushil Dhara in his Cabinet, so, that letters from district president and secretaries had strengthened his hand. Therefore, Ajay Mukherjee announced that Sushil Dhara would be the third member of the ministry of the Bangla Congress. In that way Sushil Kumar Dhara got a berth in the cabinet under Ajay Mukherjee.[25]

After settling down the names and portfolios of the ministers of the different parties of the United Front, the next question came out for consideration of the selection of Speaker and Deputy Speaker of the House.

As Nalinakshya Sanyal of Bangla Congress party could not be the Minister, so he wanted to become the Speaker. Though his demand was supported by Humayun Kabir and Dr. Prafulla Chandra Ghosh but when Jyoti Basu proposed the name of Shri Bijay Kumar Banerjee, a CPI (M) supported independent MLA, then with the support of the other members, the name of Bijay Kumar Banerjee was final as the Speaker of the First United Front Ministry headed by Ajay Mukherjee.[26]After the Speaker's issues then another problem remained unsolved regarding the confirmation of the name of Deputy Speaker. Forward Bloc wanted Apurba Lal Majumder as the Deputy Speaker on the ground that failing to become minister he was very angry. Though at first he did not want to become Deputy Speaker and later when he had given his consent of willingness then it was found that there was another candidate for the same post. He had the same problem i. e. failing of becoming Minister Sri Haridas Mitra of Bangla Congress was very aggrieved. On behalf of Bangla Congress, Sushil Dhara was handling the matter in favour of Haridas Mitra. Whenever the both parties were not agreed to leave their demand, then it was decided through votes. As the Forward Bloc already got two Ministers as per its strengths in the Assembly and along with that Shri Kamal Kanti Guha, popularly known as Kamal Guha had become the Chief Whip from the same party, so many members of the front had reservation to give Deputy Speaker again to Forward Bloc. After voting it was found that Sri Harida Mitra of Bangla Congress got the majority and ultimately became the Deputy Speaker of the first United Front Ministry. After the confirmation the names of both Speaker and Deputy Speaker in the front level then they took the responsibilities of their respective office on 8th March, 1967.[27]

First Cabinet Meeting

With the oath taking ceremony of the United Front Government, most of the people had the impression that now West Bengal would be developed. The common people also felt that the authority of the wealthy people would be subsided and the dignity of the poor people would be onward. They also hopped that corruption would be stopped and the price of the essential commodities be reduced and altogether a very happy as well as a brotherly atmosphere would be prevalent during the tenure of the United Front Government (hence forth U.F.). In that congenial atmosphere the U.F. ministry started its work. In one hand it was very positive sign but on the other there was also a negative sign. As people were with the government which might be considered as positive but the expectation of the people were sky level that might be regarded as negative sign. Thousands of people would believe that their all miseries would be abolished, but neither the government nor the common people know how that would be happened. Moreover, except Dr. Prafulla Chandra Ghosh and Ajay Mukherjee all the Ministers had no previous experience regarding Writers Buildings as well as administration. When they were in the opposition side and developed such an ideas of which there were no connection with the realities. Therefore, keeping in mind the above matters the first cabinet meeting was held on 6th March, 1967 in a very enthusiastic mood, whose main matter of discussion was food.[28] In the first meeting it was found that there was a gulf of difference between their promises during election and existing condition of food position in West Bengal. There would be no problem at all in case of providing adequate food according to the necessity to all - that was the statement of the present ministers' years after years. But, now the officers would say that the existence limit of ration quota be short cut.

The next day i. e. 7th March again the cabinet meeting was held but as per the earlier promises of the leaders it was became impossible to adopt any revolutionary food policy. It was also decided that the existence food policy of the previous Prafulla Chandra Sen Ministry would be followed until further discussion was taken up. In that meeting the ministers had taken two decisions regarding the salary of the ministers and air-conditioned machine in the office of the ministers. In order to welfare of the state as well as people the cabinet ministers thought since we were the ministers of poor country so we would draw our salary within limits. It was found that the Chief Minister himself reduced his monthly salary from Rs. 1,150 to Rs. 700 and all other cabinet ministers were also decided to take Rs. 500 as monthly salary instead of Rs. 900.[29] As per the decision of that cabinet meeting the United Front Ministers removed all the air-conditioned machines from their room in order to save money that might be used for the development of the state of West Bengal.[30]At the aim of reduce expenses regarding the use of government vehicles, Chief Minister Ajay Mukherjee himself had set an example. In spite of becoming a Chief Minister Ajay Mukherjee would bring his midday meal at the time of his coming to office in a small tiffin box at around 9 a. m. in order to save petrol costing for bringing his lunch at noon by second trip. He had continued that practices as long as he was the Chief Minister during the time of two U. F. governments. Since Ajay Mukherjee was staying with his nephew's government officer's quarter at Belvedere, therefore, he instructed his personal assistant not to draw the house rent allowances which was fixed for the Chief Minister as Rs. 350/-. In the financial matter he was furiously honest for which Ajay Mukherjee attained universal respect not only from the officials but also from the public.[31]

In a multi-party system of administration i. e. United Front government, the task of any Chief Minister was huge difficult than the Chief Minister of a single party majority government. The Chief Minister would open his lips according to the situation, otherwise, he had been pursued an interminable discussions in his office room whenever MLAs and Ministers were facing problem regarding their departmental issues and to seek his help in order to adjust in settling in the inter-party differences which took a lot of passing of time. From the very beginning, Ajay Mukherjee had played his role fairly well. As the strength of the congress in the Assembly was 127, so any division within the United Front in case of ministerial rank or ideological grounds automatically would be seized by the opposition at the aim to reduce the majority into a minority. Therefore, keeping in mind the above circumstances, Saroj Chakrabarty, personal assistant of the Chief Ministers had written, "The valuable time of the C. M. was thus consumed to play the role of an arbitrator rather than as an administrator."[32]

The first non-congress coalition ministry in West Bengal headed by Ajay Mukherjee had advised the Governor Padmaja Naidu to summon the legislature on 8th March, 1967.The Chief Minister and Deputy Chief Minister had done several joint meetings in order to prepare drafts for the address of the Governor in accordance with the tune of the political significance of the U. F. victory and its determination to work for the people at the aim of redressing the miseries of the masses.[33] Two important leaders of the united Front Ministry-Ajay Mukherjee and Jyoti Basu were never so intimate as they were in the initial days of the first U. F. government. They were so close that in fact no important decision would be taken by the ministry without prior consultation between the two. Both of them were concerned to give a reasonable trial to the system of multi-party government which was a new experiment in the political scenario of the country.

Re-election of Indira Gandhi as the Prime Minister of India

Meanwhile, in the midst of the serious electoral debacle for the congress party after independence as well as post Nehru era, as many as eight states where first non-congress government were installed throughout the country. In spite of that after defeating the top leaders of the congress party including its President K. Kamraj Nadar, Atulya Ghosh and others, in Parliamentary election, the congress had ensured its position to form the government securing altogether 277 seats out of 503 instead of 364 Lok Sabha seats in 1962.[34] As the congress party was in the majority in Lok Sabha and thereby on 12th March, 1967 Indira Gandhi, the care taker Prime Minister was again unanimously re-elected Leader of the Congress

Parliamentary Party. The President of India Dr. S. Radhakrishnan invited Leader of the Congress Parliamentary Party i. e. Indira Gandhi to form a new Government. In the meantime, resignations of outgoing ministers already been accepted. At the initial stage, Indira Gandhi's new three-member cabinet took oath in office, though in later time, the cabinet was expanded and its strength was raised from 3 to 19. Morarji Desai, one of the expectants for the post of Prime Ministership became the Deputy Prime Minister along with the charge of Finance portfolio. Since the syndicate leaders as well as pressure groups had been thrown out by the electorates, so it was possible for Mrs. Indira Gandhi to form her new cabinet which was her own handiwork in lieu of a superimposed one like the 1966 cabinet. The number of Council of Ministers at the Centre was further enlarged to 51.[35]

Khagendra Nath Dasgupta—Leader of the Opposition: Some Measures Taken by the Govt. to Gain Its Strength among the Employees

In West Bengal, Khagendra Nath Dasgupta, a senior parliamentarian and temperamentally less aggressive was elected as the Leader of the Opposition in the Assembly by the Congress Parliamentary party. In that connection it might be mentionable that Atulya Ghosh suggested the name of Dr. Pratap Chandra Chunder, a highly educated and cultural minded with good reputation as the son of Nirmal Chandra Chunder, one of the big five of the Bengal politics, as the opposition leader. But due to the controversy between Atulya Ghosh and Prafulla Chandra Sen over the name of the opposition leader, at last Khagendra Nath Dasgupta (henceforth K. N. Dasgupta), choice of Prafulla Chandra Sen ultimately became the leader of the opposition party.[36] On 16th March, at the commencement of the proceedings of the Assembly, K. N. Dasgupta, the leader of the opposition accused regarding the assaults and threat on the congress members within the Assembly building by outsiders. He complained that the withdrawal of Section 144 was a motivated move and as a protest against that step the congress members were staged a 10 minute walk-out. After that the debate in Assembly became very lively when Jyoti Basu had brought an allegation in the case of misuse of Chief Minister's fund by Prafulla Chandra Sen, the former Chief Minister. Jyoti Basu alleged that a cheque of Rs. 2 lakhs was issued by former Chief Minister (Prafulla Chandra Sen) for election purpose in favour of the General Secretary of the Pradesh Congress Committee. The another serious allegation was relating to distribution of bus permits by Saila Kumar Mukherjee, the former Transport Minister on the basis of the recommendation of a higher officer of the Transport Department. Not only that before the fall of the congress government said officer after his retirement was subsequently elevated in the post of the Chairman of the P.S.C. Thereafter the House had passed all the supplementary demands. Non-gazetted employees affiliated by the left parties were rapidly gaining their strength. Some of the top leaders of the left parties affiliated employees were dismissed by the previous congress governments on various pretexts. The Chief Minister, Ajay Mukherjee in his capacity as Home Minister had assured in a large gathering of the State government employees that the democratic rights of the employees would be recognized. That assurance of Chief Minister indicated the revision of Rules of Conduct and barring the government servants from indulging in political activities. All those employees who were dismissed or discharged during the congress rule would be reinstated as far as possible.[37]

Chief Minister, Deputy Chief Minister and Food Minister's Anxiety over Food and Their Visit to Delhi

As the United Front Government had promised to reduce the prices of the necessary commodities as well as would give the people sufficient rice through rationing system, therefore in their first cabinet meeting food was the foremost agenda of discussion. But it was found that the food situation in the state was not up to satisfaction. When after the discussion to solve the food problem times and again and failing which the leaders took a decision in one of the cabinet meetings held on 15th March, 1967 about their visit to Delhi with a view to pursuing the central government regarding the alarming food situation in West Bengal along with some other problems. Therefore, a three member ministerial committee was formed and the members were - a. Chief Minister Ajay Mukherjee; b. Deputy Chief Minister Jyoti Basu; and Food Minister c. Dr. Prafulla Chandra Ghosh. These members left for Delhi on 22nd March, 1967 accordingly. Apart from food problem, larger central allocation for the fourth five years plan, demanded for some development plans for Calcutta in case of water supply and sewerage and sanctioning of Rs. 8 crores instead of building the second Hooghly Bridge were some of their main objectives. In Delhi a long discussion was held mainly with the Prime Minister Indira Gandhi and Food Minister Babu Jagjivan Ram. In course of discussion after briefing the food situation, the state ministers demanded more allocation of food grain for West Bengal. Babu Jagjivan Ram, central food minister after informing the present status of food stock in the hands of central government, again informed that though it became possible to give to West Bengal 1, 20,000 tons per month in the previous years, but in view of present situation it would not be possible to provide more than 70,000 tons per month. The

Prime Minister also assured the state ministerial team headed by its Chief Minister Ajay Mukherjee that though food condition in central government was really deplorable, in spite of that the central government would certainly extent it's helping hand as much as possible. So, the state ministerial team had to come back with empty hand excepting being able to get assurance of central help time to time as per demand.[38]

Gherao and its Impact on Industries

Whenever food situation was alarming then the state government had to face another two devastating problems. The first problem was created in the industrial field and another one was in the agricultural sector. At that time there was a sign of depression in industries particularly in engineering industries throughout the countries. In West Bengal as many as 2, 50,000 workers were engaged in the engineering industries. On the pretext of depression in industries as the profit of the industrialists were not up to the mark, so the industrialists started reducing the number of workers from their industries. In that context, the workers would not adopt the path of strike or indignation procession. The industrial workers followed a new weapon '*Gherao*' which was once initiated by Subodh Banerjee, the then labour minister of West Bengal government to protect the interest of the working class people curbing the activities of dubious industrialists. Though, the *Gherao* movement was not something new in West Bengal, but it would continue generally for two-four hours in the head offices in a limited way for the demand of bonus. But that time the *gherao* movement would continue hours after hours for an indefinite period and mainly in the working places i. e. in the industries. It was not however, a peaceful way of movement because some coercive method of physical and mental torture was followed by the agitators so that the morale of the *Gheraod* person might break with fear and would compel to accept the demand of the agitating workers. That method of agitation was considered as an easy application and the initial results were very speedy and gainful. Due to the encouragement of the use of that *gherao* method with immediate result, within a few months in 1967 the number of *gheraos* in industrial field was reached the record figure of 811.[39] In that time, the *gherao* process was so barbarous that the industrial officers were not allowed to go into toilet and no interference of police regarding the rescue of the *gheraod* persons from that critical condition. In that context, the only alternative action of the industrialists to go for only with closure and lock-out etc. to give a suitable lesson to the offending workers and their leaders to blunt the weapon of 'gherao'.[40] The action and counter action of both sides soon landed the whole of the state into a destabilize condition of industrial unrest which was unprecedented in the industrial atlas of West Bengal. Naturally, the climate of confidence which was considered in all time as the most essential criterion for industrial growth in any state was completely shattered. Therefore, flight of capital from the state became an inevitable consequence and within a very short time the annual industrial growth rate of the state of West Bengal was fall down to a zero level.[41]

At the aim of the ending of the deadlock in the industrial field a delegation of the engineering industrialists met the Chief Minister Ajay Mukherjee. In that meeting Ajay Mukherjee with the consultation of Somenath Lahiri and others ministers of United Front decided that government would not allow any kind of violence activities in the name of agitation in the industries. As per the decision of the meeting it was instructed to the industrialists not to closure and lock out prior to the tripartite meeting among the workers, industrialists and governments. However, in case of the disturbances of the industrial field police interference was prohibited without the permission of Subodh Banerjee, the labour minister of the state. But some parties within the United Front, those who were more concern about the interest of the country than the party came to the conclusion that if that condition would continue then the situation would be gradually out of control.[42]

Forcefully Land Occupation

Amidst ongoing turbulent situation in the industries, another alarming situation was found in the agricultural sector. This was centered on the forcible occupation of agricultural land. Vested land of the government, surplus land of the zamindars and disputed land- were connected with judiciary as well as open land and houses were started to grab. Most of the cases some partners of the United Front government would lead the occupancy or indirectly support it. In that circumstances, in a statement on behalf of the cabinet ministry on 25th March, 1967, circulated which contained, "If there were any lawful complaints of anybody, then they could communicate with the government and government would try to solve the problem by giving utmost priority. In the meantime, those who had already forcefully acquired land or occupied houses or land out of mistake were directed to hand over the right of occupation to the concerned authority. Illegal activities and forceful occupation would not be allowed and in that cases government would take legal as well as police action to end the ongoing anarchy."[43] But the cautioned statement of the ministry could not bring expected result because nobody would give up the so called right of occupation at that point of time. Not only that, the tradition of illegal forceful occupation would continue bypassing the circulation of the statement issued by the ministry. In the face of the resistance of that activities a pure heartiest combined efforts were not seen among the political parties of United Front.[44]

New Food Policy of First United Front Government

Returning from Delhi the front leaders met time and again but failed to reach any satisfactory solution about food problems. The prices of rice and other essential commodities gradually started increasing. In some places people in their own responsibilities at the aim of helping the government started campaign for collection of secret stock of food grains from the hoarders. In rural areas, in the name of collection of secret stock of food grains and to stop the contraband plundering and cordoning of food grain in a large scale were started. In that pretext, Dr. Prafulla Chandra Ghosh, the Food Minister announced the food policy of United Front Government on 29th March, 1967.[45] The main features of his food policy were abolition of inter-district cordons as well as levy system and declaration of higher rates of procurement of rice and paddy. Due to heavy drought the rice production of that year was 71,000 tons less than that of the previous year. Under the new food policy the statutory rationing system in Calcutta would continue as before. In case of paddy procurement, according to quality price was fixed between Rs. 21/- to Rs. 23/- and rice Rs. 35/- to Rs. 36/50 per maund. The responsibilities of procuring rice and paddy were given to the Food Corporation of India (FCI). After that the procured food grain would go to the mills and after milling F.C.I. would store them in its go-downs. On 7th April, 1967 after six hour debate on food problems in the Assembly, Dr. Ghosh summarizing his speech with an announcement of some modifications of the government's new food policies. These were- declaration of surplus stocks within 15 days by land owners who had over 10 acres in irrigated and 12 acres non-irrigated land after keeping 9 mounds of paddy per head of the family and 2 maunds for seeds and labour. The language of his warning was "I will not hesitate to bring compulsion upon 500 persons to feed 5 lakhs of people", In the case of the non-producers including traders, the government policy was that they would have to make declaration about their stocks beyond 50 maunds of paddy or same quantity of rice instead of 100 maunds which were suggested earlier. The milling charges of food grains were brought down from Rs. 2/50 to Rs. 2/- per maund and as a result of which the millers had to agree reluctantly.[46]

On 18th April, 1967 it was declared that whole production of the rice mills would be taken by the government. But that declaration became ineffective as because there were no rice or paddy in the mills. After seven days, in an another order it was said that without prior written permission of the Block Development Officers (BDO) or local authority of Food Department it was not allowed to carry above 25 maunds of rice or paddy from one place to another in West Bengal. In spite of taking the above measures along with all precautionary steps within four months of United Front Government the food situation virtually became alarming. The prices of essential commodities were so high that even per kg rice would sell then Rs. 5, though the United Front leaders had given false assurance to the voters before election to supply 2 kg rice instead of Rs. 1.[47] In that context, the United Front Committee ordered the government to stop price hike of essential commodities and supply adequate food grains to the village areas.[48]

In spite of holding meeting after meeting in the cabinet as well as in the United Front level, it was found that there was no sign of development of ongoing food situation in West Bengal. As a protest against the failure of food policy of the government people started blockading train and other transport. At that point, some leaders within the United Front deliberately and sarcastically criticized the Food Minister, Prafulla Chandra Ghosh and his policy and he was made responsible for the crisis going on all over West Bengal. When Prafulla Chandra Ghosh refused to comment against the central government behind the food crisis and naturally an anti Ghosh propaganda was hatched out by some front leaders within and outside the government. Incidentally, some of the contemporary archival records identified the propagandists being supported by the CPI (M) party of the United Front government.[49]At last in a press statement from Darjeeling on 25th May, 1967, P. Sundarayya, all India leader of CPI (M) said, "Dr. Ghosh should be resign, he had failed." Fanning the fire of the complicated situation, Ajay Mukherjee in a press conference remarked, "Who was P. Sundarayya to claim the resignation of Dr. Ghosh? Dr. Ghosh was Minister of United Front, and as long as he was enjoying the confidence of United Front would remain Minister."[50] In response to the comment of P. Sundarayya, Pafulla Chandra Ghosh remarked, "The comment of P. Sundarayya was unjustified. That food policy was the outcome of the decision of all parties belonged to the United Front. Therefore, the accountability of that food policy would not of any individuals or any party."[51]

The food situation of West Bengal further worsened as a result of the unkindness of nature i. e. out brake of famine in certain parts of Bihar. As a neighboring state, West Bengal could not escape from that severe drought. Bankura District of West Bengal with a population of 1.8 million had to face the impact of drought from the month of April. Considering the urgency of the situation, the District Magistrate immediately had to sent an S.O.S.

seeking extension of gratuitous and relief operations. Nishit Nath Kundu, the Relief Minister rushed to the district at once for an on the spot study of the distress and arrange for relief.[52]

CPI (M)'s Attitude towards Allied Partners of the United Front Government

At the time of the blame and counter blame among the United Front partners centering the food condition of West Bengal, the Politbureau of CPI (M) in its session held in Calcutta about this time. Surprisingly, it passed a resolution accusing the West Bengal ministers for adopting their weak and ineffective policy which manifested in the failure of unearthing food stocks from the hoarders and administered a sharp criticism to the centre for discriminatory treatment regarding the supplies of food grain. P. Sundarayya, Secretary of the Party, later on advised the Party Ministers of CPI (M) to criticize the statements of United Front ministers belonging to other political parties if there were anything against the directive of the party. In that context 'Industries and Commerce' Minister as well as General Secretary of Bangla Congress Sushil Dhara's statement against 'Gherao' and Dr. Pafulla Chandra Ghosh's food procurement policy was their main target. It was thus the CPI (M) leaders who first sown the seeds of division within United Front Ministry. The Politbureau resolution concluded with "Do not walk out of the Ministry but pursue party politics within the Cabinet," [53]

The Naxalbari Episode

Apart from severe food crisis and blaming and counter blaming against each other within the leadership of United Front and by that time the ongoing *gherao* culture in one hand and termination of workers from industry, closure, lock out on the other had collectively shattered the prospect of industrial development in West Bengal. The chaotic situation in the industries of the state had drawn the attention of Prime Minister of India and other leaders as well and particularly the excessiveness of *gherao* strategy exercised by the leftists for their party interest ignoring the interest of the state as well as country shook up the central leaders to look into the affairs of West Bengal. Though Chief Minister Ajay Mukherjee and some parties were not favoring that practice, but failed to take any appropriate measures to quell those unfortunate happenings. At the same time, the forceful occupation of land and open houses were going on and government circulation time and again regarding the disallowing that activities and threatening to take police action were also unheeded. In that context, for some times back the state government had been receiving reports about the growing discontent from some rural areas at the foot hills of Himalayan Mountain. The areas were under Siliguri subdivision of Darjeeling district and known as Naxalbari, Kharibari, Phansedeoa. The reports revealed about the forcible cultivation of vested and other people's lands that intimidation of violence and leading to the cases of murder. On the 24th day of May 1967, four Police officers were attacked by the naxalites. Among the injured police personnel one died in the next day. When that reports of naxalbari had reached in the Writers Buildings' as well as Chief Minister, then aggrieved Ajay Mukherjee immediately called in the Chief Secretary and Home Department officials and issued a specific instructions at once to the Deputy Commissioner of Darjeeling district to take appropriate action against persons those who were charged with law and order violations. In the police action on 25th May, 1967; those who killed were–i. Dhaneswari Devi (Adivasi peasant woman), ii. Fulmati Devi (Adivasi peasant woman), iii. Nayaneswari Mallick (Adivasi peasant woman and wife of a Rail worker), iv. Sonamati Singh (Adivasi peasant woman), v. Simaswari Mallick, (Adivasi peasant woman), vi. Surbala Barman (Rajbangshi peasant woman), vii. Graudau Sairani and viii. Samaswari Sairani (both Mech peasant woman). Another youth named Kharsingh Mallick (Adavasi) was killed on that day due to police firings. Apart from the above mentioned names those who killed at that time were- i. Tribeni Kanu, ii. Sovan Ali, iii. Barka Manjhi and other three persons whose name are still untraced.[54]

In that burning stage of Naxalbari incident, Chief Minister Ajay Mukherjee rushed to North Bengal, the very next day i. e. on 26th May. Some very influential political leader of North Bengal like Deoprakash Rai, Kamal Guha and Sunil Dasgupta collectively apprised Ajay Mukherjee regarding the furiousness of the Naxalite activities and informed, "If you did not handle the situation in a strong hand, then the security of North Bengal would be in the face of danger."[55] On 27th May, Ajay Mukherjee warned from an open public gathering at Naxalbari saying, "Each and every citizen had the right to enjoy life and property. The owner of the land might be big or small, forcible occupation of land would be treated as the anti-social activities."[56]

First differences of opinion openly manifested in the cabinet over the question as to the way out of the resistance of violence activities at Naxalbari. Ajay Mukherjee and his party Bangla Congress, Gorkha League, S.S.P. and P.S.P. wanted to take the matter as a law and order problem. But CPI (M), CPI and some others party did not agree with Ajay Mukherjee. As the

Naxalbari movement was the manifestation of the internal chaos of CPI (M) that was why the CPI alone wished to make a hue and cry over the issues.[57] In that situation, as per the cabinet decision a six-man ministerial delegation was sent to study the condition and make on the spot decisions about law and order problems. Apart from other parties, both CPI and CPI (M) ministers were also comprised the ministerial delegation. After reaching that cabinet team on 12th June, 1967 held a series of meetings with local officials, side by side political leaders and lastly authorized the police personnel to fire if necessary at the aim to quell disturbances and maintain law and order by doing round the clock police patrol. Another three-man cabinet team had visited Naxalbari on June 29.[58]

By centering the police firing at Naxalbari, the internal conflict of United Front was again disclosed. In a press statement CPI (M) Secretary P. Sundarayya accused Chief Minister Ajay Mukherjee for sending police at Naxalbari ignoring the decision of the cabinet. Three CPI (M) ministers-Jyoti Basu, Harekrishna Konar and Niranjan Sengupta supported the statement of their leader. But Ajay Mukherjee refuted the false charges of CPI (M) leader P. Sundarayya saying that under any circumstances he never ignored any decision of the cabinet. In that way the initial relation of brotherhood of United Front leaders gradually wiped out and blame game in between one group against another continued sometimes directly and indirectly.[59]

All India Focus on Naxalbari

Meanwhile the news of violence in Naxalbari area spread all over India. The Cabinet Mission's visit at Naxalbari virtually failed to improve the situation. The picture of lawlessness was equally bad in some other districts also. In that circumstances the West Bengal Congress Members of Parliament had written the following letter to the Chief Minister on 15th June, 1967, expressing their grave concern.

Their letter was as follows:

"New Delhi

15th June, 1967

Dear Sir,

We the undersigned Congress Members of Parliament from West Bengal have learnt with grave concern the situation that is now existing in Naxalbari and other places in the district of Darjeeling. The law and order is deteriorating in the district of 24 Parganas also. We therefore feel that unless firm and positive steps are taken immediately to maintain law and order the situation in West Bengal would go completely out of control.

Yours sincerely,

Surendra Mohan Ghosh & Others." [60]

Seven Members Parliamentary team

The Prime Minister of India Smt. Indira Gandhi could not sit idle but had to draw the attention of the West Bengal Chief Minister towards the lawlessness which was prevailing in the state and suggested about the sending of a perusal team of Parliamentary delegation to evaluate the situation in Naxalbari. In response to the Prime Minister's suggestion, Chief Minister Ajay Mukherjee sent a decorous but negative reply, asserting his stand that law and order was the initial concern of the state government and as a head of the administration of the state he was taking all possible remedial measures. However, on 19th June in 1967, seven Members of Parliament who were belonging to non-congress party including M. R. Masani, A. B. Bajpayee and Hem Barua jointly had addressed a letter to the Chief Minister of West Bengal which inter alia stated:

"It cannot be maintained that normal conditions exist in the Naxalbari part of Darjeeling district. Nor can it be denied that certain extremist elements have taken to violence and sought to create a sense of fear and insecurity among the people there. In "The Statesman" of 17th June, 1967, there are reports that the villagers in areas where the S.S.P. and Forward Bloc have some following have decided to take to arms in self-defence. We have also seen statements of certain West Bengal Ministers threatening dire action against the anarchist elements which persist in disturbing the peace. In short, the situation is extraordinary and, while we do not deny the right of the State Government to deal with the situation in the area, we feel that Parliament cannot ignore the existence of these abnormal conditions.

After all, this area is strategically important for India's security. This narrow neck which connects North Eastern India with the rest of the country is a vital link in India's defense system.

Our object was to prevent a situation developing in which the Central Government might feel called upon to invoke the *Emergency provisions of the Constitution.*

Parliament is the custodian of the nation's territorial integrity and it cannot ignore the threats that the Chinese pose to our Northern frontiers.

We, therefore, thought that a representative delegation of Members of Parliament would be welcomed by the State Government.

Yours sincerely

M. R. Masani & Others" [61]

The Prime Minister Indira Gandhi requested the Chief Minister Ajay Mukherjee in the 3rd week of June 1967 to come Delhi for the discussion on West Bengal problems. Ajay Mukherjee went to Delhi on 24th June, along with Jyoti Basu and Biswanath Mukherjee. Next day i. e. on 25th June Ajay Mukherjee alone met the Prime Minister and discussed the matter for 40 minutes over the question of law and order and food condition. The Prime Minister did not hide her worry as regards to the unusual law and order situation in West Bengal. Ajay Mukherjee assured her about state government's capacity to tackle the ongoing situation provided West Bengal's quota of food supplies from the central were on time. "Give us more food and we would control the situation", Ajay Mukherjee told the waiting pressmen. Explaining the adopting measures of his government at Naxalbari, Ajay Mukherjee informed that in the meantime 1,500 armed police personnel were operating in the disturbed area in order to deal with the unusual situation of violence. Jyoti Basu and Biswanath Mukherjee met the Prime Minister separately to state their point of view.[62]

On 30thJune a very grave and alarming situation along with murder and rape in Naxalbari area again echoed in the Upper House. Congress Members of Parliament apprehended the hands of Pakistan and China behind the unfortunate incidents and mentioned it as 'Peking style Communist revolt in India'. Peking Radio in that time announced that a spot had been selected in West Bengal in order to prepare the ground for the bloody revolution.

In that context, Deo Prakash Rai of Goorkha League, one of the Ministers of United Front had threatened to resign from the cabinet unless government would adopt appropriate policy and measures to curb violence. There were two different groups within the cabinet - one group was favoring all out police action to arrest the hard core extremists against whom already arrests warrants were issued and even if necessary such action had to be taken through bloodshed. The Forward Bloc and P.S.P. Ministers of United Front Government were in favor of that policy, but the Chief Minister was some sort of less aggressive as he had to maintain a balance within the different groups for adopting a united policy. The other group i. e. Marxist and their allies opposed that form of action. After prolonged discussion, lastly a compromise formula was adopted. According to that at the aim of isolation of the extremists, a quick land reform programme was initiated in the disturbed areas to restore normalcy.[63]

Attacked of a Police Camp by Naxalites

Meanwhile the extremist Naxalite leaders warned "the struggle would continue and any amount of police repression would not be able to crush the upsurge" through their weekly mouth piece 'Deshabrati' which had started to publish on and from 6thJuly, 1967. The newly published weekly 'Deshabrati's first editor Sushital Ray Chowdhury who was expelled from CPI (M) on the charges of adventurist deviation. In the meantime, 75 Naxalite extremists were arrested from the disturbed Naxalbari area by July 13 after a successful police operation. After two days, the police took a stern action under the leadership of A. P. Mukherjee, S. P. and as a result of that completely displaced the extremists from their hidden place. On the contrary, under the leadership of Kanu Sanyal, Kadam Malik and Khokan Majumdar (he is a Muslim), as many as 2,500 people attacked a police camp in Kharibari thana. In that encounter altogether 54 people including policemen were injured and 290 of the agitators courted arrest. Though, 600 policemen had tried to encircle the agitators but the top leaders helped them to skip. The total numbers of arrest rose to 367 within two days.[64]

Dharma Vira as New Governor of West Bengal

Whenever, the Naxalbari was boiling then the appointment of Dharma Vira as the new Governor was an important turning point in the political history of West Bengal. As the tenure of Governor Padmaja Naidu was going to expire on 1st of June, 1967, so the question of the appointment of her successor drew the attention of the central government. In case of the appointment of new Governor, the state government insisted that no congressman would be acceptable as the Governor. The Chief Minister and the Deputy Chief Minister jointly demanded for the post of Governorship of a person who would be selected from the three names recommended by them.[65] But, the Government of India ignoring the three names recommended by the state government ultimately announced the name of Dharma Vira as the successor of Padmaja Naidu. Naturally, this announcement created a discontent in the ministerial circle. Dharma Vira was the former Indian Civil Service and had the experiences of holding many high posts in Central Government. As the Secretary of the Rehabilitation Ministry Dharma Vira was very much aware about some of the problems of West Bengal and showed his firmness in case of handling difficult problems. Dharma Vira took his Oath of office on June 1, 1967.[66]

U. F. Ministers vis-à-vis the New Governor

As Dharma Vira was appointed as Governor of West Bengal bypassing the recommendation of the state government, so from the very outset the ministerial circle looked upon him as 'an agent of the Central Government out to wreck the Ministry'. The resentment of U. F. was revealed publicly on 15th July, 1967 when a demonstration was held outside the Raj Bhavan by C.P.I. demanding "Dharma Vira be recalled and replaced by a person who would rigidly stick to his constitutional role and refrain from disruptive activities against West Bengal Government". [67]

Division in the United Front and Role of the Congress Party behind Dislodging the Ministry

It has already been mentioned that the congress party in West Bengal accepted the defeat in the general election of 1967 and officially declared that it would play the role of responsible opposition party in the Assembly as per the verdict of the election. But the fact was that the congress party and its leaders both from central and state level (West Bengal) were not mentally prepared to accept the unexpected defeat of the party in the last general election held in 1967. Therefore, the congress party of West Bengal with the blessing of central leadership started defecting the MLAs from other parties in order to form in such a Ministry which would be completely depended upon the congress party. In that case the congress party in West Bengal took its first step projecting Dr. Prafulla Chandra Ghosh, the first Chief Minister of West Bengal, an Independent MLA as well as Food Minister of United Front Ministry as their (Congress leaders) Chief Ministerial candidate.[68] Though there was a background behind Prafulla Chandra Ghosh's leaning to the proposal of the congress party for alternative ministry headed by him. It was well known to all that the United Front Government was not able to solve the food problem according to their pre-election manifesto. It was no doubt the failure of the food problem might be considered as the failure of United Front Ministry as a whole. But unfortunately, sometimes in and outside the cabinet the Food Minister Dr. Prafulla Chandra Ghosh was persistently heckled and criticized openly by left parties for failure of his food policy. Even P. Sundarayya, General Secretary of CPI (M) demanded the resignation of Dr. Pafulla Chanda Ghosh from the Ministry. Naturally misunderstanding and grievances gradually increased into the partners of the United Front. In that context, the congress party in West Bengal followed two separate policy to undermine the ruling United Front Ministry. Firstly, the congress party in the Assembly severely criticized the various policies adopted by the United Front Ministry.

The failure of the food policy became the main target of criticism of the opposition congress party. In that respect a procession under the caption of 'Khadya Michhil' (Food Procession) was organized by the congress party under the leadership of former Chief Minister Prafulla Chandra Sen from Wellington to Writers Buildings' via Bowbazar.[69] The second strategy of the congress party of West Bengal was to encourage the defection of the MLAs from United Front and brought them into the congress camp so that Front Ministry would be in minority and another ministry would be installed with the help of the congress MLAs. The first one was openly but the second policy was conducted very secretly. Ashu Ghosh, the congress MLC, had taken the responsibility of secret activities on behalf of the congress party and Khagendra Nath Dasgupta, leader of the opposition and Bijay Singh Nahar, a congress leader would maintain connection with him. However, when it was found that, Dr. P. C. Ghosh, the first Chief Minister of West Bengal and a front ranking nationalist as well as diehard follower of Gandhiji was being humiliated by the communists in the first United Front Ministry, then three important congress leader of West Bengal namely- Dr. Pratap Chandra Chunder, Khagendra Nath Dasgupta and Bijay singh Nahar jointly after a prolonged discussion with Dr. Prafulla Chandra Ghosh had given the proposal of defection from United Front Ministry and requested him to form Ministry under his leadership. The congress leaders also promised to extent their whole hearted support behind his move. Dr. Prafulla Chandra Ghosh was also assured if he would defect then more 18–19 MLAs from United Front under the control of congress MLC Ashu Ghosh would defect and support his Ministry. In that context Dr. Prafulla Chandra Ghosh had made up his mind to resign from United Front Ministry on 26th July, 1967. But the secret news of the resignation of Prafulla Chandra Ghosh was somehow leaked out and published in various news papers. In that pretext, the some other Ministers of the United Front along with Chief Minister Ajay Mukherjee who was the direct student of Prafulla Chandra Ghosh at Presidency College met Prafulla Chandra Ghosh and requested him not to resign from the ministry. The ministers expressed their accord with Prafulla Chandra Ghosh's grievances against the behavior of the communists and very disgusted and aggrieved Chief Minister expressing his sympathy and solidarity remarked, "Why you are leaving alone, we would all leave together, so there is no hurry at all."[70]

However, after receiving the green signal from Dr. Prafulla Chandra Ghosh of his resignation on 26th July along with other 18-19 MLAs, the Governor of West Bengal, Dharma Vira was communicated accordingly on behalf of the congress party in West Bengal. The preparation of forming alternative government headed by Prafulla Chandra Ghosh with the support of the congress MLAs was also communicated to Delhi. Governor Dharma Vira called on General Manekshaw to become ready for the changing political atmosphere of West Bengal. Upananda Mukherjee, I. G. and P. K. Sen, Police Commissioner were also alerted by General Manekshaw for their course of action in the changing situation. But whenever the news of defection of the MLAs from the United Front to the congress was published in news papers on 'Today is test of strength',[71] then a large procession of United Front blocked the Assembly gates for six hours demanding resignation of defected MLAs. The procession of three hundred people who were supporting Naxalbari movement and claimed themselves as an *anti-jotedar* and anti-capitalist were demonstrating outside the gate of the Assembly. In that situation, due to insecurity feelings of the intending defectors and lack of adequate preparation as well as providing security to the defectors on behalf of the congress party, at last the plan of dislodging the first United Front Ministry was postponed for the time being.[72]

Rift Widened in United Front and Role of the Congress Party

In the third week of July in 1967 both in the Assembly and outside a sharp division within the U. F. came to the forefront. In the Assembly on the issue of law and order the Bangla Congress, Forward Bloc and S.S.P. had strongly supported the Chief Minister Ajay Mukherjee while the C.P.I. (M) and some others took a different line. On July 20 rival student groups those who belonged to CPI and CPI (M) altercated amongst themselves at the time of holding the demonstrations on 'Vietnam Day'.[73] It is noteworthy that after the formation of the United Front Government, Chief Minister Ajay Mukherjee was very much aggrieved with the communists due to various irresponsible comments and highhandedness of its leaders and violent activities of its followers which continuously tarnishing the image of the Front Ministry. In that context some unfortunate happenings of the Left CPI (M) added the fuel behind the disillusioned of Ajay Mukherjee towards the communists, were as follows:

The Chief Minister was Assaulted by the Non-Gazetted Employees Affiliated to the Left CPI (M)

The West Bengal Government Employees Federation which was a rival employees' organization of the left dominated coordination committee sought time for an interview with the Chief Minister in order to place their demands. After hearing that news, some of his cabinet ministers straightly approached the Chief Minister to refrain from entertaining to the employees' federation. The Chief Minister however, turned down their request and decided to receive the deputation of the Employees Federation under the impression that every branch of the government employees had the right to place their demand before the Chief Minister irrespective of party affiliations. The interview was fixed on 3rd August,1967.[74] The subsequent events that followed were as such that at about 11 a.m. on the very day some employees of coordination committee met the Chief Minister and pleaded to him to cancel the proposed interview with the Employees Federation. They argued with the Chief Minister in the way that, "They are black-sheeps, a creation of P. C. Sen's Congress Government", so as a head of the U. F. Government he should not give any attention to them. Needless to say that, the leaders of the coordination committee failed to convince the Chief Minister in favour of their opinion. In the afternoon the representatives of the Employees Federation as usually entered the Chief Minister's room headed by a woman leader. Naturally, the Chief Minister gave them a patient hearing. At that time of meeting between Chief Minister and representatives of the Employees Federation, two Cabinet Ministers namely Hemanta Kumar Basu and Nishit Nath Kundu were also present there. Whenever the meeting was going on then outside the Chief Minister's chamber i. e. in the corridor facing the gathering of the number of people basically the supporters of the Coordination Committee were gradually swelled up. When the members of the deputation came out from the Chief Minister's room they were surrounded and flouted. Soon a scuffle between the two groups occurred. Hearing the shouting the Chief Minister came out in the corridor and firmly asked the employees of the two groups to stop the demonstration and fighting. But not only his interference as well as cautious voice was unheeded but he himself was subjected to be jeered at and hackled. The most important side of the incident was that whatever it happened close to the room of the Deputy Chief Minister, Jyoti Basu who preferred to remain in his room instead of coming out to stop the scuffle as well as to rescue the humiliated Chief Minister. However, the personal security of the Chief Minister and on duty police officers escorted the deputationists out of the Writers' Buildings. That incident created a commotion in the Secretariat of Writers Buildings'. It was for the first time that a Chief Minister himself was being humiliated by a group of non-gazetted employees inside the corridor of the Writers' Buildings'. Deputy Chief Minister Jyoti Basu and Chief Minister Ajay Mukherjee were so close to each other at the initial stage of the formation of the United Front Ministry that even some security guards of the Chief Minister would say, "See the Chief Minister and the Deputy Chief Minister are like two brothers, Rama and Lakshmana. Alas! they are now drifting apart!"[75]

The Pay Commission and Difference of Opinion in U. F.

The Cabinet of the United Front Government of its meetings held on 5th August, 1967 approved the appointment of a Pay Commission but was not finalized the terms of reference or the number of members. But Jyoti Basu as a Finance Minister announced the terms of reference and appointed a three men commission of whom late K.G. Basu, the veteran Marxist trade union leader was one of them. After constituting the three members commission Jyoti Basu gave it for Gazette notification, but Chief Minister Ajay Mukherjee gave the directive to stop the Gazette notification on the ground that Jyoti Basu did this without the consultation with the cabinet.[76] There was a hue and cry over the Finance Minister's unilateral appointment of the member of the Pay Commission. Non-Marxists specially Nishith Nath Kundu, the Relief Minister after severely criticizing the activities of the CPI (M) remarked, "If the Left Communists thought that the policies whichever were taken in the Cabinet did not come out from their consideration, then their only alternative was to withdraw their representatives from the Council of Ministers."[77]Jyotyi Basu's reaction to the press was: "I am not going to resign from the Cabinet because I am not here in my personal capacity. I would explain my stand to the people and would go by their verdict". A massive demonstration was organized by Marxist supported trade union workers in favour of Jyoti Basu's stand in Dalhousie Square area.[78] However, later on due to the interference of Biswanath Mukherjee, CPI, MLC and Minister of united Front, the State Cabinet raised the number of members of the pay Commission from 3 to 7 through the voting system and appointed K. K. Hajra, ex-I.C.S. as its Chairman.

Chief Minister – Prime Minister Meeting and Plan for the Decline of the United Front Ministry

Under the given circumstances in the mediation of Surendra Mohan Ghosh, former President of WBPCC and leader of Jugantar Group a communication was made for a confidential discussion between Indira Gandhi, the Prime Minister of India and Ajay Kumar Mukherjee, the Chief Minister of West Bengal. Actually after serving the congress organization for nearly half a century when Ajay Mukherjee had to quit the congress and make alliance with the anti-congress parties then Ajay Mukherjee's only one intention was to do welfare activities for the people of Bengal. But he was disillusioned when it was found that some parties and their leaders wanted to establish the influence of their parties at any cost bypassing the interest of the country then Ajay Babu decided that it would be no longer possible for him to work with them together. After getting frustration about the communists particularly the left communists, Ajay Babu looking for the path of a way out leaving his political career in an uncertain condition for the sake of the country. In his very close circle Ajay Mukherjee remarked, "If I go for with them then an irreparable loose of the country would take place. I do not want that. If I am ruined, no matter. Country is much greater than an individual."[79] In that pretext in the name of the discussion of food problem of West Bengal Ajay Mukherjee met Prime Minister Indira Gandhi on 7th August, 1967. In that an hour long discussion a future plan of action was prepared as per the proposal of the Prime Minister. A very open discussion was held between Chief Minister and Prime Minister and decided that Pradesh Congress Committee (PCC) had to be changed. Ajay Mukherjee categorically stated that as long as Pradesh Congress would be dominated by Atulya Ghosh it would not be possible for him (Ajay Mukherjee) to reconcile with him (Atulya Ghosh). Prime Minister Indira Gandhi herself was also then disgusted on Atulya Ghosh. At last it was said that Guljarilal Nanda would be sent to Bengal to investigate the situation of Pradesh Congress and political condition of West Bengal. After thorough investigation Nandaji would submit a report to Congress Working Committee (CWC). Prior to his arrival at Calcutta it was also decided that in his report Nandaji would mention that in order to rid the Pradesh Congress from group rivalries an ad-hoc committee should be formed. After its formation the power of the West Bengal Pradesh Congress Committee be transferred and obviously the power from Atulya Ghosh be handed over to the committee under consideration and thereafter Ajay Mukherjee would come out breaking the United Front Ministry and form a new Ministry with the support of the congress party.[80]

Role of Governor Dharma Vira: Prafulla Chandra Sen-Ajay Mukherjee Meet

As per the planning of Ajay Mukherjee and Indira Gandhi, Dharma Vira, the Governor of West Bengal was called in Delhi dated 20th August, 1967 in order to convey his role as well as activities in the coming political doldrums in West Bengal. Ajay Mukherjee met Governor Dharma Vira on 30th August and discussed the pros and cons of the whole matter. After two days of the meeting with Dharma Vira, Ajay Mukherjee invited four important officers in his residence namely Chief Secretary M. M. Basu, Home Secretary S. B. Roy, I. G. of Police Upananda Muykherjee and Police Commissioner P. K. Sen. Ajay Mukherjee informed them about the whole planning and gave directives for preparing accordingly. Before arrival of Guljarilal Nanda in Calcutta on 19th September, meanwhile on 16th September 1967, Dharma Vira as the Governor of West Bengal arranged a post-lunch meeting at Raj Bhavan between Ajay Mukherjee, Chief Minister and Prafulla Chandra Sen, former Chief Minister in order to mitigate the ill feeling which developed between the two at the time of the ousting Ajay Mukherjee from the congress party on the eve of fourth general election held in 1967. During the post-lunch meeting at Raj Bhavan, Nityananda Kanungo, Governor of Gujarat, was then on a visit to the city invisibly for the purpose of effecting the political discussion between the two for changing the character of the government.[81] The two leaders talked openly for an hour about the planning of Indira Gandhi, the Prime Minister and Ajay Mukherjee, the Chief Minister and in that meeting Prafulla Chandra Sen invited Ajay Mukherjee to come back in the congress party. It was almost decided that upcoming 2nd October i. e. the birth day of Gandhiji Ajay Mukherjee would resign from the post of Chief Minister of the United Front and on the same day he would form another Ministry with the support of the congress party. From 16th September to 2nd October, four secret meetings were held between Ajay Mukherjee and Prafulla Chandra Sen.[82]

Prafulla Chandra Sen and Atulya Ghosh Rupture on Ad-Hoc Debate

However, as per the instruction of the Congress High Command, Guljarilal Nanda and Sucheta Kripalini came to Calcutta on 19th September, 1967 on a six-day visit for reorientation of the congress party in West Bengal which was in a moribund condition after the general election of 1967. It was a great opportunity for Guljarilal Nanda in the factional politics of the congress party to undermine Atulya Ghosh, the old enemy of Nanda with the support of Prime Minister and help of the former and present Chief Minister of his own (Atulya Ghosh) state i.e. West Bengal. After arriving in Calcutta on 19th September to 24th September 1967, Nanda talked to all concerned except Atulya Ghosh. When the preparation was completed then Prafulla Chandra Sen talked to Atulya Ghosh face to face and informed him that an ad hoc committee would be constituted and be announced by Nanda. But Atulya Ghosh responded very angrily and remarked "who was Nanda? On what basis he would form an ad-hoc? It would never happen whenever I am here." In response of Atulya Ghosh's remark Prafulla Chandra Sen promptly responded then are you a dictator?.[83] In spite of differences of opinion between Atulya Ghosh and Prafulla Chandra Sen, strong opposition of Atulya Ghosh - once supreme commander of the PCC,

Guljarilal Nanda announced the formation of an Ad-hoc committee for the West Bengal Pradesh Congress Committee (WBPCC) on 24th September 1967. Prafulla Sen, Khagendra Nath Dasgupta, Bijay Singh Nahar, Purabi Mukherjee and other congress leaders were also present at that press conference where Nanda made his announcement and remarked, "After considering all aspects of the matter I think that formation of an Ad hoc Committee will further strengthen the West Bengal Congress Committee". Mrs. Gandhi was keen on announcing the appointment of an Ad hoc committee.[84] Though Guljarilal Nanda did not announce the name of the members of the proposed ad hoc committee and told that names would be announced from Delhi later on.

After announcing the decision of the formation of an ad hoc committee, Guljarilal Nanda went back to Delhi on 24th September by night flight and Ajay Mukherjee also went to Delhi in the morning flight of 25th September, 1967. Though at the hope of the formation of the alternative government tentatively on 1st October, 1967 and Ajay Mukherjee's coming back to the vicinity of the congress,[85] but arriving at Delhi Guljarilal Nanda faced a serious trouble as because due to the opposition of K. Kamraj, the then All India Congress President, Nanda could not able to announce the names of the ad hoc committee. Kamraj instructed Sadik Ali, one of the General Secretaries of the congress over telephone to stop the announcement of the ad hoc committee.[86] By this time, Atulya Ghosh communicated the whole matter to K. Kamraj by writing a long letter. So, the announcement of ad hoc committee was postponed for the time being. Nanda's report regarding the formation of an ad hoc committee of West Bengal was circulated in the Working Committee meeting held on 7th October 1967. In his reports G. L. Nanda mentioned that Prime Minister and some others congress leaders tried to fall a non congress government in West Bengal which was however ultimately revoked. Congress Working Committee did not take any decision about an ad hoc and the All India Congress President K. Kamraj was entrusted to take the decision about the formation of the same. After five days of that working committee meeting, K. Kamraj announced that West Bengal Pradesh Congress Committee would remain as it was. An ad hoc executive committee would be constituted by six members and Prafulla Chandra Sen would act as the convener of that committee.[87]

Unrevealed the Story of Resignation of Ajay Mukherjee

The negotiation between Ajay Mukherjee and Indira Gandhi as well as congress party was kept secret to any minister of the United Front government. Even Humayun Kabir, Vice President of Bangla Congress and Sushil Kumar Dhara, General Secretary of Bangla Congress and very close associates of Ajay Mukherjee had no any information about the impending serious move of Ajay Mukherjee. But some newspapers were publishing the news of the formation of an ad hoc committee along with the possibility of the resignation of Ajay Mukherjee from the United Front government and the formation of an alternative government with the support of the congress party headed by Ajay Mukherjee. In that context, Ajay Mukherjee at the way of the finalization of his planning to quit United Front and coming back from Delhi on 28th September 1967, divulged his planning for the first time to his cabinet colleague Nishith Nath Kundu, Hemanta Kumar Basu and requested them to join his upcoming new ministry. The next day i. e. on 29th September, 1967 at the evening Ajay Mukherjee in a meeting of the secretariat of Bangla Congress specially in presence of Sushil Dhara, Sukumar Roy and Kanai Bhattacharya expressed his entire planning and urged them to join with him. Ajay Mukherjee firmly told them that "I would not like to destroy the country remaining with CPI (M). I could not give any opportunity to the CPI (M), the enemy of the country. I must dislodge that Ministry and form a new one. So, if you want to come, you are most welcome; if you are not to come I must go alone".[88] When it was cleared that Ajay Mukherjee was going to take serious decision then in order to dissuade Ajay Mukherjee from that move in the early morning on 30th September 1967, Ashok Ghosh, leader of Forward Bloc communicated Biswanath Mukherjee, CPI leader and younger brother of Ajay Mukherjee. After being informed Biswanath Mukherjee and his wife Geeta Mukherjee rushed to Belvediare, residence of Ajay Mukherjee.[89] Both Biswanath and Geeta Mukherjee tried to influence on Ajay Mukherjee so that he could postpone his attempt to resign from united front, but failed.

After being failed Biswanath Mukherjee communicated to Sushil Dhara, General Secretary of Bangla Congress. It became clear to Biswanath Mukherjee that without the active support of Sushil Dhara he would not be able to do anything. In that situation only hope was that Sushil Dhara was also against the move of his leader Ajay Mukherjee. However, on 1st October at 8 a.m. in course of telephonic conversation Biswanath Mukherjee told Sushil Dhara to dissuade Ajay Mukherjee from his firm decision to resign on 2nd October, 1967. In response Sushil Dhara told Biswanath Mukherjee that you could talk to your 'Chhor Da' (elder brother i. e. Ajay Mukherjee)) so that he could not resign. Biswanath Mukherjee categorically informed him that, "Sushil Da, Chhorda might affectionate me, but did not believe me, he believes you."[90]

Postponement of the Resignation of Ajay Mukherjee

Under the circumstances, Sushil Dhara and Biswanath Mukherjee jointly requested Satish Chandra Samanta, M. P. of Tamluq and was the first *Sarbadhinayak* of the *Tamralipta Jatiya Sarkar* during the time of Quit India Movement, to dissuade Ajay Mukherjee from that move. Though, Satish Chandra Samanta was also the intimate friend of Ajay Mukherjee who did not take any major steps without the consultation with Satish Chandra Samanta, yet he did not able to communicate any positive response. In that context Sushil Dhara in consultation with Biswanath Mukherjee convened a meeting of the old PULF groups and some Gandhian groups at night on 1st October, 1967 in the house of Kanai Bhattacharya, treasurer of Bangla Congress at Chetla, Calcutta in order to convince Ajay Mukherjee so that he could not resign on 2nd October. The meeting was held accordingly under the Presidentship of Hemanta Kumar Basu, veteran Forward Bloc leader and a Minister of United Front Ministry. Hemanta Kumar Basu and Ajay Mykherjee had great respect to each other. They had together suffered imprisonment and anguish during freedom struggle and were comrades and courageous soldiers. Both of them had to quit the congress on principle. Both of them were extensively known for their transparency, honesty and sincerity. They had no any kind of adversity. In the U.F. Cabinet the Chief Minister had received full support and cooperation from the Forward Bloc leaders. So, when Hemanta Basu told Ajay Mukherjee to say something before them why he had taken that harsh decision, then Ajay Mukherjee very nicely elaborated his bitter experiences, soreness and grudge against some partners of United Front particularly CPI (M) and SUCI. After that each speaker from every party requested Ajay Mukherjee not to resign on 2nd October and at least continue the Ministry for some days. Then as per the request of the President of that meeting i. e. Hemanta Kumar Basu, on behalf of Bangla Congress Sushil Kumar Dhara told that as the highest leader of Bangla Congress i. e. Ajay Mukherjee had already delivered his speech, so he had nothing to say. But, due do the request from the other members of the meetings Sushil Dhara openly told them that he did not accord with the decision of Ajay Mukherjee and also said if you could refrain him from that move then he (Sushil Dhara) himself would be the most happiest person. In course of discussion Biswanath Mukherjee asked him that if Chhorda i. e. Ajay Mukherjee would go to heal then would you follow him? In response to that question of Biswanath Mukherjee, Sushil Dhara in a very emotional voice assured him and remarked, "Damu, (Small name of Biswanath Mukherjee) since the last 38 years that man (Ajay Mukherjee) is my leader, commander as well as path-finder. I am nothing but his followers only. In spite of all effort to refrain him from the decision of his resignation, I shall follow his path. I cannot leave him as well as allow him to go alone."[91] After that heartfelt speech of Sushil Dhara, President of that meeting Hemanta Basu once again requesting Ajay Mukherjee not to resign from the post of Chief Ministership on 2nd October, 1967 and declared the end of the meeting. Next day i. e. 2nd October, after short telephonic conversation between President of Bangla Congress i. e. Ajay Mukherjee and Sushil Dhara, General Secretary of the party and later on meeting with Ajay Mukherjee at his residence, at last Ajay Mukherjee had taken the decision of postponement of his resignation for at least 7 to 8 days. In the meantime, in spite of huge arrangement as well as preparation on behalf of the congress party and Governor Dharma Vira, Ajay Mukherjee went to Raj Bhavan at 8 p.m. along with Sushil Dhara and told Governor that he would not resign on that day i. e. 2nd October according to the pre-plan and want few days more time to resign.[92]

Four Points Reason as Revealed by Ajay Mukherjee behind the Decision of His Resignation from the Seat of Chief Minister

As Ajay Mukherjee wanted remedies to the leaders of Forward Bloc, CPI and Bangla Congress within 24 hours about the destructive activities in United Front at noon on 2nd October, 1967. Naturally after the postponement of the resignation of Ajay Mukherjee, the very next day i. e. on 3rd October at the aim of reunited the United Front, leaders like- Hemanta Basu, Jyoti Basu, Biswanath Mukherjee and Sushil Dhara entered into the room of Chief Minister in order to sort out the differences of opinion among themselves and to soothe the temperament of the frustrated Chief Minister. The Chief Minister made a frank and full confession regarding the secret negotiations with the congress leaders and formation of an alternative government. At the time of explaining the reason in a tearful eyes Chief Minister Ajay Mukherjee told them that the main four points which led him to come to the decision to resign were- disorderly behavior, ineffectiveness of his circular in case of prohibiting cultivators to occupy land by force from the Jotedars, ejectment by force of share croppers by the Jotedars and open invitation by some political parties to China to bring about an armed revolution.[93] Jyoti Basu repeated his assurance and requested him not to give the importance of the story of blood-revolution. In that meeting in order to assure Ajay Babu, it was also decided that in the field of the internal conflict among the partners of United Front the Chief Minister would use the police force as Home Minister.[94] Not only that in order to make happy to Ajay Mukherjee the cabinet in its meeting held on 5th October 1967 unanimously decided that in the conflict of the industries between workers and owners, police would interfere properly. A cabinet sub-committee was constituted to restore normalcy as well as peaceful environment in industries. The members of that committee were- Chief Minister Ajay Mukherjee, Jyoti Basu, Somenath Lahiri and Sushil Dhara. In that context, on 5th October 1967, in a brief statement Ajay Mukherjee said, "It is a pleasure to announce that United Front Government would remain as it was and try to serve the people according to its highest capacity." In the night of 5th October, Ajay Mukherjee also informed the Governor that he would not resign. On 7th October a meeting was convened under the Monument in the name of United Front and in that open meeting Ajay Mukherjee announced, "We are the same, what we had been"[95]

Role of the Congress Party behind the Toppling of United Front Government and Formation of an Alternative Government with Prafulla Chandra Ghosh

Congress leaders of West Bengal particularly the leaders like former Chief Minister Prafulla Chandra Sen, leader of the opposition Khagendra Nath Dasgupta, Tarun Kanti Ghosh and others had a great hope that due to the resignation of Ajay Mukherjee, the United Front Government would fall and then with the help of Ajay Mukherjee they again come back to power. Though, as a result of the changing decision of Ajay Mukherjee it would not happened, but they were not ready to leave the game very easily. So, in that changing scenario, the congress leaders followed the policy of defection the MLAs from United Front in order to oust the government from power and in that case Ashu Ghosh, the congress MLC, played a vital role on behalf of the congress party in West Bengal as well as centre. It was Ashu Ghosh against whom Prafulla Chandra Sen during his tenure of Chief Ministership brought a litigation of misappropriation of funds.[96] However, Ashu Ghosh along with the joint effort of Kabir brothers i. e. Humayun Kabir and Jehangir Kabir were able to reach their goal regarding the fall of United Front Government headed by Ajay Mukherjee, projecting Prafulla Chandra Ghosh as Chief Ministerial candidate. It was found that 15 MLAs of the B.K.D.[97]group of the Bangla Congress headed by Kabir brothers had started negotiations with the congress leaders and ultimately fulfilled their task (Congress—132 plus 15 in a house of 280). There was a story behind the rift between Humayun Kabir and Ajay Mukherjee- which were as under:

Rift between Humayun Kabir and Ajay Mukherjee

Bangla Congress had two groups from its inception one led by Ajay Mukherjee and another group was under the influence of Humayun Kabir. Actually, at the very outset behind the formation of United Front, Humayun Kabir played a very significant role. Humayun Kabir thought that it was due to his effort the United Front Government was formed and Ajay Mukherjee had become its Chief Minister. So, naturally Humayun Kabir had the expectation of gratitude from the leaders of united front and particularly from Ajay Mukherjee. But after returning from Europe Humayun Kabir found that the leaders of the united front were not giving him the due importance. Not only that at the time of selecting the 3rd minister from Bangla Congress i. e. by centering the selection of Sushil Dhara as Minister the difference of opinion between the two groups of Bangla Congress gradually increased.[98] But, the altercation between Humayun Kabir and Ajay Mukherjee accentuated by centering the opening of a B.K.D. office in Calcutta under the domination of Humayun Kabir's group. Ajay Mukherjee insisted that Bangla Congress was being recognized as the sole agent of B.K.D. in West Bengal. Naturally, there was a sharp division on that issue among Bangla Congress MLAs, although the majority members supported the Chief Minister's stance. The differences turned into intense regarding the question of sending delegates to the Indore session of the B.K.D. because, both the factions started claiming to represent Bengal. It was from that time and onwards quick political changes took place in Bengal. Humayun Kabir determined to set in toppling the ministry and initiated his spade work from September 1967. He met Prafulla Chandra Sen to explore the possibilities of forming an alternative government with his followers from Bangla Congress MLAs who were disillusioned about the performance of the U. F. Ministry in respect of law and order in addition to food and industrial relations. In the meantime, Food Minister Prafulla Chandra Ghosh was humiliated and 'gheraod' by the communist supporters in the third week of August 1967 and was equally aggrieved against the performance of the government. He did not attend the meeting of the U.F. until or unless the CPI (M) would apologize for their misbehavior to him.[99]

Rift in B.K.D. and Bangla Congress and Creation of Atmosphere of an Alternative Govt. with Prafulla Chandra Ghosh

In spite of the above differences of opinion between Humayun Kabir and Ajay Mukherejee group; Humayun Kabir and Ajay Mukherjee came back from Delhi by the same flight and Ajay Mukherjee drove Humayun Kabir in his Central Government Hostel on 28th September, 1967 and thereby relation between the two leaders seems to be improved. But When Humayun Kabir came to know that Ajay Mukherjee intended to decline the United Front Ministry on 2nd October without giving any hints to him who was still the Vice-President of Bangla Congress. So, Humayun Kabir became very much aggrieved to Ajay Mukherjee and decided not to go with him anymore and if any opportunity would come he (Ajay Mukherjee) must be given appropriate lesson. Fortunately, the opportunity of taking revenge against Ajay Mukherjee came to Humayun Kabir on 3rd October, 1967. It has already been mentioned that due to the changing decision of Ajay Mukherejee about his postponement of resignation from Chief Ministership on 2nd October, the very discontented congress leaders i. e. Prafulla Chandra Sen and Tarun Kanti Ghosh rushed to Humayun Kabir in Central Government Hostel early in the morning on 3rd October and requested him to do something regarding the oust of the United Front Ministry as well as Ajay Mukherjee with the help of Prafulla Chandra Ghosh. Humayun Kabir assured the congress leaders regarding the fulfillment of their earnest desire.[100]

In that point of time, Humayun Kabir along with Hare Krishna Mahatab, a very important leader in Orissa, went to meet Governor Dharma Vira in the evening of 3rd October. After chalking out some planning then Humayun Kabir went to the flat of Prafulla Chandra Ghosh and brought him under the confidence that after deposing Ajay Mukherjee, he would be the next Chief Minister of West Bengal within very short time. In the meanwhile, the fracture that developed among the Bangla Congress leadership started widening. A group of dissident MLAs for an alternative government became very active under the leadership of Humayun Kabir who was master-minded that plan. But the main instrumental work had done by Ashu Ghosh with the help of his two trusted associates namely-Rabi Chaudhury and Ranadhir Barman regarding the setting up the whole drama in consultation with Governor Dharma Vira, Prafulla Chandra Ghosh and as per demand of the situation of West Bengal Pradesh Congress as well as the approval of the central congress leadership.[101]

At about that time in the afternoon of 3rd November 1967, Governor Dharma Vira informed the Chief Minister Ajay Mukherjee over telephone from Darjeeling that he had received a letter over the signature of 18 MLAs including Prafulla Chandra Ghosh withdrawing their support to the U. F. Ministry. The Governor also informed him that due to the withdrawal of support of 18 MLAs, the Ministry would lose its majority in the Assembly and thereupon would not be able to continue the Government.[102]The Governor however did not divulge the names of the MLAs who were expected to withdraw their support. Cutting short his staying in Darjeeling, Governor Dharma Vira returned to Calcutta by a special plane on 4th November. After coming back to Calcutta Governor Dharma Vira first met Prafulla Chandra Ghosh and then wanted to meet defectors who had written him as to the withdrawal of support from United Front Ministry. In the afternoon, 12 of the 17 defectors arrived at Raj Bhavan with Ashu Ghosh to meet the Governor in order to remove any doubt in his mind by physical checking. On 4th November 1967, the press headlined the news regarding the resignation of Food Minister Prafulla Chandra Ghosh which was confirmed by Dr. Ghosh himself on the same day i. e. 4th November. The Chief Minister, Ajay Mukherjee met the Governor immediately after his arrival at Raj Bhavan on the same day when the Governor reiterated the confirmed decision of resignation of 17 MLAs and virtually the minority position of his ministry. At this hour he wanted to know about his next step.[103]The chief Minister wanted some time for the consultation of the emerging situation with his cabinet colleagues. A hurriedly summoned cabinet meeting held on at night on 4th November and accepted the resignation of Prafulla Chandra Ghosh who did not attend his office in the Writers' Buildings on that day. In that united front meeting it was also decided that there was no question of the resignation of the Chief Minister. The Front claimed that they were the majority and prior to the trial of strength in the Assembly Chief Minister would not resign.[104] Prafulla Chandra Sen and Khagendra Nath Dasgupta on behalf of the congress party met Dr. Ghosh at his residence in the evening of 4th November and assured him regarding the full support of the Congress Legislature Party in his attempts to form an alternative government. Humayun Kabir was also present in that meeting. On 6th November the Chief Minister along with six U. F. ministers met the Governor and urged him to summon the Assembly for trial of strength instead of taking any decision of his own. It was also hinted the mid-term poll at that meeting.[105]

The Birth of Progressive Democratic Front

Prafulla Chandra Ghosh in a statement on 6th November, 1967 announced the formation of the new party named the 'Progressive Democratic Front (PDF)' with himself as its leader and claiming the support of 17 MLAs who had already joined his party. Dr. Prafulla Chandra Ghosh demanded the termination of the U. F. Government as because it had lost majority and mentioned that the U. F. was a conglomeration of many warring groups and that is why resigning from the U. F. cabinet he did a great service to the nation. [106]

Dismissing the First U. F. Government by Governor Dharma Vira, November 21, 1967

On 6th November 1967, the Chief Minister met the Governor to inform him that as per the decision of the cabinet it would not be possible to summon the Assembly on or before 18th December, 1967. Though Governor persistently wanted to summon the Assembly as early as possible specially within 20th November. Actually, the Chief Minister himself was aware that due to lose of the support of 18 MLAs, the U. F. Government was reduced to a minority and in that case the only alternative was to save it to enforce the defectors so that they could withdraw their support to Prafulla Chandra Ghosh. In the meantime, demonstrations started to create public pressure violating Section 144 every day in front of the Writers' Buildings in favour of United Front parties.

Meanwhile, Governor Dharma Vira went to Delhi in order to consult as well as to take direction about the ongoing complicated political situation in West Bengal. There was a speculation over the situation of West Bengal, whether Governor could convene the Assembly against the desire of the decision of the cabinet, or Governor could force the cabinet to go for trial of strength. At last the experts of the Central Home and Law Ministry jointly gave the decision that in case of convening the Assembly, Governor was bound to follow the advice of the cabinet; but Governor had the right to dismiss the Ministry.[107] Governor Dharma Vira returning from Delhi to Calcutta on 14th November, 1967 gave a letter to Chief Minister Ajay Mukherjee and urged him to convene Assembly within 23rd November, 1967. After the meeting of the United Front held on 16th November and that of the Cabinet meeting on 17th November, the Chief Minister communicated to Governor in writing that prior to 18th December, 1967 it would not be possible for him to convene Assembly. In the meantime, according to the decision of the cabinet meeting specially as per the advice of Kashi Kanta Moitra and Somenath Lahiri, on 17th November two unprecedented constitutional questions were raised and appealed to the President of India to take the opinion of Supreme Court. The questions were: i) Whether the Governor had the right to compel the Cabinet to summon the Assembly according to his discretion or the day what he fixed as per his convenience? ii) Without going for trial of strength, only on the basis of his assumption or accusation that the Ministry had lost its majority, Governor would be able to dismiss any Government or not?[108]

Governor Dharma Vira sent Chief Secretary to Chief Minister Ajay Mukherjee two days prior to the dismissal of the 1st U.F. Ministry to inform him that the Governor was most reluctant to wait any more and directed him to report to the Governor whether the Assembly would be convened immediately in order to test the strength of the two opposite parties. The Chief Minister however, could give any answer to this. That was actually the final warning on behalf of Governor through the Chief Secretary.

On 21st November, 1967, the Chief Minister Ajay Mukherjee along with Sushil Dhara left Writers' Buildings in the evening to meet Chief Minister of Bihar, M. P. Sinha who on the very day halted at the Grand Hotel, Calcutta. The purpose of this meeting was to settle up a public gathering next day where M. P. Sinha was expected to deliver a public lecture. At the moment of their discussion suddenly at about 8-10 p.m. a hotel boy knocked the door of the room to inform that a messenger had come from the Raj Bhavan with an urgent letter to deliver to Ajay Mukherjee. The Chief Minister received it and after opening the letter found that the Governor of West Bengal made an office order under Article 164 (1) of the Indian Constitution that Shri Ajay Kumar Mukherjee's holding the office of the Chief Minister had ceased with immediate effect and also mentioned that the Council of Ministers headed by him stood dissolved.[109] Thereafter Ajay Mukherjee immediately asked his security to report it to his office and left the government vehicle at once. After finishing his talk to M. P. Sinha, Ajay Mukherjee returned his residence in a taxi. That fateful day Ajay Mukherjee had left his house as the Chief Minister but returned there as ex-Chief Minister.

Prafulla Chandra Ghosh Sworn in as Chief Minister: (21st November 1967- 20th February 1968)

Another magnificent drama was performed at Raj Bhavan about that time under huge secrecy i. e. Prafulla Chandra Ghosh was sworn in as Chief Minister immediately after the dismissal of Ajay Mukherjee's Ministry. Along with Prafulla Chandra Ghosh another two defectors of Bangla Congress as well as adherents of Prafulla Chandra Ghosh - Harendra Nath Majumdar and Amir Ali Molla also took oath as the Minister of Progressive Democratic Front (henceforth PDF). It was noteworthy that never before in the history of West Bengal nay India no Ministry had taken its oath in such a situation of secrecy and dramatic fashion that the PDF Ministry did in the presence of a very thin gathering. The leader of the Congress Legislature Party, K. N. Dasgupta, Humayun Kabir, Prafulla Chandra Sen, former chief minister and Ashu Ghosh, a former Minister were present there those who played key role behind the dislodging the United Front Ministry replacing the PDF Ministry headed by Prafulla Chandra Ghosh at

Raj Bhavan.[110] After the sworn in ceremony Governor Dharma Vira requested the septuagenarian Chief Minister Prafulla Chandra Ghosh to summon a session of the Assembly on 29th November in order to seek a vote of confidence. On the other hand, the reaction of U. F. was violent. They declared next day i. e. on 22nd November, 1967 as the day for general strike. Thus ended the chequered period of 8 months 19 days First United Front regime of West Bengal which was another way known as *'Mili Zuli Sarkar'*.

On 22nd November 1967, when Calcutta was observing a general strike against the dismissal of United Front Ministry in a undemocratic manner by Governor Dharma Vira and installation of P.D.F. Ministry headed by Prafulla Chandra Ghosh, reports of sporadic violence were pouring in the Secretariat through telephone, then the new Chief Minister entered his office room in Writers Buildings' just at 10 a.m. Prafulla Chandra Ghosh became the Chief Minister of West Bengal for the second time under the cover of a conspiracy that led to the development in that political atmosphere and of course it was significantly different from the context of his first term as Chief Minister (3rd July1947—22nd January 1948). During the brief period (it was 3 months) of his second term as Chief Minister Prafulla Chandra Ghosh had to rely mostly upon those bureaucrats were the Chief Secretary- M. M. Basu, Upananda Mukherjee, Inspector-General of Police-Binay Ranjan Gupta, trusted Food Secretary and Commissioner of Police-P. K. Sen.[111]

Problems faced by PDF Ministry headed by Prafulla Chandra Ghosh

The first problem before the PDF Government was to maintain law and order in the pretext of the impending civil disobedience movement as well as violence made by the parties belonged to the United Front. The Chief Minister Prafulla Chandra Ghosh retained all the portfolios in his hand except Agriculture and Community Development, Irrigation and Waterways, Animal Husbandry and Veterinary Services and Fisheries which were entrusted to Haren Majumdar who was considered as number 2 within the 3-man Cabinet. Another Minister Amir Ali Molla was given the charge of the Health and Forest Departments. The Ministry was thus initiated its activities within a hostile atmosphere as because then the statewide protest strike was observing by the left parties. In that context, once, Prafulla Chandra Ghosh told Upananda Mukherjee (I.G.), remember Gandhiji's saying "violence can be crushed only by greater violence".[112] That was perhaps the enough indication to the I. G. in the field of maintaining law and order in the wake of leftist violence.

In order to quell the disturbances, immediately after taking oath of the new Ministry on 21st November 1967, section 144 Cr. Pc. was promulgated throughout the city. On 22nd November, the U.F. leaders announced to hold a protest rally defying the Section 144 Cr. Pc. and that would be addressed by some of the erstwhile Ministers of U. F. At the time, summoning top level Home Department officials along with Police Chief of Calcutta at his room Prafulla Chandra Ghosh gave strong directives to them and said that under no circumstances the Brigade Parade Ground meeting would be allowed to take place in the afternoon. That was actually the first show-down between the Government and the Opposition. There were huge preparations on both sides. A number of Deputy Commissioners of Police were given the charge of the task force. Two former Ministers namely Biswanath Mukherjee (C.P.I.) and Amar Chakrabarty (Judicial Minister, Forward Bloc) along with four other U. F. leaders took part to address the rally. They were severely beaten up and thereupon causing bleeding injuries to them. All the leaders including the convener of the United Front, Sudhin Kumar of the Revolutionary Communist Party were arrested. The directives of the Chief Minister were carried out effectively. The Chief Minister himself with another Minister went to Lalbazar control room to supervise police operation personally.

Disturbances were also intensified on the following day i. e. on 23rd November, the second day of the general strike summoned by a body known as 'Rashtriya Sangram Samity'. In case of resistance, the police had to fire 49 rounds and thereby one person was killed and totally 700 agitators were arrested. From the view point of the United Front leaders- the strike became completely success as a result of their organizing ability and whole hearted devotion of the party workers. Curfew was imposed in some areas particularly in north and central Calcutta.[113]

Role of the Congress Leadership behind the Survival of PDF Ministry under P. C. Ghosh

Apart from suppressing the violent activities in the name of protest against PDF Ministry another issue which mostly worried the Chief Minister was to convince and agree the congress leaders to join the ministry as early as possible. As the cabinet mainly depended on the goodwill of the congress party, so Prafulla Chandra Ghosh would keep in touch frequently with Atulya Ghosh and Prafulla Chandra Sen over telephone apart from holding discussions with them and urging them to persuade with the central leadership for getting permission so that the congress party in West Bengal directly would join in the coalition Ministry. P. C. Ghosh also expressed his helplessness to the leaders of the congress party that how far was it possible for him to fight a battle against so powerful opposition only with 17 supporters. Under the circumstances, both Atulya Ghosh and Prafulla Chandra Sen on behalf of the West Bengal Pradesh Congress jointly held an hour long discussion with Prafulla Chandra Ghosh at his residence on 26th November, 1967. Both the leaders assured Prafulla Chandra Ghosh reiterating the unconditional support of the congress party to the Progressive Democratic Front Ministry under his stewardship.[114]

A Historic Assembly Session for Trial of Strength

In the meantime, after the dismissal of the United Front Ministry by the Governor, then a United Front meeting was convened on 23rd November in order to decide their future course of action. After long discussion it was decided that a committee of 5 members consisting of Ajay Mukherjee, Jyoti Basu, Somenath Lahiri, Kashi Kanta Moitra and Kamal Guha to decide the action within the Assembly House. It was also decided in the meeting that the activities of the United Front would remain as it was. Ajay Mukherjee would act as leader, Jyoti Basu as Deputy and Kamal Guha would act as Chief-whiff within the Assembly. The leaders of the Front openly declared that the Ministry of Prafulla Chandra Ghosh was illegal and they would not recognize it.[115] In that exciting situation, the day of the Assembly Session came on the 29th November, 1967. The Speaker Bijay Kumar Banerjee who earlier seceded from the congress and elected the Speaker by the members of the United Front. In order to know the final outcome every one of the Writers' Buildings was waiting eagerly. It was expected that Prafulla Chandra Ghosh with the support of the congress MLAs in that trial of strength would win if the supporters of PDF were not prevented to attend the Assembly Session.

The speaker is the supreme authority within the Assembly House. Nobody even President of India cannot do anything against the decision as well as Ruling of the Speaker. As the United Front from the beginning claiming the PDF Ministry headed by Prafulla Chandra Ghosh was unconstitutional and illegal, so everything depended upon the mentality of the Speaker. It was expected that the members of the United Front would create chaos for disruption of the Assembly Session. But they did not do that. With the entrance of the Speaker in the House all the members stood up as a mark of honour to the chair of the Speaker. In the meantime, the car of the Chief Minister already entered into the Assembly Buildings and a group of congress MLAs and volunteers under the leadership of Bijay Singh Nahar greeted him with shouting the slogan of "Vande Mataram".

No United Front MLAs or their supporters were present there to raise any counter-slogans. Everything seemed as if normal and orderly. Only a few minutes before commencing the House at 1 p.m. the United Front members rose anti Prafulla Chandra Ghosh slogans. "Dharma Vira quit Bengal, Down, Down with Prafulla Chandra Ghosh, U.F. Zindabad".[116]

Speaker's Historical Ruling

Just at 1 p.m. on 29th November 1967, the Speaker, Bijay Kumar Banerjee entered into the Assembly House and immediately after standing up he brought a paper from the pocket and started reading out his ruling which was prepared earlier with the consultation of the 5 members committee and Mohan Kumarmangalam, former advocate general of Madraj and son in law of Ajay Mukherjee and Biswanath Mukherjee. Actually, Kumarmangalam himself prepared the draft of the ruling. He was all along a man of communist mentalities.[117] However, the Speaker's 5-page ruling was started reading before understanding anything by the opposition bloc. In the historic ruling what Speaker Bijay Kumar Banerjee stated were as under:

"Honourable Members, this House meets under extraordinary circumstances, I am prima facie satisfied that the dissolution of the Ministry headed by Shri Ajay Kumar Mukherjee followed by the appointment of Dr. P. C. Ghosh as Chief Minister and the summoning of this House on his advice is unconstitutional and invalid since it has been effected behind the back of this House. Pending a full and proper examination of the matter in exercise of powers vested in me under rule 15 of the Rules of Procedure of this Assembly, I adjourn the House sine die."[118]

Quoting from the ruling of his predecessor i. e. Speaker Nausher Ali on 29th March, 1945 of pre-independent undivided Bengal,[119] Speaker Bijay Kumar Banerjee said, "No doubt, the circumstances facing Shri Nausher Ali were different. But the essence of the matter, namely, that this House is the supreme authority in regard to making and unmaking Ministers, is the same. And this statement came from the lips of the presiding officer of this House when India was not free. Today when the sovereign Indian people have given unto themselves a Constitution, surely the authority of this House, has increased and not diminished." Continuing the Speaker said, "This is why I find it extremely difficult to recognize Dr. Prafulla Chandra Ghosh as a Chief Minister and his colleagues Shri Harendra Nath Majumdar and Dr. Amir Ali Molla as members of the Council of Ministers. Both the text of the articles of the Constitution and the precedent quoted above recognize no discretion in the Governor in respect of the appointment of the Council of Ministers. He is merely a registering authority to use the expression of my predecessor; an authority whose constitutional duty is to recognize and implement the decisions of the House". [120]

The Speaker in his ruling also said, "On a prima facie examination of the constitutional question involved, I find it impossible to recognize as legal, valid and constitutional the dissolution of the Council of Ministers, headed by Shri Ajoy Kumar Mukherjee. It follows then that the appointment of the Council of Ministers headed by Dr. P.C. Ghosh as Chief Minister is invalid and unconstitutional." The Speaker further said, "The matters in issue are of the highest constitutional importance. It is my regret that when an attempt was made to refer them for the opinion of the Supreme Court under Article 143 such attempt was frustrated. It is beyond dispute that the issues go to the very root of democracy. It is obvious, therefore, that if I am to find out how exactly I should act so as to preserve and protect the privileges of this House I should need more time and then only give a considered ruling on grave issues at stake. This is why in exercise of my powers under rule 15, I have adjourned the House sine die."[121]

Attack on Chief Minister Prafulla Chandra Ghosh

With the end of the ruling of the Speaker the most unfortunate event took place in the Assembly which never happened since 1937 that a Chief Minister himself being attacked inside the House. Whenever the pandemonium was going on after the ruling of the Speaker, then some of the opposition members rushed towards the Chief Minister who was fortunately then guarded by some congress members. Amidst of chaos a piece of wood thrown by an opposition MLA to Chief Minister which hit the Chief Minister and injured him below his eye. Then a red ink-pot was thrown aiming at him. Seeing his unsafe position some more members of his group came forward and made a ring around him and left the House immediately. A doctor was then summoned in order to dress up his injured cheek. His eyes somehow escaped miraculously and blood was trickling from his face. "It would have even caused my death" Prafulla Chandra Ghosh remarked to his friends. The whole affair was really unexpected, but the most surprising event of that fateful day was that the Leader of the Opposition, Ajay Kumar Mukherjee who was a worshiper of non-violence did not raise his single finger in order to restrain his party men and spare his ex-teacher from violence.[122]

The ruling of the Speaker however completely paralyzed the constitutional experts of the central government, the congress party as well as Governor and first of all they did not understand what should they do?

But, on the other hand, Y. B. Chavan, Central Home Minister declared in the Lok Sabha on 30th November 1967, that according to the legal advice what obtained by him with the view that the West Bengal Ministry headed by Prafulla Chandra Ghosh was 'Lawfully constituted'. Then he brought the matter in Loke Sabha and got it passed by the majority voters (195 – 21). But nobody was able to give the indication how Assembly could convene coming out from the ruling of the Speaker.[123]

Expansion of PDF Ministry

In the midst of uncertainty of the fate of the PDF Ministry headed by Prafulla Chandra Ghosh in West Bengal, the meeting of the National Development Council (NDC) was convened at Delhi on the 1st of December, 1967. In that insecure political atmosphere, though Home Minister Y. B. Chavan's statement in Lok Sabha had to boost up the morale of the Bengal Government, in spite of that the Chief Minister decided not to attend the NDC meeting but to remain in the city in order to meet any developing situation. In that context on 4th December 1967, the Chief Minister P. C. Ghosh advised the Governor to appoint eight persons as members of the PDF Ministry. They were Nalinakshya Sanyal, Gangadhar Pramanick, Amiya Kumar Kisku, (who later on for sometime became a Deputy Minister under Mrs. Indira Gandhi in 1972) Dasarathi Tah, as full Cabinet Ministers and Khagendra Nath Bandopadhaya, Rajendra Singh Singhi, Chandipada Mitra and Jagadananda Roy as State Ministers.[124]

Joining of the Congress party in PDF Ministry

After inducting eight Ministers from Progressive Democratic Front, the MLAs of congress party became very much anxious to become Minister. But the congress leaders of West Bengal specially Atulya Ghosh, Pratap Chandra Chunder and Siddhartha Shankar Ray after consultation with Prime Minister, Deputy Prime Minister and Home Minister declared that with the end of the constitutional dead lock, the congress party would join in the PDF Ministry positively. On behalf of P. C. Ghosh who was repeatedly requesting to the West Bengal congress leaders and Congress High Commands to form a ministerial alliance in order to strengthen his hands. In that context, on 9th January 1968, a meeting of the Congress Parliamentary Board was held at Hyderabad. In that meeting Congress Parliamentary Board approved the demand of the congress leaders of West Bengal for joining in PDF Ministry. After that on 14th January a meeting of the congress party was convened at Congress Bhavan. As per the decision of the meeting full power was entrusted to the hands of Prafulla Chandra

Sen and Atulya Ghosh to finalize the names of the would be ministers. According to the decision of the West Bengal Pradesh Congress committee the names of Khagendra Nath Dasgupta, Rabindra Lal Singha, Bijay Singh Nahar, Pratap Chandra Chunder, Abdus Sattar and Binode Behari Manji were recommended by P. C. Ghosh to Governor to be included in his Ministry. Accordingly they took oath on 15th January, 1968.[125]

Personal and Group Politics among Three Ghoshes

At that critical hour of excitement of selecting the names of the ministers, the selectors i. e. Prafulla Chandra Sen and Atulya Ghosh did not mention the name of Ashu Ghosh who was considered as the key player of toppling the United Front Ministry. He had personal vendetta against Atulya Ghosh and Prafulla Chandra Sen. The defeat of the two top leaders of West Bengal in 1967 general elections had considerably eroded their popularity as well as prestige. When Ashu Ghosh found that his role to put an end of the first U.F. Ministry was unrewarded, then he took every possible initiatives to crack down the Congress-PDF Ministry. It was published in the newspaper on 15-01-1968 that 32 MLAs, followers of Ashu Ghosh, were going to withdraw their support from the Congress-PDF coalition Ministry.[126] Not only that Ashu Ghosh with the help of his two political emissaries namely Rabi Chowdhury and Ranadhir Barman communicated with the United Front leaders and assured them that if they (U.F. leaders) agreed to support them (Ashu Ghosh and his followers who were subsequently formed a new party named- Indian National Democratic Front) then they would form a *'Jatiya Sarkar'* jointly by the all political parties excluding congress.[127]

In order to avoid crisis Pratap Chandra Chunder, the then President of the West Bengal Pradesh Congress Committee met Ashu Ghosh in his residence but that meeting produced no result. Thereafter Ashu Ghosh sent two of his political emissaries to Delhi to inform the Congress High Command including Prime Minister, Deputy Prime Minister and Home Minister that unless his demands relating to his induction in the ministry was not positive, he would obviously bring about the fall of the new Coalition Ministry.

In this juncture, Chief Minister P. C. Ghosh made a public statement against Ashu Ghosh on 3rd February, 1968. P. C. Ghosh charged Ashu Ghosh for violation of all kinds of discipline and his effort to topple the ministry. He said, "Two of his emissaries came to me with a request to take Mr. Ghosh in the Cabinet. I pointed out that it would not be possible as a criminal case and that of another misappropriation of fund pending against him in the court. They requested me to withdraw the case against him, but I did not comply with the same".[128] Not only that P. C. Ghosh wanted to know from Pratap Chandra Chunder, the then PCC President on that 3rd February, 1968 regarding his inaction against Ashu Ghosh who openly maligning the image of the congress party. In that pretext, Dr. Pratap Chandra Chunder after consultation with other leaders of the congress party, as a PCC President he temporarily suspended Ashu Ghosh from the congress party on 3rd February, 1968 and gave a long charge sheet against him.[129]

The Indian National Democratic Front of Ashu Ghosh and his effort to form a INDF-U.F. Coalition Ministry with Barrister Shankar Das Banerjee

In that situation, on 11th February, 1968 Ashu Ghosh along with his followers founded a new party, known as 'Indian National Democratic Front' (henceforth INDF). The press in Calcutta had given wide coverage of Ashu Ghosh's day-to-day activities particularly his efforts in case of formation of an alternative party. Shankar Das Banerjee, a senior Barrister who became an MLC, then an MLA, Speaker, Advocate General and finally Finance Minister during P. C. Sen's Government (he was dropped under Kamraj Plan along with Ajay Mukherjee) was projected as the leader of the new party. Ashu Ghosh himself became the Deputy leader of his newly formed INDF party. Shankar Das Banerjee was equally pained with the West Bengal congress leaders particularly Atulya Ghosh and Prafulla Chandra Sen for crushing him out of politics under the pretext of Kamraj Plan. However, Shankar Das Banerjee after meeting the Governor informed Shankar Das Banerjee further claimed that the total number of strength in the Assembly to support INDF would rise to 150 (UF-132 + INDF-18). [130] The Governor was informed by two other letters of Shankar Das Banerjee, about the withdrawal of support of 18 MLAs from the Congress-PDF Coalition Government, of whom 12 from the Congress party, 4 from the PDF and rest 2 from nominated Anglo-Indian members. Ashu Ghosh further claimed that his party was in a position to form an alternative government with Shankar Das Banerjee as Leader and he himself as Deputy Leader.[131]

In that moment, Governor Dharma Vira asked P. C. Ghosh, Chief Minister of West Bengal whether he was prepare to face the trial of strength in the Assembly or not? In the meantime, Assembly was summoned by Governor on 14th February 1968 and P. C. Ghosh was also supported the action of Governor. At that juncture, taking advantages of summoning the assembly on 14th February, Ashu Ghosh tried to convince the United Front leaders to allow the summoning of Assembly so that they could win in the trial of strength in order to oust the Congress-PDF coalition Ministry. But the United Front leaders made it clear that as per the ruling of the Speaker on 29th November 1967, the stalemate of the Assembly was still continuing and in order to show the honour to the ruling of the Speaker at least for two hour Presidential Rule must had to be introduced in West Bengal, otherwise they would not allow to summon the Assembly under any circumstances.[132]

A Historic Joint Session and Attack on Governor Dharma Vira on 14th February, 1968

Political circles of West Bengal as well as Delhi were speculating whether after the ruling of the Speaker on 29th November, 1967 the Assembly could at all be convened. But falsifying the speculations of the political circle, the joint Session of the Assembly was summoned by the Governor on 14th February 1968, where Speaker was all in all as per regulation at the time of opening the Session. The opposition parties repeated their old tactics in order to prevent the Governor to address the session. Blocking the main door of the House, the U. F. MLAs were shouting slogans so that the Governor could not enter into the chamber for ceremonial procession. But the Governor Dharma Vira showed his remarkable courage and presence of mind through a side door securing his entry into the Assembly House. Thereafter the Governor somehow occupied a seat and started reading from a printed copy. But as and when the Governor tried to read out a few sentences of his printed address, then in the history of any legislature it was for the first time (at least from 1932-33) that voice of the Governor was drowned by shouting slogans. Moreover, some cushions were also thrown from opposition bloc to hit his head. Naturally, it was certainly impossible for him as well as for anyone to continue the speech. So, he was escorted at once and brought out of the House by a side gate and as if flee from the Assembly with the help of a number of pro-Government MLAs and employees by his car.[133]

After leaving the Assembly of Governor Dharma Vira, then wrestling started among the MLAs of both sides. One of the MLAs of violent United Front had thrown a cushion towards P. C. Ghosh. Another one thrown an ink pot and more one rushed towards P. C. Ghosh and slapped at him. Therefore, instead of resolving the constitutional crisis, the summoning of the Assembly, in other words complicated it further more when the Speaker Bijay Kumar Banerjee reiterating his previous ruling again and adjourned the Assembly sine die declaring Ghosh Ministry illegal.[134] Considering the gravity of the situation, the very next day i.e. on 15th February 1968 the Cabinet of the Central Government decided to dissolve the Legislative Assembly as well as Ministry of West Bengal.[135]

Prime Minister's Last Attempt to Reconcile between Two Groups of the Congress party

In spite of happenings the above incidents the West Bengal Congress leaders were still thinking that if they were able to show the support of the majority of the MLAs, then the Congress-PDF coalition government would exist. In the meantime, on 18th February 1968 at the invitation of the Prime Minister Indira Gandhi and the Congress High Command Pratap Chandra Chunder, P. C. Ghosh, Atulya Ghosh and Prafulla Chandra Sen left for Delhi while Ashu Ghosh was already there on the same day to have a separate talk with the Prime Minister. Both the contending parties met the Prime Minister, Home Minister and others Congress high-ups, but the possibility of rapprochement was seemed bleak.[136] After consultation with the Congress High Command in Delhi, the leaders of the congress in West Bengal felt that the central congress leaders already took the decision of the imposition of Presidential Rule in West Bengal, so the West Bengal leaders would not go for any controversy with their central leaders. In that context, according to the advice of the Governor Dharma Vira, Prafulla Chandra Ghosh tendered his resignation on 20th February, 1968.[137]

B. i. Imposition of Presidential Rule

On 20th February, 1968 the Presidential Rule was first imposed in West Bengal following the resignation of P. C. Ghosh on the same date, which ultimately led to the end of political uncertainties in the State. Thus West Bengal became the third State throughout the country to have Presidential Rule after the Fourth General Elections in 1967.[138]

Date of poll and Filing of Nomination

After continuing almost one year long Presidential Rule over West Bengal the people were sincerely waiting for the news of the date of polls in West Bengal and the installation of a popular ministry that would be elected by the electors. In that context, M.M. Basu, the Chief Secretary of West Bengal at a press meeting announced that the upcoming polling would be held on 9th February, 1969 and also expressed the hope that next ministry likely to be installed by February 16. As per the information of Mr. S. K. Mukherjee, Chief Electoral Officer that within the last date for filing the nomination papers i. e. on 8th January totally 1,000 candidates of at least 25 political parties filed their nomination papers for the 280 assembly constituencies. The United Front comprising 12 (previously it was 14) political parties i. e. CPI(M), CPI, Bangla Congress, Forward Bloc, RSP, SUCI,

SSP, Revolutionary PSP, Bolshevik Party, Gorkha League, RCPI and Marxist Forward Bloc had collectively set up 270 candidates apart from supporting 6 independent and 4 PSP candidates. The congress party filed the nomination for all the 280 seats. The Lok Dal set up 70 while Jana Sangha filed the nomination for 59 seats. The Indian National Democratic Front (INDF) of Ashu Ghosh also claimed that it filed the nomination for all the 280 seats!

The total numbers of contestants for the 280 Assembly seats in that year were 1,019 persons. Two former Chief Ministers of West Bengal, Prafulla Chandra Sen (Congress) and Ajay Mukherjee (Bangla Congress) were again locked in battle for Arambagh constituency while Jyoti Basu (CPI-M) had to contest against Amar Banerjee, a student leader of the congress party in Baranagore constituency.[140]

The Mid-term Poll and Result

At last the long awaited 9th February, 1969 came and election for the formation of Fifth Legislative Assembly was held throughout West Bengal. The election was started from early in the morning and ended in the evening within more or less peaceful environment. Mr. S. P. Sen Verma, the Chief Election Commissioner of India expressed his satisfaction for prevailing general peaceful atmosphere on the polling day in West Bengal.

After the end of the election and thereafter counting of votes the party wise comparative results of that mid-term Assembly election (in 1967 and 1969) were as under: Congress- 55 (in 1967 it was 127), CPI (M)- 80 (in 1967 it was 43), Bangla Congress- 33 (in 1967 it was 34), CPI-30 (in 1967 it was 16), Forward Bloc- 21(in 1967 it was 13), RSP- 12 (previously it was 6), SSP-9 (previously it was 7), SUCI-7 (previously it was 4), PSP-5 (previously it was 7), Gorkha League- 4 (Previously it was 3), LSS-4 (in 1967 it was 5), MFB -1 (in 1967 it was 1), WPI-2 (in 1967 it was 2), RCPI-2 (previously it was 0), Swatantra-0 (previously it was 1), Janasangha-O (previously it was 1), INDF-1, Progressive Muslim League-3, Independent and others supported by United Front-9.[141]

Landslide Defeat of the Congress Party

The result of fifth midterm general election of 1969 simply showed that it was the landslide defeat of the congress party in West Bengal. The strength of the congress party in the assembly reduced from 127 to only 55. After showing the result of that election it was found that the calculations of the congress bosses were so mistake that even the All India Congress President N. Nijalingappa also became astonished. The congress party in West Bengal never had to face such like situation in view of electoral results since independence. Actually the congress leaders were as if living their own universe. Their assessment about the changing attitude of the politically matured people of West Bengal was tragically wrong. Taking the responsibility of the unthinkable defeat of the congress party in West Bengal, Atulya Ghosh tendered his resignation as a member from the Congress Working Committee, although later on he had withdrawn the resignation letter at the request of the All India Congress President. In that very alarming situation of the congress party in the state, Siddhartha Shankar Ray was elected as the Leader of the Congress Legislature Party of 55 members. In first meeting of the CLP the name of Siddhartha Shankar Ray was proposed by Prafulla Chandra Sen and seconded by Bijay Singh Nahar. On behalf of the congress party Siddhartha Shankar Ray was authorized to elect the other office-bearers. [142]

Congress's Defeat and Atulya Ghosh's Reaction

Though there were many causes behind the defeat of the congress party in West Bengal, but as per the explanation of Atulya Ghosh- the involvement of Prime Minister Indira Gandhi herself and West Bengal congress leaders including Prafualla Chandra Sen for the toppling the First United Front Government headed by Ajay Mukherjee could not support the politically conscious people of West Bengal. As the congress party was in power since Independence throughout the country and thereupon the congressmen virtually lost the values of democratic spirit. In democracy the role of the opposition parties are always respectable. But forgetting the spirit of democracy, the congress leaders under any circumstances i. e. using the play of money and adopting various misdoing on behalf of the congress party and taking the support of Prime Minister determined for overthrowing the United Front Ministry. But the people of West Bengal did not comply that move of the congress party which reflected in the ballot box in the midterm poll of 1969.[143] It is mention worthy that Atulya Ghosh was all along against the move of knocking down the United Front Ministry and was in favour of continuing the front Ministry headed by Ajay Kumar Mukherjee. It is also noteworthy that after the defeat of Atulya Ghosh in the Fourth General election in 1967, central as well as state leadership of the congress party started ignoring him in many ways in order to diminish the image of Atulya Ghosh who was a very dynamic leader and had the record of his huge sacrifice in pre-independence era. Moreover, the congress party in West Bengal became an indomitable power and tested the victory in the last three general elections under his leadership.[144] On the other hand, on behalf of the United Front Jyoti Basu and Ajay Mukherjee in a brief press statement thanked the people of West Bengal for their political consciousness and giving massive verdict in favour of Front.

Tussle over Ministry Formation

In spite of landslide defeat of the congress party as well as massive victory of the United Front in the midterm poll in 1969, it was not easy to from the second United Front Ministry due to claiming and counter claiming for the post of Chief Minister and Home Minister between CPI (M) and Bangla Congress. Logic behind the CPI (M)'s claim was that as the single largest party (it had gained 80 seats) not only within the Front but also among the all parties those who were participated in the midterm poll in 1969, it demanded both Chief Minister and Home Ministry portfolios. But the other United Front partners specially the Bangla Congress, CPI, Forward Bloc and PSP came into an understanding and jointly claimed that Bangla Congress leader as well as Chief Minister of first United Front Ministry Shri Ajay Kumar Mukherjee would be the Chief Minister along with Home portfolios in his hand in the second United Front Ministry.[145] But on behalf of the CPI (M), Promode Das Gupta, State Secretary of CPI (M) declared "At least without getting the Home Portfolio CPI (M) would not participate in the second United front Government. It was the final decision of the CPI (M) party that under any circumstances Home portfolio must have to be retained in their hand".[146] Understanding the importance of the Home portfolio, Harekrishna Konar, CPI (M) leader and minister categorically remarked, "As the aim of the CPI (M) is to strengthen the democratic movement and it would not be fulfilled without Home portfolio in their hand, so any understanding without Home portfolio would not be meterialised."[147]

In that situation of deadlock, the CPI (M) party agreed to leave the demand of Chief Ministership but in no way the leaders of that party were ready to give up the Home portfolio. Lastly, in a United Front meeting held on 20th February it was decided that Ajay Mukherjee would be Chief Minister along with Home (political) and Finance portfolio and Jyoti Basu would be Deputy Chief Minister along with Home portfolio. The name of Ajay Mukherjee as leader of the united Front was proposed by Jyoti Basu and seconded by Jatin Chakrabarty.[148] On 21st February 1969, Ajay Mukherjee, leader of the United Front met the Governor Dharma Vira and apprised him regarding the decision of the meeting of Front Committee held on 20th February and requested him to arrange a swearing-in-ceremony. After being convinced by the claim of Ajay Mukherjee, the leader of the United Front, Governor fixed 25th February, 1969 as the date for oath-taking ceremony accordingly. It was decided in the meeting of the

United Front Committee on 20th and 21st February 1969, that a cabinet with 30 ministers would be constituted and among the total number, as per the party wise MLAs strength,- 9 from CPI (M), 4 from Bangla Congress, 3 from CPI, 3 from Forward Bloc, 2 from the RSP and one each from the S.S.P, Gorkha League, L.S.S., R.C.P.I., Workers Party and the P.S.P. The decision of the appointment of four Ministers of State was also taken in order to fulfill the demands of the smaller parties.[149]

A 30—Member Cabinet

As scheduled, with taking the oath of office by Ajay Kumar Mukherjee along with his team of 29 on 25th February, 1969 in the Throne Room at Raj Bhavan- the long one year and six (371 days)—days Presidential Rule in the state was terminated. Though, due to the disagreement among the partners of the United Front regarding ministry making, the image of the front slightly dimmed, but overall confidence of the common people were not fatigued. At the time of oath taking ceremony as well as entrance of the ministers into the Writers Buildings', the thousands of people came to wish the United Front Ministers with great hope for the betterment of the people of West Bengal. The crowed was so bigger and enthusiastic that the Chief Minister Ajay Mukherjee and Deputy Chief Minister Jyoti Basu had to come out from their room several times to address the crowd from the balcony. All the ministers of the front entered into the room of the Chief Minister one by one for holding a formal discussion. In his first press meet, Chief Minister Ajay Mukherjee said, "Though we are called the United Front, we are like a single political party and we will serve the people in a united manner."[150] Chief Minister also said, "We are cautious about the gravity of the responsibility conferred upon us. Our efforts would be succeeded if we can fulfill the rising aspiration of the people partially through our work." In that connection Deputy Chief Minister Jyoti Basu remarked, "Work is being start from today. We shall try to be worthy and reflect the aspiration of the people."[151]

The First Cabinet Meeting and Release of All Naxalites and Withdraw All Cases against Central Government Employees During Strike

In its first cabinet meeting of the United Front Government held on 26th February 1969, it was decided to release all Naxalites immediately, who were imprisoned under the Preventive Detention Act, in connection with the Naxalbari movement, subject to reconsideration by the Home Minister Jyoti Basu. It was also decided to withdraw all pending cases against Central Government Employees owing to their total strike in the month of September, 1968. The cabinet also decided to reduce the tram fare which was raised from 2nd January 1969.[152]

The Second Cabinet Meeting and Urging President–Prime Minister to withdraw Dharma Vira before Budget Session

In a cabinet meeting of the Second United Front Government held on 2nd March, 1969, decided unanimously for sending a telegram to the President of India to urge him to withdraw Dharma Vira, Governor of West Bengal prior to the Assembly Session which was expected to be held on 6th March. In response to the demand of the West Bengal Government the Union Home Minister, Y. B. Chavan rejected the demand with a firm 'no' that Governor Dharma Vira should be repealed before 6th March. Union Home Minister also disclosed that as per the Governor's request for his release on 'personal grounds' was under consideration. Following the precedence the ministers of the United Front Government prepared the address of the Governor which he had to deliver at the time of opening the Assembly Session. In that address the role of the Governor behind the toppling of the first United Front Government and his partisan activities were severely criticized. Actually the front leadership wanted to condemn the Governor's role by his own mouth. After reading the draft address when Governor expressed his unwillingness to read out the controversial portions, then Promode Dasgupta, State Secretary of CPI (M) declared, "If the Governor would not agree to read out full address and skip any parts of the same, then he would be *gheraod* within the Assembly House un till and unless he would not agree to read the whole address."[153] In that context, as per the guidance of the Central Government, Governor Dharma Vira read out the Address formally but skipping some portions which contained very critical references regarding his role behind the removal of the first United Front Ministry in 1967. Then, United Front MLAs started slogan against Dharma Vira. However, Governor Dharma Vira ended his speech describing the Centre-State relation as 'frankly intolerable'.[154]

The United Front leaders would not get much time to pick up anti Dharma Vira campaign. On behalf of Central Government, Home Minister Y. B. Chavan declared the release of Dharma Vira and he would be replaced by Shanti Swarup Dhawan (henceforth S.S. Dhawan), Indian High Commissioner in England on 19th March, 1969. At the initial stage the front leaders were not agree to accept the name of S.S. Dhawan as the Governor of West Bengal but later on they had to accord with the Central Government decision. Dharma Vira, left Clacutta on 28th March in 1969 and S. S.

Dhawan took the charge of the office of the Governor on 19th September in the same year. During that interim period as per regulation Mr. Justice Deep Narayan Sinha, the then Chief Justice of Calcutta High Court was acting as the Governor of West Bengal. [155]

Unfortunate Developments—Durgapur Steel Factory, Rabindra Sarobar Stadium and Cossipur Gun & Shell Factory:

Durgapur Steel Factory: With the end of the tussle between Centre and West Bengal State over the issue of Governor Dharma Vira, some unfortunate development took place in Durgapurr Steel Factory, Cossipur Gun and Sheel Factory and Rabindra Sarobar Stadium. The event of Durgapur took place on 24th March, 1969. The tragic event of Durgapur started centering the removal of its own security guards for the installation of central force according to the earlier decision of the Central Government. But the communist influential union of the security guards demanded no central force would be deployed under any circumstances. The Union of the Durgapur Steel Factory marched to the Head Office and when they were resisted by the C.R.P.F. and ultimately conflict broke out and C.R.P.F. was forced to fire in order to disperse the agitated workers. Then the workers raise the demand of arrest of Mr. Pal, chief security officer and Mr. Oadhera, head of the factory. Jyoti Basu, Home Minister of the Second United Front Government supported the move of the union and ultimately chief security officer Mr. Pal was arrested. Jyoti Basu himself demanded for removal of C.R.P.F.[156]

Rabindra Sarobar Stadium: One such unfortunate event took place on April 6 at Rabindra Sarobar Stadium where a musical soiree was arranged. Due to the disturbances of the microphone led to exhaust the patience of the audience and ultimately pandemonium broke out. In that context, in order to bring the situation under control the Police had to intervene and fire. Out of police firing one person died at once and huge numbers of people were injured. It was come out after two or three days from various sources that fleeing women were molested on a mass scale by anti-social elements. This incident resounded throughout the state and complains one after another started reaching to Prime Minister and Home Minister of India and demand for impartial judicial enquiry was raised. But Jyoti Basu claimed it as a conspiracy of the Central Government against United Front Government. It was alleged against Jyoti Basu that he was reluctant to go for any impartial enquiry due to the involvement of his two close associates among the organizers namely Snehangsha Kanta Acharya and Minister Ram Chatterjee. However due to the pressure from inside and outside the cabinet Jyoti Basu was compelled to appoint a one man enquiry committee headed by Justice Shambhu Ghosh on 16th April, 1969. After long days when enquiry was over then Justice Ghosh submitted his report where it was found that there was no any incident of molestation on women.[157]

Cossipur Gun & Shell Factory: In Cossipur also there was going on a trouble between authority of the factory and the workers union influenced by the communists. On 8th April, 1969 conflict started over the question of entering into the factory between the guards and the workers. In the midst of the conflict the guards of the factory had to fire to quell the disturbances and thereby four workers died at on the spot and one more dead body was rescued later on. In that context Jyoti Basu rushed to the spot and supported the claim of the workers demanded the punishment of the guards who had shot fired. But the authority argued that as the guards were the part of the Army so they would be judged only by the military court. Then on 10th April, state wide general strike was called for highlighting the Cossipur incidents and the state government was also supported the strike. Another fresh conflict started at Kancharapara between the two workers group and as a result of that one more died. Police also fired to subside the situation and lastly curfew was imposed. However in the Military Court, army authority was lastly won.[158]

Inter-Party Clash

At the beginning of the formation of the Second United Front Government, most of the parties of the front governments opposing the demand of CPI (M) having Home portfolio out of fear that after getting Home Department in their hand they would use the power of that department in order to spread sphere of influence. Hare Krishna Konar, Minister in Charge of Land and Land Revenue Department declared on 27th March, 1969 that in the field of the struggle for land among the United Front partners, police would not interfere. A circular in that regard was sent to Home Department.[159] After that CPI (M) started occupying land, embankment and school forcefully. After seeing the activities of the CPI (M) the other parties also engaged themselves in the same work and thereby inter-party bloody struggle started among the United Front parties. In Calcutta the main leaders of each party engaged themselves to impose allegation against one another but in rural areas that took the shape of a bloody struggle when the supporters of each party got involved in conflict with their traditional weapon like stick, arrows along with gun and bombs. As a result of that, murders, injuries, looting and in some cases molestation of women also became the very common phenomena in West Bengal during the second United Front Government.[160]

It might be note worthy that in most of the cases in the inter-party conflict the main accused was CPI (M). In the May Day of 1969 Calcutta witnessed violent clashes between the supporters of two contending parties i. e. on behalf of U.F. dominated by mainly CPI (M) and the newly formed CPI (ML), extremist group of the CPI (M), otherwise known as Naxalites. There was an open fight between the two groups and in due course the police had to make lathi charges and use tear gas to bring the situation under control.[161]

The Inter-Party Conflict Came to the Open Platform

At Alipurduar of Jalpaiguri district in North Bengal two party i. e. CPI (M) and RSP were involved in the inter-party conflict on 16th May, 1969 that led to the death of five person altogether. The situation was so explosive that at last Curfew was imposed in order to bring the situation normal. After that incident it was alleged on behalf of the RSP that police acted as a partisan manner and with the help of the police the cadre of the CPI (M) made that bloody campaign.[162] The Alipurduar incident was followed by many inter-party cum bloody clashes which were taken place in different parts of West Bengal. It was at Taherpur in Nadia District, conflict started between CPI (M) and RSP, in Haringhata CPI verses CPI (M). Within two or three days CPI and CPI (M) took the course of brutality in order to subdue each other. For example the places like Canning and Ranaghat were turned into common spot of clashes. On 30th May at Jadavpur CPI (M) and SUCI were involved in inter-party struggle for establishing their hold and as a result of that a number of persons were severely injured. Apart from Alipurduar incident and those which are mentioned above more such unwanted incidents were taken place in various parts of both North and South Bengal. All these events had sufficient reasons to agitate the common masses of West Bengal and all other leaders including Chief Minister were not exception.[163]

Before the outbreak of the inter-party conflict for expansion of their support base, in the meantime, the United Front Cabinet took two very major decisions on 24th and 25th March 1969. Out of anti congress feeling and taking the attitude for throwing the congress party entirely from all spheres of activities, the United Front passed an Ordinance on 24th March, by which the school boards in all district were declared null and void. By another Ordinance on 25th March, all Zilla Parishad (District Council) and Anchalic Parishad (local council) were declared nullified. After abolishing School Managing Committees, administrators were installed in the Schools and Colleges according to testing the loyalties to the parties. Those teachers were not agreed with the activities of the party nominated administrators they became subject to oppress. In some cases teachers' were forced to resign in the face of severe resistance. That practice was so exaggerated that even after a certain time Satyapriya Roy, the then Education Minister, who was very radical in his attitude, forced to raise his voice against the forceful resignation of the teachers.[164]

As the 'gherao culture' was initiated during the First United Front Government and extended in a large scale during Second United Front Government regime. The gherao tactics entered from industry to the premises of the educational institutions. The practice of gherao was so frequent that some of the ministers of the front started giving statement about the excessiveness of the system. In that context, Sushil Kumar Dhara, Minister in Charge of Commerce and Industries and Agro-Industries Corporation was himself gheraod at Jaldhaka in Darjeeling District when he went there on 24th May, 1969 to visit the 'Jaldhaka Projects', an electricity producing centre.[165]As protest against that Gherao, once well known Gandhian leader Sushil Dhara started fasting until the gherao was lifted. Though Chief Minister Ajay Mukherjee and Home Minister Jyoti Basu repeatedly requested him to use police force as much as possible to suppress the agitators and come back to Calcutta. But Sushil Dhara did not do so, rather in the fourth day of his fasting he sent a Rediogram to Chief Minister expressing his firmness i. e., "You know me best! Bless me to overcome all weaknesses and to get strength to continue my fast till the mission is successful."[166] At last the agitators were forced to withdraw their gherao programme seeing the firmness of Minister Sushil Dhara's stance against lawlessness in the industrial field in the name of gherao at night of the fourth day of his fasting. Then in the fifth day of his fasting at 7 a.m. Sushil Dhara ended his fasting after drinking fruit juice in the hands of Shiu Mangal Singh, President of Darjeeling District Bangla Congress Committee.[167]

Attack of the *Ananda Bazar Patrika* Office

Another unfortunate event took place during this time. A group of students who were representing five left parties forcefully entered into 'Ananda Bazar Patrika' office and damaged glass panes and telephone wires. They also broke and damaged some furniture of the office. These young student representatives were very much dissatisfied due to critical coverage of news along with the editorial comments relating to the activities of the U.F. Government. Jyoti Basu, as a Home Minister admitted this raid in the Assembly. This was actually the first time that a newspaper office was attacked as well as ransacked by supporters of the Government. On behalf of the opposition, the congress party described it in the Assembly as nothing short to an attempt to suppress the freedom of press and force them to 'kowtow' their line.[168]

United Front in Disarray

In Calcutta for the first time the Chief Minister gave public statement expressing his unhappiness and anxiety over the violent incidents that happened inside the State. He said to the press that he was disturbed by some recent incidents that affecting the law and order situation in the State (he was referring to the killing of five small landowners under the Police Station of Basanti in 24-Parganas in the presence of a police party) and admitted that discussions between the front leaders in case of taking measures to prevent such clashes produced little result. Most of the clashes were due to land disputes. The violence was committed by supporters of SUCI. They had strong pockets in certain areas of South 24-Parganas. In the next day's meeting the SUCI representatives were reprimanded by other party leaders for excesses committed by them.[169]

Stormy Raid of Assembly by Policemen

After becoming Deputy Chief Minister and Home Minister, Jyoti Basu at the very beginning dismissed Upananda Mukherjee, I. G. of Police, and he was replaced by Sachin Ghosh who was very much loyal to Jyoti Basu as well as CPI (M). Similarly some peoples were posted in the D. I. G.s testing loyalties. As a result of that whole police department came absolutely under the control of Jyoti Basu or CPI M) party. Most of the police officers came to the conclusion that it would be their duty to satisfy Jyoti Basu and his party. So, in that context wherever any clashes took place police started acting as a partisan manner. Moreover, when it was circulated that in case of land dispute and trade union related matters police would not interfere, in that way after making the police force inactive, the CPI (M) party started occupying land, dams, and various unions for spreading their support base. Incidentally, the communists had the long cherished grievances against the police forces, now getting the opportunities they were go for gheraoing the police stations. The police were insulted in public places which produced grudge among the police personnel against the CPI (M) leaders as well as the communists. In that context, after the murder of a police constable named Shankar Das Sharma, the angry police personnel carrying the dead body marched Assembly House at around 4.30 p.m. on 31st July, 1969.[170]

After entering into the Assembly House, the infuriated policemen started breaking the microphone stands, tables and tore up Order Papers. Minister

Biswanath Mukherjee and other several MLAs were beaten up. After showing vandalism inside the House then the agitators ran towards the Speaker's room and tried to open it by force. The angry police men then went towards the Deputy Chief Minister's room. He was the main target of the aggrieved police personnel. After entering Jyoti Basu's room more than half a dozen men who were turned brute with anger started breaking glass panels of the almirah and the flower vase on the table. At that moment, Jyoty Basu in a mild tone but firmly told, "Take your seat and tell me what you have to say". He was at first visibly shaken due to the unexpected turn of events. After that in an angry voice he roared, "It is a sinful act to raid the House while in session. I have my sympathy for the murdered policeman, Shankar Das Sharma. As a matter of fact, I have a garland ready here for him. But after your disgraceful conduct I do not feel like doing it." After that the agitators lost their nerves. Again Basu said in a violent tone, "You will have to pay a heavy price for this".[171]

Action Taken Against the Invading Policemen

However the next day of that incident i. e. on 1st August, 1969 the United Front demanded to punish four big bosses of the police department. They were- Sachin Ghosh, I. G., P. K. Sen, Police Commissioner, Ranjit Gupta, D.I.G. I.B. and Debabrata Dhar, D.I.G, Presidency Division. But instead of giving punishment, Jyoti Basu appointed an enquiry Committee headed by Ranu Gupta. Then after taking the approval of the Cabinet, Jyoti Basu dismissed Subodh Dutta, President of Police Association along with others active workers of the police association under the 311 Section of the Constitution so that the punished police personnel could not go to any appeal court. In that way creating a fearful atmosphere and in the name of punishment to the offender extreme favoritism was shown to the party men and thereby Jyoti Basu created the ground for controlling the police association in his hands.[172]

United Front Vis-à-vis Violence

In the midst of the atrocities committed by the CPI (M) only because of strengthening their organization, the United Front leaders met number of times at the aim of stopping the inter-party clashes and sometimes very good proposals were also adopted, but there was no result at all. Under the circumstances, Chief Minister Ajay Mukherjee in a reaction to the pressmen on 7th September, 1969, said, "I am really unhappy due to the inter-party conflict and if that practices were not stopped then it would create such a situation that government would not be able to continue its activities easily."[173]

But there was no sign of stopping the politics of murder, blood shedding which was going on in full swing in the tea gardens of Jalpaiguri, Mathurapur and Baruipur of South 24 Parganas. In that excited environment of inter-party clashes and blood shedding, Chief Minister Ajay Mukherjee went to Delhi and met Prime Minister Indira Gandhi on 26th September, 1969 and discussed for long time.[174]After coming back of Ajay Mukherjee from Delhi a meeting of the Secretariat of Bangla Congress was held on 7th October, 1969. The meeting was presided over by Ajay Mukherjee. The resolution of that meeting came to the public notice though the contemporary newspapers. It was brought to the news headlines that the entire West Bengal was in a violent move and the law and order was questioned. It appears from the statement that if the ongoing violence and humiliation of women were not stopped, the Bangla Congress would have no alternatives but to initiate resistance movement on Gandhian lines.[175] After distribution the resolution copies to the pressmen and openly expressed on the interrogation of the journalists that "I do not think about the dissolution of the U. F. Government and the imposition of Presidential Rule as well"[176] The main allegations which however, focused in the newspaper that - several hundred people lost their lives due to the excessiveness committed by a particular political party i. e. CPI (M).[177]

Sharp Reaction of Jyoti Basu and United Front Meeting on 16th October, 1969

As Sukumar Roy, member of the Bangla Congress Secretariat, in the meantime became very close to the CPI (M) and divulged to the CPI (M) leaders that it was due to Sushil Dhara's influence Bangla Congress adopted that resolution and party President Ajay Mukherjee had no approval on it. After getting such information Home Minister Jyoti Basu reacted sharply against that resolution saying, "Let them say so at the U.F. meeting. It is absurd" (referring to the killing of several hundred men).[178]Jyoti Basu sent a strong letter to the United Front partners on 11th October and mentioned that "untill and unless the proposal of Bangla Congress will not be placed for discussion in the Front meeting, all the joint programmes should be stopped."[179] Naturally, United Front meeting was held on 16th October, 1969. Jyoti Basu in a rude voice is said to have accused the proposals of Bangla Congress as it was completely absurd and false and with this he also raised the question and said, "Why these false allegations were given to the press and Bangla Congress must have to be answerable".[180] Hearing the statement of Jyoty Basu, Ajay Mukherjee, ever a calm and cool minded man was shocked and his face was flared up and remarked, "Am I Chief

Minister or Foolish Minister? Am I blind, deaf and dumb? Am I not watching what is happening in the state."[181] Thereafter, Chief Minister asked Sushil Dhara-"Sushil, place all the facts," Then Sushil Dhara narrated the horrible evidences of lootings, murders, injuries, bloodshed, persecution of women etc. With the end of Sushil Dhara's statement Nirmal Basu of Forward Bloc shouted at once and said, "Police was being used as per the direction of the CPI (M). CPI (M) was not abiding the instruction of the Front in the educational field. Oppression was going on everywhere. At that point of time we should instruct our followers to take actions against all vandalism."[182] Then Somenath Lahiri of CPI remarked, "Your leader Sundarayya said, there is some anti-people parties like-CPI, Bangla Congress, SUCI and Froward Bloc in the Front, so first of all you have to decide whether you would be associated with them who were supposed to be anti-people. Thereafter might be further discussion on the presence situation."[183] The CPI (M) could not give any answer, so the meeting was ended in confusion.

Deterioration of the Law and Order to the Worst Level

Meanwhile in West Bengal deadly quarrels among the U. F. partners had taken a serious turn to the worse. Three CPI workers were brutally killed by CPI (M) supporters. After two days their dead-bodies were taken to Writers' Buildings by a procession. Biswanath Mukherjee and Somenath Lahiri two CPI Ministers came near to the dead bodies and delivered speeches narrating the incidence of violence. Garlands were offered by some other Ministers of the United Front on the dead bodies except the CPI (M). The incident was followed by many more funeral processions of other United Front partners and Writers' Buildings virtually converted into a morgue. Due to large-scale murder and violent activities, the faith of common people in a multi-party system of government was rudely shaken. The administration was virtually become in a stalemate position.[184]

The Satyagraha Movement of Ajay Mukherjee

As was predicted, Ajay Mukherjee launched his Satyagraha movement on Gandhian line in order to put the end of the politics of violence and murder on and from 1st December, 1969. At least 3 to 7 days in 1450 camps and almost two lakhs Satyagrahis participated in a long monthly wide Satyagraha movement. All classes of people irrespective of male and female became the part of that gigantic effort. In the big camp of Curzon Park at least one hundred Satyagrahis would continue their fast for at least three days. Chief Minister Ajay Mukherjee himself opened the fasting camp for Satyagraha movement by doing his fast for three days in Curzon Park. Unending waves of visitors started coming spontaneously into the camp to show their respect and solidarity to the fasting Chief Minister. Lakhs of people supported the Satyagraha movement against the mischievous activities of the CPI (M). On the first day of his fasting Ajay Mukherjee faced a painful experience of violence in his fasting tent. A group of violent demonstrators rushed to the camp and smashed chairs and tables, cut telephone lines and threw shoes. Ajay Mukherjee himself was sustained injuries on his forehead and chest. There was however a continuous demonstrations in the form of slogan-shouting. At 3 p.m. police was called to avoid any mischief. Many leaders and ministers of others democratic parties came to Curzon Park fasting camp to show their support and sympathy. Bidyut Basu, President of PSP, Bhupal Basu, President of SSP along with 20-22 party workers directly participated in the fasting camp of Curzon Park. They showed their active support in order to boost up the organizers by fasting for 3 days. The 33 MLAs of Bangla Congress and 3 ministers did their fasting. Ajay Mukherjee along with Sushil Dhara and Kumudini Dakua, G.O.C. of "Shanti Fauoj" (women wings) toured all the fasting camp throughout the West Bengal and delivered their speeches for awakening the people against the violent activities in the State.[185]

On the second day of the fast, Ajay Mukherjee, the Chief Minister, addressed a big gathering outside the fasting camp and charged CPI (M) of having made the police completely ineffective. On the last day of his three day fasting, Chief Minister made a very significant remark at the time of his speech outside the camp while addressing a mammoth gathering. Ajay Mukherjee said, "If the people of West Bengal feel that the present state of lawlessness should continue, we shall silently bid them farewell. (This means that Bangla Congress would quit the U.F.) "Don't be silent", he warned the people, "against lawlessness, otherwise a catastrophe would overtake the country".[186] The Chief Minister, however, broke his fast at 8 a.m. in the morning of 4th December, 1969.

Transfer Order of the O.C. of Gazole and its Postponement

In the last week of the month of December 1969, Ajay Mukherjee, the Chief Minister went on a tour to North Bengal. While Chief Minister passing through Malda District the O.C. of Gazole Police Station, Mihiresh Barman who was under orders of transfer, met the Chief Minister and requested him to withdraw his transfer order. It was known that the O.C. was investigating some criminal cases against some of the supporters of CPI (M), and thereby he faced the transfer order. On his return to Calcutta the

Chief Minister Ajay Mukherjee sent a telex using his special power to the S. P. of Malda to keep in abeyance of the transfer order of Mihiresh Barman for a period of six months. This telex was sent on 29th December. After this, Ajay Mukherjee communicated this to his Deputy as well as Home Minister accordingly.[187]

Scenario of All India Congress Politics Following the Death of Zakir Hussain

Whenever the internal conflict among the United Front partners was going on in full swing specially due to the misuse of police force by the CPI (M) for their narrow party interests and as a result of that inter-party clashes became as if a day to day affairs which severely shaking the unity of United Front, then disagreement within the congress party by centering the election of the President of India provoked the warring United Front leaders for a while to truce their infighting. The sudden death of Dr. Zakir Hossain, a 'Bharat Ratna' awardees and the third President of Indian Republic, on 7th May, 1969 following a massive heart attack - the question of the election of the new President of India emerged that led to the difference of opinion among the top congress leadership in all India level which ultimately widened the path of the split of Indian National Congress. However, after the death of Zakir Hossain, automatically Vice-President of India, Varahagiri Venkat Giri (V.V.Giri), became the acting President as per the Constitution until the formalities of the Presidential election was over. Actually, on the issue of the election of new President the top most congress leaders divided into two parallel groups which later led to the formation of the Congress (R) and Congress (O), introducing a vast change in the entire political scenario of India.[188]

The Seeds of Strife: Division in Congress Camp

It was fact that All India Congress Committee (AICC) was then dominating by the so called Syndicate groups which was consisted by Shri K. Kamraj, Shri Nijalingappa, Shri S. K. Patil, Shri N. Sanjeeva Reddy, Shri Morarji Desai and Shri Atulya Ghosh. It was also fact that after the death of Shri Lal Bahadur Shastri, Smt. Indira Gandhi became the Prime Minister according to the will of the leaders of the so-called syndicate group. The leaders expected to her to be democratic and responsive to the public opinion. At the time of her first part of Prime Ministership in 1966-1967, Indira Gandhi generally with the consultation of the leaders would follow democratic approach in case of national problems which was something collective leadership would prevail. After the election of 1967, the same people did their best to re-elect her as Prime Minister and after that her attitude was changed and she started behaving as like as autocratic ruler.[189] The mental difference between Prime Minister Indira Gandhi and the so-called syndicate group leaders came into the forefront during the time of the nomination of the congress candidate for Presidential election. It was found that prior to the Parliamentary Board meeting on 13th July, 1969 in Bangalore, some important members of the Congress Working Committee tried to discuss about the nomination of Presidential candidate with the Prime Minister but failed to know her mind clearly. On behalf of some senior leaders of so-called syndicate first of all proposed the name of Sri Jagjivan Ram, but hearing that proposal Sri Ram at once issued a negative statement from Nainital on the ground of his comparatively young age. After getting negative reply from Sri Ram then the leaders went for a threadbare discussion about that matter and lastly majority of the leaders considered the name of Shi Neelam Snajeeva Reddy as most suitable candidate for the post of the President of India. Naturally, according to the earlier decision, on the last day of the Bangalore session of the meeting of the Congress Parliamentary Board held on 13th July 1969, the name of Sri Neelam Sanjeeva Reddy was declared as the congress candidate. But the strange was that, the Prime Minister all of a sudden proposed the name of Sri Jagjivan Ram for the nomination. The members of the Board meeting were become very much aback as because even some days ago in spite of repeated efforts of the senior leaders she never mentioned any name. However, at last the Parliamentary Board had to settle the issue following the precedence of any disagreement by a majority vote. It was showed that there was three votes went to Sri Ram i. e. Prime Minister's candidate while five votes in favour of Sri N. Sanjeeva Reddy. Therefore, as the majority members of the Parliamentary Board Meeting voted in favour of the then Lok Sabha Speaker, Shri Neelam Sanjeeva Reddy, so despite the opposition of the Prime Minister he was declared as the official congress nominee for the post of President of India. At the time of voting, the then Congress President S. Nijalingappa and Prime Minister's candidate Jagjivan Ram did not participate in the voting.[190]

V. V. Giri Stands as a Candidate for President of India

Another significant development took place that the Prime Minister herself signed the nomination paper of Shri Neelam Sanjeeva Reddy as proposer. But she had worked in the election against N. Sanjeeva Reddy.[191]It was found that another dramatic development happened following the announcement of V. V. Giri, the Vice-President of India who was acting as

President, from Delhi regarding his decision to contest as an Independent candidate for the post of the President of India. Shri Varahagiri Venkat Giri in a lengthy statement, said, "The Congress Parliamentary Board has failed to give a correct lead to the country especially at a time when they should have risen above partisan approach".[192] The date for the polling of Presidential election was fixed on 16th August, 1969. In the meantime, on 13th July, 1969 the Prime Minister declared that she would obey the decision of the Board and gave a clear indication that she would not be hesitated to fight those who attacked her policies and beliefs. On 6th August, 1969, the Prime Minister again announced that she stood by the decision of the Parliamentary Board on the nomination of N. Sanjeeva Reddy. But in practice she did not do that. On 15th August, prior to one day of the Presidential election the Prime Minister all of a sudden took a new stand. The Prime Minister suddenly advocated the principle of conscience voting at the time of the Presidential election which caused the defeat of the congress's official candidate and the defection in the party as well as bringing the split in the Indian National Congress.[193]

Reaction in West Bengal after Giri's Candidature

In West Bengal there was a mixed reaction following the announcement of V.V. Giri as his candidature for Presidential election after the announcement of the official candidate of the congress party. As the United Front came into the power in West Bengal after deposing the congress, so within the division as well as disagreement among the top congress leaders they found the ray of hope as because in spite of difference of opinion among the United Front partners they collectively would consider congress party as their main enemy. The enmity between the congress party and the United Front partners increased after the dismissal of the First United Front Government on 21st November 1967, by Governor Dharma Vira. So, in that context the United Front's reaction in West Bengal as like as jubilation over Giri's decision to contest the election. The Chief Minister Ajay Mukherjee commenting on that issue remarked that the development showed cracks in the congress. Pratap Chandra Chunder, the then President of the West Bengal Pradesh Congress Committee remarked that Mr. Giri betrayed the Congress.[194]

V. V. Giri Visits Calcutta

Vharahagiri Venkat Giri in the meantime informed Ajay Mukherjee, the Chief Minister of West Bengal about his intention to address the U.F. Legislators for the purpose of his Presidential candidature. After consultation with his colleagues, the Chief Minister on his behalf extended an invitation to V. V. Giri to arrive in Calcutta for this purpose. The meeting in between Mr. Giri and the U. F. Legislators was arranged in the Assembly House towards the last week of July 1969. In that U. F. meeting Mr. Giri emphatically declared that he had not been a congressman for years but was a trade unionist and believing in Gandhian principles.[195]

Division in Congress Camp

Reaction in Bengal

When Prime Minister of India Smt. Indira Gandhi instead of issuing a statement in support of the official congress candidate whose nomination paper signed by the Prime Minister herself, sought 'conscience voting' then in Calcutta Jatin Chakrabarty, Chief Whip of the United Front Government along with Jyoti Basu issued a joint whips to their members against cross voting. They urged to all their 217 United Front members to cast their votes in favour of V. V. Giri. On the other hand, the Legislators of the congress party met in Congress Bhavan at Chowrangee Road under the leadership of Siddartha Shankar Ray to discuss the issue related to Presidential election. After long discussion a resolution was passed in the form that "the members of CLP desire to vote in accordance with their conscience and exercise their right of free vote in the Presidential election". This resolution also authorized S.S. Ray, the leader of the Congress Legislative Party to communicate the decision to the Congress President. Among the 27 members, present 24 supported the resolution while rest of the three voted against it.[196]

Dismissal of Morarji Desai from Finance Minister and Nationalization of 14 Major Indian Banks

The month of July in 1969 would be remembered for the astonishing quick development that was coming one after the other. The headlines of the press media in the country on 16th July were like that the Prime Minister relieved Morarji Desai from the Finance Portfolio and that the latter resigned. Just after two days of the Parliamentary Board Meeting in Bangalore on 13th July Sri Morarji Desai was relieved from the Finance portfolio on 15th July, 1969 in a very unceremoniously without giving him any intimation and there was no sign of common courtesy which is generally shown as a matter of respect to Class IV employees of the government, but that was not followed to a veteran congress leader Morarjibhai who was associated with the administration since 1937.[197] However, the letter from the Prime

Minister was sent to Morarji Desai at 12-45 p.m. and the letter of resignation from Desai was received at 3-30 p.m. The Prime Minister herself assumed the responsibility of the Finance Portfolio but did not accept the resignation letter. The crisis within the congress party was fastly moving towards the climax and the political circle elucidated it as an act of reprisal for going against her desires in regard to Presidential nomination. The Prime Minister of India in a broadcast to the nation over the radio media announced the nationalization of 14 major Indian banks by an Ordinance on 19th July, 1969.[198]

The Day of Presidential Election, 16th August, 1969

At last the long awaited polling day for Presidential election came. It was 16th August, 1969. The Chief Minister Ajay Mukherjee came to Writers' Buildings first and instead of entering his office room he went straightly into the Hall and became the second man to cast his vote for the election of the country's President. Khuda Bux, an independent member of the Legislative Assembly who later joined the congress party and became an MP, was first cast his vote. Altogether out of 279 of the Legislators, 274 members had cast their votes. The numbers of absentees were 5 among whom 2 from the congress and 3 from U.F. Prior to the election due to factional feud Prime Minister Indira Gandhi in the one hand propounded the unique theory of freedom of conscience, on the other hand S. Nigalingappa, the then President of the AICC sent telegram to the congress members addressing to them to cast their votes in favour of Reddy, the official congress nominee and also mentioned in the telegram 'The question of voting according to conscience does not arise.'

Results

On 20th August, 1969 the result of the Presidential election came out and Mr. V. V. Giri was declared winner in the epic battle which opened up a new era in the political history of the country. Apart from West Bengal the surprising results in favour of Giri came from the various States like- Utter Pradesh, Bihar, Hariyana and Orissa. The result of the election unambiguously proved that the majority of the congress members exercised conscience vote.[199]The result of the election also helped Indira Gandhi to establish her authority over the government as well as party machineries. It was as if the battle in between Indira Gandhi and the senior congress leaders who were popularly known as 'syndicate group'. Therefore, it was victory of Indira Gandhi in central politics and side by side the victory of the leaders of the United Front in the State of West Bengal, because they were testing the victory due to the defeat of the so-called 'syndicate group' leaders.[200]

Congress Splits

On 1st November, 1969 it was indicated from press reports that the pro-Indira requisitionists were moving for summoning the AICC at a tremendous swiftness to oust S. Nijalingappa from the office of the President of AICC and install a new one belonging to Prime Minister's camp. The number of requisitionists of the pro-Indira group just crossed the border line and ultimately gained a marginal majority. The signed requisition was sent to Sadiq Ali, the then General Secretary of AICC immediately i. e. midnight at 2 a.m. The notable congress leaders who belonged to the Prime Minister's camp were- Jagjivan Ram, Ram Subhag Singh, Fakhruddin Ali Ahmed, Y. B. Chavan, C. Subramaniam, V. P. Naik, C. M. of Maharashtra, Mohanlal Sukhadia, C. M. of Rajasthan, S.S. Ray, K. Brahmananda Reddy, Shankar Dayal Sharma and Uma Shankar Dikshit. Incidentally Shankar Dayal Sharma was the General Secretary of the AICC. At the midnight meeting of the 1st November, 1969 the pro-Indira group took the decision in favour of boycotting the meeting of the Congress Working Committee which was scheduled to meet a day break and also decided for holding a separate meeting at Prime Minister's House on 2nd November, 1969 at 9.30 a.m. This decision indicates that there was holding of two separate and parallel CWC meetings—the venue of the meeting of the Congress President at the AICC office while the camp of Mrs. Ghandhi's at her own residence. The timing of both the meeting was the same. After the completion of two parallel CWC meeting in the capital in same day, a prominent English daily of Calcutta gave the news in the following manner:

> "Congress splits down the middle,
>
> Parallel AICCs parallel CWCs". [201]

The Division in Congress

It might be noted here that just after the Presidential election of India, when it was found that the split in the congress party was inevitable, then utmost efforts were made to restrain the split. Not only that, it was also tried to bring about mutual understanding as well as rapprochement among the senior congress leaders. But in that context, Shri Shripad Amrit Dange commenting over the development said, "Any understanding and rapprochement between the two sections of the Congressmen would be disastrous for the country."[202]However, the congress party was formally divided with the decision taken by the official CWC in Delhi on 12th November, 1969 to expel Mrs. Gandhi from the congress. After a long debate which was lasting over three hours by the last minute peace movers and lastly 11 out of 21 members of the CWC unanimously approved the decision. After expelling Smt. Indira Gandhi, the CWC also directed the Congress Legislature Party in Parliament to take necessary steps within the shortest possible time to elect a new Leader.

Next day i. e. on 13th November 1969, the strength of the party position as was revealed in a press note that pro-Indira supporters were 350 in number while on the other hand the numbers of Congress MPs were merely 70. On 13th November 1969, the Congress MPs those who were supporting Smt. Indira Gandhi met her in the usual venue in the Central Hall of the Parliament under her Presidency defying the cancellation notice issued as per the direction of Congress President, while the pro-Syndicate MPs met at the house of Morarji Desai. In the meeting of the Central Hall of the Parliament the Prime Minister received a big standing ovation and a resolution was passed undertaking the faith in the leadership of Mrs. Indira Gandhi. On 22nd November 1969, a special session of the requisitioned AICC was convened and began its deliberations under the Presidency of C. Subramaniam.[203] Thus, after the split of the congress party was over. CPI leader Mr. Dangey from Vijayawada "welcomed the split in the Congress", and said, "It was a good sign towards a better future".[204]

Impact in West Bengal

Within 3 days after convening the special session of AICC on 22nd November 1969, the new congress leaders directed the WBPCC leaders to replace the leadership of PCC. As the WBPCC was still controlling by Atulya Ghosh and his group who was widely known to all as one of the most influential member of the so-called 'syndicate group' and considered as the anti-Indira group. Naturally in order to establish their authority it was said that PCC would be replaced by appointment of an Adhoc Committee. C. Subramanium, the first President of Congress (R) in a letter suspended the members of the Executive Committee of the WBPCC and handed over their functions to an Adhoc Committee. A three-man Adhoc committee was appointed consisting of K. K. Shukla, Pijush Kanti Mukherjee and Abdus Sattar.[205]

Congress and Bangla Congress's intention to Form a New Non-Marxist Government headed by Ajay Mukherjee

On 14th January, 1970, both Shankar Dayal Sharma and Sushil Dhara, General Secretary of the AICC and Bangla Congress respectively hinted from Delhi about the possibility of the formation of the West Bengal Government excluding the Marxists. Shankar Dayal Sharma on behalf of the congress party extended all possible support in the event of unstable political situation of West Bengal and the formation of a fresh non-Marxist Government headed by Ajay Mukherjee.[206]

Jyoti Basu-Indira Gandhi Meeting and Hope of the Survival of the U. F. Ministry

At that moment of the decline of the Communist Government in Kerala on 24th October, 1969 and in the midst of the political turmoil in West Bengal, Jyoti Basu and P. Sundarayya went to Delhi for saving the West Bengal Ministry. The Marxists gave their support to Indira Gandhi in Parliament during that crucial period for survival of her government. Both the leader convinced Indira Gandhi so that the congress party would not intend to bring a change in the present form of the U. F. Government in West Bengal.[207]

Indication of Sharp Division in United Front

An incident which occurred in the Assembly of West Bengal on 21st January, 1970, that ultimately led to the situation very worst. On that day Chief Minister Ajay Mukherjee himself was manhandled in the corridor of the Assembly House by a group of outsiders, both male and female. As on 20th January the members of the managing committee of a school was *gheraod* and thereafter the frightened gheraod person directly sought help from Chief Minister and thereby as per the direction of the Chief Minister police rushed over there to rescue the victims. So, why the Chief Minister sent police to the educational institution at the aim of dishonoring the teachers - was the allegation of the angry agitators before manhandling the Chief Minister. Most significance was that even when Chief Minister was humiliating within the Assembly premises, the police remained almost silent.[208] In that situation, the United Front meeting was held on 30th January, 1970 in the CPI office at Bowbazar Street, Calcutta to restore unity among the front leaders. But at the conclusion of its midnight meeting there was a clear division among the partners of the front regarding the formation of Thana Level committees. Bangla Congress, Forward Bloc, CPI, SSP, Bolshevik, Gorkha League parties were on the one side on the other hand the CPI (M), RSP, RCPI, Forward Bloc (M), Workers Party and LSS were on the other side.

On 5th February, 1970 in the House of the Legislative Assembly during the debate on Governor's speech, the MLAs of Bangla Congress and other front partners criticized severely the U. F. Government for the dilapidation of law and order in the State. Home Minister Jyoti Basu and Land and Land Revenue Minister Hare Krishna Konar refuted all the allegation of the front partners. But Chief Minister Ajay Mukherjee said, "It is a fact that no Government can meet up all the problems of the whole people. But it is the prime duty of every civilized Government to provide security to the common people and maintain law and order, unfortunately the present Government is not able to meet that minimum necessities. I am the Chief Minister of this 'barbarous and uncivilized' Government - but helpless audience only. This miserable situation cannot continue."[209]

Reaction of the Congress Party

During the time of debate on Governor's speech, accusation and counter accusation among the united front parties about the break-down of the law and order of the state going on in the assembly house, then in a comparatively milder tone Siddhartha Shankar Ray (Henceforth S.S. Ray), Opposition Leader of the House from the Congress (R) in course of his speech straightly attacked the united front government over a wide range of subjects. S. S. Ray's main target of attack in the House was the CPI (M) and he addressed them as '80 gentlemen' (CPI-M had 80 MLAs during second U.F. Government) and narrated Governor's speech as factually and politically baseless. Both the leaders of the two faction of the congress party i. e. Congress (R) and Congress (O) sat on the front row in the opposition benches. Congress party worked unitedly under the leadership of Siddhartha Shankar Ray. As a lawyer of eminence, S. S. Ray then played very significant role for strengthening the congress party in West Bengal.[210]

Resignation of Three Bangla Congress's Ministers

Whenever the inter-party clashes and blood-shed continued in the state then in order to stop that crime during the 2nd United Front Government headed by Ajay Mukherjee, the executive committee of the Bangla Congress in its meeting held on 12th February, 1970 decided that coming 20th February three Minister of Bangla Congress namely- Sushil Dhara, Charu Mihir Sarkar and Bhabotosh Soren would resign from the Cabinet. The others parties of the front considered that move of the Bangla Congress as a kind of pressure so that the front partners would refrain from the inter-party clashes and blood-sheding. But, Promode Das Gupta, State Secretary of CPI (M) lambasted the Bangla Congress and its leader Ajay Mukherjee for resorting the 'politics of blackmail'.[211] However on 20th February, three Bangla Congress Ministers in a joint letter submitted their resignation accordingly on account of "distressing political situation owing to the intransigent attitude of the CPI (M)". The Chief Minister deferred his decision for some days about the acceptance of resignations of his party ministers.[212]

Bitterness deepened between the Bangla Congress and the CPI (M)

When the Bangla Congress and its leader as well as Chief Minister Ajay Mukherjee was mentally prepared to stop the lawlessness of the state under any circumstances even if necessary he was grounding the work of ceasing Home Portfolio from CPI (M) or otherwise he would resign from the post of Chief Ministership instead of taking the responsibility of that ongoing mischievous activities. In that context, Ajay Mukherjee's public gathering at Chatla, Calcutta on 14th February was attacked with the slogan – 'Ajay Mukherjee Murdabad, Jyoti Basu Zindabad'. On 26th February inter-party clash broke out between CPI (M) and CPI in the colliery region. On 27th February another clash broke out between CPI (M) and RSP and thereby one person died. Not only that, the news of inter-party clash and blood-sheding continuously poured in the Writers 'Building. In that situation, the very anguished Chief Minister Ajay Mukherjee remarked that the on going condition should not be continued for long time.[213] In the meantime, due to the death of Humayun Kabir, Bangla Congress M.P. from Basirhat, a by-election was held there on 3rd March, 1970. In that election Bangla Congress candidate Sarder Amjad Ali had to compete against the candidate of Congress (R) and Progressive Muslim League. Though Sardar Amjad Ali was the front candidate, in spite of that CPI (M) leaders tried their best to defeat Bangla Congress candidate and directly or indirectly supported Progressive Muslim League. But in spite of the opposition of the CPI (M) Sardar Amjad Ali came out victorious.[214]

In that unbearable situation the executive committee of Bangla Congress in an extended meeting held on 8th March, 1970 took a very drastic decision which was as under: "This meeting requests our leader C.M. Sri Ajoy Kr. Mukherjee to accept the resignation of our three party ministers immediately and directs him to quit this Govt. on a date not later than the 16th of March."[215] Therefore, according to the decision of the executive committee of the Bangla Congress Chief Minister Ajay Mukherjee accepted the resignation of the three Bangla Congress Ministers on 15th March, 1970 and sent it to the Governor for approval. The very next day i. e. on 16th March Ajay Mukherjee submitted his resignation letter from the office of the Chief Minister to the Governor S. S. Dhawan and thereafter

Governor requests him to continue his work as Chief Minister until alternative arrangement was made. In that pretext, the CPI (M) moved to explore the possibilities of an alternative Government headed by Jyoti Basu without Bangla Congress. But in response to a quarry of Governor the CPI, Forward Bloc, SUCI, Revolutionary PSP, SSP, Balshevic Party, Gorkha League and RCPI pro-Anadi Das- these eight parties informed the Governor in writing that they would not support the CPI (M)'s attempt to form an alternative Government headed by Jyoti Basu.[216]

B.ii. Imposition of Presidential Rule

Ajay Mukherjee was discharging his duties as a care taker Chief Minister after 16th March, 1970 following the instruction of the Governor S. S. Dhawan. As the law and order situation of the state broke down and that was manifested through the inactiveness of the police personnel and bloody inter-party clashes. In that context, after the resignation of Ajay Mukherjee on 16th March, 1970 from the post of the Chief Ministership, the CPI (M) party called a State wide general strike on 17th March as a protest against the decision of the out-going Chief Minister. The strike completely took the shape of violent move and thereby at least 24 persons were brutally killed on that day of strike. The notorious Saibari massacre broke out on that fateful 17th March, 1970 in presence of police and higher government officials like S.D.O, District Magistrate etc. In that event, resignation of Ajay Mukherjee was accepted on 18th March and after receiving the report from the Governor, the centre imposed Presidential Rule in West Bengal on 19th March 1970 on the ground of breakdown of Constitutional machineries.[217]

Dissolution of the Assembly on 30th July, 1970

It is worthy of mention that after the imposition of Presidential Rule in West Bengal for second time (on 19th March, 1970 – 2nd April, 1971)), the Legislative Assembly was not dissolve at once by the Governor S. S. Dhawan following the precedence of the imposition of Presidential Rule in West Bengal for first time (on 20th February 1968 – 25th February 1969). Governor Dhawan's argument behind the cherishing of the Assembly was that due to the breakdown of the constitutional machineries there were no any other best alternatives. Though, it was a speculation in the political circle that with the hope of the formation of an alternative Government headed by Ajay Mukherjee with the support of Congress (R) which was popularly known as neo Congress or Indira Congress the Assembly was not dissolved.[218] But when all the possibilities of an alternative government were faded away then on 30th July, 1970 West Bengal Legislative Assembly was declared null and void. [219]

Ajay Mukherjee's Tour All over West Bengal

During the time of Presidential Rule (19th March, 1970 – 2nd April, 1971) in West Bengal, as per the decision of the Bangla Congress on and from 4th April, 1970 to 4th July, 1970 Ajay Mukherjee toured each and every districts town, Sub-Divisional town and important places throughout the West Bengal for explaining the reasons behind his resignation from the Chief Ministership of second United Front Government. Within that three months in total 66 public gathering were organized on behalf of Bangla Congress under the efficient leadership of Sushil Dhara, where Ajay Mukherjee delivered his speech under the caption 'why this resignation' in a very lucid manner. There was a famous statement what Ajay Mukherjee generally used i. e. 'Peoples are my Supreme Court'. So at the time of his speech to his Supreme Court, Ajay Baby received huge response from the masses and his popularity in West Bengal politics as a symbol of true Gandhian and honesty reached its zenith. Haridas Mitra, former Deputy Speaker and Sarbadhinayaka of 'Shanti Fouj' of Bangla Congress, was sent to all the 66 public gathering. Others leaders of the various democratic parties like- Kashi Kanta Moitra, Sudhir Das, Bidyut Basu, Swarajbandhu Bhattacharya, Bhupal Basu, Arun Mitra etc. also delivered their speeches in that public gatherings, organized by Bangla Congress.[220]

Naxalite Violence in Calcutta

It is well known to all that the Naxalite violence reached its extreme level in the year of 1970. On 24th February, 1970 the prestigious Calcutta University campus was attacked by 30 Naxalities and rampant bombs and stones were thrown towards the student union offices. The offices were ransacked and the furniture's of the offices were destroyed. On 3rd March, 1970 as many as seven cinema halls were attacked by Naxalites with bombs and fire were also set on one.[221] In the midst of the excessiveness of the Naxalite violence, when most of the leaders of the neo-congress were leaving Calcutta out of fear and panicky then under the Chairmanship of Sushil Dhara a non-political 'Citizen Protection Committee' was formed in order to remove the fear and anxiety from the mind of the common people. During that volatile atmosphere as many as 38 public meetings were organized by the 'Citizen Protection Committee' in the most Naxalite influential areas. The meetings were held mainly in the regions of-Vijaygarh, Anwar Shah Road (Taliganj), Bagmari, Narkeldanga, Maniktala Crossing,

Kalabagan, Satyanarayan Park, Ultadanga, Amharst Street, Deshpriya Park, Garpar, Bagbazar etc. The notable persons who delivered their speech in that meetings, were- Ajay Mukherjee, Hemanta Kr. Basu, Pratap Chandra Chunder, Prafulla Chandra Sen, Bidyut Basu, Asoke Dasgupta, Swaraj Bhattacharya, Barada Mukut Moni, Bhupal Basu, Sukumar Das etc.[222]

Stand of the CPI (M) Party

At that point of time the CPI (M) party was the first political organization to come out political propaganda in favour of an election much earlier than any other parties. At the beginning of the imposition of the Presidential Rule (19th March, 1970) in West Bengal, the CPI (M) party was taking their preparation for mid-term poll.[223]

Stand of the Congress Party in West Bengal

It is obvious that centering the election of the President of India in 1969, the glorious institution like Indian National Congress broke into two wings. One part of the congress led by the senior congress leader i. e. so-called 'syndicate groups' came to be known as Organization Congress as well as Congress (O) and another part of the congress led by the Prime Minister Indira Gandhi came to be known as neo-congress or Indira Congress as well as Congress (R). As a consequence of the division of All India Congress party, Atulya Ghosh, most dominating figure as well as top most leader in the West Bengal congress since independence and one of the most influential members of the so-called 'syndicate groups' went to self-exile from active politics. In that circumstances, Prafullya Chandra Sen, former Chief Minister of West Bengal took the leadership of the Congress (O).Those who joined with the Indira Congress, there was none among them suitable and acceptable to all in West Bengal politics. But an excellent understanding between Ajay Mukherjee and Indira Gandhi already developed. Indira Gandhi wanted to bring back Ajay Mukherjee in the leadership of West Bengal Congress politics in 1967 but failed due to the opposition of the Atulya- Kamraj groups. In that context, taking into account the popularity of Bangla Congress and personal image of Ajay Mukherjee, Indira Gandhi wanted to come into an electoral alliance with Bangla Congress in the election of 1971. But on the question of seat adjustment and negative attitude of the Congress (R) leaders and their unilateral decision which led to the collapse of any hope of electoral understanding between Congress (R) and Bangla Congress in West Bengal.[224]

Date of Poll and Results

However, as per the earlier announcement of S. P. Sen Verma, Election Commissioner of India, the fifth general election along with Lok Sabha in West Bengal was held on 10th march, 1971.[225] In that election the Congress (R) announced the names of 202 candidates for Assembly and 29 for Lok Sabha constituencies. The Congress (O) also released the names of 199 candidates towards the end of January. The CPI (M) declared the names of 235 candidates out of 280 Assembly seats. Bangla Congress also filed the nomination in the 131 Assembly seats in that election. Apart from Tamlik constituency, Ajay Mukherjee also contested against Jyoti Basu, symbol of violent politics, from Baranagar Assembly seats.[226]

On 14th March, the result of the fifth general election in West Bengal came out and it changed many equations of the political parties. In the ultimate result, it was found that CPI (M) emerged as the single largest party securing 111 seats and the Congress (R) became the close second with 105 seats. The Bangla congress bagged only 5 seats while Congress (O) was able to capture only 2 seats and one of whom was Prafulla Chandra sen. [227]

Reaction in the Camp of the Congress (O)

After winning only two Assembly seats, the dispirited leaders of the Congress (O) met at the residence of Atulya Ghosh informally. The impact of the results of that election was so serious that once the key figure of the congress politics in West Bengal Atulya Ghosh and Prafulla Chandra Sen said in separate public statements, "The verdict of the people brought to an end all controversies and Congressmen should accept gracefully the decisions of the people—the organization led by Congress (R) is the Indian National Congress".[228] P. C. Sen's statement was also echoed the same.

Stand of the Bangla Congress

Infect, the result of the fifth general election was a great blow to the existence of Bangla Congress. In spite of huge public sympathy and propaganda throughout the year and its stand against politics of violence as well as clear image of its two leaders Ajay Mukherjee and Sushil Dhara to the minds of the people, the result was really astonishing. As per the analysis of the General Secretary of Bangla Congress i. e. Sushil Dhara that Pranab Mukherjee, Rajya Sabha M.P. of Bangla Congress[229] and one of the secretaries of the party wanted to contest in a Parliamentary constituency from Birbhum District, but he was restrained for two reasons, such as i).

His term as a Rajya Sabha M.P. still remained 4 years and ii). There was a suit of misappropriation of funds of Bidyanagar College against him.[230] The main conspirator behind the disastrous results of Bangla Congress was Pranab Mukherjee and Haridas Mitra. As a son of Kamada Kinkar Mukherjee (i. e. Pranab Mukherjee) and husband of Smt. Bela Bose, (i.e. wife of Haridas Mitra) nice of Netaji Subhas Chandra Bose; both Pranab Mukherjee and Haridas Mitra received all sympathy and cooperation from the top leaders of Bangla Congress particularly from Sushil Dhara. However, in the name of extended cooperation at the time of election to Sushil Dhara, Pranab Mukherjee started residing at Central Government Hostel (Nijam Palace). During that time Kalyan Roy, CPI (M) M.P., and Debi Prasad Chottopadhyay, Congress M.P. both of them were also staying there. In that tri-angular assemblage Pranab Mukherjee played his role along with Haridas Mitra very efficiently on the condition that he would break the Bangla Congress from inside and would receive its reward in time.[231]

Regarding Ministry formation Bangla Congress *Karma Parishad* in its meetings held on 19th March, 1971 decided, "The Karma Parishad resolves unanimously to give its unconditional support to the Ministry to be formed at the instance of Congress (R) in West Bengal and not to take part in the Ministry as the people of West Bengal has not given due responsibility upon Bangla Congress this time in spite of its long standing service and sacrifice to save West Bengal from political ruination and the cult of violence and vandalism." [232]

Formation of the 'Democratic Coalition' Front Government (2ndApril, 1971-28th June, 1971)

On 20th March, 1971 Ajay Mukherjee left for Delh to meet Prime Minister Indira Gandhi in a special plane sent by Jagjivan Ram, the then Defense Minister of India and President of Indian National Congress (R). In the meantime, Prime Minister Indira Gandhi had a long discussion with Jagjivan Ram, and leaders from West Bengal like Siddhartha Shankar Ray, Bijay Singh Nahar, the then President of Congress (R) in WBPCC and Tarun Kanti Ghosh were also present the meeting. After threadbare discussion it was decided that a 'Democratic Coalition' Government would be formed in West Bengal headed by Shri Ajay Kumar Mukherjee. Ajay Mukherjee also agreed provided Home portfolio had to be in his hand. Thereafter as per the proposal of the WBPCC of Congress (R), dated 23rd March, 1971, it was officially communicated to Ajay Mukherjee to form a 'Democratic Coalition' Government excluding Marxist Communists on 24th March, 1971.[233] In that Changing circumstances, Bangla Congress Karma

Parishad again met on 25th March, 1971 and resolved-"The Karma parishad though decided not to join the Ministry in its last meeting dated 19.3.71, yet in view of such changed circumstances in the political atmosphere of the state resolves unanimously that Sri Ajoy Kumar Mukherjee may like lead in forming a non-marxist democratic Govt. in West Bengal and this meeting also-(a) requests all the constituent parties, big or small, to participate in the proposed ministry from the very beginning; and (b) demands besides the Chief-Ministership one more Cabinet Minister with important portfolios in the proposed Ministry."[234]

However, in a meeting held on 26th March, 1971 at the residence of Ajay Mukherjee 'Democratic Coalition' was formed officially consisting of seven parties namely- Congress (R), Bangla Congress, Muslim League, Gorkha League, PSP (Official), PSP (Democratic) and SSP (revolutionary). On 29th March 1971 more two parties i. e. Congress (O) and Forward Bloc also joined with the coalition. CPI also promised its support to the coalition without participating in the Government. Ajay Mukherjee was elected leader of the newly formed 'Democratic Coalition' and Abdus Sattar of Congress (R) became its convener. On 31st March 1971, the parties belonged to the 'Democratic Coalition' separately sent their consent letters to Governor informing their support in favour of Ajay Mukherjee. Bijay Singh Nahar, President of WBPCC of Congress (R) met the Governor along with the names of the list of 143 MLAs those who given in writing support to Ajay Mukherjee led 'Democratic Coalition'.[235]

The Swearing-in-Ceremony

It is important to note that when Jyoti Basu, leader of the single largest party (111) as well as United Left Front (ULF) leader could not present reasonable proof of his majority to Governor, then as per the communication of S. S. Dhawan, the then Governor of West Bengal, Ajay Mukherjee, leader of the 'Democratic Coalition' placed before him 'convincing proof' of the majority's support behind his Democratic Coalition Front. In that context, Governor S. S. Dhawan invited Ajay Mukherjee to form his Ministry and thereby on 2nd April, 1971[236] the 'Democratic Coalition Front' Ministry headed by Ajay Mukherjee took its Oaths of Office at the traditional Throne Room of Raj Bhavan. There were 20 Cabinet and 5 State Ministers took their oath. Ajay Mukherjee became the Chief Minister along with Home portfolio and Bijay Singh Nahar became the Deputy Chief Minister along with Finance portfolio. Thus with the oath taking of the 'Democratic Front' Ministry the one year 14 days long Presidential Rule over West Bengal was revoked. After taking oath, Chief Minister Ajay Mukherjee told to the reporters, "The first action of his Government will be to stop the fire of violence." Reiterating the remarks of the Chief Minister, Bijay Singh Nahar, Deputy Chief Minister said, "We are determined to stop the politics of murder." [237]

Formation of Central Cabinet

Prior to the fifth general election a pro-Indira wind was blowing all over the country which was reflected in the election results of Lok Sabha. Capturing 350 seats Mrs. Gandhi's Congress (R) gained a two-thirds majority in the Lok Sabha. On 18th March, 1971, four days after the announcement of election results, Mrs. Indira Gandhi formed her new Ministry comprising 36 ministers among whom 13 Cabinet Ministers, 15 Ministers of State and 8 Deputy Ministers. Mohan Kumarmangalam (he formerly belonged to the CPI group), Siddhartha Shankar Ray, H. R. Gokhale, Raj Bahadur and Moinul Huq were the new comers among the Ministers. Mrs. Gandhi's Cabinet was however described by political commentators as "a balance between continuity and change".[238]

Assembly Session

As per the decision of the cabinet a session of the West Bengal Legislative Assembly was convened on 3rd May, 1971 to elect the Speaker and the Deputy Speaker of the Assembly House. It was in fact the first trial of strength between the Democratic Coalition Front and the Marxist-led Opposition. The Government however won in the first trial of strength when their nominee, Apurbalal Majumdar, a member of the Forward Bloc was elected Speaker and Pijush Kanti Mukherjee of Congress (R) was elected Deputy Speaker defeating the Opposition nominees. Apurbalal Majumdar was elected by 142 to 132 votes while Pijush Kanti Mukherjee was elected by 142 to 130 votes. After two days, when Governor S. S. Dhavan delivered his address then opposition members staged walkout and accused the role of Governor as partisan manner both during Presidential Rule and after the elections.[239]

Overall Law and Order Situation in West Bengal

In the midst of politics of murder and violence during the second United Front Government, Hemanta Kumar Basu, universally respected and very popular Forward Bloc leader was brutally killed on 20th February, 1971. The ghastly murder of Hemanta Kumar Basu was followed by a series of murders - Jyotish Bose, Nepal Roy, MLA and Gopal Sen, Vice-Chancellor of Jadavpur University. In a reaction of these murders the people took law in their own hands and thereby began bloody clashes in different parts of the state that led to the loss of many lives. In that popular upsurge many innocent lives were also lost.[240] But most astonishing events was that in spite of keeping Home Department in the hands of Ajay Mukherjee, the Chief Minister of the Democratic Coalition Front Government, the politics of murders and violence were not stopped. On 18th May 1971 in the by-election of Shyampukur Assembly seat of late Hemanta Kumar Basu, the Forward Bloc candidate Ajit Kumar Biswas was shot death.[241]

Resolution Regarding the Bangladesh War

In spite of taking all necessary steps to quell the disturbances, the Government of West Bengal was not able to bring the situation under control and thereupon politics of violence continued in its own way. In that grave circumstances when 'Liberation War of Bangladesh ' i. e. *Muktiyuddha* started and as a result of that lakhs of refugees started migrating into West Bengal then as a border State, West Bengal's importance as well as dealing huge numbers of influx and maintaining law and order situation strictly became prime concern to the Central Government. However, in the wake of Bangladesh war, Chief Minister Ajay Mukherjee himself mooted a proposal on 7th May, 1971, regarding immediate recognition of Bangladesh Government by the Government of India.[242] It was needless to say that all the parties unanimously supported the proposal of Chief Minister Ajay Mukherjee and promised to extend all possible help to Bangladesh and its liberators. In that critical juncture, to handle the huge refugee influx, Ajay Mukherjee convened a meeting of the Chief Ministers of Bihar, Assam, Tripura and Meghalaya in Assembly House on 8th May, 1971 thereafter all the five Chief Ministers left for Delhi for a meeting with the Prime Minister and Central leaders to deal with the situation that emerged out of the Liberation War of Bngladesh.[243]

Background behind the fall of the Democratic Coalition Front Government

It may be noted that 'Democratic Coalition Front' Government was tottering in terms of internal squabble both within the Bangla Congress and also Congress (R). The internal fray of Bangla Congress was so fatal that at last on 6th June, 1971, Bangla Congress was divided into two parts. Ajay Mukherjee and Pranab Mukherjee became the President and Secretary respectively of the one faction of the Bangla Congress whose office was 180 Bidhan Sarani, Calcutta. The other's faction of Bangla Congress office remained as it was i.e. no. 2 Basanta Bose Road, Kolkata. Purnendu

Narayan Khan and Sushil Kumar Dhara became the President and General Secretary respectively of the other faction of Bangla Congress.[244] Meanwhile results of three Assembly bye-elections showed that the Democratic Front won only one seat while the other two went to the opposition parties which were a kind of alertness to the Government relating to majority in the Assembly. Moreover, factional squabble among the leadership of Congress (R) led to the uncertainties to the existence of the Government. A section of MLAs and executive members of Congress (R) openly challenged the leadership of Bijay Singh Nahar and insisted for the implementation of the principle of 'one man one post' rule. Bijay Singh Nahar was both Deputy Chief Minister and PCC (R) President. Not only that, raising the question of gradual deterioration of law and order in the State, the Youth Congress and Chhatra Parishad, two organs of the Congress (R) in a demonstration demanded the resignation of the Ministry within 72 hours following the murder of a Youth Congress leader, namely Narayan Kar at Beliaghata in the hands of the extremists.[245]

Under the circumstances, Ajay Mukherjee, the Chief Minister himself was also not satisfied at all for the continuous deterioration of the law and order in the State. Therefore, he intended to tender his resignation from the post of Chief Ministership and his mood was communicated to Prime Minister Indira Gandhi also. Apart from the internal political equation in West Bengal, due to the *Muktiyuddha* of Bangladesh, West Bengal became the prime concern to the Government of India. Besides this, in view of the possibility of a war between India and Pakistan, a strong and stable Government was felt necessary in West Bengal. So, there were no any other alternatives to Central Government excepting the imposition of Presidential Rule in West Bengal.[246] On that pretext, taking the approval of the Prime Minister Indira Gandhi, Chief Minister, Ajay Mukherjee together with Bijay Singh Nahar went to Raj Bhavan on 25th June, 1971 with a 3-page letter and advised the Governor to dissolve the Legislative Assembly under Article 174(2) (b) of the Constitution and subsequently on 28th June, 1971 tendered resignation of his Council of Ministers.[247] The Governor suggested him to carry on the activities of Chief Minister for a while on a caretaker basis. Later the Governor in a broadcast said, "The Government had not lost its majority and therefore had the right to seek a fresh mandate from the people."[248] Thus the third Cabinet headed by Ajay Mukherjee ended only within 87 days.[249]

B.iii. Imposition of Presidential Rule and Appointment of S. S. Ray as West Bengal Affairs Minister

As per the recommendation of the Governor of West Bengal, on 29th June, 1971, President V. V. Giri issued a proclamation under Article 356 of the Constitution of India imposing Presidential Rule in the State.[250] After its issue, the Prime Minister Indira Gandhi announced in the Lok Sabha on 29th June 1971, regarding the creation of a new cabinet post of a Minister without portfolio. The post was, however, assigned to Siddhartha Shankar Ray being designated as 'West Bengal Affairs Minister'. The main responsibilities of S. S. Ray were to deal with the problems of West Bengal exclusively, specially the massive influx of refugees in view of Liberation War of Bangladesh. This was in addition to his running portfolio as an Education Minister of the Central Government.[251]

Role of S. S. Ray as West Bengal Affairs Minister

After taking the responsibility of the new assignment i. e. the West Bengal Affairs Minister, S. S. Ray's first action was to direct the military to deploy army in every Police Station in Birbhum district to bring back normal situation immediately there. In a press meet, explaining his role S. S. Ray expressed his view that he has been empowered as the sole representative of the Union Cabinet to exercise the Presidential power of 'superintendence, control and direction. S. S. Ray devoted himself whole-heartedly in the field of eradication of 'politics of murder' from the State of West Bengal. In response to the invitation of S. S. Ray, representatives of all the political parties attended on 7th July, 1971 in a conference of Assembly House for a 'meaningful discussion on the present utter lawlessness and how to eradicate this senseless politics of murder'.

After a 3-hour long discussion under the chairmanship of S. S. Ray, all those who had assembled there expressed their 'grave concern at the present situation existing in West Bengal'. The matter of discussion of the meeting exclusively was about the present lawlessness and how to put an end 'this senseless politics of murder'. Thereafter a long investigation and quarries in an all party meeting held on 30th July, 1971 in Calcutta and adopted a resolution unanimously condemning 'murder and terror from whatever quarters' to oppose and resist all murder and terror jointly. All the political parties including Jyoti Basu of CPI (M) put their signature to that resolution which might be considered as the biggest achievement of Siddhartha Shankar Ray, as West Bengal Affairs Minister.[252]

Notes and References

1. Pranab Mukherjee, *op. cit.* p. 54.
2. Saroj Chakrabarty, ... *Chief Ministers*, pp. 176-177.
3. Pranab Mukherjee, *op. cit.* p. 54.
4. Saroj Chakrabarty, ... *Chief Ministers*, pp. 200.
5. Sushil Kumar Dhara, *op.cit.* pp. 160-161.
6. Barun Sengupta, *Pala Badaler Pala, in Barun Sengupt Rachana Sangraha* (in Bengali, henceforth Pala Badaler...), Ananda Publishers, Calcutta, 2008, p. 9.
7. Sushil Kumar Dhara, *op.cit.* p. 162.
8. Barun Sengupta, *Pala Badaler* ..., p. 6.
9. Interview between Ashok Ghosh and Barun Sengupta on 18.05.1970, cited in Barun Sengupta, *Pala Badaler* ..., p. 6.
10. Barun Sengupta, *Pala Badaler* ..., pp. 8-9.
11. Interview between Ashok Ghosh and Barun Sengupta on 18.05.1970, cited in Barun Sengupta, *Pala Badaler* ..., p 10.
12. *Ibid.*
13. Barun Sengupta, *Pala Badaler* ..., p. 11.
14. *Ibid.,* p.12; Also see Shree Radhakrishna Bari, (ed.), *op.cit.* p. 158.
15. Atulya Ghosh, *Kasta...,* p.172; Also see Shree Radhakrishna Bari, (ed.), *op.cit.* p. 158.
16. Dilip Banerjee, *op.cit.* p.154.
17. Shree Radhakrishna Bari, (ed.), *op.cit.* p. 154.
18. Atulya Ghosh, *Kasta...,* p.172.
19. Shree Radhakrishna Bari, (ed.), *op.cit.* pp. 159-160; Also see Sushil Kumar Dhara, *op.cit.* pp. 168-169.
20. Barun Sengupta, *Pala Badaler* ..., p. 15.
21. Saroj Chakrabarty, ... *Chief Ministers*, pp. 201-202.
22. Dilip Banerjee, *op.cit.* p. 921.
23. Saroj Chakrabarty, ... *Chief Ministers*, pp. 205-206.
24. Dilip Banerjee, *op.cit.* pp. 921-922.
25. Barun Sengupta, *Pala Badaler* ..., p.12.
26. Sushil Kumar Dhara, *op.cit.* p. 168.
27. Dilip Banerjee, *op.cit.* pp.946, 950.
28. Barun Sengupta, *Pala Badaler* ..., p. 15.
29. Saroj Chakrabarty, ... *Chief Ministers*, pp. 205-206.

30. Shree Radhakrishna Bari, (ed.), *op.cit.* pp. 160-161; Also see Barun Sengupta, *Pala Badaler ...*, p. 17.
31. Saroj Chakrabarty, ... *Chief Ministers*, pp. 205-206.
32. *Ibid.*, pp. 203-204.
33. Barun Sengupta, *Pala Badaler ...*, p. 17.
34. Saroj Chakrabarty, ... *Chief Ministers*, p. 200.
35. *Ibid.*, p. 212.
36. Personal interview with Sukharanjan Sengupta, a veteran journalist of West Bengal, on 5th February, 2017.
37. Saroj Chakrabarty, ... *Chief Ministers*, pp. 212-214.
38. *Ibid.*, pp. 212-214; Also see Barun Sengupta, *Pala Badaler ...*, p.18.
39. Saroj Chakrabarty, ... *Chief Ministers*, pp. 214-215).
40. Barun Sengupta, *Pala Badaler ...*, p.18.
41. Saroj Chakrabarty, ... *Chief Ministers*, p.216.
42. Shree Radhakrishna Bari, (ed.), *op.cit.* p.163.
43. *Ananda Bazar Patrika,* 26th March, 1967.
44. Shree Radhakrishna Bari, (ed.), *op.cit.* p.163.
45. Barun Sengupta, *Pala Badaler ...*, p.20.
46. Saroj Chakrabarty, ... *Chief Ministers*, pp.217-218.
47. Personal interview with Kumud Bhattachara, former President of West Bengal Chhatra Parishad from 1973-1977, on 4th February, 2017.
48. Barun Sengupta, *Pala Badaler ...*, p.21.
49. *Ananda Bazar Patrika,* 29th May, 1967.
50. *Ibid.*
51. *Ibid.*
52. Saroj Chakrabarty, ... *Chief Ministers*, p.224.
53. *Ibid.*, pp.227-228.
54. *Naxalbari-50, Fire Dekha O Ajker Katha- Jangal Santal, Kanu Sanyal, Ashim Chattopadhyay (*in Bengali), Unique Printers, 5 Abul Hamid Lane, Kolkata, 2016,p.4; Also see Saroj Chakrabarty, ... *Chief Ministers*, p.228, Shree Radhakrishna Bari, (ed.), *op.cit.* p.164.
55. Barun Sengupta, *Pala Badaler ...*, p.24.
56. *Ananda Bazar Patrika,* 28th May, 1967.
57. Barun Sengupta, *Pala Badaler ...*, p.24.
58. Saroj Chakrabarty, ... *Chief Ministers*, pp.230-231.
59. Shree Radhakrishna Pari, (ed.), *op.cit.* p.164.

60. Saroj Chakrabarty, ... *Chief Ministers*, pp.234-235.
61. *Ibid.*, pp.234-237.
62. *Ibid.*, pp.238-239.
63. *Ibid.*, pp.239-241.
64. *Ibid.*, p.246.
65. *Ibid.*, p.224.
66. *Ibid.*, p.230.
67. *Ibid.*, pp.246-.247.
68. Shree Radhakrishna Bari, (ed.), *op.cit.* p.165.
69. Personal interview with Kumud Bhattachara, former President of West Bengal Chhatra Parishad from 1973-1977, on 4th February 2017.
70. Barun Sengupta, *Pala Badaler* ..., pp.28-31; Also see Shree Radhakrishna Bari, (ed.), *op.cit.* pp. 165-166.
71. *Ananda Bazar Patrika,* on 26th July 1967.
72. Barun Sengupta, *Pala Badaler* ..., pp.30-31.
73. Saroj Chakrabarty, ... *Chief Ministers*, p.247.
74. Though, Barun Sengupta mentioned the date of interview was on 2nd August 1967, see Barun Sengupta, *Pala Badaler* ..., p.33.
75. Saroj Chakrabarty, ... *Chief Ministers*, pp.248-249.
76. Barun Sengupta, *Pala Badaler* ..., p.33.
77. *Ibid.*, p.34.
78. Saroj Chakrabarty, ... *Chief Ministers*, p.250.
79. Shree Radhakrishna Bari, (ed.), *op.cit.* p.166.
80. *Ibid.*, p. 167; Also see interview between Barun Sengupta and Ashok Sen on 8-6-70, cited in Barun Sengupta, *Pala Badaler* ..., p.40.
81. Saroj Chakrabarty, ... *Chief Ministers*, p.257.
82. Barun Sengupta, *Pala Badaler* ..., p.41
83. *Ibid.*, pp. 41-42.
84. Saroj Chakrabarty, ... *Chief Ministers*, p.258.
85. *Ananda Bazar Patrika*, 25th September 1967. G.L. Nanda primarily decided that new Government would form on 1st October and meeting of the Congress Parliamentary party was also convened accordingly
86. Barun Sengupta, *Pala Badaler* ..., pp. 45.
87. *Ibid.*, pp. 56-58.
88. Interview between Sukumar Roy and Barun Sengupta, on 23-5-1970, cited in *Ibid.*, p. 46.

89. Interview between Ashok Ghosh and Barun Sengupta, on 18-5-1970, cited in *Ibid.*, p. 47.

90. Shree Radhakrishna Bari, (ed.), *op.cit.* p. 169; Also see Sushil Kumar Dhara, *op.cit.*p. 177.

91. Shree Radhakrishna Bari, (ed.), *op.cit.* p. 170; Also see Sushil Kumar Dhara, *op.cit.* pp. 178-179.

92. Shree Radhakrishna Bari, (ed.), *op.cit.* p. 171; Also see Sushil Kumar Dhara, *op.cit.* p. 180; Also see Barun Sengupta, *Pala Badaler* ..., p. 52. Though, Saroj Chakrabarty in his "My Years With Chief Ministers' mentioned that due to the Hemanta Basu's influence over Ajay Mukherjee ultimately led to the postponement of his resignation. Mr. Chakrabarty also mentioned that the credit for it, if any, must go to Hemanta Basu. See Saroj Chakrabarty, ... *Chief Ministers*, p.261.

93. Saroj Chakrabarty, ... *Chief Ministers*, p.262.

94. Sushil Kumar Dhara, *op.cit.* pp. 180-181.

95. Shree Radhakrishna Bari, (ed.), *op.cit.* p. 172; Also see Barun Sengupta, *Pala Badaler* ..., p. 56.

96. Shree Radhakrishna Bari, (ed.), *op.cit.* p. 172.

97. The first non-congress Chief Minister of Bihar, Mahamaya Prasad Sinha had written to another non-congress Chief Minister of West Bengal Ajay Mukherjee towards the end of the month of March in 1967 about the necessities for developing an alternative leadership to congress in the country. Simultaneously, almost all the non-congress Chief Ministers throughout the country and dissident all India leaders were also approached to meet at Patna on 14th May 1967. The objective of that meeting was to tackle basic problems of India and formulating a common platform of the nationalist parties for posing a democratic challenge to the Congress Party. As the Communist parties were excluded from that meeting, so, the Communist leaders did not favour the move. Even some of the Communist Ministers of the State of West Bengal tried to pursue Ajay Mukherjee not to attend the Patna convention. But disregarding their advice Ajay Mukherjee along with Dr. P. C. Ghosh, Humayun Kabir, Niharendu Dutta Majumdar and Kali Mukherjee had left for Patna to attend the convention. The new Chief Minister of Bihar Mahamaya Prasad Sinha came forward with brisk steps to welcome his counterpart and other dignitaries. The Patna convention was a hundred per cent success so far as attendance of all India non-congress leaders was concerned. From 12 States 90 delegates attended the convention and all the leaders were run-away men from the congress. Besides Bengal leaders, Singh Deo of Orissa, Charan Singh of U.P. and Chief Ministers of Punjab, Hariyana and Madras were also presented the convention. Another notable invitee was Krishna Menon. Acharya Kripalini had come to the meeting as an observer. On the second day of that conference a new political party known as "Bharatiya Kranti Dal" (B.K.D.) was formed. The immediate objective of the B.K.D. was to ensure social justice

by elimination of corruption and violence. It was also decided to provide honest and efficient administration side by side supply necessities of life and extend employment opportunities for all citizens. Mahamaya Prasad Sinha was unanimously elected Chairman of the party. After Independence it was the first major effort to form an all India party which was free from Communist and Congress influence. See Saroj Chakrabarty, ... *Chief Ministers*, p.226-227.

98. Barun Sengupta, *Pala Badaler* ..., p. 53.
99. Saroj Chakrabarty, ... *Chief Ministers*, pp.255-256.
100. Barun Sengupta, *Pala Badaler* ..., p. 54.
101. *Ibid.,* p. 59.
102. Shree Radhakrishna Bari, (ed.), *op.cit.* p.172.
103. *Ibid.,* p.173.
104. Barun Sengupta, *Pala Badaler* ..., pp. 60-61.
105. Saroj Chakrabarty, ... *Chief Ministers*, pp.262-263.
106. *Ibid.,* pp.263-264.
107. *Ananda Bazar Patrika,* 12th November, 1967.
108. Barun Sengupta, *Pala Badaler* ..., pp. 64-65.
109. Dilip Banerjee, *op.cit.* p. 416.
110. Barun Sengupta, *Pala Badaler* ..., p. 67.
111. Saroj Chakrabarty, ... *Chief Ministers*, pp.265-267.
112. *Ibid.,* pp.267-268.
113. *Ibid.,* pp.269-270.
114. *Ibid.,* pp.270-271.
115. Barun Sengupta, *Pala Badaler* ..., p. 68.
116. Saroj Chakrabarty, ... *Chief Ministers*, pp.272-273.
117. Barun Sengupta, *Pala Badaler* ..., p. 69. Mohan Kumarmangalam, a lawyer by profession and later on he joined as one of the cabinet ministers under Smt. Indira Gandhi. He married Kalyani, daughter of Phanindra Kumar Mukherjee, second elder brother of Ajay Mukherjee and Biswanath Mukherjee, and in that connection he was son-in-law of Ajay and Biswanath Mukherjee.
118. Dilip Banerjee, *op.cit.* p.1011.
119. *Ibid.,* pp. 1006-1010. On 28th March, 1945, Mr. Khwaja Najimuddin's Government was defeated in the Legislative Assembly, when the agricultural budget was rejected by 106 – 97 votes. On 29th March 1945, the then Speaker Mr. Nausher Ali ruled inter alia that refusal by the House of 'Demand for Grand' made by the Ministry for a major department was a censure on the Government and that he could not allow the existing Ministry to function as such in the Legislature and adjourned the House sine die.

120. *Ibid.,* p.1011.
121. *Ibid.,* p.1012.
122. Saroj Chakrabarty, ... *Chief Ministers*, pp.274-275.
123. *Ibid.,* pp.276; Also see Barun Sengupta, *Pala Badaler* ...,p.70.
124. Saroj Chakrabarty, ... *Chief Ministers*, p.277.
125. Barun Sengupta, *Pala Badaler* ..., pp. 72-73; Also see Shree Radhakrishna Bari, (ed.), *op.cit.* p.179.
126. *The Hindusthan Times*, 15th January, 1968.
127. Barun Sengupta, *Pala Badaler* ..., pp. 73-74.
128. Saroj Chakrabarty, ... *Chief Ministers*, pp.296-298.
129. Barun Sengupta, *Pala Badaler* ..., pp. 75.
130. *Ananda Bazar Patrika*, 12th February, 1968.
131. Saroj Chakrabarty, ... *Chief Ministers*, p.299.
132. Barun Sengupta, *Pala Badaler* ..., p. 76.
133. Saroj Chakrabarty, ... *Chief Ministers*, p.300.
134. Barun Sengupta, *Pala Badaler* ..., p. 78.
135. *Ananda Bazaar Patrika*, 16th February, 1968.
136. Saroj Chakrabarty, ... *Chief Ministers*, p.301.
137. It was a rumour that firstly- the West Bengal leaders were not willing in favour of resigning, but when they found that Delhi's leaders already decided regarding the resignation but, if they were not agree to resign then the Ministry would be dismissed, so they became agree. See, Interview between Barun Sengupta and Atulya Ghosh and Dr. Pratap Chandra Chunder, on 6-6-1970; cited in Barun Sengupta, *Pala Badaler* ..., p. 79.
138. Saroj Chakrabarty, ... *Chief Ministers*, p.301.
139. *Ibid.,* pp.304-305.
140. *Ibid.,* pp.305-306.
141. Dilip Banerjee, *op.cit.* p. 444.
142. Saroj Chakrabarty, ... *Chief Ministers*, p.308.
143. Atulya Ghosh, *Kasta*..., pp. 174-175.
144. Personal interview with Mihir Ganguly, a veteran journalist of West Bengal on 23rd February, 2017 at Konnagarh, Hooghly, West Bengal.
145. Shree Radhakrishna Bari, (ed.), *op.cit.* p.186.
146. Barun Sengupta's interview with Promode Das Gupta on 16. 7. 1970, cited in Barun Sengupta, *Pala Badaler* ..., p. 97.
147. Barun Sengupta's interview with Harekrishna Konar on 25.7.1970, cited in *Ibid.,* p. 97.

148. *Ibid.,* pp. 101-102.

149. Saroj Chakrabarty, ... *Chief Ministers*, pp.308-309.

150. *Ibid.,* p.309.

151. *Ananda Bazar Patrika,* 26th February, 1969.

152. Saroj Chakrabarty, ... *Chief Ministers*, p.310.

153. *Ananda Bazar Patrika,* 4th March, 1969. In that context, Promode Dasgupta further remarked, "If I were the Home Minister of West Bengal, then I would arrest Y. B. Chavan, chief patron of Dharma Vira as and when he would land in Calcutta under the P.D. Act as an anti-social person. See Barun Sengupta, *Pala Badaler* ..., pp.104-105.

154. Barun Sengupta, *Pala Badaler* ..., p. 105; Also see Saroj Chakrabarty, ... *Chief Ministers*, p.312.

155. Shree Radhakrishna Bari, (ed.), *op.cit.* p.189.

156. Barun Sengupta, *Pala Badaler* ..., pp. 109-110.

157. Though, till date many people believed, that committee could not able to discover the fact. See *Ibid.,* pp. 111-112.

158. *Ibid.,* pp. 110-111.

159. *Ananda Bazar Patrika,* 28th March, 1969.

160. Shree Radhakrishna Bari, (ed.), *op.cit.* p.190.

161. Saroj Chakrabarty, ... *Chief Ministers*, p.319.

162. Accusation of the State Committee of RSP. See *Ananda Bazar Patrika,* 19th May, 1969.

163. Barun Sengupta, *Pala Badaler* ..., p. 118.

164. Shree Radhakrishna Bari, (ed.), *op.cit.* p.191.

165. The date of the visit has been mentioned as 1st May, 1969. See Shree Radhakrishna Bari, (ed.), *op.cit.* p.191. But, it is mentioned as 24th May in Barun Sengupta, *Pala Badaler* ..., p. 118, but Sushil Dhara did not mention the exact date instead he mentioned the month of May, see Sushil Kumar Dhara, *op.cit.* p.191.

166. Sushil Kumar Dhara, *op.cit.* p. 193.

167. *Ibid.,* p.193.

168. Saroj Chakrabarty, ... *Chief Ministers*, p.326.

169. *Ibid.,* p.328.

170. Barun Sengupta, *Pala Badaler* ..., p. 121.

171. Saroj Chakrabarty, ... *Chief Ministers*, pp.329-331.

172. Barun Sengupta, *Pala Badaler* ..., p.121; Also see Shree Radhakrishna Bari, (ed.), *op.cit.* p.193.

173. *Ananda Bazar Patrika,* 8th September, 1969.
174. Shree Radhakrishna Bari, (ed.), *op.cit.* p.194; Also see Barun Sengupta, *Pala Badaler ...*, p.126.
175. *Ananda Bazar Patrika,* 8th October, 1969.
176. *Ibid.*
177. *Ibid.*
178. Barun Sengupta, *Pala Badaler ...*, pp. 128-129.
179. *Ibid.*
180. *Ibid.*
181. *Ibid.*
182. *Ibid.*
183. *Ibid.*
184. Saroj Chakrabarty, ... *Chief Ministers*, p .342.
185. For details see Sushil Kumar Dhara, *op.cit.* pp. 198-200.
186. Saroj Chakrabarty, ... *Chief Ministers*, p .344.
187. *Ibid.,* p .345.
188. *Ibid.,* p .320.
189. Atulya Ghosh, *The Split – Indian National Congress* (henceforth ... *Split*), Ananda Publishers Private Limited, Calcutta, 1980, p.iv).
190. *Ibid.,* pp.18-19; Also see Saroj Chakrabarty, ... *Chief Ministers*, pp .326-327.
191. Atulya Ghosh, ... *Split,* p. 45; Also see Atulya Ghosh, *Kasta...*, pp. 132-133.
192. Saroj Chakrabarty, ... *Chief Ministers*, p .327.
193. Atulya Ghosh, ... *Split,* p. 54.
194. Saroj Chakrabarty, ... *Chief Ministers*, p .327.
195. *Ibid.,* p .333.
196. *Ibid.,* p .334.
197. Atulya Ghosh, ... *Split,* p.20.
198. Saroj Chakrabarty, ... *Chief Ministers*, p .328.
199. Saroj Chakrabarty, ... *Chief Ministers*, pp .334-335.
200. Barun Sengupta, *Pala Badaler ...*, p.120.
201. Saroj Chakrabarty, ... *Chief Ministers*, pp .341-342.
202. Atulya Ghosh, ... *Split,* p.14.
203. Saroj Chakrabarty, ... *Chief Ministers*, pp. 342-343.
204. *Mail of Madras,* 2nd February, 1970. Also see Atulya Ghosh, ... *Split,* p.14.
205. Saroj Chakrabarty, ... *Chief Ministers*, p.343. Congress (R) stands for requisitioned group i.e. Indira Group.

206. *Ibid.,* p .347.
207. *Ibid.,* pp .347-348.
208. Shree Radhakrishna Bari, (ed.), *op.cit.* p. 204.
209. Saroj Chakrabarty, ... *Chief Ministers,* p .349; Also see *Ibid.,* p. 205.
210. Saroj Chakrabarty, ... *Chief Ministers,* p .349.
211. *Ananda Bazar Patrika,* 14th February, 1970.
212. Saroj Chakrabarty, ... *Chief Ministers,* p .350.
213. *Ananda Bazar Patrika,* 29th February, 1970.
214. Sushil Kumar Dhara, *op.cit.* p. 197; Also see Shree Radhakrishna Bari, (ed.), *op.cit.* p.207; Barun Sengupta, *Pala Badaler ...,* p.159.
215. Sushil Kumar Dhara, *op.cit.* p. 202.
216. Saroj Chakrabarty, ... *Chief Ministers,* p .351; Also see Barun Sengupta, *Pala Badaler ...,* pp.164-165.
217. Barun Sengupta, *Pala Badaler ...,* p.165; Also see Shree Radhakrishna Bari, (ed.), *op.cit.* p.214.
218. *Ananda Bazar Patrika,* 12th April, 1970; Also see Shree Radhakrishna Bari, (ed.), *op.cit.* p.216.
219. Dilip Banerjee, *op.cit.* p.887.
220. Sushil Kumar Dhara, *op.cit.* p.205.
221. Saroj Chakrabarty, ... *Chief Ministers,* p .350.
222. Sushil Kumar Dhara, *op.cit.* pp. 207-208.
223. Saroj Chakrabarty, ... *Chief Ministers,* p .359.
224. Shree Radhakrishna Bari, (ed.), *op.cit.* p. 220.
225. Dilip Banerjee, *op.cit.* p.884.
226. Sushil Kumar Dhara, *op.cit.* p. 212.
227. Dilip Banerjee, *op.cit.* p.882.
228. Saroj Chakrabarty, ... *Chief Ministers,* p .360.
229. Pranab Mukherjee became the Rajya Sabha Member for the first time from Bangla Congress on and from 10.07.1969 -09-07-1975; then from Indian National Congress on 10.07.1975 to 09.07.1981; 14.08.1981 to 13.08.1987; then 19.08.1993 to 08.08.1999; and again 19.08.1999 to 13.05.2004. See Dilip Banerjee, *op, cit.* p. 303.
230. "This case was lodged by Sri S. C. Roy, Chief Inspector, Secondary Education Govt. of West Bengal & the case no is 4466 Det. 1969 u/s 406 & 120 (b)" . See Shantimaya Mukherjee, *Why Bangla Congress Split,* p, i. cited in Sushil Kumar Dhara, *op. cit.* p. 213.
231. Sushil Kumar Dhara, *op. cit.* p. 218.

232. *Ibid.,* p. 221.
233. *Ananda Bazar Patrika,* 25th March, 1971.
234. See, Shantimaya Mukherjee, *Why Bangla Congress Split,* p-13.Cited in Sushil Kumar Dhara, *op. cit.* p. 221.
235. Shree Radhakrishna Bari, (ed.), *op.cit.*pp.229-230.
236. Dilip Banerjee, *op.cit.*p.925.
237. Shree Radhakrishna Bari, (ed.), *op.cit.*p.230.
238. Saroj Chakrabarty, ... *Chief Ministers*, p.361.
239. *Ibid.,* p.379-380.
240. *Ibid.,* pp.370-371.
241. Shree Radhakrishna Bari, (ed.), *op.cit.*p.243.
242. *Ibid.,* p.238. In the name of Mujib-Iahia meeting, in order to stop the voice of Bangladeshi intellectuals, modern arms and armies were sent to East Pakistan by the Pakistani Government and before leaving Dhaka according to the direction of the Iahia Khan, Military Administrator of Pakistan, the Pakistani soldiers started mass killing on Bangladeshi citizens on and from at night of 25th March, 1971. Thereafter, at the aim of gaining independence there was emerged an 'Independent, Sovereign and Republican Bangladesh' on 17th April, 1971. Sheikh Mujibur Rahaman, Awami League leader, popularly known as *'Bangabandhu'* was declared as President and Tajuddin Ahmmed as Prime Minister.
243. Saroj Chakrabarty, ... *Chief Ministers*, p.380.
244. Shree Radhakrishna Bari, (ed.), *op.cit.* pp. 252-253.
245. Saroj Chakrabarty, ... *Chief Ministers*, p .387; Also see Sushil Kumar Dhara, *op. cit.* p.224.
246. Shree Radhakrishna Bari, (ed.), *op.cit.* pp. 245-246.
247. Dilip Banerjee, *op.cit.*p.887.
248. Saroj Chakrabarty, ... *Chief Ministers*, p .388.
249. There was a speculation in the political circle that after becoming uncertain about the support of the 3 MLAs of Bangla Congress namely- Sushil Dhara, Bankim Maity and Baneswar Patra to the Democratic Coalition Front Government led by Ajay Mukherjee, the Ministry was likely to be dissolved. But, the fact was that Ajay Mukherjee had to resign following the demands of the Youth Congress and the typed letter on which Ajay Babu had to sign which was brought from Delhi. See Sushil Kumar Dhara, *op. cit.*p.224.
250. Dilip Banerjee, *op.cit.*p.887.
251. Saroj Chakrabarty, ... *Chief Ministers*, p.388.
252. *Ibid.,* pp.388-390.

Chapter

6

Progressive Democratic Alliance (PDA) Government – Promises and Performances (1972-1977)

In the midst of Presidential rule in West Bengal and under the regime of West Bengal affairs Minister headed by Siddhartha Shankar Ray, West Bengal faced its sixth general election.

The General Elections of 1972

As per the notification of the Election Commission of India, the general election of West Bengal was held on 11th March, 1972.[1] In that election Congress (R) came to an electoral understanding with the CPI and some others parties in the name of Progressive Democratic Alliance (PDA), on the other hand CPI (M) led United Left Front (ULF) was also in the electoral battle. When result of the election came out, it was found that Congress (R) having got 216 seats became the single largest party with more than absolute majority, whereas Congress (O) got only 2 seats, CPI, the main electoral partner of Congress (R) became the second power securing 35 Assembly seats and main contender of that electoral battle i.e. CPI (M) got only 14 seats. It was really a matter of astonishing in the history of success rate of the congress party in course of electoral battle in West Bengal. From the first general election in 1952 to the general election of 1971, the number of seats of the Congress party in West Bengal Legislative Assembly were— in 1952 – 150 out of 238 seats; in 1957 - 152 out of 252 seats; in 1962 - 157 out of 280 seats; in 1967 - 127 out of 280 seats; in 1969- only 55 seats got the congress party. But after the split of Indian national Congress in 1969 (in national level) the party divided into two groups in the name of Congress (R) and Congress (O). After division it was found that in 1971, Congress (R) secured 105 seats and Congress (O) only 2 seats and in the election of 1972 Congress (R) reached its climax securing

216 seats while Congress (O) got only 2 seats again.[2] It is mention worthy that during the golden period of Indian National Congress just after the independence as like as other states of India, the congress party in West Bengal came to power with its recognition as a national party as well as the main protagonist of the Indian national movement. Under the mighty leadership of Dr. Bidhan Chandra Roy and Atulya Ghosh - Prafulla Chandra Sen in the general election of 1952, 1957 and 1962 the congress could maintain its predominance in West Bengal politics. It may be noted that from 1948 to 1962 the congress party of West Bengal had a rare opportunity to enjoy the charismatic leadership of Dr. B. C. Roy but after his death on 1st July 1962, a crisis moment came over the congress party and the situation was such that a systematic decline started in the organizational platform of the party and with a result of effecting the linkages between the voters and the congress party. Not only that due to the split of West Bengal Congress and birth of 'Bangla Congress' on 1st May, 1966 under the leadership of Ajay Kumar Mukherjee, one of the architects of famous '*Tamralipta Jatiya Sarkar*' and its second *Sarbadhinayaka*[3] and his alliance with the anti-congress parties led to the congress party out of power in the general election of 1967. Then in the mid-term election of 1969, the strength of the congress party reduced and it got only 55 seats. In the election of 1971, though the Congress (R) led by Smt. Indira Gandhi, the then Prime Minister of India, got 105 seats but it was far behind from the absolute majority to form a government. But in the election of 1972 the Congress (R) in West Bengal got not only the absolute majority but securing 216 seats which broke the all previous records in the history of electoral victory of the congress party in West Bengal. Now question is that what factors were responsible for the landslide victory of the congress party in the election of 1972 and unexpected defeat of the CPI (M) led United Left Front (ULF), which gradually increased its strength from the election of 1967 to 1971 systematically. It is noteworthy that in 1967, CPI (M) got 43 seats; in 1969 and 1971 it secured 80 and 113 seats respectively. But in the election of 1972 the number of seats of CPI (M) was only 14.[4] In that context, there was a speculation regarding the large scale rigging organized by the Congress (R) as well as Progressive Democratic Alliance for winning the election and washing out the opposition parties from West Bengal. Jyoti Basu, the then opposition leader as well as Chief Ministerial candidate of CPI (M) led United Left Front (ULF), mentioned in his autobiography *Jotodur Mone Pore* about the nature of rigging in his home constituency Baranagar in the following term: "On 11th March, 1972 i. e. the day of election after reaching my Baranagar constituency I found that in most of the booths, the voting

procedures were over. There was no CPI (M) polling agents in the 100 polling booths out of 135 due to the huge atrocities of the congress party. The goondas of the congress party had snatched away the ballot boxes, stamped on ballot papers in favour of the candidates of PDA i. e. CPI candidates and drop them into the boxes."[5] It may be mention worthy that young CPI candidate named Shivapada Bhattacharjee was his rival. At about 12 noon on that polling day Jyotirmoy Basu, CPI (M) leader and MP made a complain about serious rigging in Baranagar constituency to the Governor over telephone. Later, Jyoti Basu himself talked over phone and made the same complain. Not only that Jyoti Basu made a written complain regarding that matter to S. P. Sen Verma, the then Election Commissioner by telegram and to the Governor by a letter. Following the orders of the Governor the Chief Secretary immediately made an enquiry and reported accordingly to the Governor that there was nothing wrong in the polling booths in Baranagar constituency. Naturally Jyoti Basu's demand for repeal of polling could not grant.[6]

However, when Jyoti Basu's demand for revocation of polling was not complied then Jyoti Basu withdrew himself from the electoral battle alleging rampant rigging and corrupt practices followed by the Congress (R). Not only that during the five- years rule of Congress (R) led Progressive Democratic Alliance (PDA) from 1972 to 1977, the leftists particularly all the elected CPI (M) MLAs (altogether-14), the WPI (Workers Party of India), and the SUCI (Socialist Unity Centre of India) as a mark of protest boycotted the Assembly as well as Ministry headed by Siddhartha Shankar Ray on the charge of illegal one.[7] Veteran congress leader and former President of the Pradesh Congress Committee (PCC), Soumendra Nath Mitra, popularly known as Somen Mitra and Sarder Amjad Ali, veteran congress leader and former M. P. of 'Bangla Congress' and Congress (R) expressed the same opinion that the rigging, booth capturing, fake stamping on ballot boxes were not new in the history of election in West Bengal and these tactics were imported earlier mainly by CPI (M). Both the leaders further acknowledged the fact that though in some cases riggings were held more or less but that does not mean that the congress won 216 Assembly seats only by rigging. The leaders also felt that if there was no rigging at all, in spite of that the congress would win at least 160 seats that means win of the congress party and defeat of the CPI (M) was inevitable in the election of 1972.[8]

Actually prior to the election of 1972, there were so many events took place in the political scenario in West Bengal as well as India and abroad which directly or indirectly played very significant role behind the winning of the Congress (R) and washing out of the CPI (M) in the election of 1972. Those factors which gradually led to the landslide victory of Congress (R) in the general election of 1972 were as under:

Role of Chhatra Parishad

There is a fascinating outlook of Pundit Jawaharlal Nehru, the first Prime Minister of India as well as one of the architects of modern India that in the post independent period students should not participate in the active politics of the country. As the students were not lag behind during the time of freedom movement for removing the chain of bondage which encircled our motherland, so after independence students should not participate in the sphere of active politics for attaining power on behalf of the political parties. In that case their role would be certainly different. That is why Pundit Nehru wanted complete involvement of the student communities in their education so that they would be able to become valuable citizen of the country and devote themselves for the upliftment of their motherland. So, Pundit Nehru wanted to consolidate the student community apolitically under the umbrella of 'National Students Union' (NSU) which would be absolutely free from active party or power politics. But the very necessary efforts of Pundit Nehru could not fulfill because all the political parties did not agree to accept the opinion of Pundit Nehru. In that pretext, the opposition parties particularly the name of the communists parties deserve special mention.

In the post independent period, the communist party of India started uniting the students of colleges and universities under the banner of 'Students Federation'. In West Bengal and Kerala, the 'Students Federation' established their influence among the students swiftly. The students under the banner of 'Students Federation' would participate in the students' union election in the various colleges, universities and winning the election they would adopt some well planning programme for motivating the general students towards the doctrine of communism and subsequently the communists started using the students for winning general election in order to capture power in active politics. It is noteworthy that the communist leaders ignoring the freedom with the slogan *Yea Azadi Jhuta Hai* (This freedom is fake) what inspired the youth- students to hate freedom which was obtained by the country on 15th August, 1947 and suspected the congress leaders as well as Gandhiji.[9] But many students hailed from the congress families and believer of anti-imperialism as well as ideal of the congress party also tried their best to counter the Students Federation and urged the necessity to form a students' wing according to the ideal of Indian

National Congress. In that circumstances, leaders like Bidhan Chandra Roy, Prafulla Chandra Sen, Bijay Singh Nahar, Bijayananda Chattopadhyay assessing the situation requested Atulya Ghosh, the then President of WBPCC to take appropriate steps regarding the formation of a students' wing according to the vision of Indian National Congress. Thereafter as a result of the extraordinary dealing of Atulya Ghosh with the central congress leadership and thereby considering the urgency of West Bengal and Kerala where the communists using the students for the interests of power politics, at last the central congress leadership gave the approval for the formation of a students' organization in two states. In that context, on 27th and 28th August 1954 some congress leaders and workers of Students-Youth attended in a two days conference in Indian Association Hall, Kolkata under the Chairmanship of Saila Kumar Mukherjee, the then Speaker of the West Bengal Legislative Assembly. In order to resist the gradual thriving of students' federation a proposal was accepted to form a students' organization on the basis of democratic philosophy. The name of 'Chhatra Parishad' was also accepted in that conference on 28th August, 1954. In that way 'Chhatra Parishad' was formed on 28th August, the 50th birthday of Atulya Ghosh in 1954. Besides, Atulya Ghosh, those respectable personalities remained present at the time of the birth of Chhatra Parishad were Dr. Sarvapalli Radhakrishnan, Dr. Bidhan Chandra Roy, Prafulla Chandra Sen, Bijay Singh Nahar, Shri Bijayananda Chattopadhyay, Gyan Chandra Ghosh etc. It is noteworthy that Shri Bidhu Bhushan Ghosh became the first President of Chhatra Parishad of West Bengal.[10]

In the second day of the conference of West Bengal Pradesh Congress committee held at Malda in 1955, a students' conference was held with the representatives of the students. Notable personalities like U. N. Dhevar, Babu Jagjivan Ram, Atulya Ghosh and other provincial congress leaders were present there. The third state conference of the Chhatra Parishad was held at Wellington Squire, Calcutta in 1959. Shyamal Bhattacharya was elected the State President of the Chhatra Parishad. It was decided to write a constitution of Chhatra Parishad and its Flag was also approved in that conference. In the same venue i. e. Wellington Squire the fourth state conference of the Chhatra Parishad took place in 1961 and again Shyamal Bhattacharya was elected the President. In the meantime, China attacked India in 1962 and one portion of the communist party started spreading the rumor that not China rather it was India first attacked China. As a result of the ideological conflict the Communist Party of India divided into two parts. The pro-Chinese communist leadership formed the Marxist Communists party. Under the circumstances, nationalist students' society gradually started joining with the Chhatra Parishad on the basis of ideological ground and thereupon the domination of Chhatra Parishad over the various College units gradually established. On 3rd December, 1962 a gigantic students' conference was held under the banner of Chhatra Parishad as a protest against the Chinese attack on India. In that conference the nationalist students took oath for the protection of their country. In the fifth State Conference of the Chhatra Parishad that was held at Midnapore in 1964 and once again Shri Shyamal Bhattacharya was reelected President of Chhatra Parishad. The sixth State Conference of the Chhatra Parishad was taken place at Mahajati Sadan in Kolkata on 8th May in the year of 1968 under the Presidentship of Shri Indu Adhikari. From that conference in the presence of Bijayananda Chattopadhyay, Shri Prya Ranjan Das Munshi was elected as the President of Chhatra Parishad unanimously. Actually Chhatra Parishad under the leadership of Priya Ranjan Das Munshi got a new life and always considered as the turning point in the history of constructive political movement as well as life line of Chhatra Parishad.[11]

As in the decades of 60s in the field of the establishment of 'Civil Rights' the students of the Barkley University gave birth to the awakening throughout the country and shook the administration along with political set up of the United States of America; in the decades of 70s the revolution of French students vibranted the city of Parry; in the same way-the Naxalbari movement and the contemporary wave of nationalist students' movement brought the change of political and social atmosphere in West Bengal also.[12] In the meanwhile, as a result of the split of West Bengal Pradesh Congress and birth of Bangla Congress (1st May, 1966) under the leadership of Ajay Kumar Mukherjee, emergence of United Front and the atrocities of some of its partners in the sphere of *gheraos* and its destructive politics along with gradual attack on opposition parties became day to day affairs; when the congress leaders were in a dilemma and frustrated then the students community came forward under the leadership of Chhatra Parishad in the form of protest against the foregoing activities of the left front particularly the CPI (M). In that context, Shri Nitya Gopal Dutta, a student of Birati College was brutally murdered by the Marxists cadres on 22nd April, in 1969. Chhatra Parishad under the leadership of Priya Ranjan Das Munshi made a strong protest against that brutal killing and launched a political march to the Mahakaran, the head administrative centre of the state of West Bengal on 23rd April along with the dead body of Nitya Gopal Dutta. The numbers of bomb were hurled on 13th April, 1970 in the room of the Vice-Chancellor of Calcutta University and in the house of Siddhartha Shankar Ray. Books of the university's library were set on fire and ransacked the properties of the university. Shri Bipul Roy, a Chhatra Parishad worker was murdered on the footpath of Amherst Street, Calcutta on 2nd May in 1970 at the time of public gathering addressed by Promode Das Gupta, CPI (M) leader in the Shraddhananda Park. A procession was organized by Chhatra Parishad along with the dead body of Bipul Roy from Medical College to Writers' Buildings on 4th May, 1970. Priya Ranjan Das Munshi published a death list of 22 Chhatra Parishad workers on that day. A Chhatra Parishad worker named Shuvankar Ojha was shot death pulling him from the bus in Purulia on 23rd June 1970. There was a black day in the history of Naxalite violence when the statue of Sir Ashutosh Mookherjee was broken and College Street became bloodshed. Shri Gopal Sen, the Hon'ble Vice-Chanchellor of Jadavpur University was murdered on 30th December, 1970. Hemanta Kumar Basu, colleague of Netaji Subhas Chandra Basu and most popular leader of that time was also murdered by the extremists on 20th February, 1971. Bijayananda Chattopadhyay, one of the architects of Chhatra Parishad as well as head master of Akshay Educational Institution, was brutally killed on the way from congress office to his home on 4th March, 1971. The Chhatra Parishad launched a movement for student concession in buses and trains on 12th June, 1971 and as a result of that movement at last Siddhartha Shankar Ray, the then West Bengal Affairs Minister approved the demand of student concession on 8th July, 1971.[13]

At the time of United Front Government the left parties particularly the CPI (M) unleashing the violent politics throughout the state and after becoming disgusted about the politics of murder and bloodshed of Marxist party, Ajay Mukherjee, the then Chief Minister of United Front Government tendered his resignation and observed fasting Satyagraha as a mark of protest against the bloodshed during his Chief Ministership. In that period of peril, the puzzled congress leaders became confuse and unable to make a strong resistance against the ongoing atrocities. Under the circumstances, the Chhatra Parishad under the dynamic leadership of Priya Ranjan Das Munshi and a branch of youth leaders like Subrata Mukherjee, Somen Mitra, Sudip Bandopadhyay, Kumud Bhattacharyay, Pradip Bhattacharya, Nurul Islam, Jayanta Bhattacharya, Ashok Dev, Sougata Roy, Debaprasad Roy, Goutam Chakraborty, Laxmi Kanta Basu, etc. taking all type of life risk made in such a strong resistance for the protection of West Bengal from the blood bath of Naxalites and left CPI that people of West Bengal considered them as their protector. Considering the bold leadership as well as life and death struggle of Chatra Parishad leaders the people of West Bengal as if found the reflection of Netaji Subhas Chandra Bose in Priya Ranjan Das Munshi and gave their love to him generously which ultimately led to the congress party in power partially in 1971 and overwhelmingly in 1972.[14]

Role of Siddhartha Shankar Ray

In the landslide victory of the congress party in the general election of 1972 as well as its return to power after a long time of five years in West Bengal, the name of Siddhartha Shankar Ray deserved special mention. It may be noted that after the split of West Bengal Pradesh Congress and birth of Bangla Congress (1st May, 1966) under the leadership of Ajay Mukherjee, in the election of 1967, the congress party for the first time after independence was unable to form Ministry in West Bengal and as a result of that United Front Government headed by Ajay Mukherjee came to power. In the midterm poll of 1969 it was found that the strength of the congress party became so less that it got only 55 seats in West Bengal Legislative Assembly. In that critical juncture of the congress party in West Bengal, Siddhartha Shankar Ray became the Leader of the Opposition of the congress party. In that context, taking the advantages of the inter-party conflicts within the United Front, S. S. Ray as opposition leader spearheaded the attack against the lawlessness and ongoing bloodshed throughout the West Bengal and severely criticized the activities of the CPI (M). Due to the worthy leadership of Siddhartha Shankar Ray the congress party in West Bengal gradually started regaining its lost strength which reflected in the election result of 1971. In that election securing 105 seats, the congress became the second largest party in West Bengal. Not only that during the time of Chhatra Parishad movement against the violent politics of CPI (M) and Naxalites, it got proper cooperation and timely assistance from Siddhartha Shankar Ray which also considered as one of the important causes behind the success of the congress party in West Bengal in 1972 general election.

Besides these, as a Minister of West Bengal Affairs (29th June, 1971 to 20th March, 1972) during the imposition of 3rd time Presidential Rule in West Bengal (29th June, 1971 to 20th March, 1972) Siddhartha Shankar Ray accomplished many developmental works which remained in a stagnation position for a long time due to the continuous inner struggle of the United Front and lawlessness in the State.[15] Siddhartha Shankar Ray in a strong hand tried his best to subside the lawlessness and politics of murder of ultra Marxists as well as left Communists by various measures. For example - as a mark of initial success as a West Bengal Affairs Minister, S. S. Ray convened an all party meeting in Calcutta on 7th July, 1971 for a 'meaningful dialogue about the ongoing utter lawlessness and how to eradicate that senseless politics of murder'. Though there was some controversies about Siddhartha Shankar Ray's policy of quelling the Naxalites, but it was a fact that towards the last of 60s and initial stage of 70s, the life and property of the people were not safe at all. There was no surety of life security of any individual whether he would come back to his dear and near ones after leaving home in the morning.[16] In that context S. S. Ray with the help of the state administrative machineries i.e. MISA, D.I.R, P.D. Act, declared some region as terror-prone areas along with the help of R.A.W. of Central Bureau of Investigation some squads were formed in the symbolic name like 'Ton Ton Macaute', Papa Doc' etc to quell the disturbances of the Naxalites under the leadership of Ranjit Gupta, the then DIG of Police; Devi Roy, Chief vigilance officer along with Runu Guha Neogy and Tarapada Basu.[17] On 4th-5th August in 1971, at midnight police arrested Saroj Dutta, the then state Secretary of West Bengal CPI (ML) and chief organizer of its mouth piece 'Deshbrati' from the house of his relative name Devi Prasad Chattopadhyay of 9 B, Raja Basanta Ray Road and in the morning of that day his headless body was found in the Maidan. As per the account of the Amnesty International as much as 30,000 to 40,000 people were arrested and sent to jail in West Bengal on the charge of the activities of Left extremist. Arrest warrants were issued against 30,000 to 40,000 persons. It was known from the statement of Home Minister of West Bengal Legislative Assembly in 1973 that 17,787 Naxalites were imprisoned.[18]Apart from the above facts 2,000 persons were arrested under D.I.R. and MISA and 17,000 persons were detained under the process of sub-judice.[19] However, adopting the aforesaid measures, Siddhartha Shankar Ray was successfully able to resist the Naxalites atrocities and bring back the confidence of the common people in general.

Influence of Siddhartha Shankar Ray on Muslim Community

It may be recalled here that prior to become the Chief Minister of West Bengal, as a successful barrister the monthly income of Siddhartha Shankar Ray was Rs. 60,000 which was many times more than Rs. 1,700 i. e. monthly salary of the Chief Minister. In spite of various propaganda against Siddhartha Shankar Ray regarding the way of his handling the Naxalites and various steps taken by him at the time of emergency; one thing was very much clear that he was absolutely an honest person in terms of financial matters. It is generally said to have that he was a man of complete non-communal political personality and guardian of minorities and weaker section of the society. It is again note worthy that whenever there was not a single name in the UPSC list of IAS cadre from the minorities, he would automatically turn to upset.[20] In that connection, it may be worthy of mention here that on the eve of the general election of 1972, liberation war of Bangladesh was started from the month of March 1971. In that liberation war, the whole hearted assistance of the Government of India to the *Muktijuddha* ultimately led to the victory and there emerged a free, sovereign Bangladesh in the atlas of world. It is needless to say that in the liberation war of Bangladesh India's stand against Pakistan undoubtedly aggrieved the Muslim fundamentalists on the ground that India under the Prime Ministership of Indira Gandhi in a very plan full manner breaking of a Muslim country of the sub-continent i. e. Pakistan. During the time of *Muktijuddha* of Bangladesh *Bangladesh Mukti Sangram Sahayak Samity* i. e. society for the cooperation of the liberation war of Bangladesh was formed under the joint leadership of three general secretaries of the West Bengal Pradesh Congress Committee namely Santosh Roy, Jainal Abedin and Haridas Mitra. There were also four assistant secretaries of whom most notable were Tarun Sanyal, a leading intellectual and freedom fighter and Sarder Amjad Ali, who supplied medicine, gumboot etc. to the liberator of Bangladesh. When any Muslim sympathizer to the liberation war of Bangladesh like Sarder Amjad Ali, a veteran politician and M. P. of the Bangla Congress (West Bengal) would go to Bangladesh to help the *Muktijuddha*, the citizen of Bangladesh would not easily believe any Muslim from India rather suspected they may be the spy of the West Pakistan. However, as per the observation of Sarder Amjad Ali, one of the eye witnesses of the whole incidents, it was found that though the Muslim fundamentalists of both part of Bengal were very much against the interference of India into the internal affairs of Pakistan as well as division of a Muslim country, but, in spite of that they had strong confidence on Siddhartha Shankar Ray on the ground that under any circumstances Muslims would be protected by this non-communal politician simply because he was the grandson of Desh Bandhu Chittaranjan Das who was trusted by both the Hindus and the Muslims of Bengal. It is a fact that like others people of West Bengal, the Muslims also extended their political support in favour of the congress party so that it could come back again to seat of power. It is found that most of the Muslim dominated areas the congress candidates came out victorious. Naturally, the whole-hearted support of the Muslim community to the congress in the general election of 1972 and their confidence on Siddhartha Shankar Ray may be considered as one of the significant factors behind the landslide victory of the congress party in West Bengal.[21]

Last Phase of the Political Development in 1972

The Election Manifesto[22] of the congress party and Indira Gandhi's personal image which reached its zenith just after the winning of the liberation war of Bangladesh. Some radical steps from economic point of view were taken by the central government under the leadership of Indira Gandhi i. e. bank nationalization, abolition of privy purses, land reforms and others legal administrative measures to restrain the concentration of economic power in the hands of a few, convinced a lot the common people to mould their pro-Indira mind. Not only that the famous 10-points programme and pro-poor stand of Indira Gandhi along with her brilliant slogan *Garibi hatao* (remove poverty) effectively countered the election cry of her oppositions "Indira hatao' (remove Indira) - collectively led to the resounding victory of the Congress (R) in the general election of 1972 in the Lok Sabha and also in the Assembly election of West Bengal.[23]

Formation of Cabinet and S. S. Ray Sworn-in as Chief Minister

Under the given circumstances the election was held in 1972 and the verdict of the same brought the congress to power and initiatives were taken to form a new government under the leadership of S. S. Ray. Incidentally, though, Siddhartha Shankar Ray was empowered to lead the congress party during election, but he himself did not contest in the election. It is noteworthy that after resounding victory of the congress party, it was a demand of the congress MLAs to see Siddhartha Shankar Ray in the seat of the Chief Minister of West Bengal. However, at the beginning Siddhartha Shankar Ray was not willing to become the Chief Minister but lastly due to the interference of Mohan Kumar Mangalam and P. N. Haksar,[24] Principal Secretary of the Prime Minister, S. S. Ray agreed to take the responsibility of the same. It is easy to imagine that the situation had developed due to the direct intervention and, of course, due to the willingness of Smt. Indira Gandhi. On 17th March 1972, Siddhartha Shankar Ray was elected unanimously the leader of the Congress Legislative Party. On the eve of the swearing-in-ceremony, S. S. Ray met the Prime Minister to show the list of his proposed Council of Ministers but she (Indira Gandhi) literally refused to look into the list saying that "You should do whatever you think best". Thereafter, Siddhartha Shankar Ray along with his proposed Council of Ministers took oath on 20th March, 1972 at Raj Bhavan by Governor A. L. Dias. The new Council of Ministers consisted of 16 Cabinets, 9 States and 4 Deputy Ministers.[25]

Malda- Raiganj By-Election: Victory of Siddhartha Shankar Ray & Maya Ray

It has already been mentioned that Siddhartha Shankar Ray was not the candidate of the Assembly election of West Bengal in 1972, but he was elected the leader of the Congress Legislative Party (CLP), so, it was mandatory for him to become an MLA from any constituency of West Bengal within six months. In that context, Siddhartha Shankar Ray expressed his desire to contest a seat from comparatively rural area instead of his traditional home constituency Bhawanipur in South Calcutta. As Siddhartha Shankar Ray was born and brought up within the environment of affluent society in Calcutta, that is why he wished to recognize himself with the rural people to know their problems directly. He was given the nomination by the West Bengal Pradesh Congress Election Committee for the Malda Assembly constituency and Mrs. Maya Ray, wife of Siddhartha Shankar Ray from Raiganj Parliamentary constituency from where Siddhartha Shankar Ray was elected earlier. The Power, Irrigation, Waterways and Hill Affairs Minister of West Bengal and stalwart in the politics of Malda district, Abu Barkat Ataur (A.B.A) Gani Khan Chowdhury did the ground work for winning of Siddhartha Shankar Ray from the Malda Assembly constituency. Md. Gofurur Rahaman was the sitting Congress MLA from Malda, who had to resign in favour of Chief Minister of West Bengal due to the skilful intervention of ABA Gani Khan Chowdhury. However on 6th June, 1972 Siddhartha Shankar Ray won from Malda Assembly Constituency defeating his nearest rival Thakur Prasad, an independent Left supported candidate by a comfortable margin of 37,544 votes.[26] The following day, i.e. on 7th June, 1972 Mrs. Maya Ray was declared elected from Raiganj Parliamentary constituency trouncing her nearest rival by a margin of 1,40,000 votes.[27]

Mass-scale Employment

It was decided in a special cabinet meeting held in Chief Minister's room regarding the employment of 28,000 persons within three to four months on the basis of the proportion of 100 people from the each Assembly constituency (280X100=28,000) throughout the West Bengal. As per the decision of the special cabinet meeting, Chief Minister Siddhartha Shankar Ray was empowered to form district-wise Ministerial Sub-committees for the recruitment of class III and class IV employees. It was also decided that under the purview of that scheme an MLA could recommend for employment at best thirty names from his constituency for favourable consideration to the Cabinet Sub-committee. It was a tradition that the class III recruitments would complete through the Public Service Commission (PSC) in the form of open competitive examination. By this insincere method the powers of the P.S.C. was curtailed and it was handed over to the Cabinet Sub-committee i. e. indirectly to the members of the Legislature. The inevitable outcome of that devious method was that many unemployed youths were started running to the MLAs and Ministers day by day for securing their government employment. But the fact remains that it was impossible for an MLA to satisfy the hundreds of the unemployed youths by merely having the authority for recommendation only 30 employments in his constituency. Naturally, corruption engulfed some members of the legislature that lately leading to the arrests of a few among them. Dr. Prafulla Chandra Ghosh, the veteran congress leader and first Chief-Minister of West Bengal often used to remark: "Do not corrupt the Legislature by appointing the MLAs on license and permit bodies, but put Government officers with a background of integrity. These officers can be removed or punished for malpractices, but you cannot do so against members of Legislature".[28]

Cabinet Meetings in Districts

Keeping in mind the promises in the election manifesto of the congress party on the eve of the election in 1972, as a Chief Minister of West Bengal Siddhartha Shankar Ray wanted to bring swiftness in administrative activities and to develop equally throughout the state. So, instead of running the administrative affairs from Writers' Buildings, the Chief Minister decided to hold cabinet meetings in the districts and the first of such Cabinet meeting was held at Suri in Birbhum district on 21st August, 1972. In that district-wise cabinet meetings, it became the practice to make spot decisions to expedite the solution of the problems of the districts and the Ministers were directed to visit as many blocks as possible to know the problem for taking appropriate steps. An air-conditioned train was reserved for Ministers and high officials to attend the cabinet meetings holdings in the districts.[29]

Developmental Projects for West Bengal

As Chief Minister of West Bengal, Siddhartha Shankar Ray fully utilized his cordial relation with Prime Minister Indira Gandhi for bringing various developmental projects in order to make *'Sonar Pashchim Bangla'* i. e. prosperous West Bengal. Due to his skillful endeavor for the development it was announced by the Central Government on 1st October, 1972 that an integrated ship-building yard at Haldia would be set up at a cost of Rs.73 crores and another Low Temperature Carbonization Plant of Rs. 9 crores.

The State Government under Siddhartha Shankar Ray also received firm commitments in investment of Rs. 189 crores in various undertakings public sectors. Central Government by that time issued a letter expressing its intention for materializing various projects of West Bengal amounting Rs. 85 crores. In adition to this, they agreed to expanse Rs. 42 crores for the installation an Alloy Steel Plant, Rs. 16 crores for Cement Plant, Rs. 14 crores for a Nylon Factory and Rs. 12 crores for an Automobile Tyre and Tube Manufacturing Unit. These were the initial success of Siddhartha Shankar Ray in the sphere of development as the Chief Minister of West Bengal, though lastly due to various reasons all the schemes were not materialized properly.[30]

Ordinance for Banning Strike and Lock-Outs

Development of West Bengal and creation of job opportunities had badly shaken due to the introduction of some new weapon i. e. strikes, lock-outs and *gherao* techniques in the name of immediate meet up of the demands of the working class people in the industrial sector during the period of last two U. F. Ministries. As industrial peace is always essential for the swift progress of a State that is why considering the fact Siddhartha Shankar Ray in order to end these destructive practices in the name of movement of the working class and to restore normalcy in the industrial field – the West Bengal Cabinet approved an ordinance prohibiting strikes, lock-outs and *gheraos* in the industries for the purpose of regaining the lost glory of West Bengal in the realm of industrial development on 9th January, 1973.[31]

Others Developmental Activities Initiated by the Government, Headed by Siddhartha Shankar Ray

It may be noted that many developmental programmes were initiated and successfully completed during the regime of Siddhartha Shankar Ray for all round development of West Bengal. In the sphere of the educational development as well as to promote higher education many Diploma Courses such as Journalism, Library Science and Honours Courses were also introduced in the colleges throughout the West Bengal. In order to formulate a properly articulated system of education from primary schools to universities level, Siddhartha Shankar Ray introduced the establishment of a network of Primary schools, Secondary schools and Colleges in the form of 10+2+3 system. In the light of his experience as a Union Education Minister, Siddhartha Shankar Ray considering the condition of the grass root level people introduced compulsory vocational training for the learners from different strata. As a lawyer and a very well conscious citizen of the country, it was not unknown to the Chief Minister Siddhartha Shankar Ray about the condition of womenfolk of India particularly of West Bengal. So, in order to bring the women in touch with the knowledge world, Siddhartha Shankar Ray introduced the compulsory education for girl students up to class eight and it was free from any financial burden.[32]

It appears from various sources as well as interviews of some contemporary political personalities that apart from various projects and obviously education Siddhartha Shankar Ray took up various schemes for overall development of West Bengal and these were as under: i. construction of fly-over in Calcutta as well as all over West Bengal initiated during the Chief Ministership of Siddhartha Shankar Ray. ii. Second Howrah Bridge, iii. Metro Rail, iii. Yuba Bharati Stadium, iv. Netaji Indoor Stadium, vi. Khudiram Anushilan Kendra, vii. Farakka Barrage and so on. All these were completed during his time. There were also other constructive works that he accomplished and among them was the construction of connecting bridges in all the districts of West Bengal. One of the remarkable achievements of Siddhartha Shankar Ray was to bring back discipline and work culture in the government offices and the sole purpose was to expedite the developmental process of the government. It may be noted that S. S. Ray was also concerned about the food crisis of the province and for that he paid much attention on the agriculture.[33]

Role of Siddhartha Shankar Ray for the Election of President and General Secretary of WBPCC

It is a fact that Siddhartha Shankar Ray was very close to Prime Minister Indira Gandhi and became one of her most capable advisors after the split of Indian National Congress in 1969. Indira Gandhi would often seek his advice on diverse matters. Being a reputed Barrister as well as his profound knowledge on law and as a member of the Congress Working Committee and Central Parliamentary Board, Siddhartha Shankar Ray had the immense scope to influence the decision making process both in organization and administration. His voice was also prominent whether it was in the meetings of the National Development Council or in the conference of the Chief Ministers or any other matters. He was virtually one of the main dominating voices in the All India Congress politics from early 1970s to the end of 1975. He had also the decisive voice in the Congress Politics of West Bengal. In that time Siddhartha Shankar Ray was so influential in the politics at national level that considering his frequent meeting to Indira Gandhi in Delhi earned the reputation of being a 'Delhi-based' Chief Minister.[34] In that pretext, as per the compliance as well as directives of the AICC, some organizational changes were made by Siddhartha Shankar Ray on the ground that no Minister should be an office bearer of the Pradesh Congress Committee. It is noteworthy that the posts of President and General Secretary of the WBPCC were lying vacant for quite some time. For filling up the posts of WBPCC President and General Secretary, the Chief Minister's eye fell on Arun Kumar Moitra and youth leader and MP, Priya Ranjan Das Munshi respectively. So, Siddhartha Sankar Ray called both of them separately in his room and as a result of the intervention of S. S. Ray Arun Kumar Moitra agreed to resign from his post as a Minister of Co-operation, Fisheries, Closed and Sick Industries to become the President of the WBPCC.[35] Priya Ranjan Das Munshi was also likewise agreed to become the General Secretary of the WBPCC with the request of the Chief Minister. In a meeting of the WBPCC's Ad-hoc Committee S. S. Ray proposed their names for the two posts and within a short time they were unanimously elected.[36]

Influence of Siddhartha Shankar Ray Over State As Well As Central Politics in the Early Decades of 70s

It has already been mentioned that securing 216 Assembly seats out of 280 in the general election of 1972, as an unanimous leader of the congress party, Siddhartha Shankar Ray was sworn in as Chief Minister of West Bengal on 20th March, 1972.[37] It is important to note that the number of assembly seats won by Congress (R) was 105 in 1971, but it was increased up to 216 in the election of 1972 and proportion of votes increased from 29.19 per cent to 49.08 per cent in the two consecutive elections,[38] which was enough signaling regarding the strong support base behind the Congress (R) in West Bengal. Under the circumstances, at the time of becoming the Chief Minister of West Bengal, Siddhartha Shankar Ray was not only the unparallel leader of the state but also one of the influential leaders of the All India Congress party. He used to share very close relationship with the Central leadership particularly Prime Minister Indira Gandhi's blessings with him. At the initial stage of 70s there was none among Bengali leaders who could challenge the authority of Siddhartha Shankar Ray in the political affairs at national level particularly about the affairs of the West Bengal Politics. He was so influential that even Prime Minister Indira Gandhi herself would seek the name of capable persons from West Bengal for inducting Union Government. In that case, Central Ministers from Bengal like- D. P. Chattopadhyay, Pranab Mukherjee and Shankar Ghose etc. were inducted in the Central Cabinet as per the favourable recommendation of Siddhartha

Shankar Ray.[39] As a member of the Central Parliamentary Board and Congress Working Committee, Siddhartha Shankar Ray was very much dependable and capable political personality to Indira Gandhi who rightly utilized the energetic capabilities of S. S. Ray in the field of solving the dissensions within the congress party at national level, especially in Bihar where Kedar Pande was replaced by Abdul Ghaffar Khan as Chief Minister by the recommendation of Siddhartha Shankar Ray.[40] As a mark of influence of Siddhartha Shankar Ray on central government it was found that in a letter addressed to Indira Gandhi on 24th April, 1974, the name of Fakhruddin Ali Ahmed was recommended by S. S. Ray as the proposed Presidential candidate of the congress party. In that letter S. S. Ray wrote "I think Mr. Fakruddin Ali Ahmed is our best bet. I cannot think of any other person. Apart from being a Muslim, he is also from the Eastern region, and we have never had a President from this region. He will be completely loyal and Mrs. Ahmed is eminently presentable." However, Fakhruddin Ali Ahmed became the official candidate of the congress party and was elected as the fifth President of India on 20th August, 1974.[41]

Under the given circumstances, the influence of Siddhartha Shankar Ray as one of the close advisors of Indira Gandhi on diverse matters was established at the national level. Not only that, he would enjoy overall command in the administration as well as organizational level in West Bengal. Moreover, with boycotting the Assembly by the oppositions, particularly the CPI (M), it was expected that the congress government under the spirited leadership of Siddhartha Shankar Ray would be able to perform its duty smoothly. It was also expected that the uninterrupted five-year rule under a dynamic leader like Siddhartha Shankar Ray would give an enthusiasm to the congress leaders in West Bengal which would gradually led to the foundation of a strong organization of the party and continue its domination for long time. But unfortunately all the hopes and expectations about the congress party in West Bengal as well as prospects of the personal leadership of Siddhartha Shankar Ray took a different turn within a very short span due to some unexpected circumstances.

Weak Support Base and Lack of Efficient Leadership of the Congress Party in West Bengal

In spite of landslide victory of the congress (R) party in the general election of 1972, the well-knit organization of the party as well as its efficient leadership were almost absent in West Bengal. It is a point of fact that may be appropriate to mention here the undivided congress party ruled over West Bengal uninterruptedly for nearly a period of two decades. In that connection it may be recalled that the congress (R) and its leadership failed to retain the seat of power for long time due to massive Left Front victory in 1977 general election under the charismatic leadership of Jyoti Basu. The most significant point is that after the defeat of the congress party in the election of 1977, it could not able to regain its power till to-day. Naturally, it will be an obvious question, why did the congress accomplish very poor show in the election of 1977 and it could capture only 20 seats out of 294 assembly seats while CPI (M) alone got 178, and could not come back to power as well as become a marginal power in the politics of the state in West Bengal? [42]

There were so many factors which were collectively responsible for the decline of the congress party and in the long run it led to become a marginal power in West Bengal politics. The factors were as follows:

First of all, after independence (15th August, 1947) to 1967 undivided congress ruled over West Bengal continuously by and large for 20 years as a result of the image of the congress party in the national as well as state level as a main advocator of the freedom movement in India. Moreover, during that time West Bengal congress was fortunate enough to enjoy the charismatic leadership of Dr. Bidhan Chandra Roy who won the heart of the people by introducing an era of peace and prosperity in the midst of tremendous hindrance and a viable opposition in West Bengal. He was calm, neutral and knew the pulse of the people of the state. Dr. Bidhan Chandra Roy was also one of the advisors of Pundit Jawaharlal Nehru on diverse matters. Dr. B. C. Roy utilized his close relation with top leaders of the country like Nehru, Patel, Moulana Azad etc. as an advisor or as a personal physician for the overall possible development of West Bengal. It is mention worthy that in the field of the smooth functioning of the state administration for nearly 14 years, Dr. B. C. Roy could follow the policy of division of power strictly. In that connection the name of Atulya Ghosh deserved special mention. Atulya Ghosh was the President of WBPCC from 1950 to 1958 and he again became the WBPCC chief in 1961.[43] Besides the stature of the WBPCC Chief, others PCC Presidents like Jadabendra Nath Panja (1958-1961), Rabindralal Singha (1962 – 1964)[44] etc. were belonged to mighty Hooghly Groups headed by Atulya Ghosh. Naturally, entire congress organizations were under the absolute control of Atulya Ghosh. Atulya Ghosh was the man of rare caliber regarding the organizational abilities and with the help of his innate capabilities he discovered most potential local notables from each and every district throughout West Bengal. It was Atulya Ghosh's quality of leadership through which he established organizational network from local level to top level by the superb handling the district wise stalwart like Santosh Roy of Cooch Behar, Abdus Sattar of Murshidabad, Gani Khan Chowdhury of Malda etc. and was able to make a powerful local support base of the congress party. It may be said that due to his extraordinary organizational abilities it became possible for West Bengal congress to win over three successive general elections in 1952, 1957 and 1962 respectively and as a result of that he would enjoy the confidence of the central party leadership and subsequently became one of the most important national leaders of the congress party in India.[45] Moreover, the secrecy behind the winning of consecutive three general election of the congress party in West Bengal was within the chemistry of the well understanding in between Dr. B. C. Roy and Atulya Ghosh. There was as if an unwritten agreement between the two stalwart that Dr. B. C. Roy would not interfere into the organizational affairs and while Atulya Ghosh would not intervene into the administrative affairs. It is also important to note that Dr. B. C. Roy would hardly go to the Congress Bhavan and in the same way Atulya Ghosh would seldom come to the Writers' Buildings.[46]

In case of Siddhartha Shankar Ray who was never considered as the undisputed leader of West Bengal. It is notable that Dr. Bidhan Chandra Roy inducted young Siddhartha Shankar Ray, in his second cabinet on 26th April, 1957 as Judicial, Legislative and Tribal welfare Minister. Siddhartha Shankar Ray resigned from the Minister-ship on 15th March, 1958,[47] and also from the MLA-ship on 27th March, 1958. He did not come back in congress party even with the request of Dr. B. C. Roy rather he was reelected as a Member of the Legislative Assembly as an independent candidate supported by the opposition parties in a bye-election, held on 25th August, 1958 from the same 146- Bhowanipur constituency.[48] However, he came back at the crucial time of the congress party after the death of Dr. Bidhan Chandra Roy and defended Prafully Chandra Sen's Ministry in the flour of the Assembly House against the severe onslaught of the CPI (M.) and subsequently became the opposition leader and the West Bengal Affairs Minister and thereafter Chief Minister of West Bengal. In spite of establishing absolute control over West Bengal, the main loo-falls of Siddhartha Shankar Ray was that he did not try to build his own local support base and thereby his control over party organization was always far from firm. In that respect, he had basic difference with Atulya Ghosh, the undisputed well-knit organizer of the congress party in West Bengal, and Dr. Bidhan Chandra Roy, the architect of modern West Bengal. Both the leaders while enjoying the logic of the division of power keeping aside their personal ego for the greater interest and the development of West

Bengal, Siddhartha Shankar Ray was against the division of power. Siddhartha Shankar Ray started interfering as well as controlling both state administration and overall organization of the congress party in West Bengal. These attitudes of Siddhartha Shankar Ray regarding his overall supremacy enraged the other leaders of West Bengal that led to the division among them into pro-Siddhartha and anti-Siddhartha group.[49]

Despite his complete dedication towards the fulfillment of his duty and earnest desire for improvement of the people of the State, mainly as a consequence of inter-party rivalries, Siddhartha Shankar Ray had to quit office in tragic political circumstances. There was division in the cabinet, division in the party machinery and his reputation as the congress leader suffered a serious setback due to inter-party feud and successive defeats in Lok Sabha and State Assembly elections in 1977. Moreover, Siddhartha Shankar Ray was emotionally-charged along with fluctuating temper and failed to understand the mood of his people.[50]

Wheat-Bran Scandal

The Ministry of Siddhartha Shankar Ray had to face many unwanted crisis from the very outset and as a result of that it did not get off a smooth start. The Ministry came under serious stress when news reached in Writers' Buildings relating to the arrest of Shri Arun Dasgupta, confidential assistant of Kashi Kanta Maitra, the then Food Minister of S. S. Ray Ministry on 25th July, 1973 while he was carrying with him a large amount of unaccounted money. As per the version of Shri Haladhar Patel, press reporter of *'Satya Jug Patrika'* in his book entitled *'Bhushi Kelenkari'* (wheat-bran scandal) that "in order to make his political carrier strong in the soil of Nadia District in the form of political nepotism, Kashi Kanta Maitra, the then Food Minister started giving the permits of wheat-bran selling to his party cadres ignoring all formalities and procedures. In that context, in order to secure cooperation from youth congress, Kashi Babu incorporated many influential youth congress leaders including Sudip Bandopadhyay, the then Youth Congress President of West Bengal in the wheat-bran distribution committee. The other notable personalities who were incorporated in that committee were- Somen Mitra, Debaprasad Roy, Shibdas Mukhopadhyay, Shibu Chowdhury, Swarajbandhu Bhattacharyay etc. Due to his nefarious tactics the price rate of wheat-bran increased from Rs. 20-22 to Rs. 40-44 per maund. Not only that as a result of mixing of wheat-bran (which is always used as food for cattle) with atta (smashing wheat that is used as food for men) it became the food for men and it would sell Rs. 56 to 60 per maund. In that way a black market of Rs. 9

crores was created by centering wheat-bran".[51] Kashi Kanta Maitra had also given the permit as well as license for distribution of wheat-bran to Jaydeep Mukhopadhyay, the famous tennis player with international repute and nephew of Chief Minister Siddhartha Shankar Ray. It was expected to Kashi Kanta Maitra that if there would start any enquiry regarding this matter and the name of Jaydeep Mukherjee would automatically come into surface then the Chief Minister would be forced to skip the matter and in this way Kashi Babu and his associates would be spared. But it is interesting to note that Siddhartha Shankar Ray as a Chief Minister of West Bengal took the challenge of his Food Minister Kashi Kanta Maitra. After the arrest of Shri Arun Dasgupta, confidential assistant of Kashi Kanta Maitra on 25th July 1973, the very next morning i.e. on 26th July 1973, Chief Minister ordered for an immediate investigation into the matter and said, "How many more dishonest persons there are in Writers' Buildings?" and then hand over the order to D.I.G. personally through his P. A. Mr. Saroj Chakrabarty.[52]

Following the order of investigation, when the name of Adhish Mukherejee, brother-in law of the Chief Minister Siddhartha Shankar Ray as well as father of Jaydeep Mukherjee came into the surface, then the investigating officers rolled up for the time being. Incidentally, Jaydeep Mukherjee authorized his father for running the license of wheat-bran and thereby both the father and son became accused and as per law and for the sake of impartial investigation it was necessary for the investigation officer to arrest them. As Adhish Mukherjee and Jaydeep Mukherjee were very close relative of the Chief Minister, so the investigating officers were hesitating to arrest them and before going for such harsh action they sought permission from Siddhartha Shankar Ray. In that pretext, the Chief Minister Siddhartha Shankar Ray categorically gave a strict order in the following way, "As like as others accused his relatives would also be arrested at per law and no special arrangement would be made for them."[53] As a result of the directives from the Chief Minister, Adhish Mukherjee was arrested and took bail from court and as soon as Jaydeep Mukherjee would land in West Bengal after the end of his tennis tournament in London, he would also be arrested as per the dictation of Chief Minister to enforcement branch.[54] It has also been written by Mr. Saroj Chakrabarty, personal assistant of the Chief Ministers that "into the enquiry of wheat-bran case some of the relations of Chief Minister's were involved and latter on arrested. But Siddhartha Babu had not interfered in any manner whatsoever in favour of his relations either for securing their release or by influencing the process of investigation."[55]

Whenever the investigation of the wheat-bran scandal was going on, then in the meantime, Food Minister Kashi Kanta Maitra sent two resignation letters- the first one on 30th July and the second on 4th August 1973. In his letters Kasha Kanta Maitra requested the Chief Minister to accept his resignation 'in view of a well-laid and pre-planned conspiracy against him'. He also interrogated the Chief Minister to appoint a sitting Judge of the Calcutta High Court for an enquiry regarding his activities as Food Minister.' The Chief Minister hesitated initially and at last after a brief discussion with some of the senior Cabinet Ministers on 5th August Maitra's resignation was accepted and thus Kashi Kanta Maitra quitted the Cabinet on 5th August, 1973.[56]

Wanchoo Commission

In spite of taking stern action against Food Minister Kashi Kanta Maitra, Siddhartha Shankar Ray, the Chief Minister however, failed to extricate the ministry from the crisis of corruption. A fresh allegation was brought before the Government by Sudip Banerjee, President of the West Bengal Youth Congress and Kumud Bhattacharjee, President of Chhatra Parishad through a Press conference on 7th June, 1974 and demanded immediate resignation of five Ministers and three senior officials on the plea of 'corruption and incompetence.' Both the leaders also threatened to resign from the congress party if no action were taken against them. The Chief Minister in order to assure the aggrieved leaders announced that an enquiry commission would be appointed to probe all allegations of corruption against accused ministers on 8th June, 1974. Thereafter, with the approval of Prime Minister for setting up of such a commission, the Union Government constituted a one man commission headed by K. N. Wanchoo, ex-Chief Justice of the Supreme Court and was instructed to submit its report within one month.[57]

Though, Wanchoo commission was appointed as per the demands of the top leaders of youth and student wings of the congress party in West Bengal to eradicate corruption from the state administration, but the most astonishing event was that the constitution of the Wanchoo commission as if fuelled the simmering discontent within the party. After constituting the commission, the Chief Minister remarked, "I do not think there is any other Government in the world which had followed such a liberal and open procedure."[58] Some of the leaders and cabinet colleagues of S. S. Ray found a well laid conspiracy behind the appointment of Wanchoo commission in order to place some of his co-workers in the dock. Therefore, a division in the party and within the ministry came into the forefront over the appointment of Wanchoo Commission. The dissenters of S. S. Ray insisted for 'collective decision' and considered that the appointment of such commission against the ministers and leaders of the ruling party would tarnish the image of the congress in West Bengal. However, a Gazette notification was issued on 10th July, 1974, relating to the appointment of the Wanchoo Commission for inquiry against corruption.[59]

Reports and Impact

Being authorized to investigate the corruption, Mr. Justice Wanchoo selected 10 complaints for thorough investigation out of more than 130 written complaints which had no prima *facie case* for reference. Among the 10 complaints- charges against Pradip Bhattacharya, Jainal Abedin and Prafulla Kanti Ghosh, the front ranking congress leaders were found to be forged. The complaint against Gurupada Khan regarding the appointment of his son as his Confidential Assistant (C.A.) was not at all a matter of reference to the commission. It was found that the complaints against others congress leader like Subrata Mukherjee, P. K. Ghosh on the ground of accepting bribe was absurd. So, lastly the complaints against only five congressmen i.e. Ajit Panja, Sitaram Mahato, Santosh Roy, Govinda Naskar and Suniti Chattaraj would go to the commission. On 23rd August, 1974 the five Ministers appeared before the commission in order to submit their replies. The commission completed its sittings on 22nd December and the last reports were received by the Chief Minister on 28th January, 1975. After receiving the reports of the Wanchoo Commission, Chief Minister went to Delhi at once for consultation with the Congress President and the Prime Minister. Returning from Delhi by the evening plane a special cabinet meeting was summoned at midnight on 29th January, 1975 to consider the reports of the commission. Thereafter, the Chief Minister announced the resignation of Santosh Roy, the Relief Minister and Suniti Chattaraj, Deputy Minister who had already sent the resignation letter earlier according to the advice of the Chief Minister. The three other Ministers i. e. Ajit Panja, Sitaram Mahato and Govinda Naskar were given fully cleansed by Mr. Justice K. N. Wanchoo. In his report Mr. Justice Wanchoo remarked, "A Minister's integrity should be above reproach and like Caesar's wife his conduct should be above suspicion".[60]

However, at the initial stage there was no protest as such and thereupon 180 congress MLAs in a signed statement supported the appointment of the Wanchoo Commission, yet centering the remark of Chief Minister 'I shall decide who will continue as Minister or go after I receive the report of the Commission',[61] some congressmen including his anti-groups within the party got a scope to whisper that the main purpose of the commission was to save few person who were close to the chief minister. So, it is difficult to conclude that the commission had some purpose other than identifying the corrupt ministers. Whatever the intentions it was, but the fact remains that as a result of the appointment of the commission and its aftermath intensified the factional feuds within the congress party particularly among the Yuba Congress and Chhatra Parishad activists. Reports about the physical clashes among the young congressmen started pouring from many districts and as a result of its inevitable consequences not only sapped the party's vitality but also its image was tarnished as a whole.

Breaking up of the P. D. A.

The Congress (R) led Progressive Democratic Alliance (PDA) Ministry had to face an additional problem at that time. When it was found that CPI was gradually moving closer towards the CPI (M), speculation erupted about the utility of the PDA. It may be noted that the 'All India Railway Strike' was called by the opposition parties in May 1974 where in spite of becoming partner of the congress party in the PDA Ministry in West Bengal, the CPI joined in that strike with the CPI (M). Not only that the CPI leaders brought the allegations against the Ministry on the ground that it was being dominated by the 'Rightists' and accused the Chief Minister for all that happenings. It also carried a resolution and directed the MLAs of the CPI to 'function henceforth as the Opposition'. At this juncture, Chief Minister wrote a letter to the Prime Minister on 14th June, 1974, informing her about the decision of the C.P.I. for breaking the Progressive Democratic Alliance. In fact, Chief Minister received report from intelligence service regarding the decision of the C.P.I to break the P.D.A. and accordingly a meeting was held on 11th June, 1974. The Chief Minister suspected that a conspiracy was hatched by some top congressmen and one central minister behind the breaking up of PDA to humiliate him. Being irritated and aggrieved as a result of intensified factionalism and corruption within the party and the government, the Chief Minister at one stage wrote to the Prime Minister on 30th August, 1974 in the following manner: "I am taking a firm line regarding groupism in the party here—also against anti socials or those who are connected with anti socials. I know that this may create difficulties, but I have reached the limit of my patience. I have really nothing to lose in taking this line. Bengal has no future whatsoever unless all this is stopped. If the party goes against me for taking this attitude, I am quite willing to step down. Whatever I have done in my life I have tried to do it well. I had a great success at the Bar and built up a reputation of being absolutely fearless and honest. I tried my best to keep up this reputation as a Central Minister and I do not see why at this age I shall allow people to point out to me and say that I have ruined Bengal by being soft" [62]

Thus, it was found that Siddhartha Shankar Ray's control over the organization of West Bengal congress party was not strong and he had to take external help to control the party affairs. It was not known whether the prime minister gave any reply to the letter of Siddhartha Shankar Ray or not. However, the fact as it appears was that the organization of the congress party in West Bengal was being controlled by the inefficient leaders and as a result of that the internal as well as outward cohesion of the party came under serious stress due to group politics.

Groupism in West Bengal Congress Politics and Siddhartha Shankar Ray

It is worthy to mention here that in spite of resounding victory in the general election of 1972 and installation of the congress government under the leadership of Siddhartha Shankar Ray; as a party the Congress (R) was not free from problems at all. Many veteran old guards of the congress party were unhappy because of failing to get party tickets and dissatisfied with the concession of as many as 41 seats to the CPI.[63] Not only that, though it is unfortunate but fact remains that the West Bengal Pradesh Congress was again became the victim of factional politics during the tenure of the Chief Ministership of Siddhartha Shankar Ray. In the election of 1972, breaking the traditional system in distribution of party tickets, young leaders from Yuba Congress and Chhatra Parishad were given the priority for fighting the electoral battle. It is a fact that the most of the old and reputed congressmen were remained under the fold of Congress (O) while the leaders of the new generations particularly the Yuba Congress and Chhatra Parishad were amalgamated themselves with the Congress (R) which was known as Indira Congress or Naba Congress. It was also impossible to deny that the leaders of the Chhatra Parishad and Yuba Congress played a very crucial role in the victory of the Congress (R). They became as if the main driving force of the Congress (R) and got success in the electoral battle of 1972. It was observed by Somen Mitra who was given the party tickets from Sealdah constituency instead of sitting MLA, Binay Banerjee due to the endeavour of Praya Ranjan Dasmunshi, the then all India Youth Congress President, that "as many as 80 MLAs of the 216 of the Congress (R) in 1972 whose average age groups were not above 30. If Siddhartha Babu would be able to utilize the youth force of the party properly in a united manner instead of taking every possible steps to divide them, the future of the congress party in West Bengal as well as political carrier of Siddhartha Babu himself would not had to face difficulties."[64]

Factionalism during Siddhartha Shankar Ray era initiated within the comparatively young congressmen centering the difference of opinion on some matter between Prafulla Kanti Ghosh, popularly known as Sata Ghosh (MLA, Cossipore) and Subrata Mukhapadhyay (MLA, Ballygunge). In that events Priya Ranjan Dasmunshi (henceforth P. R. Dasmunshi) supported Subrata Mukhopadhyay while Somendra Nath Mitra, widely known as Somen Mitra (MLA, Sealdah) and his close associates like Lakshmi Kanta Bose (MLA, Rash Behari), Barid Baran Das (MLA, Shyampukur) supported Prafulla Kanti Ghosh alias Sata Ghosh which bifurcated the congress organization. The far reaching consequence of this division of the congress party particularly its driving force i.e. youth congress in a parallel way whose after-taste remained long days that sapped the vitality of the congress organization in West Bengal.[65]

At this stage, the single party dominated politics of West Bengal centered round the Congress (R) and S. S. Ray was the Chief Minister. (1972-1977). The political scene of West Bengal was such that most of the non-congress parties could not obtained sufficient number of seats in the Assembly and along with the defeat of Jyoti Basu, a promising figure of the opposition parties resulted that voices of the opposition could hardly be ventilated in the Assembly Hall. Under the situation, the opposition parties had no other alternative but to boycott the Assembly accusing the election was entirely a colossal rigging and as a consequence of that the Ministry headed by Siddhartha Shankar Ray was termed as an illegal one and virtually the West Bengal Legislative Assembly turned into a Legislature without any opposition party.[66]

But fact remains that allegations of most of the opposition parties were unheeded by S. S. Ray and the accusations and criticism of the opposition parties were not so active to bring down the spirit of the Government. Rather it was the infighting and factionalism of the Congress (R) that crippled the stability and strength from within.[67] If Siddhartha Shankar Ray would want, he could easily minimize the intraparty collision, but mysteriously he indulged it.[68]

Rural Vote Bank and the Congress Party

It is also worthy of mentioning that in the years of 1964-65 a provincial-political conference was held at Mayapur, Hooghly District which was presided over by Ajay Mukherjee, the then President of West Bengal Pradesh

Congress Committee. K. Kamraj, the then all India Congress President was also present that conference. Among the various proposals of Mayapur provincial conference, the most important one i.e. 'ownership of land' was accepted unanimously. According to that proposal, the ongoing ceiling system of land in India was the fixation of upper limit and in that connection ceiling system in lower limit of the land to be introduced. Surplus land above the upper ceiling would have to be distributed among the poor people in accordance with the opinion of the experts in the form of necessity of land for the livelihood of a five member family. It was also stated that lands would be remained only in the hands of that people those who were entirely dependent for their day to day life on lands. People belonged to other professions like physicians, lawyers, teachers, businessmen etc. would not allow to retain lands in their hands. Only cultivators would become the owner of the land. Though the proposals were accepted unanimously, but most of the congress leaders did not accept the proposals willingly from the core of their hearts. As traditionally big landlords, jotedars and landed aristocrats were the main vote bank and closely associated with the congress party since long days, so, the anti jotedars proposals disillusioned them to the congress party. Though, it was accepted officially but in practice it was not executed at that moment.[69]

It is very important to note that besides featherbedding the grouping in the congress party, Siddhartha Shankar Ray, the Chief Minister of West Bengal did many welfare activities for the development of poor people. It was during his time homeless people got homes, landless got land and loan from I.R.D.P. In the time of the implementation of these projects there were no congress workers in the rural areas along with the S.D.O and B.D.Os in order to get political benefits. Not only that in spite of introducing of land reforms, operation barga, distribution of croups according to the ratio of 25:75 among the cultivators and landlords; all these went against the congress government due to lack of positive propagation among the beneficiaries. Another drastic negative impact of these welfare programmes of Siddhartha Shankar Ray was that those who were the traditional vote bank of the congress party from its inception i. e. jotedars and zaminders were disillusioned to congress due to adopting anti-jotedars stances and they started tilting to the Janata Party and CPI (M). But most irony of fact that those who were benefitted due to adoption of anti-jotedars stand by Siddhartha Shankar Ray, they did not come under the fold of the congress party rather preferred to remain in their previous stand i.e. under the red flag of the communists. So, it was found that those who were politically with the congress, after being frustrated from economic point of view they left congress; on the other hand those who became economically benefitted could not change their political stance and remained with the left politics - which drastically affected the prospects of the congress party in West Bengal. Therefore, it might be stated that despite of adopting various revolutionary measures for the ameliorating of the poor people, only due to lack of positive campaign in favour of Siddhartha Shankar Ray's Ministry or failure of countering the negative campaign of the opposition as a result of infighting and as its inevitable consequences congress systematically got de-touched from the common people which were reflected in the general election of 1977. [70]

Impact of the Verdict of Allahabad High Court (on 12th June, 1975) on the West Bengal Government vis-à-vis the Congress Party

Indira Gandhi was elected from Rai Baerily Parliamentary constituency against her contestant candidate Raj Narayan by a margin of 1,10,000 votes, in the general election of 1971. Raj Narayan Brought an allegation against Indira Gandhi for adopting illegal techniques and also immoral assistance from a Government official named Yash Pal Kapoor and also filed a suit against Indira Gandhi in Allahabad High Court on 24th April, 1971.[71] In his verdict of the case widely known as 'Rajnarayan vs. Mrs. Gandhi', Mr. Justice J. M. L. Sinha of Allahabad High Court on 12th June 1975, convicted Indira Gandhi for adopting corrupt practices and unseated her from the Lok Sabha and disqualified her membership in the House of Parliament or State Legislature for 6 years. As a direct impact of the verdict of Allahabad High Court, Chief Minister Siddhartha Shankar Ray started losing the support from the congress high command and the possibility of his replacement by Pranab Mukherjee with the blessing of Sanjay Gandhi, younger son of Indira Gandhi became clear.[72] It is a fact that Prime Minister Indira Gandhi entrusted Siddhartha Shankar Ray, Chief Minister of West Bengal and H. R. Gokhale, Central Law Minister to handle the legal affairs on behalf of her related to election centric suit of Allahabad High Court. Both the leaders assured Indira Gandhi regarding the surety of her victory in that suit. But it was Sanjay Gandhi who apprehended that the case was not handling properly. Sanjay Gandhi earlier expressed his agony to his mother about the possibility of her defeat in the suit of Allahabad High Court due to the conspiracy of Devkanta Barooh, the then All India Congress President, S. S. Ray, Gokhale and Hemabati Nandan Bahuguna, the then chief Minister of Uttar Pradesh. Naturally, after seeing the outcome of the suit of Allahabad High Court on 12th June 1975, which was considered as the great shock in the political life of Indira Gandhi who also started believing the assumption of her son about the conspiracy as well as improper handling of the suit of the Court by S. S. Ray and others. So, after becoming cautious, Indira Gandhi took over the responsibility of Allahabad High Court's suit from the hands of S. S. Ray and Gokhale and ignoring all obstacles, she handed over it to Asoke Sen to look over the case in the Supreme Court.[73]

After the judgment of Allahabad High Court on 12th June, 1975 and along with the interference of Sanjay Gandhi into the diverse matter of politics as well as his entrance into politics, the anti Siddhartha Shankar Ray's group in West Bengal politics became very much enthusiastic. In that context, those who strongly asserted themselves against Siddhartha Shankar Ray were- A. B. A. Gani Khan Choudhury, Sato Ghosh, Somen Mitra, D. P. Chattopadhyay etc. The name of Pranab Mukherjee was also incorporated in the same queue. As a result of infighting into the congress party in West Bengal that was sufficient in damaging his overall image as a leader of the party as well as chief administrator of the state.[74]

The Inner Story of Indira-Ray-Sanjay Rupture

From the above it thus became clear that there was a significant role of Sanjay Gandhi in creating disenchantment between Siddhartha Shankar Ray and Indira Gandhi. It may be recalled that Siddhartha Shankar Ray, the chief minister of West Bengal was not in the good book of Sanjay since the early days of the year of 1974. Sanjay Gandhi had personal hostility against S. S. Ray who drew the attention of Prime Minister towards certain 'irregularities' of his (Sanjay) Maruti project. Moreover, despite issuing orders from the centre to treat Sanjay Gandhi as a VIP, Siddhartha Shankar Ray never attended the airport to receive Sanjay Gandhi and did not sanction any amount of money for his frequent visit to Bengal. Shri Saroj Chakrabarty who was the personal assistant of Siddhartha Shankar Ray, the Chief Minister, later wrote, "Through some of his (S.S. Ray's) personal and confidential letters dictated to me, the Chief Minister brought to the notice of the Prime Minister certain grave irregular features of Maruti Project. This had infuriated Sanjoy Gandhi against Ray. Sanjoy Gandhi became a sore enemy of Ray and resolved to remove him from the political scene."[75]

Sanjay Gandhi and Factionalism within the Congress Party of West Bengal

Sanjay Gandhi's involvement into the arena of Indian politics towards the end of 1975, and his anti- Ray attitude was diplomatically utilized by the pro-changers i. e. anti S. S. Ray group as an opportunity to expedite their

Chandra Shekhar, Mohan Dharia, Krishna Kant, Ramdhan and even Bisheswar Prasad Koirala, former Prime Minister of Nepal unsuccessfully tried to make a compromise between them. See Bhola Chattopadhyay, *op.cit.* p.63.

90. Saroj Chakrabarty, ... *Chief Ministers*, p .434.

91. *Ibid.*, p .447.

92. *Ibid.*, p.461.

93. Personal interview with Deba Prasad Roy, a veteran congress leader, former Rajya Sabha M.P., MLA, AICC member on 18th February, 2017.

94. Saroj Chakrabarty, ... *Chief Ministers*, p.470.The experience of Calcutta on 2nd April, 1975 was so shocking to J. P. that in later time referring the incident he said in Bihar in the following manner: "What happened there, and of which I myself was a victim, was naked hooliganism and gangsterism in the presence of a West Bengal Minister, a West Bengal M. P. and possee of police officers and police force. West Bengal would be doomed unless the State is rid of Yuba Congress-Chhatra Parishad gangsterism".

95. Programme of J.P. was chalked out as per the decision of the Nava Nirman Samiti (NNS) comprising of - Congress (O), JS, BLD, SP, SSP, PSP, RPI, F.B.-Subhasist, Radical Humanist and Sarvodaya Mandal, and the seven Left Parties was held on 31st May 1975. See Saroj Chakrabarty, ... *Chief Ministers*, p.473.

96. *Ibid.*, p.473.

97. *Ibid.*, p.472.

98. *Ibid.*, pp.473-474.

99. Barun Sengupta, *Indira ...*, p. 572.

100. Devid Lockwood, *The Communist Party of India and the Indian Emergency*, Sage, New Delhi, 2016, p.115.

101. 20 points programmes were as follows: 1. Government shall control the price hike and take stern action against hoarders and black marketers. 2. Upper ceiling of lands in rural areas shall be implemented and vested lands shall be distributed. 3. Housing lands shall be given to the poor people in the rural areas. 4. 'Bonded labour' system shall be abolished as soon as possible. 5. Measures shall be adopted to provide loan among the poor and middle-class people. 6. Measures shall be adopted to increase the rate of land labour. 7. Irrigation system shall be extended. 8. Measures shall be taken for producing more electricity. 9. All types of facilities shall be provided to the tant industries. 10. Measures will be taken to sell good qualities of mill made *dhuti* and *shares* in rural areas. 11. All types of legal actions will be taken in the urban areas to

stop the activities of the speculators. 12. Stern action will be taken against those were not paying taxes properly. 13. Taking stringent measures will be continued against the contraband. 14. System of providing license to the investors will be easiest in case of opening industries. 15. Measures will be taken so that workers may take part in the administrative system of the industries. 16. National permits will be given to truck vehicles. 17. Income tax will be paid only those who will earn up to 8,000 per years instead of previous 6,000 per years. 18. Essential commodities will be provided to the students hostels in a regular price rate. 19. Measures will be adopted to provide books and khatas to the students at the cheapest rate. 20. Legal measures will be adopted so that as much as possible apprentices will be inducted in the industries. See Barun Sengupta, *Indira ...*, pp. 572-573.

102. Pranab Mukherjee, *op.cit.*p. 83.

103. Devid Lockwood, *op.cit.* p.144.

104. "*Gharer Baire Muktiyuddha - Muktir Yuddha Bhitare* 1971- 80," a Bengali article by Aurabinda Poddar in *Saat Dashak, Samakal O Anandabazar,* Ananda Publishers Private Limited, Kolkata, 2013, p. 152; Also see Bipan Chandra et.al, *op.cit.* p. 261.

105. "*Gharer Baire Muktiyuddha - Muktir Yuddha Bhitare* 1971- 80," a Bengali article by Aurabinda Poddar in *Saat Dashak, Samakal O Anandabazar,* Ananda Publishers Private Limited, Kolkata, 2013, p. 152.

106. Devid Lockwood, *op.cit.*pp.145-146.

107. In the event of the implementation of the programme, supposing political opposition from some corner Sanjay warned "so called leaders within and without the Congress' that 'any leader of any community or religion who opposes family planning ...should be thrown out". Kishen Chand, the then lieutenant-governor of Delhi, directed the civil servants of Delhi that those who had more than two children would have to sterilize- otherwise 'no promotion, no confirmation, no increment, no entitlement to government housing, no loan advances, no leave'. It was found that the chief secretary of the Uttar Pradesh issued an instruction to the district magistrates and divisional commissioners of the state to 'inform everybody that failure to achieve monthly targets of motivations will not only result in stoppage of salary but also suspension and severest penalties'. Even school teachers were also instructed to be sterilized and directed to motivate five other individuals for the operation. Those who were suitable age among the wider section of the population of India, it was found that people were denied from renewing driving, scooter, rickshaw and arms licenses on the ground of failing to show a sterilization certificate. Sometimes people were refused treatment

various groups of the congress party. The congressmen became enthusiastic to arrest the congressmen of counter groups under the MISA (Maintenance of Internal Security Act). Siddhartha Babu using his administrative power to sent one by one congress leaders to the prison under MISA. Even the members of the AICC and congress MLAs were not spared. All these actions taken by Siddhartha Shankar Ray were not considered by the common people as his success rather they considered these as corruption of the congress party. But the unfortunate was that all these were only the fruits of the intra-party rivalry of the congress in West Bengal which tarnished the image of the party and sapped its vitality as a whole. See Deba Prasad Roy, *"Doors Theke Delhi* (in Bengali), *Dharabahik Atmakatha,* Part- 15", in *Eakhan Doors,* (ed.) Pradosh Ranjan Saha, Dover Lane, Kolkata, 2016.

69. Atulya Ghosh, *Kasta...*, pp. 191-195.

70. Deba Prasad Roy, *"Doors Theke Delhi* (in Bengali), *Dharabahik Atmakatha,* Part- 17", in *Eakhan Doors,* (ed.) Pradosh Ranjan Saha, Dover Lane, Kolkata, 2016.

71. *Ananda Bazar Patrika,* 13th June 1975.

72. Sitaram Sharma, *op.cit.* 77.

73. Barun Sengupta, *Indira Ekadashi* (in Bengali henceforth *Indira...*), in Barun Sengupta *Rachana Sanghara,* Ananda Publishers Private Limited, Kolkata, 2008, pp. 566, 577.

74. Pranab Mukherjee, *op.cit.* p. 107.

75. Saroj Chakrabarty, ... *Chief Ministers*, p.515.

76. *Ibid.,* p.516.

77. *Ibid.,* p.510.

78. By this time Guljari Lal Nanda acted as the care taker Prime Minister. See Saroj Chakrabarty, ... *Chief Ministers*, p.146.

79. Sitaram Sharma, *op.cit.* p. 71.

80. *"Gharer Baire Muktiyuddha - Muktir Yuddha Bhitare* 1971- 80," a Bengali article by Aurobinda Poddar in *Saat Dashak, Samakal O Anandabazar,* Ananda Publishers Private Limited, Kolkata, 2013, p. 142.

81. Sitaram Sharma, *op.cit.* pp. 71-72.

82. Barun Sengupta, *Indira ...,* pp. 551-554.

83. *Ibid.,* pp. 556, 557, 565.

84. Jayprakash Narayan was a rare Indian politician probably after Gandhiji, who never touched any office of state power in spite of having it within his easy achieve. He was the second most popular man after Nehru in the Indian political stage and could have succeeded Pundit Nehru due to his enormous credentialities. See Pranab Mukherjee, *op.cit.*p.79. As a result of his life long struggle for restoring peace throughout the world Jayprakash Narayan was given the prestigious 'Magsaysay' award in 1966. The man of high moral values who always fought for *'shuddhi'* as well as 'reform' and had the deep grievances against corruption, misadministration and dishonor to democracy. See *"Sesh Parjanto Chhaker Baire* 1971- 80" (in Bengali), in *Saat Dashak, Samakal O Anandabazar,* Ananda, Kolkata, 2013, p. 138.

85. Barun Sengupta, *Indira ...,* pp. 555-556.

86. Bipan Chandra et.al, *op.cit.* p. 261.

87. J. P.'s comments in *Everymens Weekly,* 22nd June 1974; Also see Bhola Chattopadhyay, *Jayprakash Narayan O Sampurna Biplab* (in Bengali), Ananda, Kolkata, 1987, p.62.

88. At the beginning of the year of 1974, J. P. thought that it became compulsory to launch a movement like-42 in the wake of corruption and misadministration in the country. That movement would not be as like as to install Ram instead of Shyam or Madhu rather it would be more-wider, deeper which would bring qualitative transformation in society. Full Democracy would be established in the all sphere of society and state. In later time J.P. called these ideals of revolution as 'Total Revolution'. See *"Gharer Baire Muktiyuddha - Muktir Yuddha Bhitare* 1971- 80", a Bengali article by Aurobinda Poddar in *Saat Dashak, Samakal O Anandabazar,* Ananda Publishers Private Limited, Kolkata, 2013, p.144.

89. In that critical juncture, considering the personal relationship between J.P. and Indira Gandhi, (The personal relation between Indira Gandhi and Jayprakash Narayan since long days. Nehru and J. P. were very close to each other. Moreover, the relation between Kamala Nehru, mother of Indira Gandhi and Pravabati Devi, wife of J. P. was so intimate that it was stated that if Pravabati Devi would alive then it would probably not be possible for J. P. to take merciless attitude to the only daughter of Kamala Nehru. From the childhood days of Indira Gandhi, J. P. always called her fondly as 'Indu'.) in a response to the media persons regarding the meeting between J. P. and Indira Gandhi in Patna on 14th August 1977, J. P. said, "Indira's coming to see me proves that old connection with Nehru family still remains." see *Ananda Bazar Patrika,* 15th August,1977; also see Bhola Chattopadhyay, *op.cit.* p.57. some sympathizers towards the J. P. movement inside the Congress namely

mood that the car of J. P. was gheraod and one Chhatra Parishad supporters named 'Sabita' danced on the bonnet of his car and his supporters had to face pelting stones which were hurled by the demonstrators.[93]

But J.P. was not a man to stop there and in order to materialize his political objectives he addressed a gathering in Calcutta attended by the teachers and students. To quote J. P. as he addressed, "ground is ready for a total revolution in West Bengal. Nowhere else in India such exploitation, unemployment, poverty and a gap between the rich and the poor as in West Bengal".[94]

Intelligence Report on J. P.'s Visit to Calcutta

It may however, be noted that the Intelligence Branch of the West Bengal Government was well aware about the proposed Calcutta visit of J. P. and the government was also informed about his plans and programmes. Incidentally, the entire programme of J. P. was chalked out by a number of political parties[95] which heartily appreciated Jayprakash Narayan to lead the movement against the misrule of West Bengal. In spite of all oppositions J. P. was successful in addressing two meetings in Tamluk (4th June, 1975) and Contai (5th June, 1975) and all the more he was also able to organize a mammoth rally in Calcutta (on 5th June 1975) as a mark of unity of the anti-congress forces with not less than 20,000 followers. Not only that from the gathering of Brigade Parade ground J. P. called for the formation of *LOKA SANGRAM SAMITY* in order to unite the people for peaceful political agitation against the present rulers who were the root cause of miseries and suppression of civil liberties of the people as a whole by misusing official power on the plea of Emergency (external), MISA and DIR.[96] As a reaction, in order to give a fitting reply to J. P.'s anti congress procession the widely circulated congress factionalism in West Bengal took a dramatic turn. As per the direction of the Congress High Command the two rival groups of WBPCC temporarily resolved to sort out their differences to organize an anti-JP rally during his stay in Calcutta.[97] Accordingly, after two days of J.P's rally an anti-J.P. gathering was organized by the WBPCC at Calcutta Maidan under the leadership of Siddhartha Shankar Ray, which was attended by about 10,000 people.[98] Actually, it was the name and fame of J. P. and his wide acceptance to the oppositions despite different ideologies and his reputation as a crusader against the misadministration and corruption and his non-attraction to official power collectively created a sense of confidence among the common people. These shows an open political tussle of the Congress Party (R), its leader S. S. Ray as well as his followers and the emerging political supporters of some parties of the then West Bengal.

National Emergency and Its Impact on West Bengal

After the imposition of the emergency at the midnight of 25th June, 1975, as many as around 1,000 prominent leaders were arrested on that fateful night.[99] At the time of emergency, in order to stop the voice of any kind of oppositions over 100,000 people were arrested under Maintenance of Internal Security Act (MISA) and the Defense of India Rules (DIR).[100]

20 Points Programme of Indira Gandhi

With the imposition of emergency and taking repressive measures against the oppositions like- censorship of press, banning of assemblage, meeting and discarding many fundamental rights of the citizens; side by side with the consultation with P. N. Dhar, Principal Secretary to the Prime Minister, in order to develop the economic condition of the people as well as country during emergency, Indira Gandhi declared her famous 20 points programme on 1st July, 1975.[101]

It is impossible to deny that as a consequence of the adoption of 20 points economic programme by Indira Gandhi during emergency brought some major positive changes in discipline of public life. Not only that, it was able to bring a change in various aspects of public life such as - growing economy, controlled inflation, a reversed trade deficit for the first time, enhanced developmental expenditures and stringent action was taken against tax evasion and smugglers. But, in spite of adopting the various economic measures adverse impact fell on the congress party and its supreme leader Indira Gandhi due to her repressive measures such as- suspension of fundamental rights, large- scale arrests of political leaders and activists in the name of MISA and DIR, press censorship and extending the tenure of legislatures by not conducting elections - which collectively affected the interests of the common people and as a consequence of that the congress party and Indira Gandhi had to pay a heavy price for this misadventure.[102]

During the emergency some excesses adversely affected the congress organization in national level and state of West Bengal as well. In that context the name of Extra Constitutional Authority and Sterilization were most important.

Extra Constitutional Authority

During the time of Emergency, Indira Gandhi's younger son, Sanjay Gandhi, who held no office in the government but became all in all. He was so indispensible that as if he became the de-facto Prime Minister. With the support and encouragement of his mother (Indira Gandhi) Sanjay Gandhi

Background of J. P.'s Coming into Movement

However, in response to the joint appeal of the non-congress combined opposition parties, Jayprakash Narayan accepted the appeal.[87] Under the leadership of J. P.'s 'Youth for Democracy', the mighty students' movements in Bihar in the name of *'Chhatra Sangrasha Samity'* later on turned into the fold of 'total revolution'.[88] J. P.'s move and his organized efforts proved to be an open threat to the power and position of Indira Gandhi and she had no other alternatives but to declare rule of emergency in the country at midnight of 25th June, 1975. The turning point of the situation was such that Indira Gandhi took up the course of arresting the leading opposition leaders and they were put then in jail and obviously J.P. was not an exception.[89]

Impact of J.P. Movement and Emergency in West Bengal

The declaration of the emergency and the subsequent jail of a few national leaders including Jayprakash Narayan proved to be a political threat to West Bengal. The misrule of the congress party during emergency and the intra-party feud of the Congress (R) added fuel to the flame of the political situation and thereby the people of West Bengal were naturally seeking a relief from such a chaotic scene in the political life of West Bengal. Here one may recall that the gradual deterioration of democratic values and increasing authoritarian approach throughout the country, as a 'world peace solder' Jayprakash Narayan initiated his effort for an alliance of all opposition parties for strengthening the opponent in order to make a viable alternative for the sake of democracy. Two front ranking CPI (M) leaders namely Jyoti Basu and P. Sundarayya met J. P. on 12th February, 1973 and after 40 minutes discussion, the two communist leaders welcomed J. P.'s attempt for the realization of an apolitical platform in the defense of democracy and civil liberties. His proposal for a meeting of the leaders of all political parties in India for ensuring 'free and fair elections' was also highly appreciated by the communist leaders.[90]

J. P. Visits in Calcutta and Unity of the Opposition (July 5, 1974)

Jayprakash Narayan arrived in Calcutta on 5th July, 1974 with his three day programme. At this stage he met most of the important communist leaders namely Jyoti Basu and B.T. Ranadive of CPI (M) to form a combine opposition like Bihar under an umbrella. The ultimate aim of J. P. was to launch a movement for 'total revolution' to paralyze Government institutions and machineries by dint of mass movement. Despite their ideological differences the CPI (M) and other political parties warmly welcomed such a movement of J. P.[91]

Thereafter, according to the invitation of Prafulla Chandra Sen, veteran Congress (O) leader and former Chief Minister of West Bengal; J. P. again came to Calcutta on 30th July, 1974 for finalizing the background of a Bihar type movement in West Bengal. At the time of his addressing in a mammoth gathering at Calcutta Maidan, J. P. expressed his excitement accusing Mrs. Gandhi's congress and her way of working as the root cause of sufferings and discontent. J. P. further accused Indira Gandhi for the destruction of the democratic norms and also expressed the opinion that there was only 'skeleton of democracy' in the name of democracy. Explaining his movement in Bihar that would develop into a 'total revolution' whose ultimate goal was to complete transformation of society. He firmly reiterated that a 'revolutionary situation' existed in the country and shortly it would engulf the whole of India.[92]

Violent Demonstrations on Jayprakash Narayan's Visit to Calcutta (2nd April, 1975)

It is a fact that as a result of the internal rivalries between pro-Siddhartha and anti-Siddhartha group among the leaderships of West Bengal Pradesh Congress Committee (WBPCC); Yuba Congress (YC) and Chhatra Parishad (CP) constantly destroyed the vitality of the congress organization. The factional leaders were more concerned about their group interests rather than the interest of the congress party as a whole. It is also a fact that neither the pro nor the anti-Siddhartha Shankar Ray group taken any bold step for strengthening the support base of the congress party in the soil of West Bengal. Factional interest was so predominant that the corporate interest of the party was entirely neglected whose inevitable consequence was that the general confidence of the people on the congress party gradually eroded. Amidst factional rivalries between pro-changer and no-changer, one thing was clear that both the factional groups were pro-Indira under the fold of Naba Congress or Indira Congress i. e. Congress (R). Therefore, as and when Jayprakash Narayan spearheaded his campaign all over the country against numerous misdeeds of the central government and various state governments led by the congress (R), then as if, for the time being setting aside the group rivalries of the Congress (R), both the groups jointly showed their violent demonstration against Jayprakash Narayan in West Bengal. Here it is noteworthy that on 2nd April, 1975, J. P. came in Calcutta to address a convention of youths and students in the University Institute Hall, but he had to face a violent demonstration in front of the proposed venue and he was prevented from addressing the convention by the several thousand Chhatra Parishad and Yuba Congress supporters. The demonstration was so violent event of that time was the leave of Central Ministry and Congress (R) party by Babu Jagjivan Ram on 2nd February, 1977. Hemabati Nandan Bahuguna, Nandini Sathapathi (both had to leave Congress party due to Sanjay Gandhi) and Babu Jagjivan Ram jointly formed a new party known as 'Congress For Democracy'.[111]In that pretext, on the eve of the Parliamentary election Jayprakash Narayan, Babu Jagjivan Ram and Morarji Desai jointly in an appeal to the people said - 'in that critical juncture you (people) have to choose one option i.e. either Democracy or Autocracy.'[112]

Impact on West Bengal

As like as all India scenarios, the excessiveness of emergency was also effective in West Bengal. This had virtually shattered the prospects of the congress party in the state. At this point there was also a trend of politics which brought to light the almost forgotten chapter of the conflict between pro-Siddhartha and anti-Siddhartha groups. In the wake of emergency, the infighting reached so high that the party was virtually divided and thereupon the congress as a political party lost its credibility and was demoralized. Apart from factionalism, the style of governance of Siddhartha Shankar Ray and his activities during emergency greatly aggrieved the people. In the name of the Maintenance of Internal Security Act (MISA) more than 18,000 people were arrested in West Bengal. Not only that the excesses of police actions, arrests of senior journalists namely Barun Sengupta, Gour Kishore Ghosh, Jyotirmay Dutta,[113] reckless demolitions and press censorship in West Bengal at the time of emergency under Siddhartha Shankar Ray - were considerately reflected in the ballot box of the congress party in both Lok Sabha and Assembly elections held in 1977.[114]

Date of Election and Result

However, as per the notification of the Election Commission of India the election of all 42 Lok Sabha constituencies were held in West Bengal on 15th March, 1977.[115] As a result of infighting within the West Bengal Pradesh Congress and over all negative impact of emergency and its excessiveness among the 42 Parliamentary constituencies the congress candidates won only three Lok Sabha seats namely- Krishna Bahadur Chhetri from Darjeeling, Sougata Roy from Barrackpore and Dhirendra Nath Basu from Katwa.[116]The prospect of the Indian National Congress (R) in all India level was also not favourable.

Dissolution of State Assembly

In view of the verdict of the Lok Sabha election, 1977, a new central cabinet was formed under Morarji Desai on 24th March, 1977. One of the immediate tasks as well as first steps taken by this new Government was to give an order to dissolve the congress led state governments of West Bengal and accordingly preparation was made to arrange the election of this state assembly at the earliest.[117]

The Assembly election in West Bengal was held on 11th and 14th June of 1977 respectively.[118] In that State Assembly election, Siddhartha Shankar Ray did not contest. Interestingly, most of the cabinet ministers excepting A. B. A. Gani Khan Chowdhury were defeated and the total number of the congress MLAs in the new assembly were only 20 out of 294 seats.[119]

Notes and References

1. Dilip Banerjee, *op.cit.* p.884.
2. *Ibid.,* p.882.
3. In the wake of Quit India movement to oust the British rule from Tamluk Sub-Division in Midnapore district, West Bengal on 17th December, 1942 *'Tamralipta Jatiya Sarkar'* was formed and it continued up to 1st September, 1944. Satish Chandra Samanta, Ajay Kumar Mukherjee, Satish Chandra Shahu and Barada Kanta Kuiti became the first, second, third and fourth *Sarbadhinayak* of *'Tamralipta Jatiya Sarkar'* respectively, and Sushil Kumar Dhara was its Home Minister and G.O.C. in-Charge of Bidyut Bahini, i.e. Army division of *'Tamralipta Jatiya Sarkar'* (Tamralipta National Government), See Shree Radhakrishna Bari, (ed.), *op.cit.* pp. 108-122.
4. Dilip Banerjee, *op.cit.* p.882.
5. Jyoti Basu, *Jatadur Mone Pore — Rajnaitik Atmakathan (*in Bengali), National Book Agency Pvt. Ltd. Calcutta, 1998, p. 259.
6. Saroj Chakrabarty, ... *Chief Ministers*, pp .414-415.
7. Sitaram Sharma, *West Bengal-Changing Colours Changing Challenges,* Rupa, New Delhi, 2014, p. 55.
8. Personal interview with Somen Mitra, a veteran congress leader, former President of WBPCC, first Yuba Congress President of West Bengal and AICC member, on 20th February 2017; also see Personal interview with Sarder Amjad Ali, a veteran congress leader and former Lok Sabha and Rajya Sabha M.P, on 25th February 2017.

was able to establish his influence over politics through the administration and Youth Congress. A group of followers of Sanjay Gandhi comprised of Bansi Lal (Defense Minister from December 1975), Om Mehta (Home Minister), Kishen Chand (Lieutenant-Governor of Delhi) and R. K. Dhawan (Additional Private Secretary to the Prime Minister) were collectively operating the whole affairs through the House of the Prime Minister.[103] As per the indirect instruction of the Prime Minister, officers from most of the Departments and party leaders would present at the residence of Prime Minister to discuss and seek necessary direction from Sanjay Gandhi. The files of various departments were to send to Sanjay Gandhi for his verbal approval. In this way developing of an extra-constitutional centre of power, Sanjay Gandhi started functioning like a well-oiled 'Extra-Constitutional Authority'. During the emergency period nobody had the courage to ignore the said authority of Sanjay Gandhi. Those who would hesitate to follow the unofficial instruction of Sanjay Gandhi, had to face the punishment in the form of transfer or remove.[104]

Five Points Programme of Sanjay Gandhi

Sanjay Gandhi reached the highest limit of his power during the period of emergency. Flattering created in such an environment after mixing with fear that one of the most famous illustrated periodical of India through the voting of its readers selected Sanjay Gandhi as the number one Indian in the year of 1976.[105] So, 'helmsman of new India', 'last resort of the country' and 'future light of India' Sanjay Gandhi adopted 5-points programme in order to bring social and economic changes in the fabric of the society in the month of July 1976. The programmes were as follows: 1. Family planning; 2. Planting trees and cleaning the environment; 3. Refusal of dowry; 4. Promotion of adult literacy; and 5. Abolition of caste.[106]

Amongst the excesses during the time of emergency, probably the most well-known was the campaign for 'family planning'—which gradually converted into a wide-circulated drive for forceful sterilization.[107] The most adverse reaction of forceful sterilization was intensified among the people of the Muslim community in India. P. N. Haskar, Principal Secretary to the Prime Minister noted that 'Muslim as a whole have come out in opposition to sterilization' and were involved in resistance to it. Disturbances spread to Haryana, Madhya Pradesh, Bihar, West Bengal, Punjab and Maharastra. Detailing some incidents he warned, 'If this goes on, the congress runs the danger of losing support of Muslims, Harijans and poor people'.[108]

Therefore, it was found that the emergency and its excessiveness left an indelible imprint on the mind of the Indian people. In order to satisfy

Sanjay Gandhi, the de-facto Prime Minister during emergency whole administration in many states was utilized for the fulfillment of the sterilization programme and as a result of that the implementation of land ceiling laws as per the 20 points economic programme of Indira Gandhi almost came to a halt. The imposing sterilization in the name of 'family planning'- led to popular resistance and its inevitable outcome were killing of police and other officials in one hand and police firing and death of common people on the other. Therefore, it was obvious that the benefits of 20-points government programme were overshadowed due to the 5 points non-official programme of Sanjay Gandhi. So, as a far reaching consequence of the above happenings, discontents were shimmering into the minds of the people in a full swing which reflected in the post emergency election of 1977 throughout the country and particularly in West Bengal.

Declaration of Election during Emergency and Defeat of the Congress Party

During the period of emergency, Indira Gandhi was acquitted by the judgment of the Supreme Court Constitution Bench comprising of Chief Justice A. N. Ray, Justice H. R. Khanna, Justice K.K. Mathew, Justice M. H. Beg and Justice Y.V. Chandrachud from all the charges on 7th November, 1975. It has already been mentioned that Indira Gandhi was found guilty by Mr. Justice Jagmohan Lal Sinha of Allahabad High Court on 12th June, 1975.[109] After being confident by the verdict of Supreme Court Constitution Bench on 7th November 1975, Indira Gandhi released Jayprakash Narayan after five months detention on 12th November, 1975 due to the deterioration of his health condition.[110] Thereafter, in the midst of excessiveness of emergency, receiving the positive reports time and again from intelligence branch and leaders of her party about the sure victory of the congress party, Indira Gandhi recommended the President of India for dissolution of the Lok Sabha on 18th January, 1977 for fresh Lok Sabha election and the same was held on 12th March, 1977. With the declaration of new election all the arrested opposition leaders and activists were released from detention. In that juncture, understanding the importance of unity among the oppositions- Congress (O), Jana Sangha, Bharatiya Lok Dal and Socialist Party jointly formed 'Janata Party' on 20th January, 1977. Morarji Desai, Chaudhury Charan Singh and Surendra Mohan elected President, Vice-President and Secretary respectively of the newly formed Janata Party. These parties also had an electoral understanding with the Communist Party of India (Marxist). In contrast, the Communist Party of India supported the Indian National Congress in the election of 1977. But the most astonishing

56. William Van Schendel, *The Bengal Borderland- Beyond State and Nation in South Asia,* Anthem Press, London, 20.

Article (in English)

1. *"The Communal Award of 1932 and Its Implications in Bengal"* an Article by Bidyut Chakrabarty in *Modern Asian Studies,* Vol. XXIII, No. 3 (1989), pp. 493 -523.
2. *"Politics of Partition and Warning of the Time"* an Article by Ichhamuddin Sarker in *Dalit Lives and Dalit Visions in Eastern India,* Centre for Ambedkar studies, Jadavpur University, 2007,
3. *"The Congress Party in West Bengal- Politics, Patronage and Power, 1947-1983"* an Atricle by P. Sen Gupta in R. Chatterjee, *Politics in West Bengal.*
4. *"Intra-party conflict in a Dominant Party"* an Article by R. Zarujk in *Journal of Politics,* Vol 27(1), 1965.

Books (in Bengali)

1. Ahammad Abdul Mansur: *Amar Dekha Rajnitir Panchas Bachhar,* Dhaka-1970.
2. Ahammed Sirajuddin, *Sher-E-Bangla A. K. Fazlul Huq,* Islamic Foundation, Dhaka, 2015.
3. Ashok Mitra, *Teenkuri Dash* , Vol. II (1403 BS),
4. Bandopadhyay, Hiranmay: *Dr. Bidhan Chandra Royer Sanidhye,* Calcutta, 1882.
5. Bandyopadhyay Sandip, *Bikshubdha Bangla - Pashimbanger Birodhi Rajniti* 1947-2007,(in Bengali), Radical Impression Kolkata,2014.
6. Banerjee Sachchidananda, *Fazlul Huq Jibon O Rajniti,* Progressive Publishers, Calcutta, 2001.
7. Bari Shree Radhakrishna, (ed.), *Ajoyeo Purush- Ajoy Kumar,* Tamralipta Swatinata Sangram Itihas Committee, Parvatipur, Tamluk, Midnapore, 1990,
8. Basu Jyoti; *Janaganer Sangey*, National Book Agency, Kolkata, 1986.
9. Basu Shyama Prasad, *Jinnah: Dharmanirapekshta Banam Sampradayikata,* Dey's Publishing, Kolkata, 2006.
10. Basu, Manojit: *Bidhan Chandra,* Calcutta-1984.

11. Bose Arpita, *Udvastu Andolon O Punarbasati – Samasamayik Patra Patrikay,* Gangchil, Kolkata, 2013.
12. Chakrabarty Alok Krishna, *Pradhan Mantri – Rahasya,* Ankur Pustakalaya, Kolkata, 1999.
13. Chakraborty Rathin (ed.), *Hemanta Kumar BasuJiban O Sangram,* Hemanta Kumar Basu Janma Satabarsha Utjapan Committee, Kolkata, 1994.
14. Chattopadhyay Bhola, *Jayprakash Narayan O Sampurna Biplab*, Ananda Publishers, Kolkata, 1987.
15. Chowdhury Jamaluddin: *Raj Bidrohi Ashrafuddin Ahammed Chowdhury,* Dhaka, 1974.
16. Das Dhirendranath: *Tista Parer Katha,* Anita Press, Cooch-Behar, 2001.
17. Dasgupta Hiren et.al, *Rajnaitik Patabhumite Bharatiya Upmahadesher Chhatra Aandalon*, Radical Impression, Calcutta, 1993,
18. Dasgupta Sukharanjan, *Kachher Manush Kajer Manush – Gani Khan Chowdhury,* Dey's Publishing, Kolkata, 2006.
19. Dey Amalendu, *Pakistan Prastab O Fazlul Huq*, Parul, Kolkata, 2015.
20. Dhara Sushil Kumar, *Prabaha* -Vol. II, Janakalyan Trust, Mahishadal, Midnapore, 1995.
21. Dutta Satyabrata: *Banglar Bidhansabhar Eksho Bacchr,* Progressive Publishers, Kolkta, Feb 2002.
22. Ghosh Atulya: *Kasta Kalpita,* Ananda Publishers, Calcutta, 1980.
23. Ghosh Debabrata, *Paschim Bang Bidhan Sabhar Atit O Bartaman,* Ghosh Publishing Concern, Kolkata, 2009.
24. Ghosh Swapan Kanti (ed.), *Rastriya Santras – Naxalbari Theke Netai Gram,* Padatic, Kolkata, 2011.
25. Ghosh, Prafulla Chandra: *Jeeban Smritir Bhumika,* Calcutta; Modern Book Agency, 1976.
26. Goswami Arjun, *Deshbhager Prekshapate Gandhi – Jinnah Patralap,* Chayanika, Kolkata, 2005.
27. *Krishak Andolaner Itihasa O Samasya*, Published by the West Bengal Unit, C.P.I, Calcutta, August, 1959, pp.13-23.

21. Gene D. Overstreet and Marshal Wind Miller, *Communism in India,* Bombay, 1960.

22. Ghosh Atulya, *The Split- Indian National Congress,* Calcutta, 1980.

23. Ghosh Partha S., *Unwanted and Uprooted- A Political Study of Migrants, Refugees, Stateless and Displaced of South Asia,* New Delhi, 2004.

24. Ghosh Sankar, *Political Ideas and Movements in India*, Calcutta: Allied Publishers, 1975.

25. Ghosh Suniti Kumar, *India and the Raj,* 1919-1947, Research Unit for Political Economy, Bombay, 1995.

26. Ghosh, : *The Disinherited State,* Calcutta: Orient Longman, 1971.

27. Johari J.C, *Indian Government and Politics,* Vol. 1, New Delhi, 1996.

28. Kabir Humayun, *Muslim Politics 1906-1947 and other Essays*, Calcutta, 1969.

29. Kochanek Stanley A., *The Congress Party in India,* Princeton University Press, 1968,

30. Lockwood Devid, *The Communist Party of India and the Indian Emergency,* Sage, New Delhi, 2016.

31. Madhok Balraj, *Portrait of a Martyr: Biography of Dr. Shyama Prasad Mookherjee,* Bombay, 1969.

32. Mehta Vinod, *The Sanjay Story,* Harper Collins, New Delhi, 2012.

33. Mukherjee Pranab, Dramatic Decade- The Indira Gandhi Years, Rupa, New Delhi, 2015.

34. Narasimhan V. K., *Kamraj- A study*, National Book Trust, Publication Division, Ministry of Information and Broadcasting, Government of India.

35. Pirzada Syed Sharifuddin, (ed.), *Quid - e - Azam Jinnah's Correspondence,* (Indian Edition), New Delhi, 1981.

36. Rastogi. P.N: *The Nature and Dynamics of Factional Conflicts,* Delhi: The Macmillan Company of India Limited.

37. Rasul, M.A: *A History of the All India Kisan Sabha,* Calcutta, 1974.

38. Samanta Amiya K., *Left Extremist Movement in West Bengal- An Experiment in Armed Agrarian Struggle,* Calcutta 1984.

39. Sanyal Hitesh: *Congress Movements in the villages of eastern Midnapore,* 1921-1931, in Gaborieu, Asia du sud.
40. Sarkar Sumit, *Modern India 1885-19470,* Macmillan, New Delhi, 2001.
41. Sen Amartya, *Poverty and Famine - An Essay on Entitlement and Deprivation*, Oxford, 1981.
42. Sen Shila, *Muslim Politics in Bengal* (1937-1947), Viswakos Parisad, Kolkata, 2001.
43. Sen, A: *West Bengal: Analytical study,* Calcutta: Oxford & IBH Cal, 1971.
44. Sen. P.C: *From Here to Horizons,* Calcutta: West Bengal Government Press, 1967.
45. Sengupta Nitish, *Land of Two Rivers - A History of Bengal from the Mahabharata to Mujib,* Penguin Books, New Delhi, 2011,
46. Sharma Sitaram, *West Bengal-Changing Colours Changing Challenges,* Rupa, New Delhi, 2014.
47. Singh Jaswant: *Jinnah, India-Partition Independence;* Rupa, New Delhi, 2009.
48. Sinha Kerkhoff, K: *Tyranny of Partition, Hindus in Bangladesh and Muslims in India,* New Delhi, 2006.
49. Thaper, S. D": The Dandakaranya Project: Failure of an Ambitious Scheme, Economic and Political Weekly, Vol 15", March 2, 1962.
50. Thomas K. P, *Dr. B. C Roy*, West Bengal Pradesh Congress Committee, Calcutta, 1955.
51. Tyagi Vir Virender Singh, *The economic impact of partition on Indian agriculture and related industries,* American University, Washington, DC, doctoral dissertation, 1958.
52. Vakil C. N., *Economic consequences of divided India. A study of the economy of India and Pakistan,* Bombay, 1950.
53. Weiner Myron and Osgood Field John (ed.), *Electoral Politics in the Indian States- The Communist Politics of Bengal,* Volume-1
54. Weiner, M: *Party building in a new nation.* The Indian National Congress, Chicago, 1967.
55. Weiner, M: *Sons of the Soil, Migration and ethnic conflict in India,* Princeton, 1978.

It is generally used to be said that victory does not spare even the victor. In the case of Indira Gandhi it was found that after passing a year of her resounding victory in the election battle in various provinces in 1972 - within a very short period the widespread social and economic displeasure rapidly engulfed the country. In spite of Indira Gandhi's efforts to give a socialist orientation to the policies adopted by the congress through nationalizing the banks and abolishing the privy purses, the sufferings of the common masses were not shortened. Unkind nature as well as drought along with inflation, labour unrest, gradual rising of oil prices in international markets, fall in production, strikes in urban areas, closure of factories, increasing rampant corruption in administration, party leaders and all time low balance in the treasury - collectively shock the all sections of the people i. e. not only the poor but also the middle class people as well.[81]

Amidst of growing discontent among the common people throughout the country due to gradual price rise of necessary commodities and corruption, agitation started each and every state of the country against the government as well as the congress party. Whenever the government was very much confused to check the price rise then the demands of the congress leaders of Telengana region in Andra Pradesh for separate state led to the congress party in a very embarrassing situation. Adding fuel into the ongoing complicated situation, the congress leaders of the different states engaged themselves infighting for becoming minister or capturing government power as much as possible. In that connection infighting of the Bihar, Uttar Pradesh, Gujrat, Madhya Pradesh deserved special mention. The internal conflict of those states was so ugly that the ministry had to change and in some cases Presidential rule was imposed. In that critical juncture, observing the nature of infighting of the congress party the common people as a whole came into the understanding and became more furious on an impression that the congress leaders were more attentive to fulfill their narrow personal group interest than the collective welfare of the common people. In the meantime, Indira Gandhi earned more defame recruiting Ajit Narayan Roy as the Chief Justice of Supreme Court bypassing the rights of the three senior Justices namely- Shelt, Hegrey and Grover who resigned as a mark of protest immediately. The interference of Indira Gandhi, the Prime Minister of India into the purview of judiciary in an unprecedented manner was severely denounced by almost all the Bar Council of India and accused Indira Gahndhi's attempt to break the neutrality of Judicial Department. Educated people of the nation as a whole did not accept that action of Indira Gandhi and S.M. Sikri, the outgoing Chief Justice remarked "It was a severe attack on the freedom of Judicial Departmrnt".[82]

It was accused by the oppositions and erudite personalities that nation was moving towards dictatorial way of governance.

Era of Political Retreat of Indira Gandhi as well as Congress (R)

From the above discussion it is clear that Indira Gandhi was subject to criticism throughout the country due to her autocratic style of rule. Obviously, the days of political retreat of Indira Gandhi as well as Congress (R) after 1969 started due to misrule, corruption, disregard of democratic rights of the common people and above all her failure to put an end the intra-party feud not only in West Bengal but also some other states in India. In that connection the name of the state of Gujrat, Uttar Pradesh, Orissa, Manipur, Nagaland and Pondicherry are worthy of mention.

As a result of infighting and country wide discontent an alternative political choice became obvious that was manifested in the Gujrat Assembly election by 10th June. 1975. In that election, Congress (R) won only 75 seats while the Janata Front of the opposition comprising of Congress (O), Jana Sangha, Socialist Partry and Bharatiya Lok Dal, secured 86 seats. The result of the Gujrat Assembly election was a great blow to the political carrier of Indira Gandhi who clearly understood that in the ensuing Parliamentary election the opposition would form again the Janata Front against her and thereby the win of the election would be almost impossible for her.[83]

Moreover, in the meantime, the mid-term election was held in Uttar Pradesh, Orissa, Manipur, Nagaland and Pondicherry. The result of the election was so worse to the Congress (R) that it could not able to win any small states and lost the absolute majority in Orissa. Though in Uttar Pradesh the congress won 215 seats out of 425, but it secured only 32 percent of votes. These miserable results frightened Indira Gandhi in the one hand and the eyes of the isolated opposition political groups opened on the other to make a strong platform to bring to an end the Indira Gandhi Era. The situation convinced the leaders of the opposition groups that if they could strengthen themselves by any means, the end of Indira regime was imminent. In that pretext, all the leaders of Congress (O), Jana Sangha, Bharatiya Kranti Dal, S.S.P. etc. jointly requested Loknayak Jayprakash Narayan[84] to come forward in order to take the leadership of the combined opposition to save the country from the misrule of the Congress (R) headed by Indira Gandhi.[85]In that point one may recall that all the above mentioned parties had almost negative approach to each other and they could not able to focus any alternative programme as well as policies excepting that of the overthrowing Indira Gandhi from power.[86]

campaign against Siddhartha Shankar Ray. The anti-Siddhartha Shankar Ray group of congressmen including A.B.A. Gani Khan Chowdhury, Tarun Kanti Ghosh and Prafulla Kanti Ghosh who would obtain continuous as well as solid backing from the two Central Minister i. e. D. P. Chattopadhyay and Pranab Mukherjee and they determined to change the state party leadership. In the words of Saroj Chakrabarty, "They (anti-Ray) went in plane loads to Delhi to complain to Mrs. Gandhi. Sanjoy was there to poison the ears of his mother. The procedure was that these Congressmen would first go to Sanjoy; Sanjoy would then tell them what to say to the Prime Minister against Ray. These Congressmen then sought an appointment with the Prime Minister which Sanjoy arranged without any difficulty and they went and told Mrs. Gandhi all kinds of things about Ray. While this was going on in Delhi, one evening N. K. Seshan, Private Secretary to Prime Minister, telephoned to the Chief Minister. Seshan warned Ray that there was a conspiracy going on against him and false charges were being made. Seshan further informed Ray that Sanjoy was behind this and that two Central Ministers from Bengal were the persons in Delhi who were provoking the Prime Minister to take action against him."[76]

Being irritated and aggrieved at that point, Siddhartha Shankar Ray is said to have drafted a resignation letter also. But the supporters of S.S. Ray particularly P. R. Das Munshi, Subrata Mukherjee, Sougata Roy, Sudip Bandopadhyay, Kumud Bhattacharyay and others refrained him from that step on the ground that his resignation would imply 'yielding to Sanjay Gandhi' and urged him to fight it out. So Sanjay as well as pro-changers groups of West Bengal congress party failed to dislodge Siddhartha Shankar Ray but he was successful in replacing Nandini Satpathi of Orissa and Hemabati Nandan Bahuguna of Uttar Pradesh who were the sitting Chief Ministers of those provinces respectively. However, antipathy between pro-Siddhartha and anti-Siddhartha groups began to intensify. Though, Sanjay Gandhi failed to remove Siddhartha Shankar Ray but he at least succeeded in dividing the congress party machineries as well as Ministry of West Bengal. In a nutshell, the interference of Sanjay Gandhi in West Bengal congress politics complicated factionalism and made the situation more critical. In that connection, an intelligence Report revealed the attitude of the pro-changer as well as anti-Siddhartha Shankar Ray's group in the following manner: "The announcement of the names of candidates for contesting the Parliamentary elections from West Bengal has caused disappointment amongst the pro-changer (anti-Ray) group. At the instance of Kamal Nath, who has been made an observer of the Yuba Congress (R), they have now taken up a surreptitious move to set up independent candidates in those constituencies where the candidates of Chief Minister's choice, or favoured by the Chief Minister, as well as CPI candidates have been officially set up to contest the ensuing election. The main idea behind this move is to humiliate and lower the image of the Chief Minister."[77] The infighting became so deepened that even many congressmen filed their nomination papers in many constituencies as independent candidates which collectively paved the way landslide defeat of the congress party in West Bengal in the Parliamentary election of 1977 and the same was reflected in the Assembly election also.

Position of Congress (R) and Leadership of Indira Gandhi in All India Perspective

After the death of Lal Bahadur Shastri (11th January, 1966), when Indira Gandhi became the Prime Minister (19th January, 1966)[78] of India with the blessing of the so-called syndicate group's leader, then many leaders particularly the opposition started feeling that the inexperienced and comparatively young Indira Gandhi would only be a puppet in the hands of the then top leaders of the congress party. Even Ram Manohar Lohia would call her a *'gungi gudiya'* i.e. a dumb doll. But after defeating the official nominee for the post of President of India in 1969 and the victory of V.V. Giri as Indira Gandhi's candidate for the same, she regained confidence and could establish her authority over the party organisation.[79] Moreover, after the Liberation War of Bangladesh and side by side due to victory and triumph of the congress party in the general elections of 1971 and subsequently in 1972 in West Bengal Assembly election, the self-confidence of Indira Gandhi reached its zenith. After getting unexpected success in the power struggle, Indira Gandhi became so aggressive that she adopted various diplomatic tactics for dissolution of the coalition government in Orissa and Congress (R) led government was installed there under the leadership of Nandini Sathapathi. Accordingly in Uttar Pradesh after topple down of the sitting ministry, Congress (R) led government headed by Kamalapathi Tripathy was formed there. Thereafter in Maysore and Gujrat the Ministry of Congress (O); and in Panjab Jana-Sangha—Akali coalition governments were overthrown and most of the cases Presidential Rule were imposed which helped Indira Gandhi to control the politics of those states easily. Not only that, in the pretext of the Liberation War of Bangladesh, the imposition of emergency in order to maintain internal security i. e. MISA under whose any person would be arrested without giving any explanation. As a result of adopting these measures gradually led to the birth of autocratic mentality whose inevitable outcome was the establishment of dictatorship.[80]?

at hospitals and after enclosing in cinemas- they were checked to see the sterilization certificate. See Devid Lockwood, *op.cit.*pp.152-153.

108. See P.N. Haksar papers, Subject File Number 57. Note to the Prime Minister as Principal Secretary, 1977, 29-31; cited in Devid Lockwood, *op.cit.* p. 154; Also see Vinod Mehta, *The Sanjay Story,* Harper Collins, New Delhi, 2012, pp, 163-65.

109. Pranab Mukherjee, *op.cit.* p.74.

110. Saroj Chakrabarty, ... *Chief Ministers*, p.488.

111. Bipan Chandra et.al, *op.cit.* p. 261.

112. "*Gharer Baire Muktiyuddha - Muktir Yuddha Bhitare* 1971- 80", a Bengali article by Aurabinda Poddar in *Saat Dashak, Samakal O Anandabazar,* Ananda Publishers Private Limited, Kolkata, 2013, p. 152.

113. Saroj Chakrabarty, ... *Chief Ministers*, p.484.

114. Sitaram Sharma, *op.cit.* p. 60.

115. Dilip Banerjee, *op.cit.* p.884.

116. Ibid., pp.163-169.

117. Saroj Chakrabarty, ... *Chief Ministers*, p. 519; also see Bipan Chandra et.al, *op.cit.* p. 261.

118. Dilip Banerjee, *op.cit.*p.884.

119. Ibid.

Conclusion

The present study is by and large confined within the crucial years between1947 to 1977 in which one can experiences various issues that dictated the destiny of West Bengal. Fact remains that the present study touches in its background the most critical situation of undivided Bengal leading to the partition of India in1947. A real need for revaluation of the high politics of India's partition have largely dictated the political atmosphere of the newly created province namely West Bengal. The decades after 1947 saw the beginning of a series of development including factional politics within the congress and it considerably guided the future prospect of its governance. Our study shows in detail how most of the problems were inter-connected and in its aftermath that followed others issues which inevitably sowed the seeds of critical politics afterwards. Many political developments took place and invariably it sealed the future of Bengal politics which could not be forecast beforehand. The ultimate result was of course, the gradual deterioration of the popularity of the congress party and as a result the political forces released thereby aggravated the situation in such a position that day and after not only the congress lost its hold on politics but also due to faulty steps of the leaders were being de-touched from the people of West Bengal. In our work we have also tried to show even the Indian national congress with its capacity as central government failed to check the disasters trends in the organization of the congress party of West Bengal. Factionalism, emergence of new political organ within and outside the party and above all the increasing political polarization of the non-congress parties (specially the Communist party) became the order of the day.

The 1970s represent a more critical period for the congress as it failed to control and minimize the chaotic situation that prevailed in West Bengal and this province had to experience presidential rule. Incidentally before 1970, there were repeated presidential rule, too, even if the people of West Bengal were not prepared to entertain such an undemocratic tendency in the political process of West Bengal. At this point our study has also explored the issues that led to the repeated disillusion of government as well as its formation at short interval.

The present work has also put up the process of historical reconstruction of the province and at the same time the mistakes undertaken by the leaders,(both the congress and the non-congress political parties) so as to bypass the commitment of nation building which was entrusted to the Indian National Congress after independence. It has already been stated how the Indian National Congress inherited a responsibility to lead the nation and the leaders of West Bengal were expected to respond the call of the nation. But they failed and the relevance of the theme of our work lies here as it consciously or unconsciously intensified numerous crises with an ultimate end of the rule in 1977.

Our study tends to indicate the consequences of the growing impotence and irrelevance of the congress party and its leadership in the political platform of the province and the subsequent development rather prepared the ground for many divisive forces which have now invited suffocating atmosphere not only in West Bengal but of India. The understanding of various separatist organizations and the nature of their politics have at present laid down to such a position that whether India would survive as a nation state or might lose its integrity in future.

Bibliography

Primary Sources

Records and Proceedings

1. Bengal Legislative Assembly Proceedings Vol. LII, No.4, 1938.
2. Bengal Legislative Assembly Proceedings, 1939, Vol. LIV, No.2,
3. Bengal Legislative Assembly Proceedings, 1940, vol. LVII, No.5.
4. Bengal Legislative Assembly Proceedings-Vol. LIII, No. 4.
5. Election Commission of India; Report on the First, Second, Third, Fourth, Fifth and Sixth General Election.
6. Fortnightly Report on the Political Situation in Bengal, 2nd half of April, 1947. Govt. of Bengal.
7. Home Department's Confidential Political Records (West Bengal State Archives), (WBSA).
8. Police Records, Special Branch 'PM' and 'PH' Series, Calcutta (SB).
9. Public and Judicial Proceedings (L/P & I) (India Office Library and Records), (IOLR).
10. Summary of the Proceedings of the Congress Working Committee', AICC-1, G-30/1945-46.
11. West Bengal Legislative Assembly Proceedings 1950-1972, 1974-1982.

Private and party organizational papers

1. All India Congress committee Papers (Nehru Memorial Museum and Library), (NMML).
2. All Indian Hindu Mahasabha Papers (NMML)
3. Bengal Provislal Hindu Mahasabha Papers (NMML).

4. Kiran Sankar Roy Papers (Private collection of Sri Surjya Sankar Roy, Calcutta)
5. Ministry of Home Affairs Papers (National Achieves of India), (NAI).
6. Shyama Prasad Mookerjee Papers (NMML).

Autobiographies and Memoirs

1. Basu Hemanta Kumar, *Bhasan O Rachana Sangrahra (A Collection of Speeches and Writings),* Hemanta Kumar Basu Janma Satabarsha Utjapan Committee, Kolkata, 1994.
2. Basu Jyoti: *Jato Dur Mone Pore,* N.B A, Kolkata, 1998.
3. Chakrabarty, Saroj: *With West Bengal Chief Ministers,* Calcutta, Orient Longman, 1978.
4. Chakraborty Rathin (ed.), *Hemanta Kumar Basu- Ekti Aalekhya (Hemanta Kumar Basu: An Album),* Hemanta Kumar Basu Janma Satabarsha Utjapan Committee, Kolkata, 1994.
5. Ghosh, Atulya: *Ahimsa and Gandhi,* Calcutta, 1954.
6. Guha, Kamal: *Sangrami Jiban (A Life of Struggle)*, Lok Mat, Kolkata, 2001.
7. Guha, Kamal: *Amar Jiban Amar Rajniti,* Deep Prakashan, Kolkata 2002.
8. *Jatadur mane Pare- Rajnaitic Atmakathan* (a Bengali Book by Jyoti Basu), Calcutta, 1998
9. Ray Renuka, *My Reminiscences – Social Development during the Gandhian Era and After,* Allied Publishers Private Limited, Calcutta, 1982.
10. Talukdar, M, H, R. (ed): *The Memoris of Huseyn Shaheed Suhawardy,* Dhaka, 1987.
11. Talukdar Mohammad H. R., *Memoyors of Huseyn Shaheed Suhrawardy- with a brief account of his life and work*, The University Press Limited, Dhaka, 1987.
12. Chakrabarty Saroj, *With West Bengal Chief Ministers* (Memoirs 1962-1977), Orient Longman, Calcutta, 1978.

Personal Interviews with some important Political Leaders and Journalists of West Bengal

Personal interviews with some political leaders namely Kumud Bhattacharya (4th February,2017 at Behala, Kolkata), Deba Prasad Roy

(18th February, 2017, at E/4, Christopher Road, CIT Building, Entally, Padma Pukur, Kolkata-14), Somen Mitra (20th February, 2017, at Bidhan Bhavan, Philipse More, Kolkata), Ashim Chatterjee (23rd February, 2017, at Mahishbathan, Kolkata), Sarder Amjad Ali (25th February, 2017, Illias Road, Kolkata) and some veteran journalists i.e. Sukharanjan Sengupta (5th February, 2017, Milk Colony, Belgachhia, Kolkata) and Mihir Ganguly (23rd February, 2017, Konnagarh District Library, Hooghly, West Bengal).

Newspapers and Journals

1. Amrita Bazar Patrika.
2. Ananda Bazar Patrika
3. Asian Survey
4. Bande Mataram
5. Bartman
6. Chaturanga
7. Comparative Politics
8. Dainik Basumati
9. Economic and Political Weekly
10. Forward
11. Ganshakti.
12. Hindustan Times
13. Indian Annual Register
14. Journal of Asian Studies
15. Journal of Politics
16. Juguntar
17. Kalantar
18. Madhuparni.
19. Peoples Democracy
20. Pratidin.
21. The Statesman

Other Documents

1. Banerjee, Dilip, *Election Recorder – An Analytical Reference Bengal - West Bengal 1862-2012,* Star Publishing House, Kolkata, 2012.

2. Basu Nirmal Kumar, *Satchllisher Dairy* (ed.), Abhik Kumar Dey, Punachha, Kolkata, 2014.

3. Chakrabarty Saroj, *My Years With Dr. B.C Roy* , A Centenary Volume, Sree Saraswaty Press, Calcutta, 1982.

4. Chakraborty Rathin, *Hemanta Kumar Basu – Smaranika,* Hemanta Kumar Basu Janma Satabarsha Utjapan Committee, Kolkata, 1994.

5. G. Parthasarathi (ed.), *Jawaharlal Nehru. Letters to Chief Ministers 1947-1964,* Government of India, Delhi, 1985, vol. I, p. 99.

6. Ghosh, Atulya: *First Part of the Charge- Sheet against the CPI,* West Bengal Pradesh Congress Committee, Calcutta, 1959.

7. Islam Kazi Nazrul, *Kandari Hushiar,* Sanchita, D.M. Library, Kolkata 06,

8. *Jyoti Basu: the Authorized Biography,* Herper Collins, Publishers India, New Delhi, 1977.

9. Larry Collins & Dominique Lapiere: Mountbatten and the Partition of India, March 22 August 15, 1947, Vikash Publishing House Pvt Gaziabad, UP 1982.

10. Mukhopadhyay, Biswa Nath: Khadya Sankater Janya Dayee Ke? CPI Publication, Kolkata.

11. Partition Proceedings (06 Vols), Government of India Press, New Delhli, 1949-50.

12. Reliahabitation of Refugees. A Statistical Survey (1955), States Statistical Bureau, Government of West Bengal, Alipur, 1956.

13. *Swaranika,* Chhatra Parishad Golden Jubilee Celebration and Reunion Festival, Impression, New Bulygunj Road, Kolkata, 2004,

Secondary Sources

Books (in English)

1. Acharya P., *Education and Communal Politics in Bengal* - A Case Study, IIM, Calcutta Working Paper Series, September, 1998.

2. Azad Maulana Abul Kalam, *India Wins Freedom-The Complete Version,* Orient Black Swan, New Delhi, 2014.

3. Banerjee Sumanta: *In the Wake of Naxalbari, A history of the Naxalite Movement in India,* Calcutta, 1980.

4. Banerjee Tarun Kumar and Roychowdhury Debesh (ed.), *Colonial India – Ideas and Movments,* Progressive Publishers, Calcutta, 2001.
5. Basu Chandan, *The Making of the left Ideology in West Bengal: Culture, Political Economy, Revolution 1947-1970,* Abhijeet Publications, Delhi, 2009.
6. Bhalla Aloke, *Partition Dialogues- Memories of Lost Home,* Oxford University press, 2006.
7. Bose Ashoke Kumar, *Ruling in Bengal Legislative Assembly in West Bengal Legislative Assembly 1937-1970,* Calcutta, 1986.
8. Brass, P.R.: *Factional politics in an Indian States,* Berkeley and Los Angles: University of California Press, 1965.
9. Brecher Michael, *Succession in India: A study in Decision Making,* Oxford University Press, London, 1966.
10. Chakrabarty Prafulla Kumar, *The Marginal Men,* Naya Udyog, Calcutta, 1999.
11. Chandra Bipan, Mukherjee Mridula, Mukherjee Aditya: *India After Independence, 1947-2000;* Penguin Books, 2003.
12. Chatterjee Joya, *Bengal Divided- Hindu Communalism and Partition, 1932-1947*, Foundation Books, New Delhi, 1996:
13. Chatterjee Joya, *The Spoils of Partition, Bengal and India, 1947-1967,* Cambridge University Press, New Delhi, 2007.
14. Chatterjee Partha, *Bengal 1920 -1947, The Land Question,* Vol. 1, Calcutta, 1984.
15. Chatterjee Partha, *The Present History of West Bengal- Essays in Political Criticism,* Oxford University Press. 1998.
16. Chatterjee, Partha (ed): *State and Politics in India,* Oxford University Press, 1947.
17. Chatterjee, Rakhahari: *Politics in West Bengal;* the World Press, Kolkata, May 1985.
18. Das S.C, *The Biography of Bharat Keshari, Dr. Syama Prasad Mookherjee with Modern Implication*, New Delhih, 2000.
19. Dey Amalendu, *Islam in Modern India*, Calcutta, November, 1982.
20. Franda, F. Marcus: *Political Development and political Decay in Bengal,* Firma K.L.; Kolkata, 1971.

36. Saroj Chakrabarty, ... *Chief Ministers*, p .420.
37. Dilip Banerjee, *op.cit.* pp. 882, 926.
38. *Ibid.,* pp.977-978.
39. Saroj Chakrabarty, ... *Chief Ministers*, p.492.
40. *Ibid.,* p. 435.
41. *Ibid.,* pp. 435, 444, 451.
42. Dilip Banerjee, *op.cit.*p, 882. It is noteworthy that apart from the result of 1977 election, the congress could capture the number of assembly seats- in 1982-49 (then it became congress (I)), 1987- 40, 1991 – 43 (then only congress, i.e. no congress R or I respectively), 1996 -82, 2001- 26, 2006 -21, 2011- 42, 2016 – 44, and 2021- 00 which were far behind the absolute majority to form a Government.
43. Atulya Ghosh was the first elected President of WBPCC, after Netaji Subash Chandra Bose who was elected BPCC President in 1929 in Rangpur. Personal interview with Mihir Ganguly, a veteran journalist of West Bengal, on 23rd February, 2017.
44. See name lists of the West Bengal Pradesh Congress Committee's Presidents and their tenure from 1945-2001, inscribed on the wall of Bidhan Bhavan, Head Quarter of the West Bengal Pradesh Congress Committee, Philips More, Kolkata.
45. Personal interview with Mihir Ganguly, a veteran journalist of West Bengal, on 23rd February, 2017.
46. Personal interview with Somen Mitra, a veteran congress leader, former President of WBPCC, first Yuba Congress President of West Bengal and AICC member, on 20th February, 2017. Also see Somen Mitra, *Anubhab* (in Bengali), Punachcha, Kolkata, 2001, p. 34.
47. Dilip Banerjee, *op.cit.*p. 916.
48. *Ibid.,* p. 355.
49. Personal interview with Somen Mitra, a veteran congress leader, former President of WBPCC, first Yuba Congress President of West Bengal and AICC member, on 20th February, 2017.
50. Saroj Chakrabarty, ... *Chief Ministers*, p .413.
51. Haladhar Patel, *Bhushi Kelenkari* (in Bengali), Samabaya Press, Kolkata, (Year of publication is not mentioned)... pp. 2-11.
52. Saroj Chakrabarty, ... *Chief Ministers*, p .437.

53. Haladhar Patel, *op.cit.* p.51.
54. Ibid.
55. Saroj Chakrabarty, ... *Chief Ministers*, p. 438.
56. Ibid.
57. *Ibid.*, pp .447-448.
58. *Ibid.*, p .448.
59. *Ibid.*, pp .448-449.
60. *Ibid.*, pp .449-450.
61. *Ibid.*, p .448.
62. The text of the letter appears in *Ibid.*, pp.450-451.
63. Dilip Banerjee, *op.cit.*p. 502.
64. Personal interview with Somen Mitra, a veteran Congress leader, former President of WBPCC, first Yuba Congress President of West Bengal and AICC member, on 20th February, 2017.
65. Somen Mitra, *op.cit.* pp. 31-32.
66. Dilip Banerjee, *op.cit.* p. 502; Also see Personal interview with Deba Prasad Roy, a veteran congress leader, former MP, MLA and AICC member, on 18th February, 2017. In that election (1972) Congress (R) lonely got 216 seats and its electoral partner i. e. CPI got 35 seats. It is also mentionable that the Bangla Congress (Ajay Mukherjee) merged with the Congress (R), Kashi Kanta Maitra of SSP and Apurbalal Majumder of FB also joined with the congress. The opposition i.e. CPI (M) got only 14 seats and its electoral partners i.e. RSP-3, SUC-1, and WPI secured only 1 seat. In that pretext, when CPI (M), WPI and SUCI collectively boycotted Legislative Assembly, their total seats were-14+1+1=16 only. See Dilip Banerjee, *op.cit.*p. 502.
67. Deba Prasad Roy, "*Doors Theke Delhi* (in Bengali), *Dharabahik Atmakatha,* Part- 17", published in *Eakhan Doors*, (ed.) Pradosh Ranjan Saha, Dover Lane, Kolkata, 2016.
68. Deba Prasad Roy, *"Doors Theke Delhi* (in Bengali), *Dharabahik Atmakatha,* Part- 14", in *Eakhan Doors,* (ed.) Pradosh Ranjan Saha, Dover Lane, Kolkata, 2016. Though, it is very astonishing, but fact remains that during the last 34 years long Left Government and 6 years Trinamul Congress regime, it was not made any file named 'Congress File' in the prisons in West Bengal, but it was made each and every prisons during the reign of Siddhartha Shankar Ray. The intra-party friction became so fatal that the 'Congress File' in the prisons was prepared at the aim of giving penalty to the supporters of the

9. *"Atiter Kichhu Katha",* a Bengali article by Priyaranjan Das Munshi in *Swaranika ,* Chhatra Parishad Golden Jubilee Celebration and Reunion Festival, Impression, New Buligunj Road, Kolkata, 2004, p.69.

10. Personal interview with Kumud Bhattacharya, former state President of the Chhatra Parishad from 1973 to 1977, on 4th February, 2017; also see *"Amader Itikatha",* a Bengali article by Samir Roy in *Swaranika,* Chhatra Parishad Golden Jubilee Celebration and Reunion Festival, Impression, New Bulygunj Road, Kolkata, 2004, p.13.

11. *"Amader Itikatha",*a Bengali article by Samir Roy in *Swaranika,* Chhatra Parishad Golden Jubilee Celebration and Reunion Festival, Impression, New Bulygunj Road, Kolkata, 2004, p.15.

12. *"Swadhinata Uttar Banglar Chhatra Andolon O Chhatra Parishader Prasangikata - Atiter Kichhu Katha",* a Bengali article by Nirbed Roy in *Swaranika,* Chhatra Parishad Golden Jubilee Celebration and Reunion Festival; Impression, New Bulygunj Road, Kolkata, 2004, p.97.

13. *Amader Dinlipi,* an information of various important events (in Bengali), in *Swaranika,* Chhatra Parishad Golden Jubilee Celebration and Reunion Festival; Impression, New Bulygunj Road, Kolkata, 2004, pp.23-27.

14. *"Hathat Chhatra Parishader Janya",* a Bengali article by Dr. Partha Chattopadhyay in *Swaranika,* Chhatra Parishad Golden Jubilee Celebration and Reunion Festival; Impression, New Bulygunj Road, Kolkata, 2004, p.58; Also see *"Chhatra Andolon - Chhatra Parishad O Amader Samay",* a Bengali article by Sougata Roy in *Swaranika,* Chhatra Parishad Golden Jubilee Celebration and Reunion Festival, Impression, New Bulygunj Road, Kolkata, 2004. p.79.

15. Dilip Banerjee, *op.cit.* p. 887.

16. Personal interview with Kumud Bhattacharyay, former state President of the Chhatra Parishad from 1973 to 1977, on 4th February, 2017.

17. *Times of India*, 9th October, 1970; Also see Amar Bhattacharya, *Naxalbari Andolaner Pramanya Tathya Sangkalan - Naya Istahar* (in Bengali), Illias Road, Kolkata, 1998, p. 122.

18. *Ananda Bazar Patrika,* 17th March, 1973.

19. *The Statesman,* 1st January, 1973; Also see Amar Bhattacharya, *op.cit.* p. 124.

20. Saroj Chakrabarty, ... *Chief Ministers*, p. 413.

21. Personal interview with Sarder Amjad Ali, veteran congress leader and former Lok Sabha and Rajya Sabha M.P, on 25th February, 2017.

22. The election manifesto of the Congress party on the eve of the general election of 1972 made an appeal to elect the congress candidates in order to ensure a stable government and economic prosperity. The party's election campaign was mainly focusing the law and order. The manifesto stressed on Indira Gandhi's *'Garibi Hatao'* (Remove Poverty) call to rebuild *'Sonar Paschim Bangla'* (Golden West Bengal). It further said, "The interests of the weaker sections of society, particularly the Scheduled Castes, Scheduled Tribes and Backward Classes will be given special attention. All those below the level of subsistence today- particularly in rural areas –will be helped to improve their income, by land reform, improvement of agricultural techniques and by provision of subsidiary occupations. Land reform... will be carried through and in the towns and cities an urban ceiling will be enforced". See Election Manifesto, Indian National Congress, 1972; Also see Prasanta Sen Gupta, *op.cit.* p.134.
23. Sitaram Sharma, *op.cit.* p. 72.
24. Saroj Chakrabarty, ... *Chief Ministers*, p .416.
25. *Ibid.;* Also see Dilip Banerjee, *op.cit.*pp.926-927.
26. Dilip Banerjee, *op.cit.* pp. 481-482; Also, see Saroj Chakrabarty, ... *Chief Ministers*, p. 423.
27. Dilip Banerjee, *op.cit.*pp. 156,162.
28. Saroj Chakrabarty, ... *Chief Ministers*, p.425.
29. *Ibid,* p .428.
30. *Ibid.,* p .429.
31. *Ibid.,* p .432.
32. See *Swaranika,* Chhatra Parishad Golden Jubilee Celebration and Reunion Festival; Impression, New Bulygunj Road, Kolkata, 2004, p. 27.
33. These information are based on the interview with Kumud Bhattacharya, former state President of the Chhatra Parishad from 1973-1977, on 4th February 2017.
34. Pranab Mukherjee, *op.cit.* p. 107.
35. Dilip Banerjee, *op.cit.*p.926. Arum Kumar Maitra became the President of WBPCC in 1972 and continued up to 1977 before Purabi Mukherjee taking the charge of PCC Chief in the same year i.e. 1977. See name list of the Presidents of the WBPCC, inscribed on the wall of *Bidhan Bhavan,* Head Quarter of the West Bengal Pradesh Congress Committee, Philips More, Kolkata.

28. Krishna Bandopadhyay (ed.), *Naxal Andolone Meyera,* Peoples Book Society, Kolkata, 2017.
29. Mandal Jagadishchandra: *Matichjhapi; Udbastu, Kara Abang-Keno?* Kolkata, 2005.
30. Mukhopadhyay Dr. Binay Krishna, *Nilkantha Prafulla Chandra*, Janaswartha Barta, Kolkata, 2015.
31. Mukhopadhyay, S: *Bharater Communist Party O Amra;* Calcutta, 1889.
32. Mukhopadhyaya Upananda, *Ei Police Jiban*, 1987.
33. Pal Madhumay, *Marich Jhapi – Chhinna Desh Chhinna Itihas,* Gangchil, Kolkata, 2016.
34. *Rabindra Rachanabali,* 4th Volume (Katha o Kahini Kabyagrantha)
35. Roy Biswanath, *Paschim Banger Samajik O Arthonaitik Samiksha,* Modern Book Agency Private Limited, Kolkata, 1988.
36. Sen Manikuntala, *Sediner Katha*, Kolkata, 1982.
37. Sen Sukumar, *Bharat Bibhag: Itihasher Swapna Bhanga,* Bhasha O Sahitya, Kolkata, 1999.
38. Sengupta Barun: *Indira Ekadashi, in Barun Sengupta Rachana Sanghra,* Ananda Publishers, Kolkata, 2008.
39. Sengupta Barun: *Palabadler Pala in Barun Sengupta Rachana Sanghra,* Ananda Publishers, Kolkata, 2008,
40. Sengupta Nitish, *Dr. Bidhan Chandra Roy Jiban O Samaykal,* Dey's, Kolkata, 3rd edition-2009.
41. Sinha Dr. Dinesh Chandra, *1950: Raktaranjira Dhaka Barishal Ebang....,* Kodek, Kolkata, 2012.
42. *Somenath Lahiri Rachana Sangraha,* vol. iv, 1995,

Article (in Bengali)

1. "*Bidhan Chandra Karnadhar - Tabu Khandita Banglar Nabhishvas - 50 Dashak- Ebar Natun Pathe, Natun Laxer Dike*" a Bengali Article by Amalendu Dey in *Saat Dashak Samokal O Ananda Bazar*, Ananda Publishers, Kolkata, 2013,
2. "*Mati Theke Shikhare' Atulya Ghosh Smarane*" a Bengali Article by Mihir Gangopadhyay in *Kheal Khushir Bisesh Sankhya,* Bidhan Sishu Uddyan, Kolkata, August, 2012.

3. *Gharer Baire Muktiyuddha - Muktir Yuddha Bhitare* 1971- 80, a Bengali article by Aurobinda Poddar in *Saat Dashak, Samakal O Anandabazar,* Ananda Publishers Private Limited, Kolkata, 2013.

4. "*Doors Theke Delhi - Dharabahik Atmakatha,* Part- 13, 14, 15, 16, 17, 18, 19, 20, 21," by Deba Prasad Roy in *Eakhan Doors*, (ed.) Pradosh Ranjan Saha, Dover Lane, Kolkata, 2016.

Novels (in Bengali)

1. *Bangiya Praja Satya Natun Aain O League-er Bani,* Dhaka, 1939.
2. *Banglar Hindu Sabdhan,* (Benami), tarikhbihin.
3. Chattapadhyay Sartchandra; *Bartman Hindu, Muslim Samasya,* Sarat Racchan Samagra, Khanda-3, Kolkata, 1930.
4. Dasgupta Satischandra; *Bharater Samyabad,* Kolkata 1930
5. Devi, Mahawata; *Hazar Chusaheer Ma,* Karuna Publisher, Kolkata-1978
6. Majumder Sarmaresh: *Kalbela,* Paila Baishakh, 1390 Bangadha.
7. Tagore Rabindranath: *Gora,* Londan, 1912.

Appendices

Appendix A - A few original documents (Xerox)

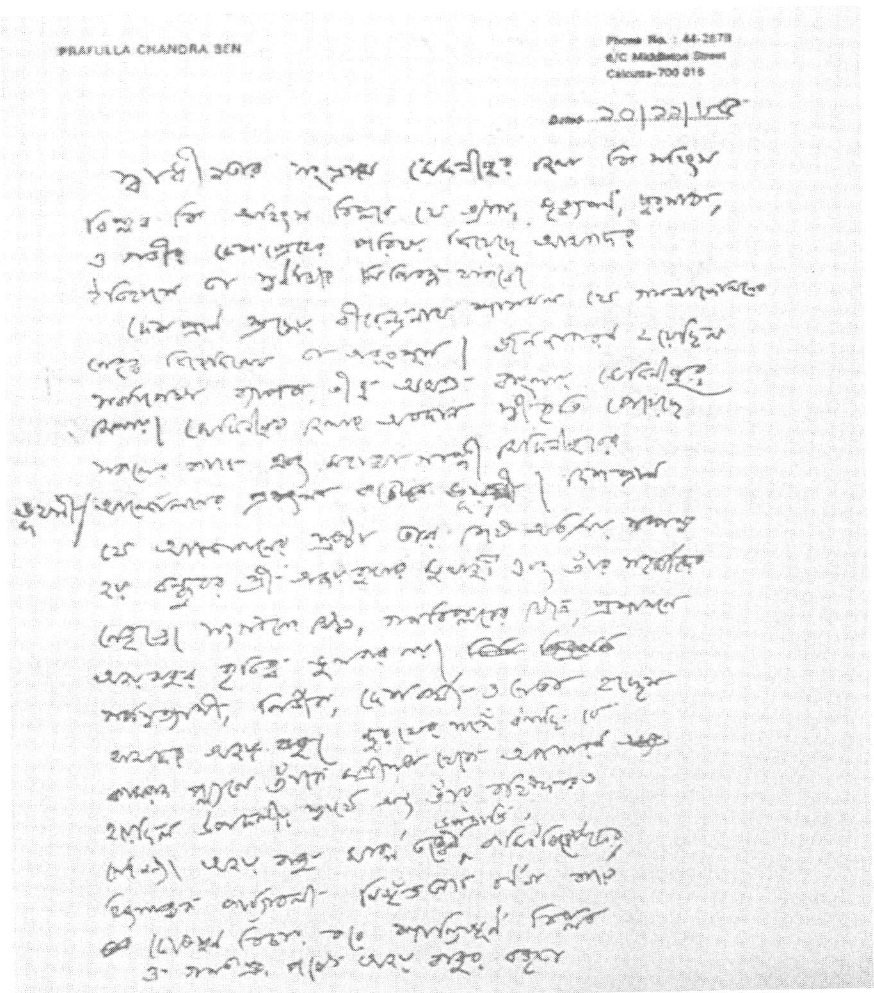

PRAFULLA CHANDRA SEN

Phone No. : 44-2878
6/C Middleton Street
Calcutta-700 016

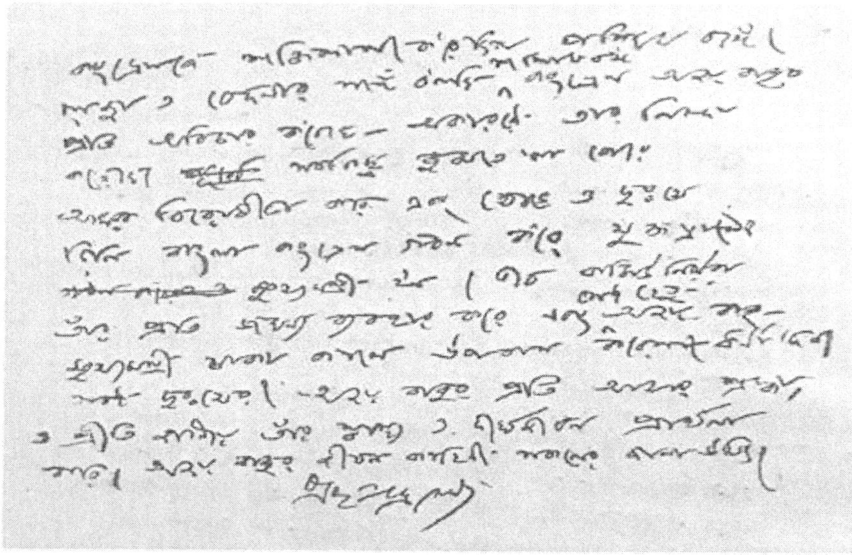

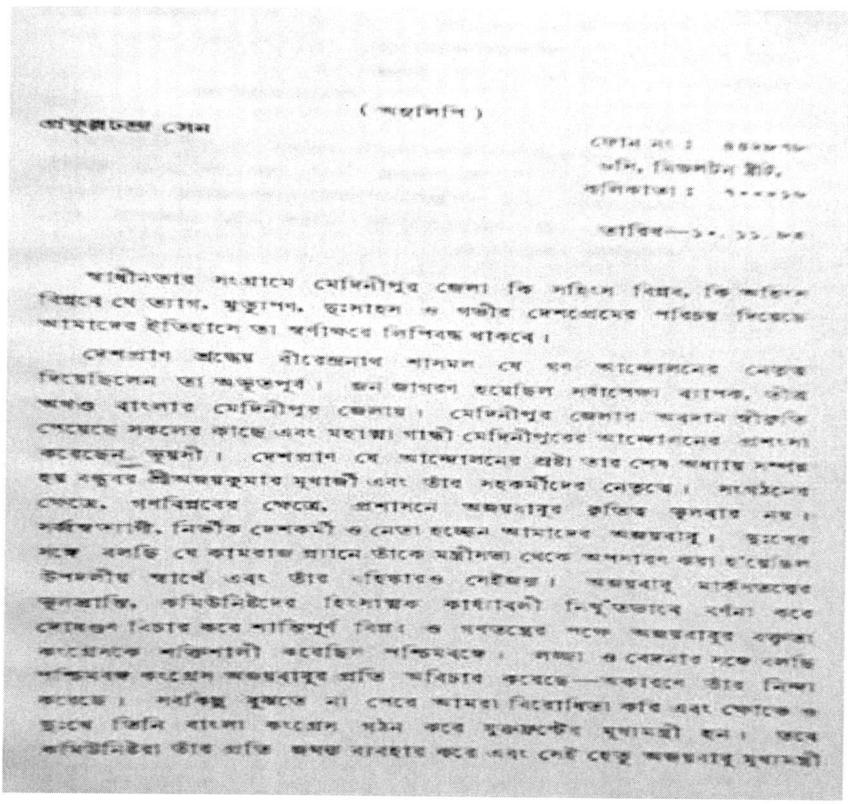

(প্রতিলিপি)

প্রফুল্লচন্দ্র সেন

ফোন নং : ৪৪৩৮৭৬
৬সি, মিডলটন স্ট্রীট,
কলিকাতা : ৭০০০১৬

তারিখ—১০.১১.৮৪

স্বাধীনতার সংগ্রামে মেদিনীপুর জেলা কি সহিংস বিপ্লব, কি অহিংস বিপ্লবে যে ত্যাগ, মৃত্যুপণ, দুঃসাহস ও গভীর দেশপ্রেমের পরিচয় দিয়েছে আমাদের ইতিহাসে তা স্বর্ণাক্ষরে লিপিবদ্ধ থাকবে।

দেশপ্রাণ শ্রদ্ধেয় বীরেন্দ্রনাথ শাসমল যে সব আন্দোলনের নেতৃত্ব দিয়েছিলেন তা অভূতপূর্ব। জন জাগরণ হয়েছিল সারাদেশে ব্যাপক, তাঁর অখণ্ড বাংলার মেদিনীপুর জেলায়। মেদিনীপুর জেলার অবদান স্বীকৃতি পেয়েছে সকলের কাছে এবং মহাত্মা গান্ধী মেদিনীপুরের আন্দোলনের প্রশংসা করেছেন ভূয়সী। দেশপ্রাণ যে আন্দোলনের স্রষ্টা তার শেষ অধ্যায় সম্পন্ন হয় বন্ধুবর শ্রীঅজয়কুমার মুখার্জী এবং তাঁর সহকর্মীদের নেতৃত্বে। সংগঠনের ক্ষেত্রে, গণবিপ্লবের ক্ষেত্রে, প্রশাসনে অজয়বাবুর কৃতিত্ব ভুলবার নয়। সর্বত্যাগী, নির্ভীক দেশকর্মী ও নেতা হচ্ছেন আমাদের অজয়বাবু। দুঃখের সঙ্গে বলছি যে কামরাজ প্ল্যানে তাঁকে মন্ত্রীসভা থেকে অপসারণ করা হ'য়েছিল উপদলীয় স্বার্থে এবং তাঁর পরিবারও সেইজন্য। অজয়বাবু মার্কসবাদের ভুলভ্রান্তি, কমিউনিস্টদের হিংসাত্মক কার্যাবলী নিখুঁতভাবে বর্ণনা করে দোষগুণ বিচার করে শান্তিপূর্ণ বিপ্লব ও গণতন্ত্রের পথে অজয়বাবুর বক্তৃতা কংগ্রেসকে শক্তিশালী করেছিল পশ্চিমবঙ্গে। লজ্জা ও বেদনার সঙ্গে বলছি পশ্চিমবঙ্গ কংগ্রেস অজয়বাবুর প্রতি অবিচার করেছে—অকারণে তাঁর নিন্দা করেছে। সবকিছু বুঝতে না পেরে আমরা বিরোধিতা করি এবং ক্ষোভে ও দুঃখে তিনি বাংলা কংগ্রেস গঠন করে যুক্তফ্রন্টের মুখ্যমন্ত্রী হন। তবে কমিউনিস্টরা তাঁর প্রতি অসৎ ব্যবহার করে এবং সেই হেতু অজয়বাবু মুখ্যমন্ত্রী

থাকাকালে উপবাস করেন, ধর্না দেন। সবই দুঃখের। অজয়বাবুর প্রতি আমার শ্রদ্ধা ও প্রীতি জানিয়ে তাঁর স্বাস্থ্য ও দীর্ঘজীবন প্রার্থনা করি। অজয়বাবুর জীবনকাহিনী সকলের জানা উচিত।

স্বাঃ—প্রফুল্লচন্দ্র সেন

বিঃ দ্রঃ—বর্তমান পুস্তকটি প্রকাশের সিদ্ধান্ত গ্রহণের পর বর্ষীয়ান নেতা ও প্রাক্তন মুখ্যমন্ত্রী শ্রীপ্রফুল্লচন্দ্র সেন যখন উপরোক্ত ভূমিকা লিখেছিলেন, তখন অজয়বাবু পি. জি. হাসপাতালে রোগশয্যায় শায়িত। ঐ হাসপাতালেই ২৭শে মে, ১৯৮৬তে তাঁর জীবনদীপ নির্বাপিত হয়।

(Source: Ajoyeo Purush Ajoy Kumar editd by Shree Radhakrishna Bari, on behalf of Tamralipta Swadhinata Sangram Itihas Committee, Parbatipur, Tamluk, Midnapore, Banirupa Press, Kolkata, 1990)

হাইকোর্টের রায়ে ইন্দিরার হার

এবার আপীল সর্বোচ্চ আদালতে

Appendix B - Lists of the Names of the Presidents of the Bengal Provincial Congress Committee (BPCC)

বঙ্গীয় প্রাদেশিক সম্মেলন
(১৮৮৮-১৯৪০)

সাল	সম্মেলন স্থল	সভাপতির নাম
১৮৮৮	কলকাতা	ডাঃ মহেন্দ্রলাল সরকার
১৮৮৯	কলকাতা	পিয়ারীমোহন মুখার্জি
১৮৯০	কলকাতা	ডিবন কেনেডি
১৮৯১	কলকাতা	রেভারেন্ড এ খাটন বেথ
১৮৯২	কলকাতা	বৈকুণ্ঠনাথ সেন
১৮৯৩	সম্মেলন হয় নি	
১৮৯৪	কলকাতা	নরেন্দ্রনাথ সেন
১৮৯৫	বহরমপুর	আনন্দমোহন বসু
১৮৯৬	কৃষ্ণনগর	গুরুপ্রসাদ সেন
১৮৯৭	নাটোর	সত্যেন্দ্রনাথ ঠাকুর
১৮৯৮	ঢাকা	কালীচরণ বন্দ্যোপাধ্যায়
১৮৯৯	বর্ধমান	অম্বিকাচরণ মজুমদার
১৯০০	ভাগলপুর	বিনয়কৃষ্ণ দেব
১৯০১	মেদিনীপুর	নগেন্দ্রনাথ ঘোষ
১৯০২	সম্মেলন হয় নি	
১৯০৩	বহরমপুর	জগদীন্দ্রনাথ রায়
১৯০৪	বর্ধমান	আশুতোষ চৌধুরী
১৯০৫	ময়মনসিংহ	ভূপেন্দ্রনাথ বসু
১৯০৬	বরিশাল	আব্দুল রসুল
১৯০৭	বহরমপুর	দীপনারায়ণ সিংহ
১৯০৮	পাবনা	রবীন্দ্রনাথ ঠাকুর
১৯০৯	হুগলি	বৈকুণ্ঠনাথ সেন
১৯১০	কলকাতা	অম্বিকাচরণ মজুমদার
১৯১১	ফরিদপুর	যতীন্দ্রনাথ রায়চৌধুরী
১৯১২	চট্টগ্রাম	আব্দুল রসুল
১৯১৩	ঢাকা	অশ্বিনীকুমার দত্ত

সাল	সম্মেলন স্থল	সভাপতির নাম
১৯১৪	কুমিল্লা	ব্যোমকেশ চক্রবর্তী
১৯১৫	কৃষ্ণনগর	মতিলাল ঘোষ
১৯১৬	সম্মেলন হয় নি	
১৯১৭	কলকাতা	চিত্তরঞ্জন দাস
১৯১৮	হুগলি	অখিল চন্দ্র দত্ত
১৯১৯	ময়মনসিংহ	যাত্রামোহন সেন
১৯২০	মেদিনীপুর	এ কে ফজলুল হক
১৯২১	বরিশাল	বিপিনচন্দ্র পাল
১৯২২	চট্টগ্রাম	বাসন্তী দেবী
১৯২৩	যশোর	শ্যামসুন্দর চক্রবর্তী
১৯২৪	সিরাজগঞ্জ(পাবনা)	এম এম আক্রাম খান
১৯২৫	ফরিদপুর	চিত্তরঞ্জন দাস
১৯২৬	কৃষ্ণনগর	বীরেন্দ্রনাথ শাসমল
১৯২৭	মাজু(হাওড়া)	যোগীন্দ্রনাথ চক্রবর্তী
১৯২৮	বসিরহাট	যতীন্দ্রমোহন সেনগুপ্ত
১৯২৯	রংপুর	সুভাষচন্দ্র বসু
১৯৩০	রাজশাহী	বিপিনবিহারী গাঙ্গুলী
১৯৩১	বহরমপুর	হরদয়াল নাগ
১৯৩২-৩৪	সম্মেলন হয় নি	
১৯৩৫	দিনাজপুর	ইন্দ্রনারায়ণ সেন
১৯৩৬-৩৭	সম্মেলন হয় নি	
১৯৩৮	বিষ্ণুপুর(বাঁকুড়া)	যতীন্দ্রমোহন রায়
১৯৩৯	জলপাইগুড়ি	শরৎচন্দ্র বসু
১৯৪০	ঢাকা	জ্যোতিষচন্দ্র ঘোষ

বঙ্গীয় প্রাদেশিক কমিটির সভাপতিবৃন্দ
ফলক উদ্বোধন
উদ্বোধক-শ্রী প্রণব কুমার মুখোপাধ্যায়,সাংসদ

Appendix C- Names of the Presidents of the West Bengal Pradesh Congress Committee (WBPCC)

(Source: Bidhan Bhavan, Head Quarter of the West Bengsl Prsdesh Congress Committee, Kolkata)

Appendix D- Photographs of a few political leaders of Bengal pre-Partition period

Chittaranjan Das

Abul Kashem Fazlul Huq

Sarat Chandra Bose

Subhas Chandra Bose

Dr. Shyama Prasad Mookherjee

Jogendra Nath Mandal

Khwaja Najimuddin

Hussein Saheed Suhrawardy

Appendix E- Photographs of the Chief Ministers of West Bengal and their tenures

Dr. Prafulla Chandra Ghosh (3rd July, 1947 – 22nd January, 1948) & (21st November, 1967 to 20th February, 1968)

Dr. Bidhan Chandra Roy (23rd January, 1948 – 1st July, 1962)

Prafulla Chandra Sen (2nd July, 1962- 1st March, 1967)

Ajay Kumar Mukherjee

(2nd March, 1967 - 21st November, 1967; 25th February, 1969 - 16th March, 1970; and 2nd April, 1971 - 28th June, 1971)

Siddhartha Shankar Ray
(20th March, 1972 – 30th April, 1977)

Appendix F- Photographs of a few political leaders of West Bengal

Atulya Ghosh

Siddhartha Sankar Ray with Smt. Indira Gandhi

Jyoti Basu

Jyoti Basu with Smt. Indira Gandhi

Sushil Kumar Dhara

Pranab Mukherjee

Humayun Kabir

Hemanta Kumar Basu

Index

Q

R

S

***